Stephen J McCormick

The Pope and Ireland

Stephen J McCormick
The Pope and Ireland
ISBN/EAN: 9783743341692
Manufactured in Europe, USA, Canada, Australia, Japa
Cover: Foto ©ninafisch / pixelio.de

Manufactured and distributed by brebook publishing software (www.brebook.com)

Stephen J McCormick

The Pope and Ireland

THE POPE AND IRELAND:

— CONTAINING —

Newly-Discovered Historical Facts Concerning the Forged Bulls

— ATTRIBUTED TO —

POPES ADRIAN IV. and ALEXANDER III.

— TOGETHER WITH A SKETCH OF —

THE UNION EXISTING BETWEEN THE CATHOLIC CHURCH and IRELAND

— FROM —

THE TWELFTH TO THE NINETEENTH CENTURY.

—✠—

BY STEPHEN J. McCORMICK,

EDITOR OF THE SAN FRANCISCO "MONITOR"

—✠—

SAN FRANCISCO, CALIFORNIA:

A. WALDTEUFEL, PUBLISHER.

BENZIGER BROTHERS,

NEW YORK.   CINCINNATI.   CHICAGO.

1889.

To
POPE LEO XIII.,
The Faithful and Affectionate
FRIEND OF THE IRISH PEOPLE
in
Every Legitimate Struggle to Obtain
their National Freedom,
THIS BOOK
is most Respectfully & Affectionately
Dedicated
As a Tribute of Homage
and a
Token of Filial Devotion.

PREFACE.

When a few of the articles which form a great portion of the chapters in this volume first appeared in the columns of the San Francisco MONITOR, it was suggested that such historical matter was well worthy of being placed in book form so as to give it a permanency which it otherwise could not acquire. The suggestion, coming as it did from many revered friends, has been acted on, and in this way the public is placed in the possession of the only volume in the English language which is devoted exclusively to defending the Popes and the Irish people against the aspersions of both ancient and modern enemies.

Viewing the present work in this aspect, the author hopes that he has added at least something to the general stock of literature and thrown a great deal of light upon a subject which has hitherto been dealt with only in a fugitive, transitory and superficial manner.

A writer in the *Irish Ecclesiastical Record*, alluding to the Bulls attributed to Popes Adrian and Alexander, says: "This question is now and again brought forth under the foolish hope of weakening in the minds of Catholics their attachment to the Holy See."

Doubtless it was for this purpose the work of which this volume is a review and a refutation, was issued. But we are proud to say that truth has been vindicated and error crushed in the following pages. We have procured evidence from sources which have not hitherto been known to the general reader, and we have treated the subjects under discussion in as extensive a manner as their importance justified. Some persons may deem it strange that two such Papal Bulls as those attributed to Popes Adrian and Alexander should have existed in the world for seven hundred years without having been proved fictitious and their falsity thoroughly and permanently established. But in this respect, to use a familiar phrase, "history repeats itself." Like the Adrian and Alexander forgeries, it was not until seven centuries of controversy had been indulged in that the False Decretals of Isadore Mercator were finally and successfully proved fictitious. These documents first came into prominence in the middle of the ninth century and they were received with credence until the middle of the sixteenth century, when public faith was withdrawn and they were relegated to the museum of fictitious literature.

It is well known that the forgery of both Papal and other documents was quite common in the twelfth century. Professor Jungmann, in the appendix to the fifth volume of his *Dissertationes Historiæ Ecclesiasticæ*, says, in support of the opinion of those who hold that the Bulls attributed to Popes Adrian and Alexander are forgeries, "it is well known from history that everywhere towards the close of the twelfth century there were forged or corrupted Papal Letters or Diplomas. That such was the case *frequently in England* is inferred from the Letters of John Sarisbiensis and of others."

Richard, the Prelate who succeeded St. Thomas in the See of Canterbury, commanded all the Bishops under his ecclesiastical jurisdiction to promulgate in all their churches the punishment of excommunication against *the public pest of forgery*. So says Peter Blessensis.

In the time of Pope Innocent III., various statutes were passed against this abominable crime, which was a source of great annoyance, as well as of insecurity, in relation to all important official documents of an ecclesiastical nature.

In the present age of the world, of course, it is easy to understand that the forgery of Papal documents has been rendered an impossibility in consequence of the vigilance exercised at the Vatican as well as from the fact that the printing press and the telegraph would soon solve any doubts concerning such documents if they were suspected. But in the twelfth century no such resources were available,—hence apochryphal documents were generally accepted as genuine when first circulated, and in this way a great deal of annoyance was encountered by ecclesiastics.

Within the past few years efforts have been made in nearly every English-speaking section of the world where Irish people congregated, to wean them from their fidelity to the Church and the Pope by means of false and malicious inventions regarding the attitude assumed by Pope Leo XIII., towards Ireland's struggles for political supremacy and National Home Government.

This movement was made with the view to "strike the Shepherd," so that the sheep of the flock of Christ might be dispersed. But in order that truth might prevail over error and malice be confuted by impartial evidence, the author deemed it a worthy task to place in the possession of the reading public all the principal points which poisonous literature had presented in antagonism to the Vicars of Christ, and then to bring forth the antidote in the shape of such facts as impartial historians furnished, in order that a correct knowledge of the historical questions under discussion might be clearly acquired.

A great deal of prejudice has been engendered in the public mind against both the Church and the Pontiffs by reason of false history and false biographies of the Popes being circulated throughout the world, and left to occupy the literary field without any contradiction on the part of Catholic authors. In this way the Church and the Vicars of Christ are prejudged and false verdicts are found against both even by Catholics themselves, who, finding all history filled with calumnies against the Church and her Chief Bishops, give up all contest in despair, and finally acquiesce in the rancorous falsehoods which teach untruth in the pages of so much nineteenth-century literature.

This volume, therefore, the author humbly hopes, will serve to stem the tide of calumny so far as concerns the Pope and the Irish people, proving, as it does, the constant fidelity of the Irish race to the See of Rome, as well as demonstrating the ready reciprocity with which that fidelity was recognized by the Roman Pontiffs.

The foot-notes and references introduced into the volume will furnish a key to those who desire to certify the proofs the author adduces or the charges he makes—as there is nothing so far from his intention as to strive to gain a point by any unfair line of argument. For this reason, therefore, he has taken great pains not to introduce his own ideas to such an extent as to shut out the evidence which he found in authors of reputation and standing, knowing full well that such evidence has far more importance and weight in the estimation of all reflecting men than any opinions which the author might advance, if such opinions were unsupported by documentary evidence.

In the treatment of the questions which have arisen between the enemies of both the Pope and Ireland during the past decade of years, the author has been at great pains to procure irrefutable evidence, so as to establish the truth of history on such a solid basis that no future calumnies against the character of the Holy Father Leo XIII., at present gloriously reigning, can be brought forward without being liable to immediate refutation by reference to these pages.

All the efforts of the author have been directed towards clearing away the clouds of calumny which ancient foes and modern enemies have heaped up against both Ireland and the Pope—both of whom are looked upon by the world as something to be hated, and thus both share in the glory of having earned the world's animosity in consequence of their steadfast fidelity to God and His Church.

Ireland will never falter in her Faith nor lose her renown as the mother of true children of the Church of Rome. As Pope Leo XIII., well says: "Irishmen take a just pride in being called Catholics—an appellation which, according to St. Augustine, means the guardians of all honor and uprightness, the followers of all equity and justice. Let them fulfill by their acts all that this word Catholic implies; and let them, while vindicating their own just rights, endeavor to be indeed all that their name suggests."

By such a course of conduct will the cause of Ireland prosper. Erin will succeed in securing temporal prosperity without the sacrifice of Catholic principle, and then indeed

>   Fixed as fate will her altars stand;
>   Unchanged—like God—her Faith;
>   Her Church will like her mountains stand
>   Untouched by Time or hand of Death!

THE POPE AND IRELAND.

CHAPTER I.

Preliminary Considerations Regarding Judge Maguire's "Ireland and the Pope."

A Brief History of Papal Intrigues against Irish Liberty from Adrian IV. to Leo XIII. By James G. Maguire, Judge of the Superior Court of San Francisco, California. San Francisco: James H. Barry, 1888.

After a careful perusal of this volume, we have come to the conclusion that it is a bad book, published through bad motives, and, in its results, it is far more likely to recoil disastrously upon the head of its author than it is to have the damaging and demoralizing affect its author's animosity against the Vicar of Christ intended.

It is an open secret that the author of this vicious volume is a great admirer of Dr. McGlynn and Henry George, both of whom he has already lauded publicly, whilst, at the same time, he has poured the vials of his wrath upon the devoted head of Pope Leo XIII as their enemy.

Any book upon "Ireland and the Pope," emanating from an author whose mind is a seething cauldron of passion and prejudice combined, must naturally be looked upon as the result of rancor, and hence it can possess but little or no value in the esteem of men who want to read the truth of history, and not the vaporings of individuals whose minds are so strongly tainted with vengeance against the Pope that they cannot permit themselves even to speak courteously of the Pontiffs whom they present to their readers as the persecutors of the Irish people, and as the barriers which have ever been stumbling blocks in the way of Ireland's independence.

Had this bad book been written by an open and avowed Orangeman, an anti-Catholic Calvinist, or an ex-priest who had turned Presbyterian, its Pope-slandering contents and its many misleading and malicious statements, would not have astonished us in the least. But being, as it is, the work of an author who was born, baptized, and brought up in the Catholic Church, and whose position on the Bench implies a decent respect for *all authority*, both civil and ecclesiastical, then indeed our wonder is excited that James G. Maguire could sully his Catholic soul and soil the ermine of his high judicial position, by placing his name and official designation upon the title-page of a book that is beneath criticism as a literary production, and which can confer no honor upon either the literary or the judicial reputation of the gentleman who generated it.

We intend to review this work *thoroughly*, for the reason that it involves questions upon which "the truth, the whole truth, and nothing but the truth," should be known. The patriotic impulses of many Catholic Irishmen very often leave them liable to have their minds filled with venom against the Vicar of Christ, because of some fancied wrong (or "outrage" as Judge Maguire would call it), which the Popes are said to have perpetrated in the past or present against the Irish people; and, in order to avoid such a calamity, it is one of the most important duties of the MONITOR to place before its readers a full, fair and candid contradiction of just such insidious falsehoods as the work under review contains.

History has been defined as "a conspiracy against truth," and in no instance is this definition more veracious than when it embraces within its scope those so called "histories" wherein occur any reference to the Popes, whose characters have been depicted in the darkest colors by hireling heretical writers, and by the enemies of the Church, for no other cause than the horrid hallucination that by traducing the Head of the Church, the body and the members would also suffer.

Such has been the conduct of the calumniators of the Pontiffs in the past, and it seems that, in this regard at least, the world has not improved, for the work before us, when contrasted with the high judicial position of its author, is truly "a conspiracy against truth," and is so malignant in its misrepresentations, and so disrespectful in its allusions to the Pope, that it will astonish and disgust all decent people who lose their time in turning over its turgid pages.

The MONITOR feels sorry for the position in which Judge Maguire has placed himself before the Catholic body at large. We have not even the scintillation of any feeling of animosity towards the gentleman for his furious but foolish attack upon the Vicar of Christ, but it would be criminal in us as a Catholic journalist to permit a poison-laden publication like the present work to be circulated all over this country, without exposing the falsehoods which figure most conspicuously upon its pages. The character of the Vicar of Christ is dear to every Catholic, and the author who imagines that he can publish any calumny he pleases against the Popes, will discover, to his sorrow and confusion, that the questions he has so dogmatically decided against the Pontiffs, have another side to them wherein Truth will prevail over error, and plain facts dominate over fanatical fictions.

The first ebulition of malice which the author of "Ireland and the Pope" manifests, appears in the "Dedication" where he alludes to the Pope as a "foreign potentate." Now, as one who was educated under Catholic influences, Judge Maguire ought to have known that the Catholic people all over the world repudiate the idea that any Pope—from St. Peter to Leo XIII.—should be contemplated under the contemptuous title of "a foreign potentate."

From the days of St. Patrick, the Irish people have always loved, honored and obeyed the Pope as their spiritual Father—after God their best and most reliable guide.

It is now about fourteen hundred years since St. Patrick converted the Irish people to Christianity, and one of those beautiful proverbs known as *Dicta Sancti Patritii*, preserved in the Book of Armagh, which was transcribed in the year 807, is to the following effect : "Thanks be to God," said St. Patrick, speaking of the conversion of the Irish people to the Catholic faith, "You have passed from the kingdom of Satan to the city of God ; the church of the Irish is a church of Romans ; *as you are children of Christ, so be you children of Rome.*" This was the legacy which St. Patrick left to those whom he had redeemed from pagan darkness and placed under the light of the Cross. The Pope represents the Church and he represents Rome, and when any writer thinks to air his wrath by styling the Pope "a foreign potentate," he insults all Catholics who—in the language of St. Patrick—are not only "children of Christ but also children of Rome."

So far from being "a foreign potentate," the Pope of Rome, the successor of St. Peter, is, in the estimation of every dutiful Catholic, the chief Pastor who holds the title-deeds of the love and loyalty of every Catholic "from Greenland's icy mountains to Africa's burning sands." The whole world is the Pope's spiritual domain. He is enshrined in the hearts of the Catholic people of every land as the Apostolic Lord and Father of Fathers, the Shepherd of the Fold of Christ, who hath charge of the lambs and the sheep, so that they may not wander into the poisonous pastures which the world has prepared for their temporal and spiritual ruin. No metes or geographical bounds, therefore, circumscribe the paternal influence of the Pope. To the faithful he is ever their dearly-beloved Father, and in calling the Vicar of Christ "a foreign potentate," the author of this volume only vents his spleen whilst he tarnishes the fair fame of his Christian education.

The object for which this book is written is set forth in the Preface thus: "To show the "wrong and injustice" of papal interference with the Irish people, and to point out the necessity and the patriotic duty of firmly and constantly rejecting and resisting every political edict, issued by a pope or inquisition respecting Irish affairs." The author, however, seems to have very conveniently forgotten that there is no instance on record where the Catholic Bishops, priests or people of Ireland ever complained of any "wrong and injustice" which they suffered through "papal interference." And the captious critic of the Vicar of Christ seems also to have forgotten that "political edicts" do not come within the Province of the Pope, save where the question of faith and morals is involved. The whole Catholic world admits that the voice of the Pope is the Supreme law in all matters appertaining to faith and morals, but Judge Maguire, of the Superior Court of San Francisco, seems to have been so anxious to punish the Pope by placing him in the pillory of Irish politics, so as to exhibit him for public execration, that he acts the part of judge, jury and public executioner!

Every man, even if he enjoys what Judge Maguire so elegantly describes in his allusion to the Pope as "the unenviable, not to say infamous distinction of being dangerous only to those who confide in him," is entitled to a full, free and impartial trial at the hands of his peers. This trial, the MONITOR has resolved the Pope shall have, even though the case has been already prejudged and passed upon without the defendant being even cited to appear in court! "Fair play is a jewel," Judge, and neither the Pope nor the Catholic Church asks more from any man or body of men. But the Pope and the Church do dread *calumny*. They have reason to fear the baneful effects of all bad literature, whether sensuous or sensational, malicious or misleading, because the people of the world are always more ready to believe evil reports of any person, whether Pope or pauper, than they are to accept the plain, substantial statements of mere matter-of-fact events in the lives of men about whom the world concerns itself.

For this, and other cogent reasons, it is only proper that "Ireland and the Pope" should be thoroughly dissected, so as to prove to the world that the Pope has "a case in court" which contains irrefutable testimony on his side whereby to secure a verdict of *acquittal* against the charges contained in Judge Maguire's indictment! "One story is good," Judge, "until the other is told." And now that the MONITOR has read your decision, we hope your Honor will read the rebutting testimony which these columns will present during the next few weeks, in defence of one who stands pre-eminent among Christians, and who shall never be hounded to death unheard, so long as the MONITOR'S guns can carry a shot into the ambush of his enemies.

In the course of his Preface to "Ireland and the Pope," the judicial author poses as a philanthropist who hates to pitch mud at the Holy Father, because he may miss his aim and some of it may bespatter the Catholic Church! Very considerate, indeed, Judge; the sentiment does you great honor, and in order that the readers of the MONITOR may not be kept in ignorance of this most gracious condescension on your part, we print the precious and peerless paragraph in full:

"I am painfully aware of the extreme difficulty if not impossibility, of *exposing* and *condemning* the *political errors* and *faults* of one who is the spiritual head of *a church*, without *working some injury* to the church which he represents."

We have purposely *italicized* those portions of the foregoing paragraph which will cause Catholics to smile serenely—even at the expense of being guilty of contempt of Court! Judging from the above extract, it is not unfair to say that the judicial power of the author of "Ireland and the Pope," is not confined to such civil or criminal cases as may come before his court, but he has elected himself as Most Magnificent Censurer-General of Popes, Cardinals and Roman Congregations! Well might this worthy legal but rather illogical luminary say:

No pent up *Civil Code* confines *our* powers
We're Pontiff of Pontiffs. The *earth* is ours!

Catholics will doubtless remark with admiration the deep feeling of sorrow which Judge Maguire evinces, when he contemplates the vast amount of injury which his wonderful book is destined to cause to "a church" over which the Pope presides. How very kind and considerate of so eminent and erudite a modern Jupiter! His power is so great that he *could* crush the Church of God entirely out of existence beneath the Juggernaut of his gigantic judgeship, but he kindly vouchsafes to express his sorrow that the Church cannot escape "some injury" from the powerful indictment which his Honor has brought against her!

And, right here, if it would not trespass too much on the patience of the Court, we would like to ask the author of "Ireland and the Pope," by what Code of Christian law his Honor came to the conclusion that the Pope presided over "*a Church*" and not *the Church?* Is there some Christian statute hidden away in the Superior Court of San Francisco which sets forth as an undeniable fact that Christ established more than *one* Church? Or is this phrase "*a church*," merely a ruse by which it is sought to belittle the One, Holy, Catholic and Apostolic Church, and to make its mountains of Faith and Truth and Apostolicity and Authority appear only the same small molehills as are Methodism, Mormonism and McGlynnism? Ah! Judge, your satire ill becomes your position, however well it may coincide with the cause which you champion. "Thou art Peter," said our Divine Saviour to the first Pope, "and upon thee I will build *My* Church," and until these words are revoked by the Second Person of the Blessed Trinity Who said them, Catholics will be compelled to accept them as even "higher law" than any judgment upon this question, even though it should emanate from "the Superior Court of San Francisco, California!"

It may be well, also, to call the attention of the author of "Ireland and the Pope" to the fact that he must either *accept* as a Catholic the Creed wherein the Church is declared to be the "One, Holy, Catholic and Apostolic Church," or he must *reject* the Creed and thus stand before the world as an open apostate. "He that shall deny Me before men," says our Blessed Redeemer, "I will also deny him before My Father Who is in Heaven," and when Judge Maguire publicly proclaims his belief that the Church of God is only *a church* among many churches, then indeed, has he denied God before all men!

So far as the future of the Church is concerned, in relation to this wonderful book, the MONITOR desires, in the most cordial and charitable manner possible, to assure Judge Maguire that he need neither fret nor fume, wonder nor worry over the amount of "injury" which his unfortunate book will cause to the Church. The quantity and quality of "chaff" which he has cast at the Church and the Pope, will all have been blown to the four winds of Heaven long before Judge Maguire will have emerged from the fog of odium in which he has enveloped himself through his unfortunate literary venture.

Further along in his Preface the bitter critic of the Chief Pastor of the Catholic Church, assures his readers that "it is not *his* fault if the spiritual heads of the Catholic Church claimed also to be, by divine right, *temporal rulers*, theoretically, over all nations, and in terrible reality over Ireland." Do not be alarmed, Judge; nobody will ever think of holding *you* accountable for any shortcomings of the Popes! God knows you have sins enough of your own to be responsible for without saddling your judicial shoulders with the peccadillos and the "political edicts" of the Popes! Besides, it would be radically in opposition to the Civil Code of California to hold an eminent and erudite American citizen responsible for the crimes of a *foreign potentate!* The idea is perfectly preposterous, and we hasten to assure Judge Maguire that so far as the MONITOR is concerned, not one of its readers shall ever harbor such a horrible thought as that which seems to harrow fearful furrows in the otherwise serene soul of the Most High and Mighty Censor-General of God's Vicegerent on Earth!

Irrespective entirely of these reasons, it is also a well and widely known fact that throughout the past nineteen centuries the Popes have always, everywhere, and under even the most adverse circumstances, managed to "hold their own" against all their assailants, whether the assaults came from heretic or apostate, king or kaiser, soldier or statesman In every conflict with the world the Pope has always triumphed in the end, and so will it be in your case, Judge; the Pope will be loved, revered and venerated by hundreds of millions of Catholic hearts long after the fly-speck with which you have tried to deface the Palace of Peter shall have been washed away completely by the tears of a prodigal's repentance!

Further on in his Preface, the candid author of "Ireland and the Pope" tells us that he speaks "neither as a friend nor as an enemy of the Catholic religion," and yet, dear Judge, it is well for all Christians to bear in mind that Almighty God has said: "He that is not with Me, is against Me; and he that gathereth not with Me, scattereth." The Pope, his Honor will please to remember, represents Almighty God in the eyes of Catholics, and he that is not the friend of Christ's Church is always ranked among her foes! There is no middle course, dear Judge. The Divine law is plain: He that is not the *friend* of God is His *enemy*. You can take which horn of the dilemma you please, although the close perusal of your unfortunate book would lead us to believe that you have allied yourself with the worst enemies the Church, the Pope, and the Irish Catholic people have to contend with — the class that would steal Catholic faith from fervent Irish souls, under the delusive plea of making them purer Irish patriots!

Alluding to just such books as the volume before us, an eminent Irish Prelate said some years ago, that they were written "not out of any love for our poor country or of historic truth," but they proceeded mainly from people who desired to proclaim their hostility to the Sovereign Pontiff and from the vain hope that their exaggerated statements, might in some way weaken the chord of Christian faith which binds the Irish people to Rome. Others who were the precursors of Judge Maguire in his attacks on the Popes, found nothing but "chaff" in the hopper when they threshed out the crop of anti-Catholic literature they had sown, and so will it be when his Honor looks around for the "injury" which he egotistically imagines his book will accomplish. He will be both chagrined and astonished to find the old Church still foremost in the world, without a dent in her sides, a rent in her sails, or a spot to show that the malice of man has cast even a thimbleful of mud at the mystic body wherein Christ dwelleth for ever!

Further on in his Preface, the ardent author of "Ireland and the Pope" says his desire is "to assist in raising my father's countrymen and my own kinsmen above that groveling *fear of the Pope*, which makes so many of them nerveless when he *strikes a blow* at their country and their race." This desire on the part of his Honor, however, is entirely uncalled for, inasmuch as *no good Catholic fears the Pope.* The Pope is only feared by those who look upon him as "a foreign potentate." Catholics love him as the Father of all the Faithful and they venerate him as the Vicar of Christ. *Fear* only enters their souls when they have sinned against the laws of God or the precepts of the Church, but so long as they are not culprits in the sight of God they look upon the Pope as their Father; they love him and pray for him, so that his reign over the Church may be productive of peace and good-will among all Christian peoples.

The Popes, may it please the Court, have never yet struck a blow at Ireland or at the Irish race. Anti-Irish authors have said so, and anti-Catholic critics of the Popes have purposely adopted and circulated the calumny. In like manner malicious men mention "the female Pontiff Joan," to this day, but this fable, like many others, has been dissipated from the minds of all intellectual men by the light of recent historical revelations which were not known to those who lived in past generations.

It may also be judicious to remind Judge Maguire that there exists a very old saying which runneth thus: "*Those who eat the Pope die of the Pope,*" and such has been the fate of many men far more notable in the world than even a judge of the Superior Court of San Francisco. The "injury" therefore, which will accrue from "Ireland and the Pope," will be quite insignificant, as most of the work is compiled from authors who are neither reliable nor respectable, and, besides, Catholics have the assurance of the Son of God that not even the Gates of Hell shall prevail against that Church which Judge Maguire is so much alarmed may be "injured" by his re-hash of "history" which has been hitherto both refuted and repudiated.

In another part of his Preface, the author of "Ireland and the Pope" assures his readers with the dogmatism of a newly-fledged Protestant Doctor of Divinity, that "a man may *reject* the tenets of the Catholic religion and yet be an equally good Irish patriot." And then he cites the names of Grattan, Emmet, Wolfe Tone, Davis, Mitchel and Parnell. Now these notable Irish patriots were all *born* Protestants, who never had the grace of Catholic faith directly bestowed upon them, nor tendered to them for their acceptance. Hence these men never *rejected* the tenets of the Catholic religion. But, on the other hand, when a Catholic publicly be-littles and belies the Church of God by slurringly styling her "*a church;*" when he slanderously charges the Pope of Rome with being "dangerous only to those who trust in him;" when he calls a member of the College of Cardinals "the red-cap-hunting-hound of the Vatican," and when he brazenly asserts that clerical influences have always kept the great mass of the Irish people in ignorance of the facts concerning the history of their country—every true Catholic will rightly doubt the genuineness of such "patriotism" when it is founded upon such apparent apostacy.

The paragraph which concludes the Preface to this unfortunate book may be likened to a scorpion—as it carries its sting in its tail! Alluding to the "political interference" which the Pope is supposed by the author's hallucination to be always "in season and out of season" forcing on the Irish people, Judge Maguire—with that dignity which is so characteristic of a Catholic gentleman when writing of the most exalted Ecclesiastic throughout the Christian world—and one whom Kings, Queens, Princes and Presidents delight to honor—thus depicts the attitude of the successor of St. Peter, the Vicar of Christ:

"The Pope, in this respect, enjoys the unenviable, not to say *infamous distinction* of being dangerous only to those who confide in him."

We are not familiar with the form of language used by the Judiciary of California, but we should most sincerely hope that the foregoing insulting garbage is not a fair specimen thereof! Catholics will feel the insult intended and they will cheerfully accept it as a part of that Cross which all true disciples are bound to carry. For the Judge of the Superior Court of San Francisco, all Catholics will ardently pray: "Forgive him Father, for he knows not what he says." But if no other assertion in his unfortunate book revealed Judge Maguire's malicious motive in compiling this literary concoction of conceit and calumny combined, the above quotation is sufficient to place his Honor among the ranks of those Pope-hating "patriots" that are the bosom friends of fanatical Frank Pixley, who, very consistently with his well-known hatred of the Catholic Church and Ireland, pats Judge Maguire affectionately on the back in the last issue of his anti-Catholic *Argonaut*, and says to his latest recruit: "Well done *my* good and faithful servant."

The author of "Ireland and the Pope," opens his volume with an imaginary conversation between himself and "a devout Catholic and brave but disheartened Irish patriot" who thought the Pope was "misinformed" when he issued the recent Rescript. Judge Maguire, on the contrary, is morally certain that the action of the Holy Father "had a political price." Of course everybody can afford to laugh at his Honor's suggestion, in view of the recent Letter of the Irish Bishops on the Rescript. But we must do Judge Maguire the justice to say that he gives some reasons—and very queer reasons they are – why he believes the Pope intended to kill the Irish National League through Mgr. Persico's agency as a "congenial confidant and general spy." Here is the principal reason:

I. "Monsignor Persico, in his letter of October last to the Pope, expressly shows that he was sent to Ireland to pave the way for the destruction of the Irish National League."

As the legal fraternity would say: We demur to the decision of the Court, for several reasons. First because Monsignor Persico *wrote no letter* to the Pope last October his Honor's assertion to the contrary, notwithstanding! Secondly, if—as we can prove—Monsignor Persico sent *no letter* to the Pope, most assuredly a document that *never existed* could hardly be made to demonstrate the fact that Monsignor Persico was sent anywhere to destroy the Irish National League or anything else under the sun!

No doubt the author of the unfortunate literary venture called "Ireland and the Pope" was misled in his views by reading only *one side of the case* before him—a handy habit in a pettifogger, but a questionable practice for a judge—and so the English-concocted cablegrams led him into this ludicrous error. If Judge Maguire had read the MONITOR of October 19th, 1887, he would have been enlightened on this matter to such an extent that he would not have fallen into the pit which the foes of both Ireland and the Pope dug for him. Here is an extract from the MONITOR of the above date which will enlarge the visual organs of his Honor considerably:

NO REPORT FROM MGR. PERSICO.

Untruthful reports concerning Mgr. Persico's opinion of the state of Ireland as derived from personal observation, having been maliciously circulated by the Tory English press, the Pope's representative has found it necessary to publicly contradict the falsehoods thus circulated for the sole purpose of damaging the Irish cause.

On a recent visit to Waterford, Mgr. Persico alluded to this disreputable action on the part of the English press in the following terms: "His mission," he said, "was one of deference to the Bishops and Catholic people of Ireland. Through his humble person the Holy Father sent his message of loving sympathy to the Irish nation. He knew that contradictory statements had been made in certain papers that he had sent a report of a certain character to Rome. He gave that statement an emphatic contradiction, but he felt that the Irish people did not need any such contradiction at his hands. He came among them not to criticize or pry, but with love and sympathy in his heart, anxious to see for himself the state of the country and what it needed to make it happy and peaceful. The Holy See had always evinced the most loving sympathy for Ireland and had received in return the warmest devotion of her people. By no Pontiff was that feeling more strongly shared than by the present Holy Father."

This extract most effectively bursts the bubble which Judge Maguire blew up out of the literary suds of sensational papers which are constantly on the *qui vive* to put the Pope, Parnell, Mgr. Persico or other prominent men in the Church or in Ireland in precisely *the wrong attitude* before the eyes of the whole world! Justice in this instance, at least, was *very blind*, and his Honor we hope will pardon us if we modestly make the suggestion that he will also be forced to reverse his decision in all that he has said condemnatory of the Pope and Monsignor Persico!

The Court will also please order the clerk to erase from its opinion on page 11 of "Ireland and the Pope" all the incorrect conclusions his Honor arrived at through false information concerning Mgr. Persico whom he very graciously condescended to notice as "this treacherous ecclesiastical statesman" who wrote to the Pope that "the Irish priest would not abandon the political struggle of their countrymen, even when urged to do so in the name of the Pontiff and for the good of the Church." All of which is untrue and naturally falls to the ground when the Court has discovered that *no letter was sent*, and that the cablegram which deceived his Honor was concocted by some scheming lover of sensational lies, who thus caused the Superior Court of San Francisco, California, to sadly blunder in its decision in the celebrated case of "The Pope *vs.* James G Maguire."

Thus we have fairly met and refuted some of the first falsehoods with which the author of "Ireland and the Pope" has seen fit to interlard his ill-starred publication.

CHAPTER II.

The Fictitious Bull of Pope Adrian IV.—Education in Ireland.—The Character of Giraldus Cambrensis Analysed by Historical Writers.

The corner-stone of the inflammatory indictment which the author of "Ireland and the Pope" brings against the successor of St. Peter, is the bogus Bull of Pope Adrain IV., which Judge Maguire accepts as true, and concerning which he coolly says:

"The subjugation of Ireland to English rule, as is well known to all students of Irish history, was not accomplished by force of English arms, but by the decree and grant of Pope Adrian IV. supplemented and enforced by the decrees and orders of Pope Alexander III.
"While, as I have said, these facts are well-known to all students of Irish history, and while they are *fully attested* by every Irish historian worthy of name, *clerical influences* have always kept the great masses of Irish people *in ignorance of them*, so that to-day not one among a hundred of the Irish people know how their country lost her nationality, and still fewer are aware of the *persistent efforts* of the successors of Adrian and Alexander to keep Ireland in *the slavery* to which *their infamous bargain* had delivered her."

Such is the dogmatic manner in which Judge Maguire decides the criminality of Popes, defines the crimes which they have committed, and renders a verdict of "guilty" in the harshest language which his Honor could invoke on the heads of innocent men whom—without producing a particle of evidence—he delivers over to the execration of even Catholics, for the "infamous bargain" they entered into!

Now it will be a most pleasing task on our part to point out the errors into which Judge Maguire has fallen in consequence of his Honor having read only *one side* of this historical question, and thus prejudging the Popes and prejudicing the Irish people against them.

In the first place therefore, it is *not true*, and consequently it is not by any means "well-known to all students of Irish history" that Popes Adrian and Alexander decreed and granted Ireland to Henry II. of England. No doubt Judge Maguire would like everybody to believe otherwise, but the weight of testimony—as we shall show further on—is greatly against him.

In the next place, Judge Maguire's "facts" (as he calls his unwarranted assertions) are *not* "well known to all students of Irish history," nor are they "fully attested by every Irish historian worthy of the name." The charge against Popes Adrian and Alexander is at best what Father Tom Burke (God rest his soul!) would call "a Thumping English Lie," and it is *adopted* only by such Irish historians as are only too willing to take the English view of the question, or too lazy to give the subject that scrutiny, which it deserves at their hands. England has often *hired* moral assassins to keep Ireland within her clutches. Unfortunately for the cause of Erin England has found even Catholics who were willing to be bribed into writing so-called "histories" which—like Scott's "Life of Napoleon," were written to order by the British Government in order to convince the world that England was right in every iniquity she perpetrated against those whom she overthrew.

The very first man whom England hired to give currency to the falsehood that Popes Adrian and Alexander gave Ireland to England, was a Welsh priest named Gerald Barry, who is known under the *nom de plume* of "Cambrensis," and who evinced his idolatry for the monarch to whom he had hired himself, by styling Henry II., "the Alexander of the West," "the Invincible," "the Solomon of the age," "the most pious of Princes," when—as we shall show further on, it is well known that Henry was not only a most immoral man, but he also caused the saintly Bishop Thomas a'Becket to be murdered in his own Cathedral!

It is really singular what unanimity exists between all enemies of the Church and the Popes concerning their fears regarding a mythical something which they all designate by the attractive title of "clerical influence." Luther lampooned it, Henry VIII., hurled defiance at it, Dr. McGlynn censured it, Henry George decried it, and now comes the Censurer-General of the Vicegerent of Christ—the disgruntled author of "Ireland and the Pope"—who declaims most violently against that ethereal hobgoblin conveniently called by critics of the Popes "clerical influence." The Judge of our Superior Court unqualifiedly asserts that the Irish people are so disgracefully ignorant that not one in a hundred of them knows anything of the "infamous bargain" of Popes Adrian and Alexander and their successors! This is a serious charge, but, fortunately, it is one of Henry George's flimsy fictions which his San Francisco disciple has copied from him. The Irish people are neither the ignorant dupes Judge Maguire depicts them, nor are they foolish enough to accept the frantic fanaticism of a frothy fireband for the truth of history. Centuries before the Superior Court of San Francisco had a Chief Censurer-General of the Popes within its bailiwick, the Irish people knew far better than Judge Maguire can now tell them, the whole history of their land as it was handed down through tradition from parent to child. And the descendants of this grand old Irish stock, who live in the present day, have no occasion to sit at the feet of any Georgeite Gamaliel in order to learn the history of the land of their birth.

Where and from whom did did this ghost of "clerical influence" assume a shape and became materialized? Assuredly not in Rome nor from the Popes, as not one of them ever exercised the slightest restraining influence over the education of the Irish people. Was it from the Irish Bishops? Decidedly not! No body of Prelates in the Universal Church of Christ ever did more to foster and to propagate among their people a knowledge of the history of their native land, than did the Bishops of Ireland. In the face of the fiercest Penal Code that ever disgraced the statute books of any country, the Irish Bishops had the history of Ireland taught to Catholic children in the shadows of the sweet hawthorne hedges of Ireland, because it was imprisonment and exile to both teacher and pupil if British spies discovered a Catholic school in Erin! It was the Irish Bishops who sent their ecclesiastical students to Rome, Louvain, Paris and other cities in Continental Europe, to be thoroughly educated in Irish literature and theology, so that they could lead their flocks both along the narrow path of true Faith, and also through the lines of legitimate agitation by which they could—and will eventually—secure the liberty of their native land.

Comparatively speaking it is only a few years since Catholic Emancipation was granted and the legal shackles of coercion of conscience unloosed from Priest and patriot in Ireland. Yet what a grand galaxy of scholars, historians, orators, statesmen, poets and theologians the Catholic body in Ireland has produced since then! The mythical "clerical influence" of Judge Maguire did not certainly use what his Honor would call its "infamous bargain" in repressing the poetical, musical, oratorical or historical genius of Ireland! No country in the world has more of its history embodied in its music and poetry than Ireland, and even the boys and girls of Ireland, as they whistle and lilt the martial air and words of "Let Erin Remember the Days of Old," could give Judge Maguire a lesson in Irish history which would actually alarm the Judge of the Superior Court of San Francisco at his own "ignorance" and at the surprising knowledge possessed by even the *gossoons* and *colleens* of old *Granuaile!*

To her glory be it said, the great majority of Ireland's best and brightest men were educated under the Ægis of the Catholic Church, and beneath the very canopy of that "clerical influence" which Judge Maguire so mistakingly and yet so maliciously designates as exercising its prerogative to keep the people of Ireland in ignorance of the history of a land whose political persecution came through the proscriptive legislation leveled at the Church herself! To keep the Irish people in ignorance of the history of their country, therefore, would be to eradicate from their minds the history of the martyrs who died for the Catholic faith, the Confessors who proclaimed it, and the persecuted people who suffered for it! Even as recent an enemy of the Pope as the Judge of the Superior Court of San Francisco, will be forced to admit that no "clerical influence" whatever, in the Catholic Church, would so stupidly stultify itself as to commit such a suicidal blunder as that !

The truth is that the history of Ireland has been told by Catholic Bishops and Priests to their people from the pulpits of Irish churches, in lectures and sermons, from time immemorial, especially during the long night of English bondage, when, in the eyes of the enemies of suffering Erin,

"It was treason to love her
And death to defend."

On the rostrum and from the altar-steps, on the verdant hillsides and by the banks of the Shannon, the Suir, the Blackwater, the Liffey and the Lee; in the cabin of the peasant and beside the sweet-smelling turf fire of the *Soggarth Aroon*, the sad history of Ireland's sufferings has been reiterated time and again, until even the women and children of that country treasured every fact of it in their ever-faithful hearts !

And in later years, when the sunlight of freedom of conscience, of speech, and of the press, was permitted to permeate the penal-law laden atmosphere of Ireland, how gladly the Bishops of that partially emancipated land availed themselves of the valuable services of the Teaching Orders of the Church in order to dispel that very murky "ignorance" which Judge Murphy asserts was fostered by ' clerical influence." The Brothers of the Christian Schools, the Brothers of St. Patrick, the Brothers of St. Francis, and even the priests themselves, founded Catholic schools wherein the very atmosphere was impregnated with Irish patriotism gleaned from a knowledge of Irish history. And what the Fathers and Brothers did for the boys of Ireland, the Jesuits, the Vincentians, the Marists, the Dominicans and the secular clergy did for the young men of Ireland in the Colleges which the "clerical influence" of Catholic Bishops established in nearly every Diocese in that Island of Saints and Sages !

And what shall we say of the "ignorance" of Irish history in which the female youth of Ireland has been kept for the past half century by those pure and patriotic Sisters who form the Female Religious Orders who have implanted virtue and holiness as well as historical knowledge in the immaculate breasts of the daughters of St. Patrick? What a sentiment of disgust must flash over the faces of the Presentation Sisters, Sisters of Mercy, Ursulines, Sisters of Charity Poor Clares, Sisters of Loretto, and other zealous teachers of Ireland's youth, when they learn from the Judge of the Superior Court of San Francisco that they are co-conspirators with certain undefined "clerical influences" to keep the rising generation of Irish girls in deep "ignorance" of the true history of their country ! Shame upon the writer who would bring such a wanton charge against the Church which gave him the Christianity and the education he thus defiles !

The facts we have cited, therefore, will impel every Irish Catholic and every Irish-American Catholic within the jurisdiction not only of the Superior Court of San Francisco, but also within the jurisdiction of the Supreme Court of the United States, to denounce in unmeasured terms the false and foul assertion of Judge Maguire, as a piece of dastardly defamation which would disgrace the already dishonored mind of even the fraudulent Froude himself ! In fact such an assertion could only emanate from a mind surcharged with hatred against the Popes, the Prelates, the Priests and the people of Ireland who belong to God's Church, a Church which entails upon itself the wrath of its enemies because she excommunicates insubordinate ecclesiastics, and which says to political demagogues who would seek to secure temporal rights at the sacrifice of Faith and Christian ethics :—" Thus far shalt thou go and no farther."

———

Recklessness of expression is characteristic of all would-be Church critics, especially when they happen to be Catholics who have fallen away from the faith of their fathers. In their over-reaching ambition to drag down other Catholic men to the deep pit into which they themselves have fallen

"Unwept, unhonored and unsung,"

these unfortunate soul-suicides make the most reckless and ridiculous charges against the Church to which they have proved renegades, and the Faith they have foolishly flung back into the Holy Face of that God from Whose Charity they received it. These unwise worldlings act thus so that they may present themselves to the world they worship as men animated by the highest motives and the purest "patriotism." But vain are their caustic criticisms, idle are their vapory insinuations, whilst their covert calumnies only recoil upon their heretical heads, to the greater increase of their deep yet well-deserved degradation.

No amount of pretended "patriotism" can conceal from the penetrating gaze of Irish Catholic people the leprous ulcers on the sin-laden souls of apostate priests or turn-coat politicians. With the Irish Catholic, whether in Australia or America, on the Continent of Europe, or in the jungles of India,

Faith and Fatherland
Go hand in hand.

They know full well that the pretended "patriot" who is a Judas to his God, will eventually prove an Arnold to the Irish cause. They realize the fact from bitter experience that a staunch Protestant like Parnell is a far safer political guide than a Catholic who has made himself believe that his soul is not large enough to contain both his religion and his Home Rule principles. Hence, those foolish writers who mistakingly think they elevate themselves by puffing up their pretended "patriotism," by lampooning and lying against the Popes, and by concocting windy and watery diatribes against "clerical influences"—which are merely meaningless, mental cobwebs of their own diseased imaginations—soon find their level when their tricks are exposed and their cant, hypocrisy and degraded demagoguism is pilloried in the public press in all its naked deformity!

In his eager desire to prove that the Bull of Pope Adrian was a genuine document, Judge Maguire vauntingly proclaims the fact that—with two exceptions—all the Irish historians from Geraldus Cambrensis in 1178, bear witness in favor of his side of the case. Now let us examine into the moral, intellectual and linguistic acquirements of Gerald Barry—who is the Geraldus Cambrensis of Judge Maguire—in order to present to "the Court" the character of the witness whom his Honor introduces as best qualified to give testimony against Popes Adrian and Alexander.

Here is the faithful pen-portrait which the Abbè MacGeoghegan draws of this hireling *Welshman* whom Judge Maguire very singularly selects as foremost among *Irish* historians! Here is the character of Judge Maguire's principal witness in the hopeless task his Honor has undertaken of proving his charges against certain Popes of Rome.

In the opening chapter of his elaborate *History of Ireland*, the Abbè MacGeoghegan thus dissects the "history" which Geraldus Cambrensis concocted by order of the King of England who was determined to make falsehood appear as truth, and to foster forgery through fraud--in order to adduce even suborned evidence in proof of his pretended right to retain Ireland in the grasp of England.

"The English, having in the twelfth century, put an end to the Irish monarchy, and wishing to give *a color of justice to their usurpation*, and to the tyranny which they exercised against the inhabitants of the country, have, without any other title than a *fictitious bull of Adrian the Fourth*, and the right of the strongest, represented the Irish as savages, who inhabited the woods,[*] and who never obeyed the laws, as if these titles were sufficient for stripping them of their properties.[†] What! that people so renowned in the first ages of Christianity for their piety and learning, and among whom the Anglo-Saxons themselves went, according to their own historians, to be instructed, during the centuries, which preceded the invasion of the English, are all of a sudden reduced to the condition of savages![‡] The metamorphosis is too difficult to be admitted, and at the same time too obvious for us not to feel how absurd such an accusation must be. * * * *

Gerald Barry, a priest, and native of the country of Wales, in England, called in Latin Cambria, (from whence is derived the name of Cambrensis, under which he is known), was the first stranger who undertook to write the history of Ireland,

---

[*] Sylvestres Hiberni.

[†] Camd. edit. Lond. p. 730.

[‡] "They retired hither, for the sake either of divine study, or a more chaste life."—*Bede's Church History*, b. 3, c. 27.

in order to perpetuate the calumnies which his countrymen had already published against its inhabitants.

Circumstances required that they should make the Irish pass for barbarians. The title of Henry the Second was founded only upon a bull obtained clandestinely from Pope Adrian the Fourth, an Englishman by birth. The cause of this bull was a false statement which Henry had given to the Pope of the impiety and barbarism of the Irish nation. Cambrensis was then *ordered to verify, by writing*, the statement upon which the granting of the bull had been extorted. He did not fail to intermix his work with calumnies, and groundless absurdities; however, the credit of a powerful king knew how to make even the court of Rome believe them. *It was in this spirit that Cambrensis wrote his history*, *and from thence the English authors have taken the false coloring under which ancient Ireland has been represented*. Passion and interest made them pass over the *recantation* which Cambrensis felt himself obliged to make, in the latter part of his life, of several false and calumnious imputations, with which his history has been filled. *Cambrensis did not possess the necessary requisites for an historian*. History is not a mere production of the mind; it is an assemblage of facts, the arrangement of which depends alone upon the author. To write the history of a country it is essential to know it, likewise the character and genius of its inhabitants, and to be capable of consulting its annals. Cambrensis possessed none of these qualities with respect to Ireland, the history whereof he undertook to write. It is true, that he had been twice in that country, first through curiosity, in 1171, to witness the advancement of his relations and friends; secondly, as preceptor of John Earl of Montayne, son of Henry the Second to whom, the king, his father, had given the title Lord of Ireland. In those two voyages he remained but eighteen months in Ireland, and saw about one-third of it, which alone obeyed the English; he could not with safety put his foot into any other part of the kingdom. Being incapable of consulting the records of the country, (written in a language to which he was altogether a stranger,) *he was obliged to substitute, instead of truth, falsehoods, and the productions of a prejudiced mind, to swell his volumes.*   *   *   *

Like certain animals, which wallow in mire, and prefer it to the sweetest flowers*

he attached himself to whatever he could discover meanest and most vile among the people; unsupported likewise by any written authority, or the evidence of any correct or impartial man, he composed an absurd collection of old women's, sailors' and soldiers' stories, which he seasons with scandalous aspersions, satires and invectives against the nation; neither prince nor people, clergy, secular or regular, are spared; *he respects nothing; everything becomes the object of his calumnies and detraction†* Having spent five years in composing this fine work, the five books of his pretended history of Ireland came forth. In raptures with that new production of his genius, and unable to conceal his vanity, Cambrensis repaired to Oxford‡ where, in presence of learned doctors and the assembled people, he read, after the example of the Greeks, his topography, during three successive days, giving to each successive book an entire day. To render the comedy more solemn, he treated the whole town splendidly for three days; the first was appropriated to the populace; the second to the doctors, professors and principal scholars of the university; and lastly the third day he regaled the other scholars soldiers and citizens of the town; "a noble and brilliant action," says Cambrensis himself, "whereby the ancient custom of the poets has been, for the first time, renewed in England." But unfortunately for him, the success did not answer his expectations; it was easily seen, particularly at court, that the bad choice he had made of the materials whereof his history had been composed, and the fables he had introduced into it, *could be but the effect of his ignorance, or hatred for the Irish nation*. They were not astray for the cause of that hatred; besides the private quarrel which he had with Aubin O'Molloy, monk of the order of Citeaux, and abbot of Bahinglass, in which he was defeated, and which excited his anger against that nation, he wished *for the ruin and destruction altogether of the Irish*, who might prove an obstacle to the aggrandizement of his relatives and friends,

---

* "He hath defiled his writings with the filthiness of the rabble; he resolved to stuff the whole nation with the imperfections of the populace, recorded by himself, like the spider which draws poison from the thyme

† Grat. Lucius, cap. 5, p. 38.
‡ Usser. Silog. edit. Par. Epist, 49, p. 84, et, 85.

from which the bee extracts honey. He has thus formed from among the most abandoned of the Irish, a package; leaving those things which he found most eminent, unnoticed. Whatsoever filth he discovered, appeared as a gem to him; with it, as if most precious. has he arranged his productions and work, so that, like the swine, he delights more in the dunghill than to enjoy himself amidst the sweetest odors."--*Gratianus Lucius*, p. 5, c. 41.

as appears from his second book on the conquest of that people. Nothing tends to discover* more easily the malignity and inconsistency of Cambrensis' mind, than the extremes into which he lets himself be carried. Sometimes he extols with warmth the merit of his relations, newly established in that country; again he exclaims violently against the English and Normans engaged with them in the same cause, against the Irish.

While King Henry II. lived, that prince was, according to him, "the Alexander of the west," "the Invincible," "the Solomon of his age," "the most pious of princes," who had the glory of repressing the fury of the Gentiles, not only of Europe, but likewise of Asia, beyond the Mediterranean. The most extravagant phrases which the refined flatterer could invent were not spared in extolling him, contrary to reason and common sense; for example, he did not blush to say of that prince, that his victories and conquests were limited only by the circumference and extremities of the earth. However, so soon as the king was dead, (as David Powell remarks,) he broke forth into a thousand invectives against his memory in the book entitled "The Instructions of a Prince," and gave free vent to his ancient enmity against him. That alone should suffice to characterize this author, and to show what little credit every thing else which he advanced is entitled.

The reproaches which were directed against Cambrensis *for having inserted in his writings so much fabulous matter obliged him to recant* what he had advanced both by an apology, inserted in the preface of his book, called, "The Conquest of Ireland," and a treatise on "Recantation." In these he acknowledges that, although he learned from men of that country, worthy of belief, many things which he mentions, he had followed the reports of the vulgar in many others; but he thinks as St. Augustine, in his book on the "City of God," that we should not positively affirm, nor absolutely deny, the things we have only from heresay. Sir James Ware in his "Antiquities of Ireland," knew how to appreciate with justice the merit of our author. The following is the opinion he holds of him: "Cambrensis," said he "has collected into his topography *so many fabulous things*, that it would require an entire volume to discuss it correctly." In the mean time he warns the reader to peruse it with caution; he then adds, "That it astonishes him how men of his time, otherwise grave and learned, could have imposed upon the world, *by giving as truths the fictitious of Cambrensis.*"

But, notwithstanding the incontestable proofs of the fallacy and imposture in the writings of this discredited author, and although they had lain 400 years in obscurity until 1602, when Camden had them published at Frankfort, *all who have spoken of the Irish since that period, but particularly the English, have no other foundation for their abuses against them than the authority of that impostor.* The evil has become so general throughout Europe, that in most books and geographical treatises, wherein there is mention of the manners and customs of nations, we find upon the Irish only the poisoned darts which Cambrensis had directed against them.†

After the character now drawn of Cambrensis, let the judicious and impartial reader judge if he can be considered as a grave historian, and one worthy of credit; or if he should not, on the contrary, be looked upon as a *libeller* and *impostor*, who sought, by amusing the public with absurd tales, to disgrace, against all truth and justice, an entire nation. All others among the English who have undertaken to write the history of Ireland, particularly since the Reformation, have, "like the asp that borrows the venom of the viper,"‡ taken the same tone as Cambrensis, and faithfully followed his tracks; among the number are Hammer, Campion, Spencer, Camden &c. By breathing the same air as he, they were animated by the same spirit, and have inherited *all his hatred against the Irish.*

What must intelligent and impartial people think of Judge Maguire's *principal* witness *against* the Pope and *in favor* of the bogus Bull? A *hireling* writer is like a *perjured* witness, and Gerald Barry, as the Abbé MacGeoghegan clearly shows, was the purchased tool of one of England's tyrannical monarchs who hired the Welshman to malign the people of Ireland, and to fabri-

---

* Grat. Luc. c. 7, p. 49, 50, 51, 52, 53 etc.

* "Many things concerning Ireland could be noticed in this place as fabulous, which Cambrensis hath heaped together in his topography. To analyze or descant upon each would require a whole tract. Caution should be particularly applied by the reader to his topography, which Giraldus himself confesses. I cannot but express my surprise, how men now-a-days otherwise grave and learned have obtruded on the world the fictions of Giraldus for truths."—*Ware's Antiquities of Ireland*, c. 23,

† Grat. Luc. c. 1, p. 4.

‡ "They are borne by a similar propensity to traduce the Irish, (as it is expressed in the proverb) the asp borrows poison from the viper."—*Gratianus Lucius*, c. 1, p. 3.

cate reasons why a fraudulent, forged and fictitious Bull should be considered genuine!

A nice witness *that* to support the animosity which Judge Maguire's antagonism to the Pope's clearly demonstrates! A *bad* cause is consistently backed up by *bad* men and *bad* books, and in selecting the malignant, mercenary Cambrensis as the cornerstone of his testimony against Pope Adrian, Judge Maguire has virtually broken down his own case, and every candid person will say with the MONITOR that it should be thrown out of Court!

It will be noticed in the above extract that the Abbè Mac Geoghegan says " the title of Henry II. to Ireland was founded only upon a Bull obtained clandestinely from Pope Adrian IV. The cause of this Bull was a false statement which Henry had given to the Pope of the impiety and barbarism of the Irish nation." This at first sight might appear as if such were the sentiment of the writer, but as the Abbè MacGeoghegan had perviously made use of the condemnatory expression " *a fictitious Bull* of Adrian the Fourth," it is easily seen that the writer *was merely stating the case as set forth by the enemies of the Church*, who were always desirous of discovering some pretext by which to break the chains of faith and love which have ever bound the hearts of the people of Ireland to the Pope of Rome.

So much for the wretch Gerald Barry, whom Abbé MacGeoghegan justly styles " a libeller and an impostor," and whom Judge Maguire places most prominently in the witness-box in order to give *perjured testimony* against the Popes of Rome!

CHAPTER III.

The Character of Giraldus Cambrensis Depicted by Different Writers.

THIRD ARTICLE.

The fraudulent motives which prompted the hireling Giraldus Cambrensis to accede to the request of King Henry II. of England, which the Abbè McGeoghegan so lucidly exposes, have also drawn down upon the head of that disreputable Welshman the just indignation of numerous other Irish historical writers.

Assuredly Judge Maguire could not have known the true character of Giraldus Cambrensis, or he would never have cited that pensioned libeler of the Irish people as a witness to the authenticity of the bogus Bull of Pope Adrian IV. Already we have shown the diabolical mendacity of Judge Maguire's principal witness against the Popes, upon the evidence of such veritable testimony as that given by the Abbè MacGeoghegan, and now let us place on the witness stand of the Superior Court of San Francisco other trustworthy witnesses whose evidence will not only fully corroborate the truth told by Abbè MacGeoghegan, but some of whom go even to further extremes in their just condemnation of the bribe-taking calumniator of both the Pope and the Irish people, the stool-pigeon of Henry the Second—Giraldus Cambrensis.

Speaking of the inhuman brood of bloodthirsty Welshmen whom the iniquitous Irish traitor MacMurrough gathered around him in Wales, when he applied to King Henry II. of England for help to avert the threatened vengeance of the Irish people, Professor Martin A. O'Brennan, in the first volume of his *Irish Antiquities*, draws the following brief but graphic picture of the peculiarities which adorned their characters:

"Almost every history on Irish matters, even Wright's, (brought out by Tallis), has agreed that the cause of religion in Ireland, at that very time, [the time of Henry's invasion] did not require any reformation—and could not expect it from the allies of the adulterous, perjured Mac Murrough. Who were his first adherents in Wales? The Fitz Henrys, *illegitimate sons* of Henry I., and other children of Nesta, the concubine of the said Henry, viz. De Gros, Fitz-Gerald, Fitz Stephen, *the three De Barris*, one of whom was *the infamous Cambrensis*—all the offspring of the harlot Nesta—a vicious monarch, with Cavanagh, his bastard son, were the nest of robbers who, at first, gave their adhesion to Dermod. God! how awful is the reflection, that an island which was so powerful in resources should become the prey of such an infernal banditti—*all the issue of sin!* The soul shrinks back from the contemplation of, and the flesh of the hand that writes these lines, creeps with disgust at the mere recording of such turpitude. From the origin of the gang of English plunderers we refer to Wright's 'Ireland,' chap. ix. p. 1. The idea of Satan quoting Scripture is not more repugnant than religious reform from *such sinful reptiles*. What a precious company Dermod brought with him to the Abbot of Ferns, in Wexford. Cambrensis says that the *Helen of Ireland*, Dervorgilla, wife of O'Rourke, was one of the company at the Abbot's table. Can it be? We cannot answer. What a fraternity! Only the presence of the murderer of the glorious à Becket was wanted to complement one of the most remarkable brotherhoods that ever existed!"

What do Catholics think of the *origin* of Giraldus Cambrensis, the first and foremost witness whom the author of "Ireland and the Pope" has presented in Court in order to convict, upon *perjured* testimony, Popes Adrian IV. and Alexander III. of committing a most heinous crime against the Catholic people of Ireland? Are our readers prepared to give *any credence whatever* to this Welsh calumniator of the Irish people? We think not. The iniquitous birth, the corrupt blood, and the evil company kept by Giraldus Cambrensis, at once stamp him as the perjured tool of King Henry II., and the fitting sycophant to first concoct the story of Pope Adrian's gift of Ireland to that disreputable monarch!

Judge Maguire is cheerfully welcome to all the credit he can achieve by introducing to the American public the malodorous memory of Giraldus Cambrensis, as his first and *best* witness against a Pope who was raised up by Almighty God from the position of a beggar boy to the highest position which man can achieve on earth! Pope Adrian IV. was an Englishman, and the fact of his nationality has been used by the enemies of truth in order to prejudice the whole Irish Catholic race against him. Every English historian, and every enemy alike of Catholicity, Ireland, and truth, parades the fact that Pope Adrian IV., was "the only Englishman that ever occupied the Chair of Peter." Numerous other nationalities have had but a single representative in the person of the Vicar of Christ, but not a single biographical or historical writer makes allusion to the fact! Why, therefore, do the historians of England and the opponents of the Papacy in this country, so steadfastly harp upon the fact that Adrian IV. "was the only Englishman that ever occupied the Chair of Peter"? Simply in order to try and create in the hearts of Irish Catholics a virulent antipathy to the Vicar of Christ, and thus cause a schism in the Catholic Church. Catholics, therefore, should view with suspicion any assertions made by writers who form their false charges against a Pontiff upon the prejudices which they hope to arouse through working upon the well-known national antipathy which the Irish people have against English rulers—whether civil or religious.

The next witness whom we shall produce in order to further illustrate the infamous character of Giraldus Cambrensis, is Mr. John J. Clancy, whose work, "Ireland: As She Is, As She Has Been, and as She Ought to Be," Judge Maguire no doubt is familiar with. In the opening of the second chapter of that work, the author alludes to Giraldus Cambrensis as "*the lying Welshman,*" and, in another portion of the volume, he thus portrays the vile character of Judge Maguire's most prominent witness against the Popes:

"Gerald Barry (Cambrensis), Welshman by birth, monk by profession, *knave and sycophant by nature*, was the first British historian to deal with Anglo-Irish affairs. James A. Froude, Englishman by birth, ex-theologue by profession, bigot and partisan by temperament and education, is the latest adventurer who has donned the cap of Cambrensis.

Each may be accurately described as the historian laureate of England, bound to earn his porridge by praising his master through thick and thin, and halting at no obstacle of rude fact while doing so. The Welshman was commissioned by Henry II. to paint the Irish as a lawless, graceless, godless crew; so Gerald promptly reported that "their chief characteristics were treachery, thirst for blood, unbridled licentiousness, and inveterate detestation of order and rule"! Of the scribe who penned these words it has been said that *he never spoke the truth, unless by accident.*"

A man whose moral character is so bad that "*he never spoke the truth except by accident,*" is hardly up to the standard of historians who are worthy of belief. Cambrensis may be good enough authority for Judge Maguire, but we feel assured that Catholics must have more credible and respectable testimony before they will adjudge Popes Adrian and Alexander guilty of having made over Ireland to the murderer of Thomas à Becket, on the testimony of a witness who has the reputation of "never having told the truth except by accident!"

The next witness we will call in order to enlighten Judge Maguire upon the character of Cambrensis, is the celebrated Irish poet and historian Thomas Moore, who thus outlines the reasons which should impel all impartial-minded people in *refusing* to give credence to a single statement made by this mercenary maligner of both the Popes and the Irish people. "In estimating the value of Cambrensis' testimony," says Moore, on page 342 of the second volume of his "History of Ireland," "the character of the man himself ought to be taken into account; and, finding him so ready a believer and reporter of all sorts of physical marvels and masters, we should consider whether a taste for the morally monstrous may not also have inspired his pen, and induced him in a similar manner, *to impose as well upon himself, perhaps, as his readers.*"

Such is the estimate which Thomas Moore places upon Judge Maguire's stalwart witness. And now, let us introduce into the Superior Court of San Francisco the well-known history of Thomas Mooney, and learn the corrupt character of the Popelibeling Cambrensis, as described by him in the presence of his Honor James G. Maguire. Here is Thomas Mooney's testimony, as recorded on pages 107-9-11 of his "History of Ireland":

"The man who stands conspicuous on the page of time, as the historian *and traducer of Ireland, is Gerald Barry, commonly called Giraldus Cambrensis;* he was the first stranger who undertook to write a history of Ireland. Giraldus was a Welsh priest, who followed the fortunes of his relatives and friends, in their invasions of Ireland, from 1169 to 1171. Henry the Second of England had made claim to the Irish soil, at the court of Rome; he represented the Irish people to Pope Adrian (an Englishman) as destitute of religion, law, morals, or government; and to support this representation, with a view to induce the Pope to join his cause, *he employed Giraldus to write his book.* The Popes of that epoch had much temporal power awarded to them by the nations of Europe. They were, by a kind of universal consent, referred to as arbiters in all national or princely disputes. Their decisions were bowed to with implicit obedience by the whole Christian world. Hence the anxiety of Henry to procure *a corrupt witness* against Ireland, which Giraldus proved himself to be. It appeared that Henry obtained a clandestine bull from Pope Adrian, which (though the genuineness of this document has been disputed by O'Connell and others) conferred authority on Henry to invade Ireland, and force it into subjection to England, and, through the English monarch, more immediately than it had been, to the Pope. To sustain the king, Cambrensis wrote his "History of Ireland." He was only twice in Ireland, once with the adventurers under Strongbow, and once with Prince John, the son of Henry the Second, both visits not occupying more than eighteen months; he only saw about one-third of the country; he, or his, durst proceed no farther; he understood not the language of the people, to whom he was a total stranger, and could not, therefore, consult the records of their ancient archives; he was obliged to substitute inventions, and tales, picked up after the manner of our modern travellers, for historical facts; he mixed only with the most common and illiterate, and such tales as he obtained from the lowest, he distorted and mixed up with the most ridiculous inventions of his own, representing the people as little better *than barbarians,* and their civilization by *conquest* a *meritorious* act. * * * * The "History of Ireland," written by this *half-witted calumniator,* represents the river Shannon as discharging itself into the *North Sea,* whereas it discharges itself into the South or Atlantic. He scarcely mentions who were the first inhabitants of Ireland; as to the Scoto-Milesians, who were the peaceful possessors of it for two thousand years, he gives no account whatever, either of their government, laws, battles or inventions; he says, indeed, there had been one hundred and eighty-one monarchs of that race before his time, but does not give us so much as their names.

Such was the authority on which the majority of subsequent English writers have deprived Ireland of her two thousand years of literature and glory. The learned Abbé McGeoghegan, from whom, in O'Kelly's translation, I have condensed some of the foregoing, asks, with great force, "Have not the Irish an equal right to complain of him, as Josephus [in his first book against Appion] complains of some Greek authors, who undertook to compose the history of the Jewish war, the destruction of Jerusalem, and captivity of the Jews, from hearsay, without having ever been in the country, or seen the things of which they wrote, and who, he said, impudently assumed to themselves the title of historians!" * * * * * *

Men "grave and learned" *have* adopted, age after age, the falsehoods of Cambrensis; have added to these falsehoods, and have piled them up with unblushing effrontery; for this they have been well rewarded with fat places and easy chairs by the British government; and the worst of it is, there are plenty of "grave and learned men," in our day, who pursue the self-same course in reference to unhappy Ireland, and who are rewarded by the self-same power that instigated and rewarded Cambrensis. The works of this *false witness* lay buried in obscurity for four hundred years, until republished by *Camden,* at Frankfort, in 1602; and thus was the poison generated anew through the mind of Europe. Those old, confronted, and *discredited falsehoods* were reproduced by the host of calumniators, who grew up after the Reformation, and who methodically and unblushingly followed Cambrensis, building up their histories on his fictions; for the same motives that actuated Cambrensis, in the twelfth century, have guided the pens of most of the English historians of Ireland since the Reformation. Hammer, Campion, Spenser, Camden, and Leland, are amongst the most conspicuous of the English defamers of Ireland; whilst it must be confessed, with deep humility, that Ireland has vomited forth monstrosities, who have undertaken, for English pay, to disparage and vilify the glorious, though oppressed, land that bore them."

We have other witnesses by whom we

might also prove the contemptible, corrupt and untruthful character of Judge Maguire's chief witness, but we think it entirely unnecessary to call them into Court, as the evidence we have already adduced is sufficient to satisfy every unprejudiced person that neither Popes Adrian IV., Alexander III. nor the Irish people, were guilty of the crimes he charged against them. That is, Adrian never sent a Bull to King Henry II., bestowing Ireland upon him; Alexander III. never sent a Bull sanctioning it; nor were the Irish people the savages which this libellous hireling depicted them.

And now that we have torn the mask away from Judge Maguire's most treasured witness, and shown him up in all his naked deformity, we will turn our attention to the Bull itself, and next week we will introduce as our first witness in defence of Popes Adrian and Alexander, his Eminence Cardinal Moran, whose learned essay upon that interesting historical question is purposely deprecated by the prejudiced author of "Ireland and the Pope," for the sole purpose of undermining its influence and predisposing Irish Catholic readers to reject its truthful statements.

The name of Cardinal Moran carries with it great weight. He is among the most ardent Irish patriots that ever wore a mitre. As an Irish annalist and student of Irish ecclesiastical history he has no equal in our day. He has made the question of the genuineness or the fraudulency of the supposed Bull of Pope Adrian to Henry II., the subject of close study for a number of years. His Eminence visited Rome frequently in order to search among the Vatican Archives for documents bearing on this great Irish Catholic question, and he spent much valuable time in compiling authorities which add great weight to his able argument, which, by the way, Judge Maguire superciliously throws aside with the curt and caustic criticism that it is "a very ingenious but radically defective essay."

Notwithstanding Judge Maguire's *ipse dixit*, however, our Catholic readers have sufficient intelligence to peruse, digest, and decide for themselves whether Cardinal Moran's able contribution in defence of the supposed criminals whom Judge Maguire has prejudged and condemned, is the "defective essay" the author of "Ireland and the Pope" designates it, or an unanswerable argument in proof of the fact that Henry II. of England, and some of his courtiers, *forged* the so-called Bull of Pope Adrian IV. in order to frame for him and them an excuse for invading Ireland.

CHAPTER IV.

Pope Adrian's Bull Proved Fictitious by Cardinal Moran. — An Able Historical Essay. Conclusive Proofs that the Bull was a Forgery.

There was a time when it would be little less than treason to question the genuineness of the Bull by which Pope Adrian IV. is supposed to have made a grant of Ireland to Henry the Second; and, indeed from the first half of the thirteenth to the close of the fifteenth century, it was principally through this supposed grant of the Holy See that the English Government sought to justify their claim to hold dominion in our island. However, opinions and times have changed, and at the present day this Bull of Adrian has as little bearing on the connection between England and this country, as it could possibly have on the union of the Isle of Man with Great Britain.

On the other hand, many strange things have been said during the past months in the so-called nationalist journals, while asserting the genuineness of this famous Bull. I need scarcely remark that *it does not seem to have been the love either of our poor country or of historic truth that inspired their declamation. It proceeded mainly from their hatred to the Sovereign Pontiff, and from the vain hope that such exaggerated statements might in some way weaken the devoted affection of our people for Rome.*

Laying aside such prejudiced opinions, the controversy as to the genuineness of Adrian's Bull should be viewed in a purely historical light, and its decision must depend on the value and weight of the historical arguments which may be advanced to sustain it.

The following is a literal translation of the old

LATIN TEXT OF ADRIAN'S BULL:

"Adrian, Bishop, servant of the servants of God, to our most dear Son in Christ, the illustrious King of the English, greeting and the Apostolical Benediction.

"The thoughts of Your Highness are laudably and profitably directed to the greater glory of your name on earth and to the increase of the reward of eternal happiness in heaven, when as a Catholic Prince you propose to yourself to extend the borders of the Church, to announce the truths of Christian Faith to ignorant and barbarous nations, and to root out the weeds of wickedness from the field of the Lord; and the more effectually to accomplish this, you implore the counsel and favor of the Apostolic See. In which matter we feel assured that the higher your aims are, and the more discreet your proceedings, the happier, with God's aid, will be the result; because those undertakings that proceed from the ardor of faith and the love of religion are sure always to have a prosperous end and issue.

"It is beyond all doubt, as your Highness also doth acknowledge, that Ireland, and all the islands upon which Christ the Sun of Justice has shone, and which have received the knowledge of the Christian faith, are subject to the authority of St. Peter and of the most Holy Roman Church. Wherefore we are the more desirous to sow in them an acceptable seed and a plantation pleasing unto God, because we know that a most rigorous account of them shall be required of us hereafter.

"Now, most dear Son in Christ, you have signified to us that you propose to enter the island of Ireland to establish the observance of law among its people, and to eradicate the weeds of vice; and that you are willing to pay from every house one penny as an annual tribute to St. Peter, and to preserve the rights of the churches of that land, whole and inviolate. We, therefore, receiving with due favor your pious and laudable desires, and graciously granting our consent to your petition, declare that it is pleasing and acceptable to us, that for the purpose of enlarging the limits of the Church, setting bounds to the torrent of vice, reforming evil manners, planting the seeds of virtue and increasing Christian faith, you should enter that island and carry into effect those things which belong to the service of God and to the salvation of that people; and that the people of that land should honorably receive and reverence you as Lord; the rights of the churches being preserved untouched and entire, and reserving the annual tribute of one penny from every house to St. Peter and the most Holy Roman Church.

"If, therefore, you resolve to carry these designs into execution, let it be your study to form that people to good morals, and take such orders both by yourself and by those whom you shall find qualified in faith, in words, and in conduct, that the Church there may be adorned, and the practices of Christian faith be planted and increased; and let all that tends to the glory of God and the salvation of souls be so ordered by you that you may deserve to obtain from God an increase of everlasting reward, and may secure on earth a glorious name throughout all time. Given at Rome," &c.

SOME PRELIMINARY REMARKS.

Before we proceed with the inquiry as to the genuineness of this letter of Pope Adrian, I must detain the reader with a few brief preliminary remarks.—First: Some passages of this important document have been very unfairly dealt with by modern writers while purporting to discuss its merits. Thus, for instance, Prof. Richey, in his "Lectures on Irish History," presenting a translation of the Latin text to the lady pupils of the Alexandra College, makes the Pontiff to write: "You have signified to us, our well-beloved son in

Christ, that you propose to enter the island of Ireland *in order to subdue the people*, etc. . . . . We therefore, regarding your pious and laudable design with due favor, etc., do hereby declare our will and pleasure, that for the purpose of enlarging the borders of the Church, etc., you do enter and *take possession of that island.**
Such an erroneous translation must be the more blamed in the present instance, as it was scarcely to be expected that the ladies whom the learned lecturer addressed would have leisure to consult the original Latin text, or the document which he professed to translate. This, however, is not the only error into which Professor Richey has been betrayed regarding the Bull of Adrian IV. Having mentioned in a note the statement of Roger de Wendover, that the Bull was obtained from Pope Adrian in the year 1155, he adds his own opinion that "the grant appears to have been made in 1172."† However, at that date, Pope Adrian had been for about thirteen years freed from the cares of his Pontificate, having passed to a better world in the year 1159.

Second: Any one who attentively weighs the words of the above document will see at once that it precinds from all title of conquest, while at the same time it makes no gift of transfer of dominion to Henry the Second. As far as this letter of Adrian is concerned, the visit of Henry to our island might be the enterprise of a friendly monarch, who, at the invitation of a distracted State, would seek by his presence to restore peace, and to uphold the observance of the laws. Thus, those foolish theories must be at once set aside which rest on the groundless supposition that Pope Adrian authorized the invasion and plunder of our people by the Anglo-Norman adventurers.

Third: There is another serious error which must also be set at rest by the simple perusal of the above document. I mean that opinion which would fain set forth the letter of Pope Adrian as a dogmatical definition of the Holy See, as if the Sovereign Pontiff then spoke *ex cathedra i. e.*, solemnly propounded some doctrine to be believed by the Universal Church Now it is manifest from the letter itself that it has none of the conditions required for a definition *ex cathedra*; it is not addressed to the Universal Church; it proposes no matter of faith to be held by all the children of Christ; in fact it presents no doctrine whatever to be believed by the faithful, and it is nothing more than a commendatory letter addressed to Henry, resting on the good intentions set forth by that monarch himself. There is one maxim, indeed, which awakens the suspicions of the old Gallican school, viz.: that "all the islands are subject to the authority of St. Peter." However it is no doctrinal teaching that is thus propounded; it is a matter of fact admitted by Henry himself, a principle recognized by the international law of Europe in the Middle Ages, a maxim set down by the various States, the better to maintain peace and concord among the princes of Christendom. To admit, however or to call in question the teaching of the civil law of Europe, as embodied in that maxim, has nothing whatever to say to the great prerogative of St. Peter's successors, while they solemnly propound to the faithful, in unerring accents, the doctrines of Divine faith.

Fourth: To many it will seem a paradox, and yet it is a fact, that the supposed Bull of Pope Adrian *had no part whatever in the submission of the Irish chieftains to Henry the Second*. Even according to those who maintain its genuineness, this Bull was not published till the year 1175, and certainly no mention of it was made in Ireland till long after the submission of the Irish princes. The successes of the Anglo-Normans were mainly due to a far different cause, viz., to the superior military skill and equipment of the invaders. Among the Anglo-Norman leaders were some of the bravest knights of the kingdom, who had won their laurels in the wars of France and Wales. Their weapons and armor rendered it almost impossible for the Irish troops to meet them in the open field. The crossbow, which was made use of for the first time in this invasion, produced as great a change in military tactics as the rifled cannon in our own days. When Henry came in person to Ireland his numerous army hushed all opposition. There were 400 vessels in his fleet, and if a minimum of twenty-five armed men be allowed for each vessel, we will have an army of at least 10,000 men fully equipped, landing unopposed on the southern shores of our island.‡ It is to this imposing force, and the armor of the Anglo-Norman knights, that we must, in great part, refer whatever success attended this invasion of the English monarch.

---

* "Lecture on the History of Ireland," by A. G. Richey, Esq., delivered to the pupils of the Alexandra College during the Hilary and Easter Terms of 1869. Dublin, 1869, pages 122, 123.

† *Ibid.* page 121.

‡ The authorities for the statements made in the text may be seen in *Macariae Excidium* edited by Mr. O'Callaghan for the R. I. A., in 1850.

HISTORICAL CRITICISMS ON THE BULL.

To proceed now with the immediate matter of our present historical inquiry, the following is the summary of the arguments in favor of the authenticity of Pope Adrian's letter, inserted in the *Irishman* newspaper of June 8 last, by J. C. O'Callaghan, Esq., editor of the *Macariae Excidium*, and author of many valuable works on Irish history: "We have, firstly the testimony of John of Salisbury, Secretary to the Archbishop of Canterbury, and one of the ablest writers of the day, who relates his having been the envoy from Henry to Adrian, in 1155, to ask for a grant of Ireland, and such a grant having been then obtained, accompanied by a gold ring, containing a fine emerald, as a token of investure, with which grant and ring the said John returned to Henry. We have, secondly, the grant or Bull of Adrian, *in extenso*, in the works of Giraldus Cambrensis, and his contemporary Radulfus de Diceto, Dean of London, as well as in those of Roger de Wendover, and Mathew Paris. We have, thirdly, several Bulls of Adrian's successor, Pope Alexander III., still further to the purport of Adrian's, or in Henry's favor. We have, fourthly, the recorded public reading of the Bulls of Adrian and Alexander, at a meeting of Bishops in Waterford in 1175. We have, fifthly, after the liberation of Scotland from England at Bannockburn, and the consequent invitation of Bruce's brother Edward, to be King of Ireland, the Bull of Adrian prefixed to the eloquent lay remonstrance, which the Irish presented to Pope John XXII. against the English; the same Bull moreover, referred to in the remonstrance, itself as so ruinous to Ireland; and a copy of that Bull, accordingly sent back by the Pope to Edward II. of England, for his use under those circumstances. We have, sixthly, from Cardinal Baronius, in his great work, the *Annales Ecclesiastici*, under Adrian IV., his grant of Ireland to his countrymen in full, or, as is said, '*ex codice Vaticano, diploma datum ad Henricum, Anglorum, Regem*. We have seventhly, the Bull in the *Bullarium Romanum*, as printed in Rome in 1739. The citations and references in support of all the foregoing statements will be found in the 'Notes and Illustrations' of my edition of *Macariae Excidium* for the Irish Archeological Society in 1850, given in such a manner as must satisfy the most skeptical.''

THE TESTIMONY ANALYZED.

Examining these arguments in detail. I will follow the order thus marked out by Mr. O'Callaghan.

I.—We meet, in the first place, the testimony of John of Salisbury, who, in his *Metalogicus* (lib. iv., cap. 42,) writes, that being in an official capacity at the Papal Court, in 1155, Pope Adrian IV., then granted the investure of Ireland to the illustrious King Henry II. of England. I do not wish in any way to detract from the praise due to John of Salisbury, who was at this time one of the ablest courtiers of Henry II. However, the words here imputed to him must be taken with great reserve. Inserted as they are in the last chapter of his work, they are not at all required by the context; by cancelling them the whole passage runs smoother and is more connected in every way. This is more striking, as in another work of the same writer, which is entitled *Polycraticus* we meet with a detailed account of the various incidents of his embassy to Pope Adrian, yet he there makes no mention of the Bull in Henry's favor, or of the gold ring and its fine emerald, or of the grant of Ireland, all of which would have been so important for his narrative.

We must also hold in mind the time when the *Metalogicus* was written. The author himself fixes its date; for immediately before asking the prayers of "those who read his book, and those who hear it read," he tells us that the news of Pope Adrian's death had reached him a little time before, and he adds that his own patron, Theobald, Archbishop of Canterbury though still living, was weighed down by many infirmities.† Now, Pope Adrian departed this life in 1159, and the death of Archbishop, Theobald happened in 1161. Hence, Gile and other editors of John of Salisbury's works, without a dissentient voice, refer the *Metalogicus* to the year 1159.

QUEER ACTION OF HENRY II.

Now, it is a matter beyond the reach of controversy, that if Henry the Second obtained the investure of Ireland from Adrian IV., he kept this grant a strict secret till at least the year 1175. For twenty years, *i. e.*, from 1155 to 1175, no mention was made of the gift of Adrian. Henry did not refer to it when authorizing his vassals to join Diarmaid in 1167, when Adrian's Bull would have been so opportune to justify his intervention; he did not mention it when he himself set out for Ireland to solicit and receive the homage of the Irish princes; he did not even refer to it when he assumed his new title and accomplished the purpose of his expedition. The Council of Cashel in 1172 was the first episcopal assembly after Henry's arrival in Ireland; the Papal Legate was present

† Metalogicus, lib. iv. cap. ult.

there, and did Adrian's Bull exist it should necessarily have engaged the attention of the assembled Fathers. Nevertheless, not a whisper as to Adrian's grant was to be heard at that famous Council. Even the learned editor of "Cambrensis Eversus" while warmly asserting the genuineness of Adrian's Bull, admits "there is not any, even the slightest authority, for asserting that its existence was known in Ireland before the year 1172, or for three years later"—vol ii., p. 440, note z). It is extremely difficult, in any hypothesis, to explain in a satisfactory way this mysterious silence of Henry the Second, nor is it easy to understand how a fact so important, so vital to the interests of Ireland, could remain so many years concealed from those who ruled the destinies of the Irish Church. For, we must hold in mind that throughout that interval Ireland numbered among its Bishops one who held the important office of Legate of the Holy See; our Church had constant intercourse with England and the continent, and through St. Lawrence O'Toole and a hundred other distinguished Prelates, enjoyed in the fullest manner the confidence of Rome.

HISTORICAL CONTRADICTIONS CONSIDERED.

If Adrian granted this Bull to Henry at the solicitation of John of Salisbury in 1155 there is but one explanation for the silence of this courtier in his diary, as set forth in the *Polycraticus*, and for the concealment of the Bull itself from the Irish Bishops and people, viz., that this secrecy was required by the State policy of the English monarch. And, if it be so, how then can we be asked to admit as genuine this passage of the *Metalogicus*, in which the astute agent of Henry, still continuing to discharge offices of the highest trust in the Court, would proclaim to the world as early as the year 1159, that Pope Adrian had made this formal grant of Ireland to his royal master, and that the solemn record of the investiture of this high dignity was preserved in the public archives of the kingdom?

It must also be added that there are some phrases in this passage of the *Metalogicus* which manifestly betray the hand of the impostor. Thus the words *usque in hodiernum diem* imply that a long interval had elapsed since the concession was made by Pope Adrian, and surely they could not have been penned by John of Salisbury in 1159. Much less can we suppose that this writer employed the words *jure hæreditario possidendam*. No such hereditary right is granted in the Bull of Adrian. It was not dreamt of even during the first of the Anglo-Norman invasion, and it was only at a later period, when the Irish chieftains scornfully rejected the Anglo-Norman law of hereditary succession, that this expedient was thought of for allaying the fierce opposition of our people.

Thus we are forced to regard the supposed testimony of John of Salisbury as nothing more than a clumsy interpolation, which probably was not inserted in his work till many years after the first Anglo-Norman invasion of our island.

THE MAIN ARGUMENT CONSIDERED.

I now come to the second and main argument of those who seek to defend the authenticity of Pope Adrian's Bull. We have Giraldus Cambrensis, they say, a contemporary witness, whose testimony is unquestionable. He asserts in full this letter of Adrian IV. and he nowhere betrays the slightest doubt in regard to its genuineness.

Some years ago we might perhaps have accepted this flattering character of Giraldus Cambrensis, but at the present day, and since the publication of an accurate edition of his historical works, it is impossible for us to do so.

It was not till many years after the death of Pope Adrian that Gerald de Barry, better known by the name of Giraldus Cambrensis, entered on the stage of Irish history. Twice he visited Ireland after the year 1183, and on both occasions he discharged those duties which, at the present day, would merit for him the title of special court correspondent with the invading army. The *Expugnatio Hibernica*, in which he inserts Adrian's Bull, may justly be said to have been *written to order*. Hence, as a matter of course, Giraldus adopted in it as genuine every document set forth as such by his royal master, and any statements that strengthened the claim or promoted the interests of his brother Welsh adventurers were sure not to be too nicely weighed in the scales of criticism by such an historian. The editor of the works of Giraldus, just now published under the direction of the Master of the Rolls, has fully recognized this special feature of the historical writings of Giraldus. The official catalogue describing the *Expugnatio Hibernica*, of which we treat, expressly says: "It may be regarded rather as a great epic than a sober relation of facts occurring in his own days. No one can peruse it without coming to the conclusion that it is rather *a poetical fiction than a prosaic truthful history*."

GIRALDUS CAMBRENSIS CORNERED.

In the preface to the fifth volume of the Historical Treatises of Giraldus, the learned editor, Rev. James F. Dimock, enters at considerable length into the inquiry, whether, the *Expugnatio Hibernica* was to be accepted as genuine and authentic history. I need do no more than state the conclusions which he enunciates:

"I think I have said enough to justify me in refusing to accept Giraldus' history of the Irish and of their English invaders as sober, truthful history." And again he writes: "My good friend and pre-laborer in editing these volumes of Giraldus' works (Mr. Brewer) says of the *Expugnatio*, that Giraldus would seem to have regarded his subject rather as a great epic, which undoubtedly it was, than a sober relation of facts occurring in his own days. . . . . .

This is a most true and characteristic description of Giraldus' treatment of his subject; the treatise certainly is, in great measure, rather a poetical fiction than a prosaic truthful history."

I must further remark as another result from Rev. Mr. Dimock's researches, that the old text of Giraldus in reference to Pope Adrian's Bull, from which Mr. O'Callaghan's citations are made, is now proved *to be singularly defective.* I will give the pithy words of that learned editor, which are stronger than any I would wish to use: "*No more absurd nonsensical a muddle was ever blundered into by the most stupid of abbreviators.*" It is of course from the ancient MSS. of the work that this corruption of the old text is mainly proved; but it should indeed be apparent from an attentive study of the very printed text itself, for, as Mr. Dimock remarks, being accurately translated, its words "marvellously contrive to make Henry, in 1172, apply for and procure this privilege from Pope Adrian, who died in 1159, and with equally marvellous confusion they represent John of Salisbury, who had been Henry's agent in procuring this privilege in 1155, as sent, not to Ireland, but to Rome, for the purpose of publishing the Bull at Waterford in 1174 or 1175."

I will only add, regarding the testimony of Giraldus Cambrensis, that in the genuine text of the *Expugnatio Hibernica* he places on the same level the Bull of Adrian IV. and that of Alexander III. Nevertheless, as we will just now see he elsewhere admits that there were many and grave suspicions that the supposed Bull of Alexander had never been granted by the Holy See.

OTHER AUTHORITIES ANALYZED.

The other names mentioned together with Giraldus will not detain us long. They are all writers who only incidentally make reference to Irish matters, and in these they naturally enough take Giraldus for their guide.

Ralph de Diceto wrote about 1210, and like Giraldus, received his honors at the hands of Henry the Second. Irish historians have not yet accepted him as a guide in reference to matters connected with our country. For instance, the Synod of Cashel of 1172, which was one of the most important events of that period of our history, is described by him as held in Lismore.

Roger de Wendover was a monk of St. Alban's, who died 6th of May, 1237. His *Flores Historiarum* begin with the creation of the world, and end two years before his death, in 1235. He merely compendiates other sources down to the beginning of the 13th century. It is only the subsequent portion of his work which is held in esteem by our annalists.

Mathew Paris was a brother religious of Roger de Wendover, in St. Albans, where he died in 1259. Mr. Coxe, who edited a portion of the *Flores Historiarum* for the English Historical Society (1841–1844), has proved that down to the year 1235 Mathew Paris only commendiates the work of Wendover. At all events his *Historia Major* is of very little weight. A distinguished German historian of the present day, Schrodl, thus conveys his strictures on its merits:

"Se trompe a chaque instant, et, entraine, par son evaugle rage de critique, donne pour des faits historigues des anecdotes piquantes qui n'ont aucune authenticite, des legendes, deraisonnables et toutes sortes de details suspacts, exageres et calomnieux.

To the testimony of such writers we may well oppose the silence of Peter de Blois, Secretary of Henry the Second, though chronicling the chief events of Henry's reign, and the silence of all our native annalists, not one of whom ever mentions the Bull of Adrian.

THE THIRD ARGUMENT CONSIDERED.

But it is time to pass on to the third argument which is advanced by our opponents. It is quite true that we have some letters or Bulls of Pope Alexander III., connected with the Irish invasion. Three of these, written in 1172, are certainly authentic. They are preserved in the "Liber Niger Scaccarii" from which they were edited by Hearne, and in later times they have been accurately printed by Mr. O'Callaghan and Rev. Dr. Kelly. They are addressed respectfully to the Irish Bishops, King Henry and the Irish princes. So far, however, are these letters from corroborating the genuineness of Pope Adrian's Bull, that they furnish an unanswerable argument for wholly setting it aside as groundless and unauthentic. They are entirely devoted to the circumstances of the invasion of our island and its results, and yet the only title that they recognize is "that monarch's power and the submission of the Irish chieftains." They simply ignore any Bull of Adrian, and any investiture from the Holy See.

BULL OF POPE ALEXANDER III.

There is, however, another Bull of Alexander III. preserved by Giraldus Cambrensis, which he supposed to have been granted at the request of King Henry in 1172, and is confirmatory of the gift and investiture made by Pope Adrian. Mr. O'Callaghan holds that this Bull of Alexander III. sets at rest forever all doubt as to the genuineness of the grant made by Adrian IV.

The question at once suggests itself: Is this Bull of Alexander III. to be admitted as genuine and authentic? If its own authority be doubtful, surely it cannot suffice to prop up the tottering cause of Adrian's Bull. Now its style is entirely different from that of the three authentic letters of which we have just spoken. Quite in opposition to these letters, "the only authority alleged in it for Henry's right to Ireland is the Bull of Adrian" as Dr. Lanigan allows. The genuine letters are dated from Tusculum, where, as we know from other sources, Alexander actually resided in 1172. On the other hand, this confirmatory Bull, though supposed to have been obtained in 1172 is dated *from Rome,* thus clearly betraying the hand of the impostor. Such was the disturbed condition of Rome at that period that it was impossible for His Holiness to reside there; and hence we find him sometimes holding his Court in Tusculum, at other times in Segni, Anagni, or Ferrara. It was only when these disturbances were quelled that Alexander III. was able, in 1178, to return in triumph to his capital.

BUT THERE IS STILL ANOTHER REASON

why we must doubt of the authority of this confirmatory Bull. The researches of Rev. Mr. Dimock have proved what Ussher long ago remarked, that this Bull of Alexander originally formed part of the work of Giraldus Cambrensis, although later copyists, and the first editors, including the learned Camden, recognizing its spuriousness, excluded it from Giraldus' text. The matter is now set at rest, for the ancient MSS. clearly prove that it originally formed part of the *Expugnatio Hibernica.* Thanks, however, to the zeal and industry of Mr. Brewer, we are at present acquainted with another work of Giraldus, written at a later period than His Historical Tracts on Ireland. It is entitled *De Principis Instructione,* and was edited in 1846 for the *Anglia Christiana* Society. Now, in this treatise, Giraldus refers to the Bull of Alexander III., of which we treat, but he prefixes the following remarkable words. "*Some assert or imagine that this Bull was obtained from the Pope; but others deny that it was ever obtained from the Pontiff.* "Sicut a quibusdam impetratum asseritur aut confingitur; ab aliis autem unquam impetratum fuisse negatur." Surely these words should suffice to convince the most skeptical that the fact of the Bull of Alexander being recited by Giraldus in his "Expugnatio Hibernica" is a very unsatisfactory ground on which to rest the argument for its genuineness.

AS REGARDS THE SYNOD OF WATERFORD

in 1175, and the statement that the Bulls of Adrian and Alexander were published therein for the first time, all these matters rest on the very doubtful authority of Giraldus Cambrensis. We have no record in the Irish Annals that any general meeting of the Irish Bishops was held in Waterford in 1175. The circumstances of the country rendered such a Synod impossible; for war and dissensions ranged throughout the length and breadth of our island. It was in that year, however, that the first Bishop was appointed by King Henry to the See of Waterford as Ware informs us; and, perhaps, we would not err were we to suppose that the Synod so pompously set forth by Giraldus was a convention of the Anglo-Norman clergy of Waterford under their newly appointed Prelate, all of whom would, no doubt, joyfully accept the official documents presented in the name of the King by Nicholas of Wallingford.

Leland supposes that this Synod of Waterford was not held till 1177. The disturbed state of the kingdom, however, rendered a Synod equally impossible in that year, and all our ancient authorities utterly ignore such a Synod.

IN THE REMONSTRANCE ADDRESSED

by the Irish princes and people to John XXII., about the year 1315, repeated mention is made of the Bull of Adrian. But then it is only cited there as a conclusive argument *ad hominem* against the English traducers of our nation, "lest the bitter and venomous calumnies of the English, and their unjust and unfounded attacks upon us and all who support our rights, may in any degree influence the mind of your Holiness." The Bull of Adrian IV. was published by the English, and set forth by them as the charter deed of their rule in Ireland; yet they violated in a most flagrant manner all the conditions of that Papal grant. The Irish princes and people in self-defense had now made over the sovereignty of the island to Edward de Bruce, brother of the Scottish King; they style him their adopted monarch, and they pray the Pope to give a formal sanction to their proceedings. Thus, throughout the whole Remonstrance, the Bull of Adrian is used as a telling argument against the injustice of the invaders, and as a precedent which John XXII might justly follow in sanctioning the transfer of the Irish crown to Edward Bruce. But in all this the historian will find no grounds for asserting the genuineness of the supposed Bulls of Adrian or Alexander. We will just now see that at this very time the Irish people universally regarded these Bulls as spurious inventions of their English enemies.

Baronius, the eminent ecclesiastical historian, inserts in his invaluable *Annals* the Bull of Adrian IV., "from a Vatican Manuscript." This is the sixth argument advanced by Mr. O'Callaghan.

IT IS NOT MY INTENTION TO QUESTION

in any way the services rendered by Cardinal Baronius to the cause of our Church history; but at the same time no one will deny that considerable progress has been made in historical research during the past three hundred and fifty years, and many documents are now set aside which were then accepted as unquestioned on the supposed reliable authority of preceding chroniclers.

In the present instance we are not left in doubt as to the source whence Baronius derived his information regarding Adrian's supposed Bull. During my stay in Rome I took occasion to inquire whether the MSS of the eminent annalist, which are happily preserved, indicated the special "Vatican Manuscript" referred to in this text, and I was informed by the learned archivist, of the Vatican, Monsignor Theiner, who is at present engaged in giving a new edition and continuing the great work of Baronius, that the *Codex Vaticanus* referred to is a MS. copy of the history of Mathew Paris, which is preserved in the Vatican Library. Thus it is the testimony of Mathew Paris alone that here confronts us in the pages of Baronius and no new argument can be taken from the words of the eminent annalist. Relying on the same high authority, I am happy to state that nowhere in the private archives or among the private papers of the Vatican, or in the *Regesta*, which Jaffe's researches have made so famous, or in the various indices of the Pontifical Letters, can a single trace be found of the supposed Bulls of Adrian IV. and Alexander III.

THE LAST ARGUMENT ADVANCED

by Mr. O'Callaghan will not detain us long. The insertion or omission of such ancient records in the *Bullarium* is a matter that depends wholly on the critical skill of the editor. Curious enough, in one edition of the *Bullarium*, as may be seen in the references of Dr. Lanigan, Adrian's Bull is inserted, while no mention is made of that of Alexander. In another edition, however, the Bull of Alexander is given in full, while the Bull of Adrian is omitted. We may well leave our opponents to settle this matter with the conflicting editors of the *Bullarium*. They probably, like Baronius, merely copied the Bull of Adrian from Mathew Paris, and erred in doing so. Labbe, in his magnificent edition of the Councils, also publishes Adrian's Bull; but then he expressly tells us that it is copied from the work of Mathew Paris.

THE IRISH OPINION OF ADRIAN'S BULL.

We have thus, as far as the limits of this article will allow, examined in detail the various arguments which support the genuineness of the supposed Bull; and now it only remains for us to conclude that there are no sufficient grounds for accepting that document as the genuine work of Pope Adrian.

Indeed, the Irish nation at all times, as if instinctively, shrunk from accepting it as genuine, and unhesitatingly pronounced it an Anglo-Norman forgery. We have already seen how even Giraldus Cambrensis refers to the doubts which had arisen regarding the Bull of Pope Alexander; but we have at hand still more conclusive evidence that Adrian's Bull was universally rejected by our people. There is, happily preserved in the Barberini archives, Rome, a MS. of the fourteenth century, containing a series of official papers connected with the Pontificate of John XXIII., and among them is a letter from the Lord Justiciary and the Royal Seal, and presented to His Holiness by William of Nottingham, Canon and Precentor of St. Patrick's Cathedral, Dublin, about the year 1325. In this important, but hitherto unnoticed document, the Irish are accused of very many crimes, among which is insidiously introduced the rejection of supposed Bulls: "Moreover, they assert that the King of England under false pretences and by false Bulls obtained the dominion of Ireland, and this opinion is commonly held by them." "Asserantes etiam Dominum Regem Anglia ex falsa suggestione et ex falsis Bullis terram Hibernie in dominium impetrosse ac communiter hoc tenentes."

This national tradition was preserved unbroken throughout the turmoil of the fifteenth and sixteenth centuries, and on the revival of our historical literature in the beginning of the seventeenth century was registered in the pages of Lynch, Stephen White, and other writers.

It will be well, also, while forming our judgment regarding the supposed Bull of Adrian, to hold in mind the disturbed state of society, especially in Italy, at the time to which it refers. At the present day it would be no easy matter indeed for such a forgery to survive more than a few weeks. But at the close of the twelfth century it was far otherwise. Owing to the constant revolutions and disturbances that then prevailed, the Pontiff was oftentimes obliged to fly from city to city; and frequently his papers were seized and burned, and he himself detained as a hostage or a prisoner by his enemies. Hence it is that several forged Bulls, examples of which are given in "Cambrensis Eversis," date from these times. More than one of the grants made to the Norman families are now believed to rest on such forgeries; and that the Anglo-Norman adventurers in Ireland were not strangers to such deeds of darkness, appears from the fact that a matrix for forging the Papal Seal of such Bulls, now preserved in the R. I. Academy, was found a few years ago in the ruins of one of the earliest Anglo-Norman monasteries founded by De Courcy.

HOW THE BULL WAS PROMULGATED.

The circumstances of the publication of the Bull by Henry were surely not calculated to disarm suspicion. Our opponents do not even pretend that it was made known in Ireland till the year 1175, and hence, though publicly granted with solemn investiture, as John of Salisbury's testimony would imply, and though its record was deposited in the public archives of the kingdom, this Bull, so vital to the interests of the Irish Church, should have remained dormant, for twenty years, unnoticed in Rome, unnoticed by Henry's courtiers, still more, unnoticed by the Irish Bishops, and I will add, unnoticed by the Continental Sovereigns so jealous of the power and preponderance of the English Monarch. For such suppositions there is indeed no parallel in the whole history of investitures.

It is seldom, too, that the hand of the imposture may not be detected in some at least of the minor details of the spurious document. In the present instance more than one ancient MS. preserves the concluding formula of the Bull: "Datum Romae," dated from Rome. Now, this simple formula would suffice of itself to prove the whole Bull to be a forgery. Before the news of the election of Pope Adrian to the Chair of St. Peter could reach England, that Pontiff was obliged to seek for safety in flight from his capital. Rome was in revolt, and Arnold of Brescia sought to renew there a spectre of the old Pagan Republic. John of Salisbury, in his "Polycraticus" faithfully attests that on his arrival in Italy, the Papal Court was held not in Rome but in Beneventum; it was in this city he presented to Pope Adrian the congratulations of Henry II., and he mentions his sojourn there during the three months that he remained in Italy. This is further confirmed by the Italian chronicles. Baronius saw the inconsistency of the formula, Datum Romae," with the date 1155, and hence, in his Annals, he entered Adrian's Bull under the year 1159; but, if this date be correct, surely then that Bull could not have been brought to Henry by John of Salisbury, and the passage of the "Metalogicus" referring to it must at once be admitted a forgery. Other historians have been equally puzzled to find a year for this supposed Bull. For instance, O'Halloran in his History of Ireland, while admitting that the Irish people always regarded the Bull as a forgery, refers its date to the year 1167, that is eight years after the death of Pope Adrian IV.

A CONCLUDING REFLECTION.

There is only one other reflection with which I wish to detain the reader. The condition of our country and the relations between Ireland and the English King, which are set forth in the supposed Bull, are precisely those of the year 1172; but it would have required more than a prophetic vision to have anticipated them in 1155. In 1155 Ireland was not in a state of turmoil or verging toward barbarism; on the contrary, it was rapidly progressing and renewing its claims to religious and moral pre-eminence. I will add, that Pope Adrian, who had studied under Irish masters, knew well this flourishing condition of our country. In 1172 however, a sad change had come over our island. Four years of continual warfare, and the ravages of the Anglo-Norman filibusterers, since their first landing in 1168, had well nigh reduced Ireland to a state of barbarism, and the authentic letters of Alexander III., in 1172 faithfully describe its most deplorable condition. Moreover, an expedition of Henry to Ireland, which would not be an invasion, and yet would merit the homage of the Irish Princes, was simply an impossibility in 1155. But owing to the special circumstances of the Kingdom, such in reality was the expedition of Henry in 1172. He set out for

Ireland, not avowedly to invade and conquer it, but to curb the insolence and to punish the deeds of pillage of his own Norman freebooters. Hence during his stay in Ireland he fought no battle and made no conquest; his first measures of severity were directed against some of the most lawless of the early Norman adventurers, and this more than anything else reconciled the native princes to his military display. In return he received from a majority of the Irish chieftains the empty title of *Ardrigh*, or "Head Sovereign," which did not suppose any conquest on his part, and did not involve any surrender of their own hereditary rights. Such a state of things could not have been imagined in 1155; and yet it is one which is implied in the spurious Bull of the much maligned Pontiff, Adrian the Fourth.

CHAPTER V.

A Historical Contrast.—The Characters of Pope Adrian IV. and King Henry II. Compared.

Having in our previous chapters thoroughly diagnosed the disreputable character of Giraldus Cambrensis, whose literary services King Henry II. of England secured in order to introduce into his history of Ireland the *forged* Bull of Pope Adrian IV., by which that Pontiff was supposed to have granted Ireland to Henry Plantagenet, it is now in order to introduce historical testimony which will forcibly demonstrate the fact that the character of King Henry the Second of England was not of that calibre which would entitle him to receive the confidence of any Pontiff, much less to have bestowed upon him unlimited authority over an *independent people*, such as the Irish were up to the time of the English invasion.

In order that our readers may the more readily understand this important historical question, it is well to bear in mind a few important facts and dates, so as to more clearly understand the character which King Henry II. presented to both the Pope and the Irish people at the opening of the very year when the *forged* Bull of Giraldus Cambrensis was first brought to light.

Nicholas Breakspeare was elected to succeed Pope Eugenius III., on December 2nd, A. D., 1154, and took the name of Adrian IV. By birth he was an Englishman, and —as a notable historian truly remarks—the extraordinary circumstances attending his promotion to the Pontifical Chair of St. Peter plainly indicated the workings of the Almighty Hand. Almighty God called this Servant of Servants from the lowest rank of human society to the most supereminent position man can occupy, and no Catholic can for a moment harbor the thought that Almighty God placed Nicholas Breakspeare in the Chair of St. Peter for the sole purpose of enslaving the Irish people by handing them over to the brutality of a British king.

The lives of all the Popes have lessons in them for every Catholic, hence, in order that our readers may have an intimate knowledge of the genius displayed by this much-maligned Pontiff, we will briefly sketch his life and his labors, so that every person interested in knowing the truth may conclude at once that Pope Adrian was the last man in the world who would be guilty of making such a concession to Henry II. of England as to bestow Ireland upon that monarch in order to purify the morals of the Irish people, and for the propagation of religion.

The father of Pope Adrian IV. was a servant in the English monastery of St. Alban's, where the son was supported through the charity of the Religious. After a few years of penury and parental cruelty, young Nicholas Breakspeare wandered off to work his own way in the world, and after spending some time in England he crossed over to France, where he enjoyed for a period the hospitality of the monks in the monastery of St. Rufus, near Arles. He had not been long in the company of these Religious until they discovered in his character a religious zeal, a remarkable regularity of life, a lofty and generous disposition, and an amount of genius and superiority which prompted them to elect him Abbot. His strictness of discipline, however, caused some of the monks to complain to Pope Eugenius III., and when that holy Pontiff heard their story he said to them: "Go and choose an Abbot with whom you may be able, or rather with whom you are willing to live in peace; your present Superior shall not long be a burden to you; *I appoint him Cardinal of Albano.*"

From these two circumstances it may easily be surmized that the future Pope Adrian IV. was no ordinary man. Honors sought him, and not he them. He was far from being the sycophant implied by those who foolishly assert that he bestowed Ireland upon Henry II., because he was an Englishman; and his future course in the government of the Church proved his dignity and sterling justice in every cause that came before him.

The new Cardinal stood so high in the estimation of Pope Eugenius III., that he sent him as Apostolic Legate to the northern Kingdoms of Denmark, Sweden and Norway. In each of these lands he endeared himself to the people through his prudence, piety, eloquence, and gentleness of disposition. He was the Apostle of Norway, and the bosom friend of the great St. Eric, or Henry, the martyred Bishop of Upsal, whose feast falls on January 19th. Thus every Catholic can readily understand that the experience which Pope Adrian IV. gained by his Apostolic labors among the Danes, Swedes and Norwegians, as well as the constant intimacy which existed between him and the saintly Bishops who were then planting the faith among these different nations, developed in him those qualities which made him afterwards illustrious as one among the many notable Pontiffs that occupied the Chair of St. Peter.

On the return of the Cardinal of Albano to Rome, his high reputation at once gained for him the unanimous vote of the College of Cardinals as the successor of Pope Anastasius IV., then recently deceased. But scarcely had Nicholas Breakspeare assumed the title of Pope Adrian IV., ere he was called upon to do battle against *royal encroachments* upon the rights of the Roman people. And yet, unreflecting writers say that the same Pontiff permitted and authorized the *royal encroachment* of Henry II. of England upon the *independent* Irish people.

Arnald of Brescia was in Rome, developing his plans for the revival of paganism, but Adrian IV. was equal to the occasion, and by placing Rome under Interdict circumvented the designs of the enemy of Christianity, who was beheaded in 1155.

The next enemy of the Church over whom Pope Adrian prevailed was William the Bad, who succeeded his father Roger on the throne of Sicily. He then faced no less a foeman than Frederick Barbarossa whose path through Lombardy was marked by rivers of blood and by mountains of ruins. Barbarossa sought to make the whole world a single Empire, with—as history records him saying—"the Sovereign Pontiff as its spiritual and the Emperor as its temporal chief." But Pope Adrian IV. scorned the bribe. He determined at all hazards to *defend the rights of the people* of Lombardy against this second Attila, and the Pontiff triumphed over the persecutor in the end, going so far as to excommunicate the Archbishop of Milan for falsely asserting that the will of Frederick Barbarossa was "right, justice and law." The Pope also severely censured the Bishops of Lombardy for their slavish compliance to every demand of this ambitious tyrant. Here again we may well ask: Was such a Pontiff likely to act in opposition to all his antecedents by quietly enslaving Ireland to England whilst he used all his powerful influence to prevent the people of Lombardy and of Italy from the loss of their freedom?

Pope Adrian died at Anagni on September 1st, A. D., 1159, leaving behind him a brilliant record, unsullied by a single speck of iniquity. "He is described by his contemporaries," says Rev. John Miley, in his

"History of the Papal States," "as a man full of kindliness and good nature; mild, patient, profound: versed in Greek and Latin literature: eloquent: a complete master in ecclesiastical music: powerful in handling the Word of God, not easily ruffled, prone to forgive, liberal of alms and gifts, and altogether a most amiable and perfect character."

Now let us place in contrast with Pope Adrian IV., the character of King Henry II. of England, so that we may discover, if possible, a single reason why Henry Plantagenet should be authorized to propagate what is styled his "glorious renown," in the bogus Bull published in Judge Maguire's pamphlet, wherein this fictitious document is dated as "Given at *Rome*, in the year of Salvation, 1156.

The first pen-portrait of King Henry II., whose "glorious renown" Pope Adrian IV. is falsely accused of desiring to propagate, is taken from an address delivered at Fort Wayne, Indiana, on St. Patrick's Day, 1881, by Hon. Edmund F. Dunne, LL. D., ex-Chief Justice of Arizona. Speaking of the English invaders of Ireland, Judge Dunne says:

"But neither was it from the Normans proper that the troubles of Ireland began. There was a tribe came after William the Conqueror worse than the Normans, the Angevins, and they were the devils incarnate who began the present troubles of the Irish people. They were descended from one of those moral monsters with which God in his wrath sometimes afflicts the world, from the infamous Fulc the Black, wife-murderer of Anjou. Henry II. was his representative in England. This was the man who began English rule in Ireland. According to the accounts of even English historians, *he was a devil incarnate* if there ever was such a thing in this world, and his end as told by English writers was so fearfully horrible, not from physical torture, for no man touched him, so fearfully horrible I say that I would not dare shock you to-night by a repetition of the *blasphemies which preceded it.*"

A nice man this to "teach the Christian faith to the ignorant and rude Irish," and to extirpate the roots of vice "from the field of the Lord," as the fictitious Bull makes Pope Adrian IV. say to "His dearest Son in Christ, the Illustrious King of England!"

"You have heard of a King of England who, enraged because he could not chastise the people of Wales as he wished, turned upon the hostages he held, the sons and daughters of the noblest families of Wales and rooted out the eyes of the youths and amputated the ears and noses of the daughters. This was the king who did it."

Yet the bogus Bull tells us that this same inhuman monster was authorized to "extend the borders of the Church" in Ireland! He was also deputed by the Pope to "restrain the progress of vice," to increase religion and to do all things whichsoever pertained *to the honor of God!*

"You have heard of St. Thomas A'Beckett, who was murdered in the house of God while participating in the vesper chant; stricken down within the chancel, his brains dug out with a sword and smeared upon the altar. This King Henry was the instigator of the murder."

What a charming character to send into Ireland as a Christian Apostle! The king's mission, according to the fraudulent Bull of Pope Alexander III. was to reform the barbarous Irish people who were "Christians only in name!"

"There were four sons of a King of England once. One of them, afterwards Richard I. of England, said: 'The custom of our family is that the son shall hate the father; our destiny is to detest each other. This is our heritage which we shall never renounce. From the devil we came; to the devil we will return.' These were the sons of this King Henry."

A bad tree produces bad fruit, and King Henry's genealogical tree may be well called the Upas tree whose deadly odors poisoned the atmosphere surrounding it.

"There was a King of England once who said: 'Accursed be the day on which I was born, and accursed of God be the children I leave behind me.' That was also this same King Henry."

No doubt when Henry Plantagenet drew down this malediction upon the heads of himself and his offspring, he had in mind the *bogus* Bull which he had forged and which worked such iniquity upon the independent Catholics of Ireland.

"But there was another malediction he uttered before his death, more fearful than any of these. A malediction which I dare not repeat to you. I will not say go to the histories and find it. You can find it if you look for it, but you cannot read it without horror, nor afterwards think of it without terror. The rule of these Angevin devils lasted about 300 years. This Henry II. was the first of the brood; the crooked-back tyrant, Richard III., was the last. I have said that England had men of genius to foresee, and iron hearts to execute. These were some of them, and all English rulers of Ireland since, in everything relating to Ireland, seem to have inherited their cruelty of character, determining every Irish question not upon any principle of natural justice but solely upon the cold-blooded policy of how most to injure Ireland and prevent her in any way rivalling England. Do my American friends smile a little at this, thinking it a Celtic exaggeration? Ah! if they do, it only proves how necessary it is for us to show them what enormities have been perpetrated upon the Irish people, under the forms of English law. Did you ever hear of the Penal Laws in force in Ireland down to a late day? King Henry was not more enraged by Welsh resistance than his successors were by Irish obstruction. King Henry was not more cruel to his Welsh hostages than his successors were to their Irish subjects. They forbade to the Irish people all liberty of religion; forbade them to speak the Irish language, to have Irish books, or to instruct Irish children. It was declared by these laws that the life of an Irishman, or the honor of an Irishwoman might be taken at will, anywhere outside the pale, that is, anywhere over fifty miles from Dublin; and to mark their hatred of the Irish race, they enacted that if an Englishman dared to marry an Irishwoman, he was to be half hanged, his heart cut out before he was dead, his head struck off and his lands forfeited to the crown. Do you ask whether these laws had not been left simply a dead letter on the Statute book? Many of them were not only in force but enforced down to 1829.

This Henry II. was the first English king who claimed to govern Ireland, and he did it on the pretence of wishing to improve the morals of the people. He knew that the deepest, strongest love which the Irish people had, was for their old Catholic faith, and that they had unmeasured respect, love and affection for the Holy Father, visible head of their Church. Now, how do you suppose he applied that knowledge? *He forged a Bull, as coming from the Pope,* giving to him the sovereignty of Ireland, and calling upon the people of Ireland to render him allegiance.

Thus the very beginning of English rule in Ireland was built *on a foundation of fraud,* and ever since, it has been continued by fraud, treachery, robbery, rapine, murder, slaughter and every other crime known in the calendar."

It will be noticed in one of the paragraphs of the foregoing extract, that Judge Dunne alludes to the inhumanity of King Henry the Second toward the children of his Welsh hostages. Lingard makes this blood-red record of that horrible barbarity:

"Henry II., in his excursion into Wales in 1164, having received as hostages the children of the noblest families of that country, gave orders that the eyes of all the males should be rooted out, and the ears and noses of the females should be amputated."

It is also reported of this brutal king that on one occasion his anger became so fierce that he actually became crazy. The occasion arose as follows: "The king being at Caen, he was provoked against Richard de Harnet, because he said something in defence of the king of Scotland. Breaking out into a rage of passion, king Henry called him a traitor, and thereupon, beginning to be inflamed with his wonted fury, he flung his cap from his head, ungirted his belt, hurled away his cloak and garments wherewith he was apparelled, cast off with his own hands a coverlet of silk from his bed, and sitting as it were upon a dunghill of straw, began to chew the straws in order to glut his demoniacal rage!"

On another occasion a page carried a letter to King Henry II., the contents of which were not pleasing to his Majesty, so, in order to give vent to his vengeance, he grasped the unfortunate messenger by the throat and attempted to pluck out his eyes with his royal fingers!

A man infuriated with such diabolical passion and such brutal propensities, was not exactly the kind of ruler Pope Adrian IV. would place over the Irish people or address as a monarch of "glorious renown."

Now let us turn to the treatment which St. Thomas A'Becket, Bishop and Martyr, received at the hands of this monarch who was the first accessory to the Archbishop's murder. King Henry II. ascended the English throne on the 20th of December, A. D., 1154, and three years later he elevated the distinguished divine whose murder he subsequently suggested, to the high position of Lord Chancellor of England.

From the first day he entered upon the duties of his office, until he resigned it into the king's hands, St. Thomas was constantly annoyed by the petty tyranny and the usurpation by the king of ecclesiastical authority over even the Catholic Prelates. At length King Henry determined to persecute St. Thomas to death if possible. Accordingly, Henry called a Council of the Bishops and nobility at Northampton, on October 8th, 1164, during which he pronounced sentence of exile against the saintly Archbishop of Canterbury, and declared all his goods confiscated to the Crown. St. Thomas fled to France, where he had an audience with the Pope, to whom he related all the trouble which Henry II. had caused the Church in England.

In the meantime the English monarch was greatly incensed against both the Pope and the Archbishop, because the latter had escaped his wrath and the former had commended him for his course. In order to gratify his passion, therefore, Henry confiscated not only the goods of the innocent Archbishop, but he actually seized upon all the property belonging to all the friends, relatives and domestics even of Saint Thomas, banished them from his dominions, not sparing even year-old infants or tottering age! Then he compelled them by oath to proceed in a body to the place where the Archbishop was residing at Pontigny, in a monastery of the Cisterian Order, so that he might be compelled to shed tears of sorrow at the sight of so much helpless poverty and undeserved destitution! Not satisfied with these acts of inhuman tyranny, the brutal butcher of the Welsh Innocents, actually wrote to the Cistercian monks that he would close up and confiscate every Cistercian monastery in England unless the monks of Pontigny turned St. Thomas out of their house!

The Pope and some of the Princes of Europe tried to bring Henry II. to effect a reconciliation with St. Thomas, but the Plantagenet persecutor went so far as to threaten the Holy Father with his direful vengeance if he dared again to address him on the subject!

The saintly Archbishop not desiring to bring down the King's ungovernable wrath upon the innocent members of the Cistercian Order, left their hospitable roof, and proceeded to Sens, where the King of France provided him with the few necessaries of life required by this living martyr of a brutal monarch's vengeance. From the monastery of St. Columba, adjacent to Sens, the exiled Archbishop of Canterbury sent Pastoral Letters over to England, excommunicating all those who should obey the late orders of the King of England in seizing the estates of the Church, and exhorting that monarch to repentance. In the meantime King Henry sent some of his deputies to Rome in order to influence the Cardinals against St. Thomas. But his secret diplomacy availed him nothing in the end, as Cardinal Otto, one of the two Legates appointed by the Pope, wrote to Henry that he must return the ill-gotten property he had gained by unjust confiscation.

The King of France then undertook to act as arbitrator between Henry and the saintly Archbishop of Canterbury, but the audiences subsequently held availed nothing. The Pope then sent two new Legates—Gratian and Vivian—to the turbulent King, and, after them, two more, but the surly monarch would not accede to their terms of required restitution. As adding insult to injury, Henry caused his son to be crowned King by the Archbishop of York, in the very Diocese of Canterbury from which St. Thomas a'Becket had been expatriated. The cruel monarch moreover, obliged his subjects, even by inhuman torments, to renounce their obedience not only to the Archbishop but *also to the Pope!*

At lenght a reconciliation was brought about by the Archbishop of Sens, but it was of the nature of a reconciliation which a wolf might make with a lamb in order to satiate its craving for flesh and blood. King Henry, finding that he could not wreak his vengeance with sufficient severity upon the Archbishop of Canterbury, so long as he remained in France, patched up a peace in order to get the innocent victim of his terrible wrath into the kingdom where his death would pay the penalty of the blood-thirsty monarch. Archbishop Becket—who well knew there were no bounds to King Henry's hatred—had a premonition that the English king meant him grevious bodily harm, as he said to the French King when taking leave of him: "I am going to seek my death in England." The monarch answered: "So I believe," and pressed St. Thomas to stay in his kingdom where he could live in peace and religious happiness, but the innocent victim of King Henry's wrath answered with true Christian resignation: "The will of God must be accomplished."

St. Thomas proceeded to England, where he landed in safety, but during his journey into the interior he miraculously escaped ambuscades set for him by assassins hired no doubt by Henry to murder him. This is evident from the fact that when, a few weeks afterwards, a deputation of dissatisfied Prelates arrived in Normandy to have an interview with King Henry, in order to inform him that St. Thomas would not remove the Censures which were promulgated against them in consequence of their quiet acquiescence with King Henry's robbery of the temporalities of the See of Canterbury, the wrathful monarch cried out in a voice quivering with demoniacal passion, that "He cursed all those whom he had honored with his friendship, and enriched by his bounty, seeing that none of them had the courage *to rid him of one Bishop*, who gave him more trouble than all the rest of his subjects."

These words at once suggested to several of his courtiers who surrounded him, the propriety of *murdering* St. Thomas, in order to please the detestable tyrant. Accordingly on Christmas Day, when St. Thomas came to preach, he took for his text: "Peace to men of good-will on earth," telling his flock that it was his last discourse, as he should shortly leave them. In the meantime five assassins and a troop of armed men were approaching Canterbury Cathedral, which they reached next day. It was the Vesper hour, and the Archbishop was in the sacred edifice when the murderers entered with drawn swords. One of the ruffians advanced towards the venerable Prelate exclaiming:

"Now you must die!" The Archbishop calmly answered: "I am ready to die for God, for justice, and for the liberty of His Church. * * * I have defended the Church as far as I was able during my life, when I saw it oppressed, and I shall be happy if by my death at least I can restore its peace and liberty." He then slowly sank to the ground on his knees and spoke these his last words: "I recommend my soul and the cause of the Church to God, to the Blessed Virgin, to the holy patrons of this place, to the martyrs St. Dionysius and St. Elphege of Canterbury." The saintly Prelate, with the true courage of a Christian martyr, then prayed for his murderers and placed his head so they could strike it with their swords. The hirelings of King Henry desired to remove him from the Cathedral, but he courageously exclaimed: "I will not stir; do here what you please, *or are commanded.*" The assassins then fell upon him, hacking his head and scattering his brains upon the consecrated floor of the Cathedral. When Henry's minions had thus accomplished their master's will, they proceeded to the martyred Archbishop's residence which they rifled of all its valuables as their booty for the bloody deed they had performed. This horrible murder occurred on the 29th of December, 1170.

In justice to the murderers of the Archbishop of Canterbury, and the monarch who suggested the horrible butchery, it is proper to state that, with one exception, they all repented their fearful crime, but the fact still remains that it was at the suggestion of King Henry II. of England, the martyred Archbishop was ruthlessly slaughtered, and it requires no great stretch of the imagination to conclude that a ruler who would suggest the murder of a saintly Archbishop, merely because he defended the Church against the King's injustice, would not hesitate to cause *a forged Bull* to be manufactured in order to fortify injustice towards the Irish people by perpetrating a fraud against Rome.

CHAPTER VI.

The Bull of Adrian Tested.—Analysis of the Pontificate of Alexander III.—More of Judge Maguire's Mistakes.—Pope Adrian's Bull Viewed from a Critical Standpoint.

The three principal characters that figure most prominently in the historical question: "Did Pope Adrian IV. bestow Ireland upon King Henry II. of England?" are, the Pontiff who is *supposed* to have *made* the grant, the King who is *said* to have *received* it, and Pope Alexander III., the Pontiff who is *reported* to have *confirmed* it. Already we have made a sufficient analysis of the characters of Pope Adrian and King Henry to satisfy any reasonable mind that the former never *made* the grant and that the latter never *received* it. Now let us make an analysis of the character and policy of Pope Alexander III., and ascertain whether a single action of his whole Pontificate points him out as a spiritual ruler likely to use the *uncharitable* and *untruthful* language in which the Bull attributed to him is couched. All men, whether Popes, Presidents, or private individuals, are to be judged by their works, and not by a single act *attributed to them* by parties deeply interested in sustaining their own iniquitous proceedings, and which stands in direct opposition *to all their other official proceedings*.

The Pontificate of Pope Alexander III. commenced September 7th, A. D., 1159, and ended August 30th, 1181. The *bogus* Bull, printed in Judge Maguire's bad book, bears date thus : "Given at *Rome*, in the year of Salvation, 1172," although the Pope was *not in Rome at that time*. The absence of day or month from the document is also another *fatal* omission which goes far to prove the aforesaid document a clumsy *forgery*. These facts, however, we will develop in their proper place, and we will now proceed at once to give a sketch of the character which Pope Alexander sustained throughout his occupancy of the Chair of St. Peter, and offer irrefutable proof showing that he loved popular freedom far too dearly to permit himself to be a party to such enslavement of a whole independent nation as that contemplated by King Henry II.

Pope Alexander III. was the emancipator of the slaves in the middle ages. In a Council held in the twelfth century, this great Pontiff abolished, as far as lay in his power, the curse of slavery throughout the world. His prudence, wisdom and justice gave him a great victory over Frederick Barbarossa. He it was who—as a French historian says—"restored the rights of nations and curbed the passions of kings." Voltaire says of him : "If men have recovered *their rights*, it is chiefly to Pope Alexander that they are indebted for them ; to him so many cities owe their new or recovered splendor." This is a grand eulogy coming from such an enemy of the Church as Voltaire, but Pope Alexander well deserved such praise for the fortitude and prudence which he constantly manifested during his twenty years exile from Rome, in the midst of threatened schism, persecution, and a constant struggle against the armed hosts of the ambitious Barbarossa, who desired to bring the whole world under his regal sway.

Alexander III. had scarcely received the news of his election to the Pontifical throne ere he had to quit Rome and hurry to the monastery of Santa Nympha, where he was consecrated, whilst the anti-Pope Victor III. reigned in Rome. The Emperor Frederick favored Victor, and a number of the Cardinals did the anti-Pope homage, but Alexander faced the fierce storm with cheeks unblanched with fear, and when deputies were sent by Barbarossa to call the true Vicar of Christ before a council which Frederick had called to meet at Pavia, Alexander replied to the request in these courageous terms: "We recognize in the Emperor," said the exiled Pontiff, "the armed defender of the Roman Church, but never shall the prerogative given by JESUS CHRIST to St. Peter be violated in our person. The Roman Church judges all others, and is subject to the judgment of none. We are prepared to give our life in defence of her rights."

Notwithstanding the Pope's declaration, the council met and the anti-Pope Victor was placed upon the Pontifical throne by the Emperor Barbarossa, who proclaimed that all Bishops should obey the authority of Victor on pain of perpetual banishment. The true Pope replied by solemnly excommunicating Frederick, together with the anti-Pope and all his partisans, both lay and clerical.

This was the first act in a drama which lasted for many years, and which engaged the attention of the whole of Europe, arraying against the patient Alexander III. the bitter animosity of a world conquering tyrant who has been well-named "the modern Attila." The ancient and beautiful city of Milan was reduced to a heap of shapeless ruins, because the inhabitants recognized Alexander as the true Pope. Other cities did likewise, until Alexander III. became the head and the leader about whose sacred person all the Italian cities rallied when they saw their independence threatened by the despotic ambition of the German Emperor, Frederick Barbarossa.

In order to get beyond the reach of the would-be Emperor of the world, Pope Alexander III. retired in 1163 to France, where he heard of the death of the anti-Pope Victor, and also of the election of the anti-Pope Paschal III. through the influence of Barbarossa. Yet the undismayed Vicar of Christ was determined to die in exile if necessary, sooner than submit to the enslavement of a single people to the sway of the tyrant who persecuted the Church in the person of its Pontiff. And thus it came about that at last the warlike Barbarossa yielded to the exalted ecclesiastic whose only weapon was his crozier and whose only shield was the Cross. The Vicar of Christ was called back to Italy, and as the exiled Pontiff saw himself surrounded in Venice by the Prelates of the Church and the representatives of the Emperor who sought peace at his hands, he must have felt that his triumph came from God. "Well-beloved sons," said Alexander, "it is a miracle of God's power, that an aged and unarmed priest should have resisted the rage of the most powerful king on earth; by this let all men know that it is impossible to war against the Lord and against His Christ."

Such was the courageous hero of liberty whom Catholics are asked to believe helped to hand over the independent Irish people, bound hand and foot, to Henry II of England, in order to confer upon the English monarch the Apostolic power of "teaching the truth of the Christian faith" to a people who had about thirty Archbishops and Bishops, as well as hundreds of secular priests and members of Religious Orders! Is there any sensible Catholic in America who would harbor such an idea for a moment? What? A Vicar of Christ to *ignore* the Bishops and priests of a country, and to confer Episcopal powers on an alien layman? Such an outrage never was perpetrated by any Pontiff that ever sat in the Chair of St. Peter.

It is true that Henry did penance and was forgiven for the part he acted in the horrible butchery of St. Thomas A'Becket, but it by no means follows that Pope Alexander would make such a rebellious, immoral and ruffianly character as he knew King Henry to be, the second Apostle of Ireland to "propagate the righteous plantation of faith" in an island whose fame for sanctity was known all over the world through the numerous saints it had sent to convert the nations of Europe! The Bull was made by King Henry's order, and Pope Alexander never saw it!

Another feature in the character of Pope Alexander III, which goes very far towards proving that he never signed the Bull attributed to him, is the fact that *he knew King Henry to be a bad man and the promoter of the murder of St. Thomas A'Becket, Archbishop of Canterbury.*

In order to escape from the fury of the ferocious King of England it became necessary for St. Thomas A'Becket to fly to France in 1164, in order to lay before Alexander III. the injustice, robbery and sacrilege done by a monarch who became a perfect demon in his passion, presenting, as Lingard says, "the raving of a mad man with the fury of a savage beast. In his paroxysms his eyes were spotted with blood, his countenance seemed to flame, his tongue poured forth a torrent of abuse and imprecation, and his hands were employed to inflict vengeance on what ever came within his reach."

Pope Alexander received the exiled victim of Henry's hatred with open arms. He directed the Archbishop to promulgate a *Bull of excommunication against Henry II.*, and against all who abetted his tyranny and his thievery. The Letters containing these Pontifical censures had to be secretly conveyed into England by some monks, in consequence of the caution used by Henry, who determined to prevent the Pope from laying an Interdict* upon his kingdom. In order also to accomplish his antagonism to both Pope and Prelate, the King caused these *humane* regulations to be published along the whole English coast: "If any Religious attempt to bring Pontifical Letters into England, he shall lose his feet; if a cleric, he shall lose his eyes; if a layman he shall be hanged, and if a leper, burned." This barbarous order from a King who is foolishly supposed to have been delegated *by the same Pope to Christianize* the Irish people—who in the bogus Bull are called "Christians only in name"—was promulga-

---

* For the benefit of readers who may not fully understand the severe nature of an ecclesiastical Interdict when issued against a nation, and also for a better appreciation of the dread felt by Henry II., it may be well to state that in a district or country under Interdict the churches were closed; the bells were silent; solemn religious services ceased; the sacraments were administered only to infants and the dying; and the interment of the dead took place without any religious services. Thus the sovereign was punished through his subjects, to whom, in a short time, the deprivation of all the aids and ministrations of religion became intolerable. Hence the offender was eventually compelled to submission, pleading with a most penitential spirit to the Sovereign Pontiff to forgive his obstinacy, to raise the Interdict, and thus restore again the sacraments and services of the true Church of God to the suffering people.

ted in Normandy and throughout the English possessions in France.

The Letters excommunicating King Henry II., when promulgated in England, threw the whole kingdom into a state of consternation; the excommunicant could not find a priest to celebrate Mass in his presence. And in this crisis the unfortunate monarch turned to the Pope, plying him with all the vast influence at his royal command, in order to have the Interdict raised. But *Pope Alexander sternly refused every petition*, referring both the King and his advocates to the Archbishop whose sentence of excommunication against the hateful Henry, Pope Alexander most heartily confirmed!

The brutal murder of St. Thomas has already been described, and when the news of this most atrocious crime reached the ears of Pope Alexander III. he shed bitter tears to the memory of the saintly Thomas A'Becket. Such indignation did the Pontiff manifest that *he refused to see any Englishman*. "Hold! hold!" exclaimed the Pope, to one who was about to utter the detestable name of the King of England in his presence: "Such a name may not be spoken before a Sovereign Pontiff." Pope Alexander then hurled the anathemas of the Church against the assassins, with all their advisors and protectors. All this occurred only *two years* before the *spurious* date (1172) ascribed to the *fictitious* Bull!

The Pontificate of Pope Alexander III., the victorious champion of Italian liberty, the courageous asserter of the sovereignty of the Apostolic See against Kings in their fury and people in their infatuation, came to a close in glorious victory. After twenty years of struggle, persecution and exile, the great Vicar of Christ rested in peace on August 30th, 1181, bequeathing to the Church that peace which he had won for her through his pious courage, prudence and love of justice and liberty, which were the brightest ornaments of his character. The Pope was preceded in death by King Louis VII. of France, who died on September 18th, 1180, and as this King will figure in the controversy over the *two* bogus Bulls of Adrian and Alexander further on, we allude to the matter in this place so as to fix the dates upon which these two characters in this long-disputed question ceased to exist. About this time, also, there disappeared from this earthly scene, John of Salisbury, called by some authors "Johannes Parvus," John the Little, who is said to have received the *bogus* Bull from Pope Adrian. This character in the drama, the plot of which we are developing, died at Chartres, France, on October 25th, 1180. He was the author of several works, two of which we expect to refer to hereafter. These are the *Polycraticus* and the *Metalogicus*, into the latter of which was first *injected* (by an anonymous interloper) the *fraudulent* account of the Bull claimed to have been received from Pope Adrian by John of Salisbury himself. Of this more anon.

Now that we have given pen-pictures of several of the principal actors in this twelfth century historical melodrama, let us take up Judge Maguire's "Ireland and the Pope," so as to refute a few more of the false statements therein which he picked out of the works he quotes, without any regard whatever for the author's reasons prefixed or affixed thereto. The first wisp of wisdom which we pluck therefrom is the following:

"In the year 1152 Ireland was a prosperous and independent nation. . . . Her people were Catholics, and had for many generations looked lovingly to the Pope of Rome as their spiritual father, but they neither owned nor recognized any political allegiance to him."

Such wisdom as is manifested in the foregoing extract must have a very debilitating effect upon Judge Maguire's mental vitality! And so there were no *Protestants* in Ireland in the year 1152—three hundred and thirty-one years before Martin Luther was born! *Mirabile dictu!* Ah! dear Judge,

'Twas well for poor humanity
You undertook to write,
Your *amazing* erudition
Is so *very* erudite!

How important it is to know that in the year 1152 there were no Methodists in Mullingar; no Baptists in Ballinasloe; no Congregationalists in Cork; no Presbyterians in Portarlington; no Dunkers in Dublin; no Campbellites in Castlecomer; no Lutherans in Lismore; no Shakers in Shanagolden; no Sabbatarians in Stradbally; no non-Conformists in Newtownmountkennedy; and no Salvation Army in Sligo! Such information, coming as it does to Irish Catholics whom his Honor calls a people "crushed in ignorance," and from so supereminent a dignitary as the Superior Judge of the Superior Court of a superior city like San Francisco, is worthy of being framed for exhibition among the curiosities of California in the cabinet of the Pioneers' Association!

And now, dear Judge, since you have so most graciously condescended to enlighten the Irish people, who have been "crushed in ignorance," on this point, will your Honor so far descend from your high dignity as to write a pamphlet in answer to this query: "Why is it that there were no inhabitants in Ireland until people first settled there?"

The next specimen of Judge Maguire's sapience comes to the crushed "ignorant" Celts in this fashion:

"In that fatal year (1152) Cardinal John Paparo appeared in Ireland as a special legate of Pope Eugenius III. He was the first Italian legate ever sent to Ireland—may Persico be the last! He summoned the bishops and principal priests to the Synod of Kells, and there delivered palliums to the archbishops, taking their oaths of obedience to the Pope. From that hour dates the downfall of Irish nationality."

Here we have it on the authority of the electric legal light who illumines the Superior Court of San Francisco, that it was *palliums*, and not Papal Bulls, which caused the downfall of Irish nationality! What profound knowledge! What beguiling balderdash! The conferring of the terrible *palliums* which seems to have made his Honor's anti-Papal heart palpitate with extraordinary emotion, had no more to do with "the downfall of Irish nationality" than Judge Maguire had with framing the Ten Commandments!

As one of those Catholic Irishmen who have been "crushed in ignorance," we also most respectfully desire to correct his Honor concerning the baneful *influence* which the bestowal of the apostate-scaring *pallium* is supposed to have exercised on Ireland's destiny. The first papal Legate in Ireland was St. Malachy, Archbishop of Armagh, who visited Rome about twelve years before Cardinal Paparo was sent to Ireland, and, while in the Eternal City, the great Irish saint was appointed by Pope Innocent II.— who reigned from 1130 to 1143—Apostolic Legate for all Ireland. The Pope also promised St. Malachy the mysterious *pallium* which Judge Maguire seems to think is a kind of dynamite bomb invented by the Pope specially for the destruction of Ireland !

When St. Malachy was in Rome he asked the Pope for *palliums* for the other Archbishops of Ireland, but the Holy Father said he preferred to have petitions presented from the ecclesiastics of the several Dioceses presided over by Archbishops, before sending palliums to the incumbents. Here the matter rested until the year 1145, when Pope Eugenius III. sat in the Chair of St. Peter. Two years after his election, a National synod comprising 15 Bishops and 200 Priests was assembled at Holmpatrick, by order of the Primate Gelasius, and there both Bishops and Priests petitioned the Holy See to confer *palliums* on the Metropolitans of Armagh and Cashel. They also elected St. Malachy as their representative to the Vicar of Christ. The saint set out on his journey but died before he reached his destination.

The death of St. Malachy delayed matters for some time. Finally, however, Christian, Bishop of Lismore, was appointed Papal Legate, to succeed St. Malachy, and a short time thereafter, Pope Eugenius III. sent Cardinal Paparo to Ireland, in order to *carry out the wishes of the ecclesiastics of that country.* A National Synod convened at Kells, on March 9th, 1152, and the Pope's Legate conferred the *pallium* upon the Metropolitans of Armagh, Cashel, Dublin and Tuam. The *pallium*, as all Catholics know, is merely a woolen insignia of the fullness of the Episcopal office, and it has no more political significance than has the archiepiscopal cross of a Metropolitan.

Judge Maguire says that the Irish Archbishops "took the oath of obedience to the Pope," as if this also was some new-fangled notion which some "foreign potentate" had imposed upon the Irish episcopate. The truth is that from the early ages this rule existed, just as it does down to this day, and its effect no more circumscribes the mental or political independence of a Bishop than does the band of linen which is bound round his head during the ceremonies of his consecration.

From all this it follows that neither the visit of Cardinal Paparo to Ireland and the reception of the *palliums* by the Archbishops, nor the oaths taken by the Metropolitans, had a single feather's weight in "the downfall of Irish nationality," even though the High and Mighty Censuror-General of Popes, Cardinals, and the "ignorant" Irish gives a contrary opinion.

Judge Maguire next says that one of the benefits which accrued to "Pope Adrian's financial and political advantage," was that the Pope "desired to put Ireland under tribute to the Vatican; the Irish people having previously paid those small dues called Peter-Pence to the See of Armagh, which the rest of Europe paid to Rome." His authority for this assertion is *O'Halloran's History of Ireland*; but as the greater part of that work was compiled by a number of anti Irish Englishmen, it possesses no value as a History of Ireland. The truth is that Peter-Pence was *not* paid by Ireland previous to the invasion, nor, though it was expressly promised by the invaders (admitting for argument's sake that Adrian's Bull was genuine), does it anywhere appear that a single penny of such contribution was ever sent to Rome! Right here arises *another doubt* concerning the genuineness of the Adrian Bull, inasmuch as if that document was of Papal origin, would not Pope Adrian or Alexander or some of their immediate successors have forwarded a *just claim* to England for *damages*, and would not the Papal authorities have declared the Bull null and void in consequence of the King of England not having carried out the *money* stipulation in that *supposed* agreement between himself and the Pope? But no Pope ever uttered a word of remonstrance; no Cardinal ever carried to England a single complaint. And why ? Because the Bul was *bogus* and its terms were *binding on nobody!*

Again, if the Bull were genuine, England forfeited every iota of authority which that document gave Henry II. over Ireland. The *specific purpose* for which the Bull is said to have been given was that King Henry should have certain rights in Ireland, provided—as the document quoted by Judge Maguire, says—"that you (King Henry II.) are willing to pay from each house a yearly pension of one penny to St. Peter, that you will preserve the rights of the churches of the land whole and inviolate." Did King Henry fulfill these stipulations? Most assuredly not! He not only never paid a single penny in Peter-Pence—nor was he ever asked for it—but, instead of "preserving" the rights of the Catholic Church in Ireland, he saw churches demolished, monasteries destroyed, and he quietly acquiesced whilst robbery and rapine worked the ruin of numerous holy Irish shrines! Did any Pope chide him for thus breaking his bond? Most assuredly not. And why? Because no Papal official in Rome had any authoritative knowledge of the existence of such Bulls as those fraudulently represented to have emanated from Popes Adrian IV. and Alexander III.

Now, even as prejudiced a critic of the rights of the Catholic Church as his Honor the Judge of the Superior Court of San Francisco, will be forced to admit that when King Henry II. *failed to fulfill these obligations*, the Bull ceased to have any binding force either upon the Pope or the Irish people. The document became so much waste paper, just as it really was from the first hour of its forgery. These are plain, palpable *facts* which no amount of pettifogging can push aside!

In accordance with the unfortunate habit he has acquired of *manufacturing* historical facts and distorting them to suit his own side of the case, Judge Maguire puts this very untruthful text into his remarkably unreliable publication:

"That everlasting yearly ' penny from every house' again—the price of poor Ireland's liberty. It has been faithfully paid. England's promise to the Vatican has been faithfully fulfilled to the letter; but alas, every penny of the tribute has been stained with the blood and tears of Erin's subjugated children."

This paragraph is as clear a perversion of truth as we have yet caught Judge Maguire in telling. There is not a single word on record to prove that England ever paid a single farthing of Peter-pence in fulfillment of the fraudulent Bull.

Rev. P. J. Carew, in his "Ecclesiastical History of Ireland," decides the whole matter by saying—on the 171st page of his work—"Henry's promises to Adrian respecting the Peter-Pence appears to have been wholly forgotten by him. The exaction of this tribute *he never attempted to enforce on Irish subjects."* Thus we correct *another* of Judge Maguire's "mistakes," and we advise his Honor to reserve his tears in future in order to shed them over his own false history, rather than to waste them in weeping over supposed wrongs which Ireland never suffered!

CHAPTER VII.

The Peter-Pence Proviso Continued.—More Proof Exhibiting the False Character of the Stipulation.—King John's Surrender of England to the Pope.—Important Documents Relating Thereto.—Additional Evidence of the Fictitious Nature of the Two Bulls of Adrian and Alexander.—The Editor of Cambrensis Criticises that Falsifier's Fabrications.

In our last chapter we showed from reliable historical authority that Ireland never paid Peter-Pence to the Pope, in accordance with the clause of the bogus Bull attributed to Pope Adrian. But we have still further proof to offer in this direction. During the Pontificate of Pope Innocent III., a demand was sent by that Pontiff to the Bishops of England, (*but not to those of Ireland*) demanding some over-due Peter-Pence from them. This is strong evidence that Pope Innocent III., either never knew of any Bulls by Popes Adrian and Alexander, requiring Peter-Pence from the Irish people in accordance therewith, or, if he had ever heard of them he looked upon them as utterly unreliable.

On page 189 of the first volume of the *Chronicles* of Rymer, *Fœdora, etc.*, will be found a document from Pope Innocent which still more forcibly sets forth the fact that the Pope never knew that any Peter-Pence was promised by King Henry II., on the part of the Irish people. The document in question is a Letter which Pope Innocent addressed to Cardinal Nicholas, Bishop of Tusculum, Legate of the Apostolic See in England, and also to Pandolphus, Sub-Deacon, and a familiar friend of the Sovereign Pontiff. In that Letter Pope Innocent says :

"As every house throughout all England—as you very well know—must give every year a penny as the revenue due to the Holy See, the Prelates of England, who have collected the revenue in Our name, have disposed of it against the will of the owner, and they have not feared to keep the greater part of it for themselves. They have sent to Us only three hundred marks ; and they have kept more than one thousand marks in their own hands. Wishing, therefore, that the rights of the Roman Church be protected, We command you, by the authority of this letter, and We ordain expressly, that you receive in the first place from their hands the sums that have been paid up to this time, and to oblige them, if necessary, by ecclesiastical censures without appeal. Then you shall enjoin them formally, in Our name, to pay integrally the balance. We do not see what title they can allege ; they cannot produce a privilege granted to them by the Holy See, nor can they prove a prescription of one hundred years against the Roman Church.

Given at the Lateran, on the 5th kalends of February, in the 6th year of Our Pontificate."

Here we find that Pope Innocent III., was afforded a most suitable opportunity for demanding the Peter-Pence due to his Holiness from Ireland under the bogus bond which is attributed to King Henry. But the Pope never once alludes to it ; he *insists* upon being paid the collections made in England to the last penny, but he leaves Ireland entirely out of the question. Now, we ask any reasonable individual, what would be the line of argument used in the above Papal document, if Pope Innocent had the slightest claim on England for any Peter-Pence collected in Ireland ? Would not the Pontiff have included Ireland in the text ? Most assuredly he would, as his Holiness was not to be cheated out of his dues with impunity. It is clear, therefore, that down to the year 1206 the Bull of Adrian had no *status* whatever in the mind of the Vicar of Christ, and here again we have *another* proof that the Bull attributed to Pope Adrian IV. was a flagrant forgery.

Now let us cite another historical event wherein additional evidence lucidly appears against the Peter-Pence proposal in the fictitious Bull of Pope Adrian. It is a matter of history that in the year 1213 King John of England (Lackland, or *sans-terre*) seeing himself without resources and on the brink of ruin, placed his person and his kingdom under the suzerainty of Pope Innocent III. The Golden Bull which concluded that compact may be found in

Rymer, as well as the agreement of King John, wherein occurs this passage :

"Not determined by force, nor constrained by terror, but of our own free and spontaneous will, and of the common council of our Barons, we offer and freely concede to God, to His Apostles Peter and Paul, to the Holy Roman Church, our Mother, and to our Lord Pope Innocent III., and his Catholic successors, the whole kingdom of England and the whole kingdom of Ireland," etc.

Then the prince promises, among other things, to pay to the Pope one thousand pounds sterling every year, being £700 for England, and £300 for Ireland, under pain of forfeiture for himself as well as for his successors.

When offering his kingdom to the Holy See, John had a splendid opportunity whereby to refer to the Bull of Adrian, who, about seventy years previously, had, it is alleged, generously given over the spiritual and temporal affairs of Ireland to the tender mercies of his father, King Henry II. The prince was aware of the alleged existence of the Bull, because the king-worshipping Cambrensis had dedicated to John a few years before, the third edition of his *Expugnatio Hibernica*, into which the dubious document was inserted. In fact, so eager was Cambrensis to attract the attention of King John to the bogus Bull, that he overshot the mark by a special appeal to the king in the dedication of the work, calling the particular attention of his Majesty to that document! This of itself looks very much like one of the many disreputable tricks which Cambrensis was famous for, and it also tends to cast additional doubt upon the authenticity of the Adrian Bull.

Another query arises in our mind right here : If King John had any faith in the authenticity of the Adrian Bull, *why did he keep silence concerning it?* Would it not have been more in accord with common sense on his part, as well as on the part of his counsellors, to tell the Pope that he was already the feudatory of the Holy See in Ireland, he being the immediate successor of his father King Henry II.

Instead of acting in this rational way, however, we find the ruling monarch addressing the Holy Father as if he, the King of England, was entering for the first time into negotiations concerning Peter-Pence with the Pope of Rome. We must, therefore, come to the conclusion that, even in the estimation of the son and successor of King Henry II., the Bull of Adrian had no value as an official document—even when he was in treaty with a legitimate successor of the Pope who is said to have made it !

If we are astonished at the silence of King John regarding Pope Adrian's Bull, what excuse can be given for *the silence of Pope Innocent III. on the subject?* It will be also remarked that the Pope to whom King John became submissive, says nothing of the Bull of Alexander, although that document decrees that a very large sum should be paid as Peter-Pence by the people of Ireland to the Pope, whereas John offered the paltry sum of three hundred pounds sterling.

Now we ask any common-sense citizen, who has the slightest idea of diplomacy, if documents of such vast importance as the Bulls of Adrian and Alexander would not have been alluded to on such an important occasion as the one we have described—*provided they were known in Rome?* Every person familiar with the mode of procedure in the execution of important trusts in Rome, where the interests of a whole nation are at stake, will admit that there is no Court in Europe where *genuine* documents are more frequently cited and quoted than by the Chancellor of the Papal Court. That official has ever been noted for declaring that the Sovereign Pontiff "walks in the footsteps of his predecessor Pope So-and-so," that he "continues the work they have commenced," and then reference is made to Bulls, Briefs, Concordats or Letters which formerly treated of the question under immediate consideration.

The case of King John was precisely the opportunity which the Roman Chancellor would have been delighted to take advantage of by introducing the ancient official style of " *Praedecessorum nostrorum vestigiis inhaerentes, eorumque concessionem appro-*

bantes et confirmantes, etc.," if he was afforded the opportunity. But that official found no document of any "predecessor" of Pope Innocent, in whose footsteps his Holiness could "walk," nor could the Chancellor coerce his Pontiff to "continue" a course of conduct which neither Adrian nor any other Pope ever *commenced!* It is perfectly certain, therefore, that neither the Pope himself, nor any official connected with the Papal archives, knew anything of the so-called Bull of Adrian during the Pontificate of Pope Innocent III.

We now come to another very important feature in this surrender of his kingdom on the part of John to the Pope. It takes two to make a bargain, and although King John *offered* "the kingdom of Ireland" to the Holy Father, the Vicar of Christ *entirely ignored the gift!*

A reference to Rymer's *Chronicles* (Vol. I, pp. 179) will disclose a Letter which the Pope addressed to the Irish people on October 27th, 1213, in which his Holiness alludes to the kingdom of England, but he never joins therewith the name of Ireland. The Pope styles John "King of the English," without adding that he is also King of Ireland. He says that "the Kingdom of England belongs—through the act of donation made by King John—to the Church, and that she possesses "a special right over that kingdom," but does not say that the Church also received by John's act any temporal power whatever *over Ireland!*

Need we comment on these facts? We think not. They prove, with all the force of truth that Pope Innocent III. well knew that although King John of England offered his Holiness full temporal authority over the "kingdom of Ireland," still that monarch did not possess a single particle of title to an inch of that island. Hence the Pope wisely ignored John's proposition because he knew that his title was mythical.

In counselling the people of Ireland as to the best course they should pursue in their diplomatic relations with England, Pope Innocent never makes use of the terms "obedience" or "submission" to any English monarch. His Holiness recommends "benevolence" and "friendship" on the part of the Irish people towards King John. Nor do we see how the Pope could do otherwise, because the Vicar of Christ was fully cognizant of the fact that he—as the custodian of the English kingdom—possessed no temporal power whatever over the Bishops, princes, nobles and people of Ireland. Hence his Holiness could never think of asking them to submit their allegiance to King John and his successors.

Pope Innocent was also well aware of the fact that only a small fraction of Ireland was in the possession of the English, and that the greater portion of the island preserved its independence. The Kings of Ireland generally continued to exercise their regal functions in peace; and the districts of Ireland which the English did not occupy preserved their independence inviolate. But even supposing that the Pope had required submission to King John on the part of the Irish people, such a mandate could only affect those within the English Pale, or the territory which Strongbow and his satellites had stolen by force and fraud.

Returning to the Letter which King John sent to the Pope, we call the attention of our readers to the £300 which that prince promised to send to Rome as his tribute from Ireland. But so little value did Pope Innocent III. place upon the king's voluntary offering, that his Holiness entirely avoided *all mention of it* in his Letter to the Irish people! Like the "gift" of "the kingdom of Ireland" which John presented to the Pope, his Holiness received the promised £300 as a myth which looked far more substantial upon the bond of surrender than it was in reality!

In point of fact King John derived no regal title whatever from Ireland. Henry VIII., who scandalized the world about three centuries after King John, wrote a book against Luther, and, in dedicating it to the Pope, he styles himself King of England and Lord of Ireland. But the Lord knows his "lordship" in Ireland hardly amounted to anything, as he never added a solitary inch of land to the territory his henchmen usurped! On the other hand, it is known to all readers of history that it was not until the time of Pope Paul IV., that Ireland was erected into a kingdom, and this occurred some three hundred and fifty years after King John had offered "the kingdom of Ireland" to a Pope who had no idea of becoming a receiver of stolen goods!

Whilst we are treating of this era in English history, it may not be amiss to introduce another instance where the Peter-Pence paragraph in the pretended Bull of Pope Adrian helps materially to prove that document to be a rank forgery. Four years previous to the events just narrated, Giraldus Cambrensis had represented to King John that one of the causes which led to the severe reverses which the English forces had met with in Ireland, arose from the fact that both Henry and his hopeful son had neglected to establish the collection of Peter-Pence in Ireland, in accordance with the provision of that Bull, the text and terms of which were far more familiar to Cambrensis than they were to any Pope or Cardinal in the Catholic Church.

In conformity with the advice of Cambrensis, John should have made this proposition to Pope Innocent, instead of offering the paltry sum of fifteen hundred dollars to the Holy See. But King John was—like his father—wise in all things wicked. He had his suspicions that the Adrian Bull was bogus, and so he studiously avoided all mention of it, and although several donations of £1,000 were sent from England to Rome, the whole sum was *credited to England*, and no mention whatever made of any part of it coming from a country which Rome knew was no party to the compact!

In the year 1234, when King Henry III., occupied the English throne, the Peter-Pence collection was due for several years. So the Pope's Chancellor wrote over to England to remit the back dues. The response of King Henry III., as quoted by Rymer, is dated February 25th, 1235, and states that from the *first* concession of the tribute, it was stated in the document of *King John*, that the sum of £1,000 would be given to the Roman Church in an undivided manner. Here again we find the Adrian Bull ignored, the document sent by King John to the Pope, when he surrendered his kingdom to his Holiness, being quoted as *the first concession of the Peter-Pence tribute!* The force of this evidence will be better appreciated when it is brought to mind that the Adrian Bull was manufactured by order of his Majesty Henry the Second, nearly seventy years previously!

These historical proofs entirely overcome any assertions that can be advanced against the bogus character of the Adrian Bull, and now, having conclusively proved that the Peter-Pence clause in both Bulls was false, misleading, and inoperative, we will present some new phases of historical evidence in support of the claim of truth and justice on the part of both the Catholic Church and the Irish people.

We have before us as we pen these lines the *Topographia Hibernica* and the *Expugnatio Hibernica* of Giraldus Cambrensis, edited by James F. Dimock, M. A., Rector of Barnburgh, Yorkshire, and published in London in 1867.* Now let us open this volume and hear the editor describe for our edification the *moral* and *intellectual* character of Cambrensis, whom Judge Maguire endeavors to glorify, simply because that ancient perverter of truth is a *perjured* witness against the Pope of Rome and the innocent Irish people.

The Editor of the works of Cambrensis in the first part of the Preface thereto, when speaking of Cambrensis, whom his Honor falsely styles "a *leading* Prelate," (*misleading* would be the proper term) gives these reasons why the works of that disreputable author were not transcribed by the monks of his own time:

"We cannot be surprised at these treatises having been no favorite subject of transcription in the scriptoria of our larger English monasteries, the great source of all English mediæval manuscripts, where Giraldus and the See of St. David would be held in a vastly *lower* degree of importance than that in which he regarded it and himself. His bitter abuse of monasticism,

*Official edition published under the auspices of the Master of the Rolls.

moreover, would make him far from a welcome inmate generally of monastic libraries. His *Speculum Ecclesiæ*, especially, could only have been looked upon by monks *as a piece of gross, lying, blasphemous ribaldry*, which it would be no venial sin for any monk to transcribe. No wonder that some of his works have *so barely survived to our days.*"

Such is the estimation formed of Giraldus Cambrensis by the English Protestant Editor of his works, in 1867 ! The Editor further contradicts Judge Maguire's assertion that Cambrensis' "history" appeared in 1178, during the lifetime of Alexander III. Now as Pope Alexander departed this life in 1181, it is scarcely possible that he came out of his tomb to read the falsifying "history" of Cambrensis, even supposing that author's first attempt at libelling the Irish people was issued as early as 1182 ! This rectifies *another* of Judge Maguire's "mistakes."

On another page of Mr. Dimock's Preface we read that Cambrensis did not complete his first work until the years 1185 or 1186, so that by no possibility can Judge Maguire squirm out of his very peculiar manner of anticipating events and manufacturing history to suit the sentiments of splenic hate which impelled him to commit the blunder of issuing his bad book.

Turning to page 42 of Mr. Dimock's Preface, we come to a disclosure which throws very considerable light upon the bungling manner in which the bogus Bulls were manipulated by Cambrensis and his co-conspirators against both Ireland and the Catholic Church. Alluding to the *omissions* and *subtractions* in the Cambrensian manuscripts, Mr. Dimock makes this damaging revelation :

"There is one other case of subtraction to be mentioned and a most strange one. In the 5th chapter of the 2nd book (*Expugnatio Hibernica*) the early MSS. gives under the year 1174 or 1175 a privilege long before obtained from Pope Adrian IV. authorizing Henry II.'s invasion of Ireland ; and a confirmatory one of the then Pope, Alexander III, with some prefatory matter principally relating to the persons employed in bringing these privileges for publication into Ireland at this time, and to the agency of John of Salisbury in having procured the first from Pope Adrian in 1155. But the later MSS. *omit Alexander's privilege* and all mention of him, and give Adrian's privilege only. The prefatory matter had to be *altered* accordingly. In doing this they marvellously contrive to make Henry in 1172 apply for and procure this privilege from Pope Adrian who died in 1159 (!!!) And with equally marvellous confusion they represent John of Salisbury, agent in procuring this privilege in 1155, as sent, *not* to Ireland, but to *Rome*, for the purpose of publishing it at Waterford in 1174 or 1175. (!!!)

In a foot-note to page xliii., from which this extract is taken, Mr. Dimock adds this explanation which throws another *very serious doubt* upon the genuineness of the Adrian Bull :

"But the cause of the suppression of Alexander's Bull, and the germ of the blundering in the prefatory matter, were both perhaps supplied by Giraldus, in his copy of this chapter, as given in the *De Instr. Princ.* (p. 51, etc.) He there states, in introducing Alexander's privilege, that *some asserted it to be a forgery* (!!!) and hence perhaps its *suppression* afterwards in the *Expugnatio* by some rectifier of his history of Henry's papal rights over Ireland."

The plain meaning of this paragraph shows that—*even during the lifetime of Cambrensis*—there were persons who *suspected* Adrian's Bull *to be a forgery.* This completely nullifies Judge Maguire's boast that the genuineness of the Bulls of Adrian and Alexander was not challenged when first published. Here we have *prima facie* evidence that Pope Adrian's Bull *was forged*, as no candid, honest or truthful historian could make such fearful blunders or such a jumble of facts or dates, unless his mind was beclouded by the darkness of doubt through a departure from truth and the adoption of falsehood. A manuscript that had to be altered, amended, revised and corrected after the manner in which Mr. Dimock proves the miscalled "history" of Cambrensis to have been changed and corrupted by that author himself, is entirely *unworthy* of any respect from reasonable men as an authority upon *any* question of fact whatever.

It has been already clearly demonstrated in these pages that Cambrensis did not possess a single necessary qualification to entitle him to be ranked as a historian of Ireland, but in case any person might demur to this sweeping charge, we will again have recourse to the testimony of Mr. Dimock— the Editor of the works of Cambrensis and the man who is supposed to have been most deeply versed in his writings. Here is that gentleman's verdict, showing how entirely *valueless* Cambrensis is for any purpose:

"As to his history of the English invasion, it must have been wholly derived *from the English themselves*, and in great measure from his own near friends. If Giraldus had been the most cool and fair and unbiassed of writers still a history so derived could not well have been *anything but one-sided.* * * * Giraldus was replete with the exact qualities *the very reverse* of what are needed to form an impartial historian. * * * Giraldus asserts that from the time of St. Patrick there had never been a single Irish Bishop who had manfully striven to instruct and correct the people, and this he asserts though St. Malachi's fame could not possibly be unknown to him. St. Malachi had been dead only about forty years; and few, if any, more earnest and laborious instructors and reformers can perhaps be named amongst the Bishops of all Christendom of all times, and he had contemporaries and followers not unworthy of him. And this, too, he (Cambrensis) asserts of the Isle of Saints, for ages after Patrick's time the great nursery of missionary Bishops, Apostles of the Faith, throughout the wide district of the Continent of Europe, where the name of many an Irish saint and martyr is still held in reverence; to whom also was due the conversion of Scotland and of a large part of Saxon England."

In requires no comment on our part to add any additional force to the plain truth of the foregoing caustic criticism which Mr. Dimock makes regarding the utterly worthless character of the writings of Giraldus Cambrensus, so we will leave the character of this historical hireling in the keeping of our readers while we pass under review other matters connected with this period.

CHAPTER VIII.

Proof that Giraldus Cambrensis knew the Adrian Bull was a Forged Document.—His Spiteful and Slanderous Sermon in Dublin.—The "Synod of Cashel" Critically Analyzed. More of Judge Maguire's Mistakes Made Manifest.

We will now reveal to our readers another action of Giraldus Cambrensis, which will serve to show that he himself *knew* that the Bull attributed to Pope Adrian was *a forgery*. Giraldus composed numerous works (such as they were) and whilst at Rome in the year 1199, he presented copies of them to the Pope and several notable Italian Church dignitaries, but—with the cunning of a genuine conspirator against truth—he was very careful *not* to present anybody in the Eternal City with a copy of his *Expugnatio Hibernica*, which contained *the spurious Bull of Pope Adrian!*

In the year mentioned, Cambrensis presented Pope Innocent III., with six of his works, but the *Gemma Sacerdotalis*, the infamous *Conquest of Ireland*, was studiously kept from the sight of that Pontiff or any of his Cardinals!*

In the *Symbolum Electorum*, there occurs a letter written by Cambrensis to the Premicarius and Chancellor of the Roman Court, to whom he presented his works entitled "The *Topographia* of Ireland," and the "Description of Wales," but he was cute enough to conceal from the prying eyes of that Pontifical Official the "Conquest of Ireland."†

Here again we have explicit proof which will help all who are interested in this intricate question in forming a just opinion, and of coming to a correct conclusion, that Giraldus Cambrensis knew in his heart and soul that the Adrian Bull was the outgrowth of early British "conspiracy against truth," and hence he kept it carefully concealed from the sight of those who *would have discovered the fraud!*

Alluding to the "sermon" which Giraldus preached in Dublin, and which Judge Ma-

---

*Brewer's Ed. Cambrensis, Edition of 1861, Vol. I., pp. 70.

†Brewer, pp. 308.

guire ignorantly cites as evidence that Cambrensis was "a leading Catholic Prelate of the time of Popes Adrian and Alexander," Mr. Dimock gives this not very complimentary explanation:

"Giraldus first made this assertion [his attack upon the Irish Bishops cited last week] in a sermon which he preached before a Synod of the Clergy in Dublin, and he deliberately repeats it in the *Topographia* of the present volume, and again long afterwards in his *De Rebus*, etc. The preacher of the day before, an Irish Abbot, had denounced, and very justly, as was proved, the incontinence of the English Clergy, who had followed the invaders into Ireland. Giraldus retaliated in his sermon, with a sweeping charge of excessive drinking against the Irish clergy, but adds not a word as to any attempt being made *to prove the charge*; and not content with that, he then makes this charge of utter neglect of duty against the Bishops of Ireland, without one exception since the time of St. Patrick. It was *bad enough*, in a moment of exasperation, to make so *reckless* an assertion; it was *worse* to persist deliberately in it afterwards. It seems incredible that he should not have well known *its gross falsehood*, if not at the time he first uttered it, at any rate long before he repeated it in the *De Gestis* etc. But there was nothing that Giraldus had once said, which in his opinion was not well worthy of being said again. There can be *but one opinion* of a historian who could thus *recklessly make an untrue statement, and thus deliberately persist in it.*"

What can honest people think of a "historian" who would make a false, dastardly and calumniating charge against the Prelates and the Priests of Ireland, and then—well knowing it to be a most outrageous and unfounded slander—repeat it over and over again *ad nauseiem*? Would such an unscrupulous scribe hesitate for a moment to assist the king he idolized in *forging* a fictitious Bull? Besides, Cambrensis frankly admits that in writing his book on Ireland "*truth was not his main object*," but that the volume was especially concocted "for the purpose of *sounding the praises* of King Henry the Second." Expect truth, honesty, or even ordinary impartiality, from such a villifying villian! As well look for Truth in the pit of perdition! But perhaps some reader may doubt that even as debased a character as Cambrensis so completely stultified himself as to admit these telling facts so clearly showing that *no reliance whatever* can be placed in a single word ever written by this champion conspirator against truth. In order, therefore, to meet any such objection, let us turn again to the work before us and we will find that on page lxix of Mr. Dimock's Preface, the Editor of the works of Cambrensis thus explicitly states the disreputable reason which that author had in writing his miscalled "history." Mr. Dimock says:

"I think I have said enough to justify me in refusing to accept Giraldus's history of the Irish and of their English invaders *as sober, truthful history*. Somewhat to the same purpose will be found occasionally in my notes, when it has seemed to me allowable to compare his statements with those of other authorities. Giraldus, indeed, seems himself to allow, in the case of the *Topographia*, that *truth was not his main object*. He says that he compiled the work for the purpose of sounding the praises of Henry II."

Here, therefore, we ask any candid reader, what estimate he would place upon a Papal Bull which made its first appearance in the world through the works of such an obsequious scribe and such a malignant calumniator of the whole Irish Episcopate? The only conclusion every impartial person can come to is that King Henry II., cm-employed Giraldus Cambrensis, John of Salisbury and other traitors to truth, to concoct the *bogus* Bull of Pope Adrian, which was filed away and not taken from its hiding place until about *twenty years after* the fictitious year forged on a document which is dated from *Rome*, although Pope Adrian was not in Rome at that time!

A great deal of stress is laid by those writers who suppose the spurious Bull of Pope Adrian IV. to be genuine, upon what is generally known as a Conference of the Irish clergy called at "Cashell" by order of King Henry, in some year from 1171 to 1177, regarding the date of which there are as many different opinions as there are disputants concerning the issuance of the Bull itself.

Judge Maguire, with his usual blundering derived from ignorance of the facts in the case, says on this point:

"Armed with these Bulls, King Henry, who,

before receiving the last, had entered Ireland (October 18th, 1171), claiming it under that of Adrian IV., immediately summoned the principal clergy of Ireland to meet in conference at Cashel.

"This conference is historically known as the 'Synod of Cashel.' Here the Bulls of Adrian and Alexander were read, and, 'in the name of the Sovereign Pontiff, the clergy and people of Ireland were called upon to receive Henry the Second of England as their king.'

"At this Synod the Pope's Legate presided, St. Gelasius, the Primate of Ireland, having refused to attend."

These paragraphs are all right, save that the date (October 18th) is *wrong:* the year (1171) is *inexact*: the "arming" of King Henry *a bad bull:* the Synod of "Cashell" is *a myth*: and the whole matter a *misleading fiction* manufactured by English writers in order to cover up King Henry's iniquitous invasion of Ireland! So far from being "armed with these Bulls," as Judge Maguire stupidly asserts, the bogus documents were *lying* (in far more senses than one) in some dark corner of Winchester Castle, ready to be removed into the light as soon as the parties whose names were *forged* thereto had "shuffled off this mortal coil." A pretty extensive reading of Irish history in connection with this question, justifies us in boldly asserting that no Conference of the Irish Hierarchy or Clergy was held in "Cashell" on October 18th, 1171. Rev. P. J. Carew, in his "Ecclesiastical History of Ireland," says that the Synod at which the bogus Bulls were for the first time publicly read in Ireland, was in the year 1175, and he mentions *Waterford* as the place.

In the Appendix to his work, Father Carew has given a list of the "Principal Synods held in Ireland before the Thirteenth Century." This list is copied from Lanigan's History, and the only Synods mentioned from 1162 to 1172 are the following:

1170. Synod of Armagh. This Synod decreed that all the English who were detained in servitude in Ireland, should be restored to liberty.

1172. Synod of Cashel, by order of Henry II., convened for the purpose *regulating some matters of ecclesiastical discipline.*

Judge Maguire's statement concerning the Synod of October 18th, 1171, will have to be added, therefore, to the other numerous "mistakes" for which his Honor is becoming daily more notorious.

Thomas Moore in his History of Ireland, also gives the year 1175 as the date when the manipulated manuscripts first saw the sunlight of Ireland fall upon their fictitous faces. This writer thus describes the manner of their introduction:

"It was about this time (A. D. 1175) that the Bull of Pope Adrian, granting the kingdom of Ireland to Henry II., and obtained by this Sovereign by the Holy See as far back as the year 1151, was for the first time publicly announced to his Irish subjects. * * * The persons appointed to carry these documents to Ireland were, William Fitz-Aldelm, and Nicholas, the Prior of Wallingford; and a Synod of Bishops being assembled, on their arrival, the Papal grants were there publicly read."

This extract does not look as if King Henry was "armed" with Bulls to any very alarming extent when he went to Ireland, although as eminent a legal authority as his Honor the Judge of the Superior Court of San Francisco says so! Tom Moore's history, therefore, is far more likely to be correct than Judge Maguire's miserable literary failure.

Let us now hear what the Abbé Mac-Geoghegan has to say on this subject. This celebrated historian makes no mention whatever of any Synod of Irish Bishops being held in Cashel on October 18th, 1171, nor does he allude to the introduction of the bogus Adrian Bull at any time during the twelfth century, except in the following paragraph:

"About this time, says Ware, *following the English authors by whom alone it is mentioned*, Henry II. sent Nicholas, Prior of Wallingford, and afterwards Abbot of Malmsbury, and William Fitz-Aldelm to Ireland, A. D. 1175, with the Bull of Alexander, which, *they say*, was read and approved of at an assembly of the Bishops at *Waterford*. This Bull, *according to them*, confirmed that by which Adrian IV., had already granted to this prince, the title of Lord of Ireland, and other privileges."

The portions of the above paragraph

which we have placed in *italic*, will demonstrate at a glance to our readers how entirely valueless is the whole assertion! In the first place, every person familiar with the manner in which Irish history has ever been concocted by English authors, is well aware of the fact that such works are generally genuine "conspiracies against truth." In the second place, this event is mentioned by *English authors alone*, and upon *their authority* "it is said" that the Alexander Bull was read and approved of in an assembly of Bishops! This whole paragraph, therefore, may be set down as partaking of that fradulent character which good Father Tom Burke (God rest his soul!) so graphically described as "a Thumping English Lie!"

Among the most valuable Annals of Ireland, are those of Maurice Regan, secretary and interpreter of Dermod MacMurrough, last King of Leinster, and the man through whose evil ways the English first entered Ireland. The Chronicles of Regan embrace that important era in Ireland between the years 1167 and 1173, and most assuredly King Henry the invader could not have been "armed" with the ammunition of the bogus Bulls, without the chronicler making some mention thereof. Yet *Regan is as silent as a Sphinx on the subject.*

The work‡ is one of the rarest books on Irish history extant, and it contains some very valuable statistics, as well as specimens of the singular title-deeds which the King of England made to the different invaders of the lands of Ireland. As a specimen of the orthographical combinations of the English language in the last century we append the opening paragraph in the preface, which was written in 1747:

"It apperith that this History following was written by one callid *Maurice Regan* (some tymes mentioned in this Discourse) who was Servaunt and Interpreter unto *Dermott Mac-*

‡ "HIBERNICA: Or, some Antient Pieces relating to Ireland. Part I. Containing the History of Ireland by Maurice Regan, Servant and Interpreter to Dermod MacMurrough, King of Leinster, translated from the Irish into French and from thence into English by Sir George Carew, Lord President of Munster. Dublin: Printed for John Milliken (at No. 10) in Skinner-Row. M,DCC,LXX."

Murrogh, Kyng of *Leinster*, and put into French Meetre by one of his familiar Acquaintaunce: * * * It endith abruptly at the winning of Limerick, which was not full three Yeres after *Robert Fitz-Stephen* his first arrivall in Ireland."

Concerning the manner in which King Henry of England became connected with Ireland, the chronicler of this work (under date of 1168-9) after recounting Dermod MacMurrough's visit to Henry the Second, says:

"When he came to the presence of Kyng Henry, he related at large unto hym the Cause of his Comyng, telling hym, that his vassals had forsaken hym; that he was forced to runne into Exile, and beseeching hym to gyve hym Aide, whereby he mought be restorid to his Inheritance; which yf it shuld plese hym in his goodness to graunt, he would acknowledge hym to be his Lorde, and serve him faithfully during his Life."

"THIS petiful Relation of the distressed Kyng so much movid Kyng *Henry* to Compassion, as that he promised him Aid, and willed him to return to *Bristoll*, ther to Remayne untill he herd futhir from hym; and with all he wrot to *Robert Harding*, requireing hym to receve Kyng *Dermod* and his Followers into his House, and to intreat them with all the Courtesie and Humanitie he could; wherof *Robert* failed in Nothing.

"AFTIR that Kyng *Dermod* had remaiued more than a Moneth in *Bristoll*, and seeing no hope of Aide from Kyng *Henry*, weary of delaye, and Comfortless, he went to the Erle *Richard*, intreating Succours from hym, and promising, that yf by his Means he mought be re-established in his Kyngdome, that he would gyve hym his Daughter to Wife, and with her the whole Kyngdom of *Leinster* for his Inheritaunce. The Erle tickled with so fair an Offer, made Answeare, that if he culd obteyne leave of the Kyng his Mastir, he would not fail to Assiste him in his Person, and bringe sufficiaunt Aid; but for the present he desired to be excused; for unless the Kyng wuld give his Assent ther unto, he durst not entertaine a Business of that Importance.

"THIS faire and discreot Answear so well contentid the exiled Kyng, as he solemnly Sware, that whensoever the Erle did bring Aide unto hym, he wuld gyve him his Daughter in Marriage, and after his Death the Kyngdome of *Leinster*. These Conditions bring agreed on either Party, *Dermond* departid, and went to St. *David*'s, where he staid untill Shipping was provided to Transport hym into *Irland*.

"IN the meane tyme while the banished Kyng's Shipping was in prepareing, he was Advised to goe and Visite a King in *Wales*, called *Rice*, to Desyre hym to Enlardge out of his Prison a Geutilman callid *Robert Fitz-Stephen*; but how the sayd *Robert* was taken, or for what Offence Imprisoned, I doe not understand; but that he was Enlargid by King *Rice*, at the request of the Kyng of *Leinster*, I am well Assured.

"HAVING obteyned his Request, he returned to St. *David's*, carrying no more *Englishmen* with him than one Gentilman called *Richard Fitz-Godobert*, who had many good Parts in him, but so slenderly attendid, as they were of small use for King *Dermond*, when he came into *Irland*; wherfore he licenced them to depart home.

"THE Kyng of *Leinster* findinge it to be an Impossibility for hym to recovir his Kyngdome, and to prevaile in hys Designs without Aid out of *England*, Dispatched his Trusty Servaunt and Interpreter, *Maurice Regan*, with Letres into *Wales*, and with Auctority in hys Name to promise all souche as wuld come to serve hym in his Wars in *Irland* large Recompence in Landes of Inheritaunce to souche as wuld staye in the Country, and to those that wuld returne, he would gyve them good Intertainment eyther in Money or in Cattle. As soone as these Promises were divulged, Men of all Sortes, and from divers Places, preparid themselves to goe into *Irland*, first, especially *Robert Fitz-Stephen*, a Man of good Esteeme in *Wales*, (who had lately been enlargid out of Prison by the Mediation of *Dermond*) undirtooke the Imployment, and with hym some nine or ten Knights of good account, namely."

We cite these passages in order to show our readers that the *invasion* of Ireland was decided upon by Henry of England long before he thought of forging the two bogus Bulls. And now let us turn to this author's account of King Henry's landing in Ireland, which appears under date of 1171-2 3, in the following quaint style of spelling :

"A. D. 1171. As soon as the Winde served, Kyng Henry, attended by Erle Richard, Fitz Aldelme, Humfrie de Bohun, Hugh de Lacy, Robert Fitz-Bernard, with divers others Lordes, Erles and Barons, besides four Hundred Knights and four Thousand Soldiers imbarqued for Irland, and landid nere unto Waterford; which City the Erle Richard deliverid unto hym, and did Homage for the Kyngdome of Leinster, the Inheritaunce whereof was graunted unto hym; the Government of Waterford was bestowed upon him Robert Fitz-Bernard; but before the Kyng's departur the Men of Weixford, as they promised, brought Robert Fizt-Stephen, and delivered him unto the Kynge, where in the presence of all that were present he sharply reproved Fitz-Stephen for his past Misdemeanours. He made his humble Excuse, and all the Lordes, as well English, Normans, and Flemings, became Suretie for his future Behaviour.

"A. D. 1172. THE Kyng, making but little Staie at Waterford, marched into Dublin, whych City the Earle deliverid unto him; who committed the keepeinge thereof to Hugh de Lacy.

AFTIR some small abode at Dublyn, the Kynge tooke his Jorney into Mounster, where the Archbishop of Cashell came unto him hym; at Lismore he gave Direction for the building of a Castle; from whence he returned into Leinster.

"THE Kynge made his aboade at Dublin, and the Earle Richard at Kildare; and in thys Tyme of the Kyng's beinge in Irland all sorts of Victualles were at excessive Rates.

"WHILE the Kynge remained at Dublin, by Messingers and Intelligence out of England he was certified, that his Son, the yonge King Henry had rebelled against him, and that Normandie was in Danger to revolt unto hym.

"THIS ill News troubled the Kyng beyond all Measure; and enforced him to hasten his return out of Ireland. The Cittie of Waterford he left in the Custodie of Robert Fitz-Bernard, and Dublyn unto Hugh de Lacy. Robert Fitz-Stephen, Meyler Fitz-Henry and Myles Fitz-David were in a sort restrained, and to remain at Dublyn with Lacy. Before his Departure from Dublyn he gave unto Hugh de Lacy the Inheritaunce of all Meath, to hold of hym at fifty Knight Fees, and unto John de Courcey he gave all Ulster if he could conquer it.

"A. D. 1173 WHEN the Kynge had taken provisional Order for the Affairs of Irland, he went to Weixford, where he imbarqued, and arrived at Portfinan in Wales, halfe a League from St David's, and in his Companie Miles de Cogan, whom he carryed with hym out of Ireland; and from thence with all possible Expedition he passed through England, and so into Normandie."

Here we find that the only allusion to "Cashell" is that King Henry, being in the province of Munster in 1172, the Archbishop of "Cashell" *paid him a visit.* There was *no Synod,* therefore, or assuredly this chronicler who was living at that period would have mentioned such an important assemblage of the Irish Ecclesiastical body.

We now turn to the "History of Ireland" by Sister Mary Francis Clare, popularly known as "the Nun of Kenmare," whom Judge Maguire vain-gloriously alludes to as one of the Irish historians who "attest to the genuineness of the Adrian Bull." But in this regard, as in a great many other matters in his bad book, Judge Maguire misjudges this author's opinions from a random foot-note. If the careless author of "Ireland and the Pope" had opened the Nun of Kenmare's work at page 259, he would have saved us the trouble of exposing his shallowness, as therein he would have read the following opinion of that estimable Sister, upon the favorable Letter which King Henry gave to Dermod MacMorrough when he asked the English monarch for help to reinstate him in his Irish possessions:

The royal letter ran thus: "Henry, King of England, Duke of Normandy and Aquitaine, and Earl of Anjou, to all his liegemen, English, Norman, Welsh and Scotch, and to all the nations under his dominion, sends greeting. As soon as the present letter shall come to your hand, know that Dermod, Prince of Leinster, has been received into the bosom of our grace and benevolence: wherefore whosoever, within the ample extent of our territories, shall be willing to lend aid towards this prince as our faithful and liege subject, let such person know that we do hereby grant to him for said purpose our licence and favor."

"Commenting on this Letter, the Nun of Kenmare says:

"In this document there is *not even the remotest reference to the Bull of Adrian*, conferring the island of Ireland on Henry, although the Bull had been obtained some time before. *In whatever light we may view this omission it is certainly inexplicable.*"

This extract *proves* that the good Nun of Kenmare was not *thoroughly convinced* of the genuineness of the Adrian Bull. But we have other proofs from this author, that also offset Judge Maguire's claim upon this gifted writer as coinciding with the *English* writers on this subject. Alluding to the Synod of Cashel—regarding which *no date is given*—the Nun of Kenmare says:

"The Synod of Cashel, which he (Henry) caused to be convened was *not attended* as numerously as he had expected, and the regulations made thereat, were simply a *renewal of those which had been made previously*. The Primate of Ireland *was absent*, and the Prelates who assembled there, far from having *enslaved the State to Henry*, avoided any *interference in politics either by word or act*. It has been well observed that whether "piping or mourning," they were not destined to escape. Their office was to promote peace. So long as the permanent peace and independence of the nation seemed likely to be forwarded by resistance to foreign invasion, they counselled resistance; when resistance was hopeless they recommended acquiescence, not because they believed the usurpation less unjust, but because they considered submission the wisest course. But *the Bull of Adrian had not yet been produced*; and Henry's indifference about this document, or his reluctance to use it, shows *of how little real importance it was considered at the time.*"

This extract, taken in connection with the preceding one, does not look as if the Nun of Kenmare had the unreserved faith in the genuineness of the Adrian Bull which Judge Maguire credits her with. That estimable friend of Ireland, on the contrary, seems to have had *very serious misgivings* on this point, even when she wrote her history a quarter of a century ago, and we have little doubt but when Sister Mary Francis reads the MONITOR'S revelations on this subject, she will become thoroughly convinced that both the Adrian and Alexander Bulls *were bogus.*

The next extract we make from the anti-Maguirean pages of the Nun of Kenmare's history is entirely in opposition to his Honor's idea that King Henry had "armed" himself with bogus Bulls before he left the British shores in order to invade Ireland. In fact he was in England for several years before the spurious documents were completed sufficiently to present them in public.

"Henry now considered it time to produce the Papal Bulls, A. D., 1175. He therefore dispatched the Prior of Wallingford and William Fitz-Aldelm to Waterford, where a synod of *the clergy* was assembled to hear these important documents. * * * Our historians have not informed us what was the result of the meeting. Had the Papal donation *appeared a matter of national importance, there can be little doubt that it would have excited more attention.*"

A Synod of "the Clergy of Ireland" could have no standing in Canon Law unless presided over by some Prelate and authorized by the Pope's Legate or the Archbishops and Bishops of that country. It is sheer folly, therefore, to speak of a "Synod of the Clergy of Ireland" having ever convened in that Island of Saints for any such purpose. A Synod even of "the Clergy" which was so insignificant in size, substance and sacerdotal character as not to be worthy of being chronicled by Irish historians, must have been a very mythical body! Even *Waterford*, the place where—according to English writers *only*—the supposed Synod was held, would be the *last place in Ireland* which the Irish Bishops would select for assembling. This fact will not fail to strike our readers when they have learned the character of the class of people who forcibly entered and occupied Waterford both at the time of the Anglo-Norman invasion as well as for centuries previous.

We will now give our readers some idea of the early inhabitants of *Waterford*, which will go far towards showing why a *bogus* Bull should be brought before a *bogus* Synod—even supposing that such a gathering ever took place.

CHAPTER IX.

A Description of Waterford's Inhabitants.—A Favorite Abiding Place of Danes, English and other Enemies of Ireland.—When that See was Established.—Why no Synod Ever Met There.—Pope Alexander and the Irish Bishops.—Another of Judge Maguire's "Mistakes" Made Minced-meat of.

Waterford is one of the most ancient maritime ports of Ireland, and was known as far back as the second century by the name of *Cuan-na-grain*, or "The Harbor of the Sun." But its present name of Waterford is generally supposed to be a corruption of the Scandinavian *Vader Fiord*, or the "Ford of Father," and this name it received from the foreign freebooters from the North of Europe who landed there as early as the ninth century.*

For nearly three hundred years prior to 1175, Waterford had been the headquarters in Ireland of the piratical Danes, who established a regal dynasty there under Sitrack, which continued to exist down to the Norman invasion. It was in Waterford that the first body of Norman freebooters landed, and it was the same place which King Henry selected as his landing place so as to arrive in the midst of *his friends*.

Waterford was also the scene of one of the most barbarous deeds that ever blackened the pages of history, and one well worthy of being the first act in the bloody drama which English tyranny has acted upon Ireland's stage since it first baptized that beautiful land in blood, seven centuries ago.

The advance guard of the Anglo-Norman invaders under Strongbow, built a small fort near Waterford, and seized all the cattle in the surrounding district. They had invaded the land of a peaceable people, and to pilfer the personal property of the rightful owners of the soil, was a most suitable action with which to open the Anglo-Norman campaign in Ireland. The robbery of their cattle so incensed the native Irish that they very naturally assembled in order to drive off the piratical pilferers from their locality, but an unarmed and undisciplined crowd was no match for the Welsh and Anglo-Norman soldiers, encased in coats-of-mail and armed with warlike weapons. The result was that five hundred Irish were slain and a large number taken prisoners, among whom were some of the principal inhabitants; and although large sums of gold were offered for their ransom, these proto-martyrs in defence of their homes and property were most brutally murdered by England's savage hirelings. According to an English annalist, these unfortunate Irishmen were marched up on the high cliffs adjoining the sea, where their limbs were

*Marmion's Ancient and Modern History of the Maritime Ports of Ireland.

broken in the most brutal manner, and their bleeding bodies then cast headlong on the rocks beneath! Such was the first scene enacted by England's minions when the shadow of their blighting presence fell upon the virgin soil of virtuous Ireland! It was, as already stated, in Waterford, also, that King Henry landed, when he went to Ireland in 1172 with 500 knights and 4,000 soldiers, many of whom settled in that country, and, amongst others, a number of English, Norman and Welsh priests, whose morals were such as to scandalize the Irish people and to receive the just condemnation of numerous Irish historians.

Waterford, therefore, at the time when the very suspicious skeleton Synod already mentioned, is *supposed* to have been held, was the hive into which had gathered the greater number of the Irish-hating adventurers who had followed the fortunes of Strongbow and King Henry to Ireland, in order to improve their finances by filching the lands and property of the Irish people by means of force of arms, forged Bulls, or in any other iniquitous manner which suggested itself to such a squad of piratical invaders.

It is very certain, therefore, that if any Synod was held in Waterford during any year from 1171 to 1177, very likely it was composed of the foreign ecclesiastical element which had colonized there, and who were ready to accept any document presented to them through the influential agents of King Henry, and to ask no questions as to its genuine character or its justice.

Those writers who copy from hired English historians, repeat the romance that the bogus Bull of Alexander was read to an assembly of "Bishops," but these "Bishops," we may safely surmise, were merely the foreign ecclesiastics who are thus described in Carew's *Ecclesiastical History of Ireland:*

"Of the English Clergy who settled in this country, there were many whose lives were a reproach to their sacred calling. These, we are assured, had scarcely taken up their abode in Ireland, when several of them were found to live in the violation of the solemn obligations which are annexed to the Priesthood. That, under the pretense of introducing a more strict morality into Ireland, the country should have been made tributary to England, was in itself sufficiently mortifying to the Irish Clergy. But, that such spiritual instructors as had been imported by the invaders, should be employed to enlighten the piety of the Irish people, provoked their utmost indignation."

With such ecclesiastical material as these Anglo-Norman and Welsh Priests formed, King Henry would have no trouble whatever in molding them to suit his views. A Pope's Bull, without date or location, would be approved and accepted without a dissenting voice, especially if—like the Alexander forgery—it calumniated the Catholic Bishops, Priests, Religious and people of Ireland, by designating them under the diabolical aspersion of being "Christians only in name." Even, therefore, supposing there was a Synod at Waterford, in the twelfth century, there is no proof extant that any of the Irish Bishops assisted thereat, and a Synod in which the Irish Bishops took no part would be nothing more than a convention of unauthorized clerics who would incur excommunication for their contumacious conduct in thus usurping an authority solely vested in the Irish Prelates.

It is said by English writers and repeated by their American imitators in the propagation of falsehood, that the bogus Bulls were seen by the Irish Bishops and accepted by them as genuine. Now, if such were the fact, was it not an act of rank disobedience to, and of actual rebellion against, the Holy See, for each of those twenty or thirty Bishops then in Ireland, to live and die without ever once asking their flocks for a single penny for St. Peter's successor? Does any person who has even the remotest idea of the ready obedience and the scrupulous punctiliousness of the Irish Bishops, in carrying out the provisions of all genuine Bulls received by them from Rome, harbor for an instant the idea that St. Gelasius, the Primate of Armagh, St. Laurence O'Toole, then Archbishop of Dublin, and all the other saintly Prelates who at that period presided over God's Church in Ireland, would rebel against the Roman Pontiff whom they had sworn to obey in all things just? It is very clear to our mind, therefore, that no Irish Bishop believed the Adrian Bull to be genuine, allowing even that any of them saw it, and, if we had no other evidence of the spurious character of this document, the scornful and scurvy treatment that it received at the hands of the entire Hierarchy of Ireland, would satisfy us that they saw through the fraud at the first glance, hence they paid no attention to it.

No Bishops in the world were more in harmony with Rome in the twelfth century than the Irish Prelates. Popes Adrian and Alexander were personally known to many of them, and the idea that not a single one of the Bishops would obey those Pontiffs' demand for "a penny from each house in Ireland," as Peter-Pence, is a statement so contrary to the saintly obedience of these noble successors to St. Patrick as to cast the shadow of diabolical calumny athwart the sacred shrines in which their blessed ashes repose! No! a thousand times No! The Irish Bishops of the twelfth century who saw the bogus Bulls, set them down at their true value and—to a man—they silently spurned with sacerdotal scorn the spurious documents—and may God increase their heavenly happiness for having done so!

The next witness we call into the Superior Court of San Francisco in order to convict its Judge of a very serious "mistake," is Dr. John Lingard, the eminent historian, who, speaking of the first introduction of the Adrian fraud into Ireland, says, after alluding to King Henry's return to England:

"It was during this period, when his authority in Ireland was nearly annihilated, that Henry bethought him of the letter which he had formerly procured from Pope Adrian. I had been forgotten during almost twenty years now it was drawn from obscurity, was intrusted to William Fitz Aldelm, and Nicholas, Prior of Wallingford, and was read by them with much solemnity to a Synod of Irish Bishops."

It seems, therefore, from Dr. Lingard's language, that Judge Maguire's assertion about King Henry being "armed" with double-barreled Bulls, when he set out for Ireland, was one of those "mistakes" which superficial readers of Irish history so often purposely make in order to mislead their dupes. Dr. Lingard says that the Adrian Bull was read at a Synod of the Irish Bishops: but a Synod held *no where*, and on a day in a month and year *not designated*, would be *precisely* the place for introducing a *forged* Bull *without date*, and issued from *Rome* by a Pope who was *not* permitted to occupy the Eternal City during *the fictitious year* attributed to the *fraudulent document!* The fitness of the *bogus Bull* and the *bogus Synod*, will, therefore, be both *apparent* as well as *transparent* to all our readers!

Another fact which we desire to impress upon our readers in connection with this very suspicious Synod which is supposed to have been held in Waterford, is, that from the time of St. Patrick (about the year 456) down to the year 1175, there were a great number of National Synods held in Ireland, but not one of them ever assembled in Waterford! Nor is there any account in Irish history of any such Synod ever being held in that locality for more than a hundred years thereafter.†

It is well to understand that so few Catholics were there in Waterford during the six centuries intervening between the years 456 and 1096, that the See of Waterford had no existence. This is another evidence of the fact that Danes, Scandinavians, Normans and people from other portions of Pagan Europe, must have predominated in Waterford, especially when we have historical proof of the fact that twenty Catholic Sees were formed in Ireland between the founding of the Dioceses of Armagh, Clogher, Meath, Clonmacnoise, Down and Ardagh in the fifth century, down to five hundred years thereafter, when a See was established in Waterford. Thus it came about that Waterford was created a See only about seventy-five years before the English invasion, and six hundred and forty years after the See of Armagh. It is not likely, therefore, that not only St. Gelasius, the Irish Primate, was absent from this very suspicious Synod, but that every other Irish bishop carefully and dutifully made

†Carew's Ecclesiastical History.

themselves absentees from such an assembly of scandal-giving English and Welsh ecclesiastics.

Judge Maguire seems to imagine that he has made a point in favor of the genuineness of the Adrian Bull, by copying the assertion of a writer who says that "St. Lawrence O'Toole, and other leading Bishops of Ireland, conversed with Pope Alexander III. about the Adrian Bull as well as the reigning Pontiff's own confirmatory Bull," during the time these Irish Prelates were in Rome attending the Third Lateran Council in 1179.

Admitting, for the purpose of illustrating the falsity of the foregoing statement, that St. Laurence O'Toole and the Irish Bishops conversed *every day for a year* about the two Bulls above mentioned, and that each Prelate could recite every word of these documents from memory, we claim that this very fact, so far from proving anything in favor of the authenticity of the Bulls in question, actually helps to show their fraudulent nature, thus adding another link to the chain we are making in order to demonstrate their spurious character.

Now we ask any reflecting Catholic to consider this phase of the case as we present it from a Catholic standpoint:

Irish Bishops go to Rome ;‡ while there two Bulls calling for an annual alms of one penny from every house in Ireland, as Peter-Pence for the propagation of the Faith, are presented to them by one of the Pontiffs who *is said* to have issued a Bull of his own in confirmation of that of one of his predecessors. The Pope lucidly explains the two documents to the Prelates; he points out the Peter-Pence clause particularly; he causes certified copies to be made of the Bulls, hands them to the Bishops at their departure from the Eternal City, gives them his blessing, and bids them God-speed.

St. Laurence O'Toole and his Episcopal brethren arrive in Ireland; they publicly and privately recite their experience in Rome during the Council, and particularly allude to their frequent conferences with Pope Alexander III., on the two Bulls calling for Peter-Pence every year, and yet, *not one of these Bishops ever sent to Rome a single penny in response to the double request for Peter-Pence made by Popes Adrian and Alexander!*

Is there a single Catholic on the face of God's footstool who will charge the saintly St. Laurence O'Toole and the other Bishops of Ireland with having thus heaped insult and injury upon Pope Alexander III. and the Holy See! Yet this is precisely the unenviable position these Prelates must inevitably occupy in the estimation of a just public opinion, if the statement in Judge Maguire's bad book is to be credited.

Laurence O'Toole, Archbishop of Dublin, was canonized and is duly recognized as a great Saint in the Church of God, but if, during the process of the proceedings prior to his Canonization, the Devil's Advocate had adduced evidence to prove that this holy Prelate had been disobedient, insubordinate and contumacious towards Popes Adrian and Alexander, the nimbus of canonization would never have encircled his brow !

It is worse than folly, therefore, for Judge Maguire, or any other anti-Catholic to say that any Bishop in Ireland ever had a conversation with any Pope upon Bulls that never were issued by the Pontiffs named, nor were ever properly registered in any official record of evidence belonging to the Church of Christ. Pope Alexander never saw them; St. Gelasius never saw them; St. Laurence O'Toole never saw them— either in the Vatican or any other place within the walls of the Eternal City, and thus it came about that the Irish Prelates never collected a single cent of Peter-Pence as laid down in both the criminally-concocted bogus Bulls !

---

‡There were six Irish Prelates in Rome in attendance at the Council of Lateran. These are said to have been St. Laurence of Dublin, Catholicus of Tuam, Constantine O'Brien of Killaloe, Felix of Lismore, Augustine of Waterford, and Brictius of Limerick. Pope Alexander III. bestowed the kindest attention on them all, taking the Church of Dublin under under his own special protection ; confirmed the jurisdiction of St. Laurence O'Toole over the Sees of Glendaloch, Kildare, Ferns, Leighlin and Ossory; and appointed the saintly Metropolitan of Dublin the Legate of his Holiness throughout the Kingdom of Ireland.—*Carew's Ecclesiastical History.*

CHAPTER X.

The Synod of Windsor Criticised.—King Henry's Treaty with the King of Connaught.—Neither the Adrian nor the Alexander Bulls Known in England even as late as the Year 1175.—Cardinal Vivian's Visit to Ireland.—The Right of Sanctuary in Ireland.—More of Judge Maguire's Malignant Mistakes Melted in the Crucible of Historic Truth.

Now that we have clearly shown the sham character of the Waterford Synod, let us turn to the Synod of Windsor, in order to ascertain the fact that—*even in England*—no person had knowledge of any Bulls from Popes Adrian and Alexander relating to England and Ireland, down to the year 1175.

According to the Annals of Roger de Hoveden,* in 1175, King Henry II., held a Council at Windsor, in England, at which assisted the Archbishops of Tuam and Dublin, as well as Cantordis, Abbot of St. Brandan and Master Laurence, Chancellor of Roderic, King of Connaught. This fact introduces new evidence to prove that the Bulls of Adrian and Alexander *were not in existence* in 1175, although one is dated 1156, and the other forgery 1172.

The Council of Windsor was held for the purpose of making a treaty of peace with Roderic O'Connor, King of Connaught, on whose behalf the Irish Prelates were present. The terms which bound the King and Roderic to keep the peace, help to elucidate the fact that up to this date no one in England or Ireland had any knowledge of the Bulls, the fradulent character of which we are exposing. Here is the agreement as printed in Leland's History of Ireland, copied from the Annals of Rymer :

Roderic, on his part, consented to do homage, and pay tribute, as liege-man to the king of England ; on which conditions he was allowed to hold the kingdom of Connaught, as well as his other lands and sovereignties in as ample a manner as he had enjoyed them before the arrival of Henry in Ireland. His vassals were to hold under him in peace, as long as they paid tribute, and continued faithful to the king of England ; in which Roderic was to enforce their due obedience, and for this purpose to call to his assistance the English government if necessary. The annual tribute to be paid was every tenth merchantable hide, as well as from Connaught as the rest of the island, excepting those parts under the immediate dominion of the king of England and his barons, Dublin with its appurtenances, Meath with all its appurtenances, Wexford and all Leinster, and Waterford with its lands, as far as to Dungarvan inclusive ; in all which districts, Roderic was not to interfere, nor claim any power or authority. The Irish, who had fled from hence, were to return, and either to pay their tribute, or to perform the services required by their tenures, at the option of their immediate lords ; and if refractory, Roderic, at the requisition of their lords, was to compel them to return. He was to take hostages from his vassels, such as he and his liege lords should think proper ; and on his part to deliver either these or others to his lord as Henry should appoint. His vassels were to furnish hawks and hounds annually to the English monarch, and were not to detain any tenant of his immediate demesnes in Ireland, contrary to his royal pleasure and command.

Here we find an agreement by the conditions of which the King of Connaught retains his kingdom, "as well as his sovereignties and other lands in as ample a manner as he had enjoyed them before the arrival of King Henry in Ireland !" This is certainly a very singular agreement for King Henry to make, if—as is falsely supposed—he had the Adrian Bull in his possession ! King Henry exacts from Roderic an annual tribute of "every tenth merchantable hide" for *himself*, but he never once thinks of asking Roderic O'Connor for that "penny from every house" collection for the Pope who gave him all Ireland for a free donation ! Was not Henry a most ungrateful wretch ? To capture every tenth *hide* and to leave not a *hair* for the Popes who made him both Pope and King of Ireland ! Deeper ingratitude than this no man ever committed ! But was it ingratitude ? Or, rather, does not Henry'

---

*An English historian in the age of Henry II. He was born at York, was Court Chaplain to Henry and also one of his Majesty's legal advisers. He wrote annals which began in the year 731, where Bede left off, and continued to the third year of King John.

conduct and the contents of his agreement with Roderic O'Connor clearly prove that the English King had not a scrap of Adrian's or Alexander's Bulls among his archives even as late as 1175!

If these Bulls existed, both the English and the Irish Prelates present at the Synod of Windsor, would most assuredly have known of them, and have alluded to them and their peculiar Peter-Pence clauses, before closing the above treaty of peace! King Henry would certainly have alluded to the collection of Peter-Pence (provided he had the Popes' authority therefor) when he entered into a treaty with Roderic as *King of Ireland*. The Irish Bishops, too—had they an inkling of any Bulls by which the Papal treasury was entitled to certain specified donations—could not do otherwise than to see that such a clause was put into the treaty of peace as would make the collection of the Peter-Pence just as binding on the two kings as Henry made the obligation of furnishing "a *tenth* merchantable hide" obligatory upon the part of Roderic. This is very clear, and these circumstances cast an additional shadow of doubt over the genuineness of both the apocryphal Bulls attributed to Popes Adrian and Alexander.

Again, if, as Cambrensis and his copyists say, there was a Synod of Bishops in Cashel or elsewhere in 1172, at which the bogus Bulls were read and accepted by the Irish Bishops, would not the Archbishop of Tuam's memory have carried him back three years prior to 1175 and revived that fact?

And when that Prelate read and signed a treaty of peace in which *an annual tribute* of "every tenth merchantable hide" was to be paid to King Henry, would not such a proviso prick his conscience that in signing such a document he was virtually *robbing Peter of his pence* in order to favor a foreign prince?

We leave every intelligent reader to answer these questions to the satisfaction of his own reason, but for ourself we can freely say that no Irish Bishop could act in the fraudulent, dishonest, disrespectful and degrading manner English falsifying historians chronicle, simply because such nefarious actions belong to the lives of the scheming, the ambitious, the unscrupulous, and the irreligious, but not to the saintly lives of the humble, pious, virtuous Apostles of Almighty God who ruled over His Church in Ireland in every century from the fifth to the nineteenth!

The Irish Bishops, like the Round Towers of that holy land, stand as monuments of the Faith in an island where Christianity took root as spontaneously in the hearts of the people, as did the shamrock in its native soil! More loyal men to Faith, truth, justice and honor than the Bishops of Ireland never lived! And to falsely charge these Prelates with double hypocrisy towards the Vicar of Christ on one hand, and against King Henry on the other, is to charge the very sun in the heavens with giving forth no light!

It is clear, therefore, that no Synod of Irish Bishops ever saw the bogus Bulls, nor did Henry the Second issue his order to have them forged and fraudulently signed even as late as the year 1175.

Let us now carry our readers back to Dublin, where, as some historians assert, and some copyists repeat, a Synod was summoned in the year 1177, by, and immediately held under Vivian, the Pope's Legate to Ireland. Judge Maguire, copying from Carew, who copied from Lanigan, who copied from the falsifying calumniator Cambrensis, says "the Legate set forth Henry's right to the sovereignty of Ireland, in virtue of the Pope's authority, and inculcated the necessity of obeying him under pain of excommunication." The *inventor* of this falsehood was Cambrensis, and every reader of these lines already knows what reliance can be placed upon any expression of that publicly-convicted perverter of each truth, fact and circumstance his pen ever treated of. Cambrensis says that Cardinal Vivian proclaimed publicly (but *verbally*) in the Dublin Synod, the right of the King of England over Ireland, and the confirmation of Pope Alexander, "with the rigorous precept, both to the clergy and people, to remain faithful to the King, under pain of excommunication."

In regard to this assertion, as well as to all others made by Cambrensis, it is clear that it will not stand the test or critical scrutiny. The Council of Dublin could not have been attended by any Irish clergy outside the English Pale, as Cambrensis himself tells us that during the same year in which the Dublin Council was held (1177) the entire Provinces of Ulster and Connaught remained *inaccessible to the English*, whose attacks the natives constantly repelled. It is safe to say, therefore, that not *one-half* of the clergy of Ireland attended the Dublin Synod.

When, therefore, Cambrensis says that a *verbal* proclamation of excommunication against the whole Episcopate, the clergy and people of Ireland, was made by Cardinal Vivian, that untruthful scribe fairly outdoes himself as the champion historical falsier of the twelfth century ! There is not *a single word of truth* in that part of his statement concerning Cardinal Vivian or the threat of excommunication ! And now for the proof:

Leaving aside altogether every copyist of Cambrensis—from the mercenary Giraldus himself down to the malignant Maguire— let us take up the ancient Chronicles written by men who were not *hired* to calumniate the Catholic Church, nor whose *hate* against the Pope was not so malignant as to lead them into the filthy habit of picking up every scrap of rotten rubbish which they found floating along the scum of libellous literature flowing from the foulest sources of English bigots—for no other purpose than to cause a separation between the Vicar of Christ and the children of St. Patrick.

When *honest* men desire to investigate the dogmas of the Catholic Church, for the purpose of learning the *truth* concerning them, they do not consult the works of anti-Catholic writers whose prejudices preclude the possibility of truth having any existence in their mental regions. In like manner, when any *honest* investigator of Irish events desires to learn the truth concerning them, he does not consult the works of Ireland's worst enemies (as Judge Maguire does) in order to blacken the character of the Catholic Church and to justify his own Judas-like apostacy.

Now let us open the Annals of Ireland, written by Irishmen, and see how far they will assist in convicting Judge Maguire of another of those "mistakes" which are prompted by his anti-Papal prejudices and vitalized by his vicious attack upon the Church of his holy Irish ancestors.

The ancient annals of Ireland mention the arrival in that country of a Cardinal Vivianus, (or Vivian as it is abridged by recent writers). This Legate of the Pope is recorded as having arrived in Ireland in 1177. Under that date we find, in the Annals of Dublin, the following :

"Cardinal Vivianus came to Ireland, and convened a Synod of Irish Bishops and Abbots at Dublin, on the first Sunday in Lent, at which they enacted many ecclesiastical regulations."†

The Chronicles of the Four Masters say :

"In the year 1177 Cardinal Vivian arrived in Ireland. A Council of the whole Irish clergy, with its Bishops and Abbots was assembled by the Cardinal on the first Saturday of Lent ; he promulgated several ordinances which now are not known ";‡

Even if we had no other evidence to offer, these two extracts are sufficient to prove that the Synod of the Irish Bishops, clergy and people was never—in 1177 or at any other time—threatened with excommunication by any Pope if they refused to remain faithful to the King of England. In the first place the crime (if crime it was ?) and the punishment, are opposed in fact and essence to the ever just laws of God and of His Church. Threaten with excommunication Bishops, Priests and millions of people, if ever they were unfaithful to a foreign invader who was a murderer, a robber and a sacrilegious violator of God's consecrated sanctuaries ? Is there a single sane person whose mind is acquainted with even the elementary principles of God's justice, the integrity of the Holy See, and the code of Canon Law, who harbors the thought for an instant that such a transaction ever transpired ?

Now let us apply the rules of Catholic justice to the Dublin Synod, and see how far they prove that Cardinal Vivian could not act in the manner that Cambrensis states.

Giraldus says of the Pope's Legate that

†Irish Miscellany, Vol. I., pp. 195.
‡Quoted by Cambrensis, Vol. V. pp. 345.

when he called the Ecclesiastical Council of Dublin, he announced publicly (but *verbally*, be it borne in mind) the right of the King of England to rule over Ireland, and the confirmation of Pope Alexander, with the unusual and extraordinary penalty against all the Bishops, the Clergy and the people of Ireland, to remain faithful to the English King *under pain of anathema*.§

This assertion may be all *right*, coming as it does from *Cambrensis*, who could scarcely tell the truth even by accident, but when it is weighed and measured by the scale of Canon law, and long-established custom in the Catholic Church, it immediately (if we may be permitted to imitate King Henry, and *fabricate a Bull*) weighs *nothing* and measures *less!*

Rome has certain laws by which all documents emanating from the Vatican are brought to the notice of those who come under their provisions and upon whom they are binding. But no one will pretend to say that in the Code of the Catholic Church there is any enactment by which even Cardinal Vivian would be justified in making a *verbal* announcement of a Bull to *a few* of the Irish Bishops, and then threaten the whole Episcopate, clergy and people of Ireland with the vengeance of *anathema*—if they were disloyal to the English King.

Rome does not disseminate her Bulls after any such loose fashion, nor does she expect that they will be propagated by *word of mouth*, or obeyed by Prelates and people who know their contents *only by hearsay*. Rome never countenances an injustice against her children, nor does she expect obedience in anything impossible.

In 1177 neither the Province of Ulster nor Connaught were embraced in that portion of Ireland invaded by King Henry.

§ Few persons have a clear comprehension of the awful spiritual punishment which is comprised within the simple word "anathema." Anathema is rarely pronounced, but when promulgated it is conducted with far more imposing ceremonies than excommunication, in order to strike terror into the hearts of the culprits and to bring them back to repentance. The ceremony is performed by a Bishop and twelve priests, who hold lighted candles in their hands, which, after prescribed prayers, they cast upon the earth, and trample upon them the moment the awful sentence is pronounced, uttering maledictions and execrations against the guilty parties.—*Leg. 13: Fit. 9, p. 1.*

And for this reason we are safe in asserting that no Bishop, Priest, Monk of Friar *outside the English Pale*, ever set foot in the Synod of Dublin.

The English chronicler Hoveden speaks of Cardinal Vivian, and his journey to Ireland in 1177, but he says not a word about any Synod at Dublin or anywhere else in Ireland during that year. Here is what his chronicles say on that subject:

"The same year (1176) Vivian, Cardinal-Priest of the title of St. Stephen on the Cecilian Mount, Legate of the Apostolic See, passed the Christmas in the Isle of Man, with King Guthred. After the Feast of the Epiphany (1177) he set sail for Ireland and landed at Dun‖ in Alvestre.¶ As he was going to Dublin, by the shore, he met the army of John de Curci, by whom he was arrested and detained, but when his ecclesiastical character was revealed he was released.

"John de Curci laid seige to and captured Dun," the chief city of Alvestre,¶ where repose the bodies of the holy Confessors, Patrick and Columba, as well as the body of St. Bridget, Virgin. Roderick, King of Alvestre,¶ on hearing this, collected a large body of Irishmen and gave battle to John de Curci, but the latter was victorious. The Bishop of Dun‖ was captured in the combat, but subsequently liberated at the entreaty of the Cardinal."

When the Pope's Legate had procured the best terms he could for the defeated Irish, he proceeded to Dublin, where—as the Nun of Kenmare says—"he held a Synod. The principal enactment referred *to the right of sanctuary*." The Nun says *nothing* about any excommunication for a crime *not committed*, and thus Judge Maguire's witness gives evidence for the Pope and against the English Cambrensis and his California imitator!

ARCHBISHOP COMYN'S CHARACTER.

In his attempts at exposing what he calls "Humiliating the Irish priests and people and Papal interference with Irish struggles for liberty after the Conquest," Judge Maguire is just as inaccurate as he is in every other portion of his bad book. His honor must have had a bad attack of anti-Catholic

‖ Downpatrick.
¶ Ulster.

rabies when he wrote the following foolish fusillade of fanatical hate:

"In the year 1180 King Henry, who persecuted the Holy Prelate, St. Laurence, for his ardent attachment to the land of his birth, resolved that an office of so much importance (the Archbishopric of Dublin) should not be entrusted to an Irishman. * * * Accordingly on the monarch's recommendation, his chaplain, John Comyn, a native of England, was elected to the Archbishopric of Dublin, by some of the clergy who had assembled at Evesham for that purpose. *John was not then a priest*, but was in the following year ordained, and was consecrated by Pope Lucius III."

After reading the foregoing paragraph, Catholics will naturally conclude that Judge Maguire has a very small stock of Catholic knowledge, inasmuch as he tells his readers that John Comyn was *chaplain* to Henry II., but was not *ordained!* Was ever man in such a dual position? A priest and a layman at the same time! Now the *truth* of the circumstance is that John Comyn, ("Cumyn," or "Cummin" as it is variously written by Irish historians) was a good *Irish* Prelate, although an Englishman by birth. Here is what Judge Maguire's favorite author, the Nun of Kenmare, says of the Archbishop of Dublin:

"The English Archbishop resented the wrongs of the Irish Church as personal injuries, and devoted himself to its advancement as a personal interest. We are indebted to Archbishop Comyn for building St. Patrick's Cathedral in Dublin, as well as for his steady efforts to *promote the welfare of the nation*."=

Judge Maguire seems to think Henry did a most iniquitous deed when he sent John Comyn to Dublin, but if the English monarch never did anything worse, the Irish people would have little cause to censure him. John Comyn, when selected for the See of Dublin was not a *chaplain* to Henry II., but one of his secretaries. He was an eloquent and learned layman.° The election took place in the monastery at Evesham, where *the clergy of Dublin elected him*, September 6th, 1181. The candidate proceeded to Italy, studied theology, was ordained Priest, and subsequently consecrated Archbishop at Veletri, by Pope Lucius III., as the successor of St. Laurence O'Toole, in the See of Dublin. Now, what is wrong about all that? Assuredly Pope Lucius knew fully as much about the needs of the Catholic Church in Ireland in the twelfth century, as Judge Maguire *thinks he does* in the nineteenth century! But his Honor thought he would make a point against the Pope and so—as usual—he put his own foot in the hole he dug for his Holiness!

In order to create and foster animosity against the Pope, Judge Maguire says that the British Government has generally dictated the appointment of most of the Catholic Archbishops and Bishops of Ireland. While this is not exactly true, except in some special cases, it by no means follows that the Archbishops and Bishops so selected were not true to Ireland. To a man they were with their people in every laudable and Christian effort which was made to benefit Erin. These Bishops did not believe as Judge Maguire seems to imagine, that a man's patriotism is promoted by his apostacy, nor did they suspect that the best way to serve Ireland was to curse the Pope. On the contrary, these holy Prelates guided their flocks on the lines of Christian law and human justice in their struggles for freedom, and, when the sword was invoked, the Irish Prelates blessed the green banners of the brave Irish patriots!

CONCERNING THE RIGHT OF SANCTUARY.

On the twenty-fifth page of Judge Maguire's bad book, we read this malignant and monstrous concoction of calumny and anti-Catholic hatred combined:

"Until that time (1177) the Catholic churches were inviolable sanctuaries into which the hunted people might flee, and in which their lives were safe from murder and their property from spoliation. At this Synod of Dublin, the Pope through his Legate made Ireland an exception to this rule, and gave leave to the English soldiers to enter the churches and strip the people of the food brought there for safety. Since these things were done by the Vicar of Christ how terrible to contemplate what the Vicar of Hell would have done under similar circumstances."

°McGeoghegan.
• =The Patriot's History of Ireland.

To the closing sentence of the above diabolical diatribe we may justly reply: When such sentiments are the product of Judge Maguire's mind, the Vicar of Hell must have gained full possession of that mental region from which the Vicar of Christ has been ruthlessly evicted !

Concerning the first portion of Judge Maguire's malignant aspersion upon the Pope's Legate we are happy to state that it is about as mean a piece of pettifogging as ever was perpetrated. Now for the facts and the historical proofs of our assertion.

The first witness whom we shall introduce in order to convict Judge Maguire of not telling "the whole truth," is no less a personage than the Nun of Kenmare, who says:

"Cardinal Vivian now proceeded to Dublin, where he held a Synod. The principal enactment related to the right of sanctuary. During the Anglo-Norman wars, the Irish had secured their provisions in the churches; and, it is said, that in order to starve out the enemy, they even refused to sell at any price. It was not decreed that sanctuary might be violated to obtain food; *but a fair price was to be paid for whatever was taken.*"*

With this paragraph staring him in the face, Judge Maguire mendaciously *kept back the truth* in order to stab the Pope and to draw down the maledictions of evil-minded men upon the Church of Christ ! Since such things are done by Judge Maguire, the Vicar of Hell must indeed have made the Satanic suggestion !

Moreover, Judge Maguire accuses the Pope and Cardinal Vivian with having made this rule, when the fact is it was *the Irish Bishops themselves who voted it into existence !* No Pope, no Legate, no power on earth could coerce a Synod of Bishops (in Ireland or anywhere else) into adopting domestic rules during the existence of warfare, without the consent of those most interested. The matter rested in the hands of the Irish Bishops. If they had voted the matter down no such regulation could have been made, but when they—in Synod assembled —determined by their votes that, during the continuation of hostilities, provisions should be furnished to those *who paid for them*, it was solely the act of the Bishops, with which neither Cardinal Vivian nor Pope Alexander III. had anything whatever to do.

The conclusion every candid-minded reader must come to in regard to this point, therefore, is that Judge Maguire is again convicted of another "mistake" in which he is caught purposely keeping back a fact which changes the entire face of the charge he so disreputably fabricated against the Church of his former Faith but now the victim of his virulent calumny.

---

*History of Ireland, pp. 287.

CHAPTER XI.

Strong Evidence of English Chroniclers, Irish Historians and other Writers from the Twelfth to the Nineteenth Centuries against the Authenticity of the Adrian Bull.

Among the numerous proofs of the spurious character of the Bull attributed to Pope Adrian IV., by which that Pontiff was supposed to have donated Ireland to King Henry II. of England, the fact that the forged document first made its appearance in a work written by the notorious falsifier Giraldus Cambrensis, is not the least worthy of consideration. The despicable character of that untruthful and unreliable hireling of Henry II. which even the Protestant editors of his works acknowledge, make it entirely unnecessary on our part to particularize the many disqualifications which a man who "could tell the truth only by accident" possessed for writing a history of the Irish people, and the great doubt with which every statement of his should be received by the reasoning public of any century from the time of his existence down to the end of time.

The Adrian Bull is *supposed* by some writers to have been issued about the year 1151, others *guess* at the date of this gross fraud anywhere about or between the years 1152 to 1166.

Now if this Bull were *a genuine document*, there would be no trouble whatever in settling not only the exact *year* of its issuance, but also the very *day*, *month* and *place* when and where it was sealed with the *Bulla* of Pope Adrian IV. It is clear, therefore, that when those English and anti-Catholic American writers whose interest it is to support the genuineness of the Bull in question, fail to prove with certitude the *day*, *month and year* when it was issued, as well as the *city* from whence Pope Adrian promulgated it--there is truly a mountain of doubt erected as a mausoleum over this document which should bury it forever among the rotten rubbish where repose all similarly spurious Papal instruments.

Even in the lifetime of Cambrensis--as we have already shown--the *authenticity* of the Adrian Bull was publicly challenged. And right here the question naturally arises: Why did not King Henry II., or Cambrensis--who were each personally responsible for its production and publication--take means to prove its authenticity at that early period? A simple letter sent to the Sovereign Pontiff would have dispelled all doubts regarding the document and set at rest for ever all contention as to its authenticity. But when we find King Henry and his obsequious hireling historian, both possessing a full knowledge of the disbelief of many readers of the Cambrensian work in which the fictitious document first appeared, and yet not making a single effort to disabuse the public mind of all doubt--then, indeed, it is reasonable to conclude that they were cognizant of the spurious character of the document, and, furthermore, that they did not desire to apply any test that would reveal their rascality.

Another suspicious feature about the fraudulent Adrian Bull arises from the fact that it is found to be mentioned in the works of only a couple of early *English Chroniclers alone*. And now let us trace this Bull down the course of time, from the twelfth to the nineteenth century, and learn from the evidence of reliable annalists, Irish historians, and other reputable writers how much credence they placed in that English-made Roman document.

THE EVIDENCE OF BARONIUS.

Cardinal Baronius, the celebrated official compiler of the Pontifical Annals of Rome, who flourished in the sixteenth century, and whose Ecclesiastical Annals include the twelfth century, does not mention the name of King Henry II., of England in connection with any Bull issued under the signature of Pope Adrian IV., by which *a donation of Ireland* was made to that English monarch.

To any person who is acquainted with the careful fidelity with which Baronius notes every important act of each Pope of Rome, in his official records, the omission we have mentioned will be considered *fatal*, and will close all further controversy on the subject.

In his annals for the year 1159, Baronius makes record of the death of Pope Adrian; then he gives a lengthy biographical sketch of the deceased Pontiff's life, noting with great minuteness the principal events in which he was prominent during his Pontificate. These events having all been detailed, Baronius—in order that his Annals might not lack completion—makes this *addendum*:

"In order to leave out nothing which may have reference to the memory of so great a Pontiff, he desires to quote, according to a manuscript of the Vatican,* a diploma given to Henry, King of England, for the purpose of re-establishing religion in Ireland; *but in what year of the Pontificate of Adrian the diploma was given is uncertain.*"

More "uncertainty" regarding the date of this remarkably doubtful diploma! When there is any "uncertainty" about the *date* of as highly important a document as a Papal Bull; when the *year* in which it was issued *is not known;* and when the *suspicious* document is *said* to have issued from *Rome*, at a time when the Pontiff to whom it is attributed, was *not in that city*, the document is at once stamped "*spurious*" by virtue of these shortcomings!

Rome is most severely critical in her scrutiny of official Papal documents, and if there is the least doubt concerning any Bull, Brief, Concordat, or other ecclesiastical or diplomatic epistle, a Council of the most erudite Cardinals is called, and upon their decision the document is adopted or condemned, according as the evidence may justify.

Baronius clearly *doubted* the genuineness of the Adrian "diploma," for the potent reason that he could not discover the *year*, the *day*, nor the *place* of its issuance, and with such a skilled compiler of ecclesiastical records as Baronius, *such omissions* cause all documents in which they occur to be classed among those looked upon as apocryphal.

No annalist expresses himself more perspicuously than Baronius whenever there is question of the authenticity of any document upon which there is no doubt. But by affirming the absence of any date, in the present instance, Baronius flatly contradicts every English and Irish author who pretends to fix a year to this "doctored" diploma, which, as Baronius cautiously remarks, was not a "Bull," but merely a "document" which he found among some other unimportant papers in the Vatican Archives. This document says nothing about any "donation" of Ireland to King Henry II., it being issued entirely, as Baronius says, "for the purpose of re-establishing religion in Ireland."

Doubtless the paper found by Baronius was a transcript of the spurious "Bull" which was concocted to order for King Henry in England, and a copy of which was surreptitiously introduced among the Vatican manuscripts so as to give the color of authenticity to the original which King Henry kept carefully concealed from public gaze in the secret archives of Winchester castle.

EVIDENCE OF BZOVIUS.

Bzovius, a Polish Dominican, examined authoritatively the Archives of the Vatican, and published different works, besides continuing the Annals of Baronius.† Although his predecessor in recording the Vatican chronicles alludes in a peculiar way to "a document" in which King Henry's name is mentioned, Bzovius is entirely silent concerning it. He quotes, however, John of Salisbury, gives three extracts from the *Polycraticus*, but he altogether ignores the *Metalogicus* and the donation of Ireland.

---

*It was the Chronicle of Mathew of Paris, an Englishman who flourished in the 13th century, which was smuggled into the Vatican, and of whom Lingard says but little credit is due, because "his narrations abound with errors."

†The first volume of his continuation of the Annals of Baronius appeared in the year 1615 and was dedicated to Pope Paul V.

THE ANCIENT CHRONICLES AND ADRIAN'S BIOGRAPHERS.

It is a very remarkable fact, and one not to be easily forgotten, that outside a few of those of England, the ancient Chroniclers of Europe make no mention whatever of the Adrian and Alexander Bulls, until we come down to the sixteenth century, when these forgeries were copied from English works.

It is also a notable fact that all the biographers of Pope Adrian outside of English influence, make no reference in their lives of that Pontiff to his ever having made any donation of Ireland to King Henry II. of England. A strong instance of this character is found in the sketch of the Pontificate of Pope Adrian IV. written by the great Dominican St. Antoninus, who flourished in the fifteenth century, and who is silent concerning any donation. This saintly scribe quotes the *Polycraticus* of Salisbury, but he omits altogether the interpolated *addenda* which constitute the forty-second chapter of the *Metalogicus*, treating of Ireland and the fictitious donation.‡

TWO OTHER BIOGRAPHERS OF ADRIAN IV.

In the fourteenth century so little was known of the Papal Bull attributed to Pope Adrian, that even the eminent Ecclesiastics who were denizens of the Papal Court had no knowledge of its existence. Two elaborate biographies of Pope Adrian IV., were written during that period by eminent men who resided at the Pontifical Court of Avignon, neither of which contain the slightest allusion to any compact said to have existed between that Pontiff and King Henry of England.

The first biography was the work of the learned Dominican, Guidonis, who died in 1331. The other work was composed by Cardinal d'Arragon, who was raised to the purple in 1356, by Pope Innocent VI. The two biographies are contained in Muratori's *Scriptores rerum Italicarum*.

In his biographical notice of Pope Alexander III., which follows that of Adrian IV., Cardinal d'Arragon quotes the oath of Henry II., in the Cathedral at Avranches,

and he also inserts other documents showing his intimacy with all the events of that Pontiff's career. But as he kept silence in regard to the Bull of Adrian, it is a clear proof that he did not find any mention of it in the Pontifical Archives.

GRAFTON'S ENGLISH CHRONICLES.

A minute search through *Grafton's Chronicles*, published in London in the year 1809, and which contain all the public acts of King Henry II., from his birth to his death, failed to reveal any allusion whatever to either the Adrian or the Alexander Bulls. In fact this English chronicler says plainly that Henry *won* Ireland by force of arms, whilst this author's account of Henry's invasion also clearly implies that the English monarch neither possessed nor required any Papal Letter, Bull, Diploma or document of any kind whatever in order to invade Ireland. He had a large army and also 400 ships strongly manned, so that by force of arms alone he was prepared to successfully invade a portion of the island, entirely regardless of any interference from Rome. If no successor to St. Peter existed in the Eternal City in the twelfth century, the Invasion would still have occurred, for Dermod MacMorrough's invitation to King Henry; as well as to Strongbow, and other soldiers of fortune whose swords were at the service of any person who wanted them for conquest or defence, was the primal and principal cause of Ireland's becoming a prey to unprincipled Norman, English and Welsh adventurers.

Alluding to the precipitate flight of King Henry from England, and the cause that lead to it, *Grafton's Chronicles*—after alluding to the murder of St. Thomas a'Becket and the departure of the King's ambassadors to Rome in order to placate the Pope—gives this quaint account of that eventful transaction:

"The King's ambassadors, lying, as is sayd in Rome, could find no grace or favour for a long tyme at the Pope's hande. At length, with much ado, it was agreed that two Cardinalles should be sent down, to enquire out the matter concernying them that were consentying to Becket's death. The King perceyving (perceiving) what was in preparing at Rome, neither

‡St. Antoninus, Pars historialis, Tit. 17, chap. 1, §9.

being yet certaine, whereto the intent of the Pope and the commying downe of the Cardinalles would tende, in the mean tyme addressed hymself with a greate power to enter into Irelande, giving charge and command that no messenger from Rome shuld be permitted to enter his kingdome or to pass unto Ireland."

Here is a plain statement of the reasons which impelled Henry to invade Ireland. He had heard that the Papal Legates were coming over to England in order to lay his possessions under Interdict, and he flew over to Ireland so that he could not be brought face to face with the Pope's representatives. He had neither Bull, Rescript, or Letter of any such ecclesiastical character in his possession at that time, nor did he require any documentary justification whatever for his iniquitous encroachment of a neighboring country which even the Romans never invaded.

PLOWDEN'S PLAIN EVIDENCE.

The next historian to whom we desire to call the attention of our readers in order to furnish evidence wherewith to refute the idea that the Bull of Pope Adrian IV. was a genuine document, is Francis Plowden, author of an Historical Review of Ireland from the Invasion down to the year 1800. Here is his testimony. Speaking of the bogus Bull, Plowden says:

"The Irish nation, however, drew the true line of demarcation between the spiritual and temporal power, by *resisting* this *mock donation of the kingdom to a foreigner;* a distinction which the nation has generally made, but which before the accession of his present majesty it had not been allowed to give earnest of upon oath. If anything can strongly paint *the abusive profanation of religion* it is certainly Henry's *attempt* to gloss over with a *sanctified varnish of spiritual sanction* the infamous support of an adulterous tyrant and the more iniquitous efforts of his own ambition *and usurpation.* Possibly King Henry may have relied more upon the devotion of the Irish to the Roman mandate than upon the power of his arms. In the first he was disappointed, and he would have failed in the latter had Ireland been united in itself."§

§Plowden's History of Ireland, pp. 27-8

It is scarcely necessary to dilate at any length upon this denunciatory language of Plowden, as every reader can easily comprehend the indignation which that writer manifests at the outrage perpetrated by King Henry in order to cast a religious cloak over his rascally invasion of Ireland.

Plowden plainly points out that the Irish people resisted the mock donation of their kingdom to a foreigner, and that they clearly recognized the infamy of King Henry, in attempting to gloss over with Englishmade "spiritual varnish," the infamous designs of his iniquitous invasion. The Irish people saw at once through his ill-concealed "profanation of religion," and hence they repudiated both Henry and his spurious Bull—as innovations upon their vested rights and their ancient liberty. Thus Irish perspicuity and patriotism combined in the rejection of both the bogus Bull of Adrian IV., and the British King who tried to invade Ireland under the false cloak of religion.

"BOWER'S HISTORY OF THE POPES."

Archibald Bower, the author of this work, was a Scotchman who was born in 1685, educated for the Priesthood in Douay, went to Rome, thence to England, where he apostatized in 1726, recanted in 1745, and cast himself into the arms of heretics again in 1777. Like all the Priests who became perverts he followed the example of Luther, having married the neice of a Protestant bishop in 1749, and then he died September 2nd, 1766, in the 80th year of his age.

We narrate these events in the life of this unfortunate changeling in order that our readers may fully understand that Bower was not partial to the Popes whose lives he has written, as the evidence he gives concerning the Adrian Bull gains much additional strength when this fact is fully understood. Mr. Bower was a Scotchman, and, being *an apostate*, of course he hated the Irish people for their consistent fidelity to the Catholic Faith, even at the expense of life, liberty and property. This fact should also be borne in mind in order to

History of the Popes from the Foundation of the See of Rome to the Present Time. By Archibald Bower. London: Vol. vi. pp 107.

understand that his sentiments were purely the result of his experience in reading and his knowledge of Irish history, and not from any partiality for the Pope or the Irish people.

Having followed other English authors in saying that King Henry made the Pope acquainted with his designs on Ireland and that the English monarch begged the advice and favor of the Apostolic See, Bower says:

"It were to be wished that Hadrian* had told us upon what he grounded his undoubted claim of Ireland, and to all other islands that had embraced the Christian faith. But neither he nor his successors have to this day thought fit to let the world into that secret.

"What the King and the Pope meant that the end of the intended expedition against Ireland was to extend the bounds of the Church, I know not. The Christian faith had been planted in Ireland many ages before, and they had at this time a settled Church, governed by its proper Bishops and Metropolitans, who had a few years before received their Palliums from Rome, and they were, for aught that appears to the contrary, as orthodox in their faith, and as regular in their discipline, as most other nations."

Here we find even *an apostate* from the faith of his forefathers who bears testimony to the fact that the Catholic Church in Ireland was in a far better moral and spiritual condition than is designated by the denunciatory terms of the manipulated Adrian and Alexander Bulls! In the Adrian Bull the Pope is made to say that Ireland was in a state of moral iniquity and religious darkness, whilst Mr. Bower expresses his astonishment that any such charges could be brought in a Papal document against a Church that was "as orthodox in faith and as regular in discipline as most other nations." Evidently Mr. Bower surmized that no Pope ever saw the Adrian Bull, and he was thoroughly correct in his conclusion.

---

* Hadrian. Nearly all the old Chroniclers print Adrian thus.

CHAPTER XII.

Continuation of the Evidence of Historical Writers in proof of the False Character of the Adrian and Alexander Bulls.—Absurd Statements of English and Irish Historians.—How "Iniquity Hath Lied to Itself."

In addition to the testimony which we have already compiled, in order to show the spurious character of the Adrian Bull, we now desire to introduce the evidence of other writers regarding that dubious document.

ABBE MACGEOGHEGAN'S TESTIMONY.

In the first article of the present series, we have given a portion of the strong evidence which Abbè MacGeoghegan's History of Ireland furnishes, in order to prove the spurious nature of both the Adrian and Alexander Bulls. The annexed paragraphs from the same work, are, therefore, confirmatory of what has already been said by that distinguished Irish historian. Commenting on the text of the Adrian Bull Abbè MacGeoghegan says:

The above was an edict pronounced against Ireland, by which the rights of men, and the most sacred laws are violated, under the specious pretext of religion and the reformation of morals. The Irish were no longer to possess a country. That people, who had never bent under a foreign yoke, *nunquam externæ subjacuit ditioni*, were condemned to lose their liberty, without even being heard. But can the Vicar of Jesus Christ be accused of so glaring an act of injustice? Can he be thought capable of having dictated a Bull which overthrew an entire nation, which dispossessed so many ancient proprietors of their patrimonies, caused so much blood to be shed, and at length tended to the destruction of religion in the island? It is a thing not to be conceived.

In truth were we to consider the circumstances and motives of the Bull, it has all the appearance of *a fictitious one, under the borrowed name of Adrian IV.* Baronius quotes it, without giving *any date of year or day*, which would make it *suspicious*; it remained unpublished for seventeen years; it is said that it was fabricated in 1155, and not made public till 1172. * * *

The Bull gains but little authentication from the authority of John of Salisbury, afterwards Bishop of Chartres, in his treatise "*de nugis curialibus.*" The writer is made to say, at the end of the last chapter of his fourth book, that "Pope Adrian had granted Ireland to King Henry, at his request, it being the patrimony of his Holiness by hereditary right, inasmuch as all the islands belonged to the Roman Church, by the concession of the Emperor Constantine the Great." But this nonsense is considered by the learned as having been *added to the chapter by a strange hand;* since the author, in speaking particularly in the sixth and eighth books of his visit to the Holy Father at Benevento, where he remained with him for three months, states most minutely the various conversations he had with his Holiness, *without making any mention* of the Bull in question, though it was a matter of particular importance, and that was naturally the fit time to have mentioned it. Pierre de Blois, a zealous panegyrist of this Prelate, who publishes his praises in various epistles, *makes no mention of it* either.

It is well known that King Henry, who found creatures sufficiently devoted to him to revenge his quarrel with the holy Prelate of Canterbury, did not want *for venal writers to add to, and retrench from, the writings of the times, in order to give an appearance of authenticity to a document so necessary for the justification of his conduct.* Besides, it appears that Salisbury had gone to Italy of his own accord, and through curiosity, to visit his countryman Adrian, and not with any commission from the King of England; while the Bull, according to Mathew of Westminster, was obtained by a solemn embassy, which Henry had sent to the Pope. In my opinion, however, this circumstance appears to be *another fable* added to the former, as he is the first who mentions this embassy, and that two centuries afterwards. The silence, too, of Nubrigensis, an English contemporary author, respecting this embassy and the Bull which it is affirmed was granted, is an argument which, though negative, deserves some attention. This author, who was so zealous for the glory of Henry II., and his nation, commences his narrative by saying that the English had entered Ireland in a warlike manner, and that, their forces increasing every day, they subjugated a considerable part of it.[*] *He makes no mention of a Bull granted by any Pope;* and I consider it highly improbable that

---

[*] "At this time the English made a descent upon Ireland in a warlike manner, and their numbers having increased, they became masters of no inconsiderable part of it by force of arms."—*Nubrigensis, de Rebus. Anglic.* b. 2, c 26.

he would have forgotten to speak of a circumstance so necessary to give an appearance of justice to the unprecedented conduct of his nation. However this be, it may be affirmed that no Pope, either before or after Adrian IV., ever punished a nation so severely without cause. We have seen instances of Popes making use of their spiritual authority in opposition to crowned heads; we have known them to excommunicate emperors and kings, and place their states under an interdict, for crimes of heresy, or other causes; but we here behold *innocent Ireland* given up to tyrants, without having been summoned before any tribunal, or convicted of any crime.

It would be entirely a work of supererogation on our part to add a single word of comment to the clear, concise and convincing testimony which the learned Abbè MacGeoghegan offers in order to show that he had no doubts whatever upon his mind in regard to the spurious character of the bogus Adrian Bull. Hence we will leave our readers to draw their own conclusions from the foregoing extracts, and proceed to produce other witnesses in support of the Catholic side of this question.

FATHER THOMAS N. BURKE'S EVIDENCE.

The next witness whose evidence we introduce in order to show the fallacy and the fraudulent character of the Adrian and Alexander Bulls, is the celebrated Dominican, Father Thomas N. Burke, of cherished memory, who was both a great Catholic Priest and a distinguished Irish Patriot.

In his first Lecture in answer to Froude, which was delivered in the Academy of Music, New York, on the evening of November 12th, 1872, Father Burke alluded to the Norman Invasion of Ireland and the forged Bulls of Adrian and Alexander, in the following terms of unqualified condemnation:

Henry landed in Ireland in 1171. He was after murdering the Holy Archbishop of Canterbury, St. Thomas a'Becket. They scattered his brains before the foot of the altar, before the Blessed Sacrament at the Vesper hour. The blood of the saint and martyr was upon his hands when he came to Ireland to teach the Irish, "Thou shalt not kill." What was the occasion of their coming? When the adulterer was driven from the sacred soil of Erin as one unworthy to profane it by his tread, he went over to Henry and procured from him a letter permitting any of his subjects that chose to embark for Ireland to do so, and there to reinstate the adulterous tyrant King Dermot in his kingdom. They came there as protectors and helpers of adultery to teach the Irish people, "Thou shalt not covet thy neighbor's wife." * * *

But suppose that Pope Adrian *had* given the letter to King Henry, and Henry had kept it so secret because his mother, the Empress Matilda, did not want him to act upon it. Well, when he did act upon it, why did he not produce it? That was the only warrant on which he came to Ireland, invaded the country and never breathed a word to a human being about that letter. There is a lie on the face of it! Oh! Mr. Froude reminded me "to remember that Alexander III., his successor, mentions that rescript of Adrian's, and confirms it." I answer, with Dr. Lynch and the learned author Dr. Moran, of Ossory, and with many other Irish scholars and historians, that *Alexander's letter is a forgery as well as Adrian's.*

I grant that there are learned men who admit the Bull of Adrian and Alexander's Rescript; but there are equally learned men who deny that Bull, and I have as good reason to believe one as the other, and *I prefer to believe it was a forgery.* Alexander's letter bears the date 1172. Now, let us see whether it is likely for the Pope Alexander to give Henry such a letter, recommending him to go to Ireland, the beloved son of the Lord, to take care of the Church, etc. Remember it is said that Adrian gave the Rescript and did not know the man he gave it to. But Alexander knew him well! Henry in 1159 and 1166, supported the Anti-Popes against Alexander, and, according to Matthew of Westminster, King Henry II., obliged every one in England from the boy of twelve years of age to the old man, to renounce their allegiance to Alexander III. and go over to the Anti-Popes. Now, is it likely that Alexander would give him a Rescript telling him to go to Ireland then and settle ecclesiastical matters? Alexander himself wrote to Henry, and said to him: "Instead of remedying the disorders caused by your predecessors, you have added prevarication to prevarication; you have oppressed the Church, and endeavored to destroy the canons of Apostolic men." * * *

It was this man that was sent over as an Apostle of morality to Ireland; he who was the man accused of violating the betrothed wife of his own son, Richard I.; a man whose crimes will not bear repetition; a man who was believed by Europe to be possessed of the devil; a man of whom it is written "that when he got into a fit of anger he tore off his clothes and sat naked, chewing straw like a beast." Furthermore, is it likely that a Pope who knew him so well, who suffered so much from him, would have sent him to Ireland—the murderer of Bishops, the robber of churches, the destroyer of ecclesiastical liberty, and every form of liberty that came before him. No! I never will believe that the Pope of Rome was so very short-sighted, so unjust as by a stroke of his pen to abolish and destroy the liberties of the most faithful people who ever bowed down in allegiance to him.

Like the evidence of the Abbé MacGeoghegan, the truthful and trenchant testimony of the great Father Burke cannot but carry conviction to the soul of every reader that is not blinded by prejudice or political passion. Both these eminent and immortal sons of Holy Mother Church looked at this vexed question from a truly Christian standpoint; they were anxious solely to state the truth, and they have done so in such a manner as to stamp entirely out of existence any pretensions to authenticity which the spurious Bulls, to which the names of Popes Adrian and Alexander were forged, may have gained during the past seven centuries.

THOMAS MOONEY'S TESTIMONY.

Thomas Mooney, whose History of Ireland is doubtless familiar to many of our readers, thus alludes to the two Bulls which were fabricated by order of King Henry the Second of England:

It was *pretended* by King Henry that *Adrian the Fourth* had made over the whole of Ireland to him. He lost no time, therefore, on his arrival, in inviting the clergy of the South and the West to a grand Conference, at the ancient seat of legislation in Cashell. The *pretended Bull of Adrian* which had been dead eighteen years, was produced. It set forth the anxieties of the Holy See to have virtue and religion cultivated in Ireland, and the chief pastors obedient and submissive to the Sovereign Pontiff; and the better to insure this object, the clergy and people of Ireland were called upon to receive Henry the Second of England as their king. A *second Bull*, confirming the foregoing, *purporting to be from Alexander the Third*, was also read; *and though this one also has since been proved a forgery*, yet it had an astounding effect on the assembly.

No wonder the bogus Alexander Bull had "an astounding effect on the assembly!" It would have had "an astounding effect on any assembly" inside or outside of Ireland! If ever Irish Bishops, Priests or laymen listened to the libelous assaults upon their race and their religion, their morals and their very manhood which that anti-Christian concoction contained, they would have torn it into shreds and have flung the fragments into the face of King Henry himself were he present on the occasion! There is not a single Bishop of the Catholic Church who ever lived—we care not what his nationality may be—that would dare to defend the Alexander Bull as a Papal document. The very idea that the Irish people are styled therein "*Christians only in name,*" is enough to brand this document as fraudulent on its very face, and enough is known of the aggressive character of the Irish people to warrant us in saying that it would be unsafe for any reader to proclaim such a scurrilously falsifying document even in the presence of an assemblage of Irish disciples of the God of Peace! It is clear, therefore, that no Pope ever issued such a scandalous document, nor did any assemblage of the Irish clergy ever undergo the dishonor of listening to its libelous language.

REV. J. J. BRENNAN'S TESTIMONY.

The next witness we desire to introduce on the side of historical truth and justice is Rev. J. J. Brennan, the author of a text-book History of Ireland from which we make the following extract:

In 1154 Henry II. succeeded to the English throne, and in the same year, Nicholas Breakspere, an Englishman, was elected Pope, under the title of Adrian IV. Seeing his opportunity, Henry is said to have asked and obtained permission from the new Pontiff to invade and conquer Ireland. A Bull, giving the requisite authority, is indeed attributed to Adrian, but historians are about equally divided as to its authenticity. If the Pope did issue the document, he had no right whatever to do so, as Ireland never belonged to Rome, and such an action on his part would be wholly unjust. Adrian IV., however, was a man of piety, and, as long as we are without positive proof of his guilt, it is wrong to blacken his character by attributing to him the lies and the base motives contained in the Bull in question.

JAMES J. CLANCY'S EVIDENCE.

The next witness we desire to introduce in order to give his testimony showing that, even if the Adrian Bull was authentic, it possessed no binding force on the Irish people, is James J. Clancy author of a very interesting work on Ireland,* wherein he thus speaks of the supposed Bull by which Henry II. claimed to possess spiritual and temporal sovereignty over Ireland:

Meantime Henry II., who had long yearned to acquire the mastery of Ireland, grew alarmed lest his vassal, Stronghow, should assume an independent sovereignty (which the latter might claim through his marriage with MacMurrough's daughter). The consequence was that in 1172 Henry arrived with four thousand five hundred men, and exhibited a Papal Bull investing him with the sovereignty of Ireland. This document, *alleged* to have been given by Adrian IV.—the only Englishman that ever wore the Roman tiara—is a grievous stumbling-block to some people, and countless are the controversies based upon it. There is little practical value in such discussions, whether the Bull was forged, as some say, or genuine, as is commonly conceded. Had Henry brought a shipload of such Bulls, and every one of them authentic, they would not have improved his title one jot, and would have no more essential bearing on the case to-day than so many military orders signed by Julius Cæsar. No document can sanctify injustice or vindicate deliberate fraud. Above and beyond all trafficking parchments rest the inalienable rights of mankind. It is an amusing fact that this Bull of Adrian is the one solitary Papal utterance for which the English people profess gratitude and respect. They hoot and howl at Rome, yet they would be ineffably thankful if Rome engaged in the holy and wholesome work of forcing loyalty down the Irish throat. It is to be regretted that the Irish Clergy (who of course were an influential class) took no decisive and resolute stand against Henry's impudent claim. A large portion of them deceived by the Bull and desirous of peace at almost any price, advised the recognition of Henry's authority, which be it remembered, was claimed to be a merely titular sovereignty. Acting on this advice, Roderick O'Connor signed a treaty defining their mutual relations, and expressly stipulating that the English monarch should occupy only the position of feudal *suze rain* in Ireland. Every subsequent act of English aggression was a violation of that first solemn compact.

THOMAS MOORE'S TESTIMONY.

It was about this time (A. D. 1175) that the Bull of Pope Adrian, granting the kingdom of Ireland to Henry II., and obtained by this sovereign from the Holy See as far back as *the year 1151*, was for the first time publicly announced to his Irish subjects.†

Here is an historical muddle worthy of Judge Maguire himself ! Let us see what complications arise from this short paragraph from the pen of Ireland's bard ?

Henry II. was born in 1132, and ascended the English throne in 1154, so that if the mis-called "Adrian" Bull was issued in 1151, it must have been sent to Stephen, Earl of Blois, who reigned as King of England until the year 1153 !

Again, if the Bull signed "Adrian IV ," was issued in 1151, it must have emanated from Pope Eugenius III., as Pope Adrian IV., was not invested with the tiara until December 3rd, 1154 !

If, therefore, we take Moore's statement of the case, we will be forced to believe the "Adrian" Bull, addressed to "Henry II." to have been issued by Pope Eugenius the Third, and sent over to England to Stephen, Earl of Blois !

This is a complicated historical enigma, the solution of which we leave to Judge Maguire as a penance for issuing his *very bad book !*

MONSIGNOR BERNARD O'RIELLY'S EVIDENCE.

The name and literary fame of Dr. Bernard O'Rielly, D. D., L. D., is doubtless familiar to all our readers. His numerous letters upon Irish subjects which have appeared in the MONITOR, as well as his unequalled biography of Pope Leo XIII., have made the name of this distinguished Prelate a household word in every part of world.

Monsignor O'Rielly has also written a work on Ireland,‡ in which he casts an additional doubt upon the Adrian Bull, and thus adds new strength to the numerous proofs we have produced in order to clearly demonstrate its spurious character.

In the work alluded to Mgr. O'Rielly says:

He (King Henry II.) produced, *it is said,* the

---

*Ireland: As She Is, as She Has Been, and as She Ought To Be. New York: 1877.

†History of Ireland, Vol. II., pp. 276.

‡" The Cause of Ireland Pleaded Before the Civilized World." New York, 1886.

Bull of Pope Adrian, bestowing on him the lordship of Ireland. But the latest and ripest scholarship has discovered, in what must be accounted *the genuine Letter of Pope Adrian*, instead of an absolute gift of the island, *a positive injunction* laid on Henry in his projected expedition to Ireland, that "*he should attempt nothing of the kind without the consent of the Princes, Bishops and people of Ireland.*"

Monsignor O'Rielly is eminently correct when he intimates that so far from Pope Adrian ever having granted any Bull, Brief, Rescript or Letter even, to King Henry of England, authorizing him to invade Ireland for any purpose whatever, that learned and just Pontiff actually *forbade* the invasion of that country, unless it was done with the consent of the princes, bishops and people most interested in the matter. This phase of the question we are elaborating will be treated fully in a subsequent chapter.

GEOFFREY KEATING'S EVIDENCE.

This author was born in Ireland in the sixteenth century, during the reign of Queen Elizabeth. His work was composed in the Irish language, and he states that his history was written in order to develop the rank injustice with which Anglo-Irish authors before him had treated every Irish subject. Speaking of the Bull of Pope Adrian IV. Keating says:

It must be surprising to every one who makes himself acquainted with Irish history, to find such an expression in the Bull of Pope Adrian as that the King of England was to enjoy the crown of Ireland, upon the condition that *he would revive the ancient faith and restore it to its former lustre;* as if Christianity had been expelled, and the people had returned to a state of paganism and idolatry. Whoever gave this account to the Pope was as great an enemy to truth as he was to the glory of the Irish nation.§

In the light of facts already developed, we join with Dr. Keating in his laudable indignation. No Pope, either in the twelfth or any other century since Christianity came into the world—had a *scintilla* of evidence before him to justify the outrageous expressions employed in the Adrian and Alexander fictitious Bulls.

§Vol. 2, pp. 368.

Dr. Keating, in order to show the untruthfulness of the Adrian Bull, next points out the fact that the Pontiff must have known different, because, he says : "*it was the custom of the times*" for numerous Irish pilgrims to journey to Rome, and he mentions the names of many of them. In order also to show the absurdity of the Bull wherein it is intimated that Catholic faith was dead in Ireland in the twelfth century, Keating says that new churches, abbeys and monasteries were at that period in course of construction all over Ireland. This assertion he supports by the following facts and figures :

St. Mary's Abbey, Dublin, built by Maolseachluin, King of Meath and Monarch of the Island, in 1139; Abbey of Mellifont, built by Donough O'Carroll, Monarch of Oirgialluch, 1142; St. Malachias, Bishop of Each Dun, built the Abbey of Jobbair Cintragha, in 1144. Diarmod MacMorrough, King of Leinster, laid the foundation of the Abbey of Baltinglass in the year 1151. The Abbey of Beictiff, in the County Meath, the Abbey of O'Dorma in the County Kerry, and the Abbey of Boyle, were erected in 1161; Daniel O'Bryen, King of Limerick, built the Abbey of Holy Cross, in the County Tipperary, in 1169; the Abbey of Fermony, in the County Cork, was completed in the year 1170.

Many other instances, says Keating, might be produced of churches, abbeys, monasteries, and other religious foundations erected in those pious times before the English came upon the Irish coast; and consequently it follows that those foreigners did not plant the Catholic faith in the Island, but found it as it was believed and established for many preceding ages.

Such a Bull, therefore, as that to which the name of Adrian IV. was signed by some English forger, never could have emanated from any other source than the mind of a bad, designing English monarch.

CHARLES O'KELLY'S EVIDENCE.

Charles O'Kelly, author of *Macariæ Excidium* says "King Henry thought that the moment had come to execute a plan which he had long previously conceived. In fact he prepared the artifices which he was to employ in order to subjugate Ireland and to extend his kingdom by the annexation of so large a territory. For that purpose *he fabricated a Bull* of the Sovereign

Pontiff, a Bull which granted to him, *said he,* the domain of Ireland, on condition that he would protect the Priesthood, re-establish in its ancient splendor Catholic worship, and the temples and altars that were overturned."

Inasmuch as King Henry failed in the performance of any single one of the clauses of the Adrian Bull, it is certainly good proof that he had it manufactured himself for his own base purposes.

EVIDENCE OF LELAND.

Thomas Leland, the Protestant author of the History of Ireland, which bears his name, was born in Dublin in the year 1702. He was educated in Trinity College, and afterwards became Prebendary of St. Patrick's Church in that city. He died in 1785. His work is hostile to the Catholic Church, and—like many other so-called "Histories of Ireland," it seems to have been written entirely in the interest of England.

After a passing allusion to the Adrian Bull, Leland furnishes us with evidence in proof of the fact that in his time the long chain of doubt which had commenced to be formed in men's minds even when Cambrensis lived, still continued to be woven, link by link, down to the eighteenth century. Here is what Dr. Leland says upon this phase of the spurious Bull:

"Some Irish writers, scandalized at the gross representations of the corruptions and barbarisms of their country," (as depicted in the Adrian Bull) "seemed willing to question the authenticity of this Bull."[*]

[*] Vol. I., pp. 11.

CHAPTER XIII.

Further Evidence in Proof of the Spurious Character of the Adrian and Alexander Bulls.—O'Halloran's History Dissected.—Extracts from the Historical Writings of Hume, Lingard, Father Theband, S. J., and others.

TESTIMONY FROM O'HALLORAN'S HISTORY.[*]

The work we design peering into at present is one of those so-called Irish Histories which are bound in *green cloth*—so that those who buy them may actually judge the book "by the cover." On the back of the work is stamped the name O'Halloran, so as to lead Irish people into the false idea that some person with that Celtic patronymic was the author, while on the title-page appears the thoroughly English name of "Dolby." This work, therefore, is, to all intents and purposes, a *spurious* History of Ireland, only one-third of which was written by an Irish historian, whilst the other two-thirds are the concoction of some hireling Cockneys who were bitterly anti-Catholic as well as anti-Irish, as we intend to prove when we come to cite certain passages.

[*] "The History of Ireland from the Invasion by Henry II., to the Present Times." By William Dolby. New York.

This O'Halloran-Dolby mixture is cited very frequently in Judge Maguire's bad book, for the reason that—as an English publication—it just suited his anti-Catholic views on the question of the bogus Bulls, hence he drew many of his worst falsehoods from the prejudiced pages of this fraudulent volume.

In the so-called O'Halloran portion of this Irish-English History,[†] we are told in the body of the work that King Henry "entered the harbor of Waterford, October 18th, 1172," but the modern Editor of O'Halloran's part, it appears knew more than the Irish historian did, and so he added this foot-note:

The reader will remember that Dr. Leland and others, have unfortunately followed the authority of Giraldus Cambrensis for this date (1172). It has lately been ascertained that the right year is 1171. Dr. O'Connor is severely indignant at the mistake. When such learned

[†] Pages 314-306-308.

Doctors disagree, surely my friend O'Halloran may be excused. T. Moore equitably observes that it is "a mark of carelessness, unquestionably, but by no means meriting the grave severity with which Dr. O'Connor remarks upon it."

Here, then, we have the date of King Henry's arrival in Ireland decisively settled as having taken place on October 18th, 1171. Very well! Now let us glance at the text of the Alexander Bull as it appears on another page of this Irish-English "history," and we find to our great astonishment that it bears date 1172! And yet O'Halloran says that both the Adrian and Alexander Bulls were presented by the English monarch before the Synod of Cashel, held within a couple of weeks after King Henry's arrival in Ireland!

This Cashel Synod, O'Halloran says, "was splendid and numerous," but were it the largest and most gorgeous assembly of notables ever convened in the world, how, we ask, in the name of all the mathematicians that ever lived from the time of Euclid down to our own Davies—could King Henry present to any body of men in the month of October, 1171, a document purporting to have been issued at Rome in the year following?

The only way we can account for such a blunder in the date of the spurious Bull is that King Henry II., when he had that fictitious document drawn up, did not intend to invade Ireland until the year 1172, and he had that date inscribed upon it, but the murder of a Becket, and the news that two Papal Legates were coming over to England to lay his country under Interdict, hastened his departure by several months, and in his flurry the King *forgot to alter the date on the spurious document!*

Under the date 1171, in the O'Halloran section of this spurious Irish "history," we are told that King Henry of England had completed his rupture with Rome by the murder of a'Becket. Then the English-Irish writer conveniently sends Henry to Normandy to meet the Papal Legates; then he says that Henry took the oath at Avranches, and *then* and *there* he was presented with the Alexander Bull, and journeyed to Ireland in the October following!

In this statement O'Halloran stands "alone in his glory!" Not even Cambrensis, with all his inventive faculty for falsehood, ever pretended that King Henry went to Avranches and became reconciled to Pope Alexander before he entered Ireland. The English-Irish O'Halloran, therefore, is guilty of a wilful perversion of truth!

We now come to the Dolby "donation" to this badly-doctored Irish-English "history," and on the very first page of the English-Irish portion of the work the Cockney Editor *flatly contradicts* O'Halloran after this fashion:

While Henry was busy in Ireland, his sons became treacherous and refractory. Their disobedience was instigated by the jealousy of his Queen, Eleanor, on account of the untimely attachment of their father to "Fair Rosamond" Clifford. The same messengers who secretly brought him information of the conduct of his sons also reported that the two Cardinals, Albert and Theodine (who had been delegated by the Pope to make an investigation of the death of Thomas a'Becket) were now impatient of any further delay, and required Henry's immediate presence in Normandy, where they had already waited for him about a year.

Here our readers will at once discern the value of the O'Halloran-Dolby literary decoction, when they find the English continuator contradicting the Irish originator!

In the O'Halloran section of this two-sided historical hodge-podge, we were told that King Henry exhibited the Adrian and Alexander forgeries to a grand Synod of the Irish Clergy in the year 1171. Now comes the English Editor in his section, and he flatly refutes O'Halloran again by assuring his readers that Henry obtained the Adrian Bull as far back as the year 1151,‡ and that the twin forgeries were first seen in Ireland in 1175 or thereabouts!

There are several other instances in this English-Irish volume where contradictions occur similar to those we have exposed, but we will not stop to notice them. Before laying down this work, however, it is well that our readers should know its anti-Catholic character, and here are instances thereof. Speaking of the Protestant Reformation, the English Protestant editor says:

It is to be hoped that these slight and im-

---

‡O'Halloran-Dolby History, p. 28.

perfect notices of the state of Ireland during the fifteenth century will enable the reader to judge how the great "Reformation" of the succeeding century should be estimated, with reference to the *domestic and educational benefits proposed to be thus conferred on the Irish people;* and also its effects on the *welfare* of mankind generally.*

On another page of the Dolby addition occurs a virulent attack on "that fatal delusion" Monasticism, and on still another page† we are told that "the Reformation in England was supported by the majority of the people and a great body of the Clergy, *weary of the Papal yoke.*" On the same page "the Romish Church" is alluded to in no very complimentary terms, showing the virulence of the English Protestant Dolby. On another page‡ Queen Mary of England is said "to have fully proved her right" to the title of "Bloody," and Queen Elizabeth is painted as an angelic creature who had all the virtues of her sex !

Such is the source from which Judge Maguire drew most of his calumnies against the Popes and the Catholic Church, and when he went to such a work for the purpose of fortifying his falsehoods, he at once exposed his venomous hatred towards that holy Church which made him a Christian. The double-faced Dolby and his *coterie* of English contributors were just the men Judge Maguire should have fellowship with, as they are in perfect unanimity with him in their hatred of all things Catholic.

HISTORIAN HUME'S TESTIMONY.

It is scarcely necessary to tell our readers that David Hume, the English historian, was no friend either of the Catholic Church or of the Irish people. Hence it is reasonable to conclude that his account of the so-called "Conquest of Ireland," was written from a thoroughly anti-Catholic and anti-Irish standpoint. The man who could say that the "Irish from the beginning of time were buried in the most profound barbarism and ignorance," could not be expected to write impartially on any question wherein the interests of Rome and Ireland were at stake.

In view of this fact, it is not surprising

---
* Page 97. † Page 104. ‡ Page 174.

to learn from Hume§ that the Irish were "imperfectly converted to Christianity by some missionaries from Britain." "Pope Adrian, therefore," continues Hume, "in the year 1156, issued a Bull in favor of Henry, in which," says the English historian, "the Pope exhorts the King to *invade* Ireland," gives the English King "entire right and authority over the island, commanding all the inhabitants to obey him as their sovereign, and invests with full power *all such godly instruments* [!] as he (the king) should think proper to employ in an enterprise they calculated to undertake *for the glory of God and the salvation of the souls of men.*"

What irony ! Is it possible that we are asked to believe that any Pope of Rome would ever delegate his supreme spiritual authority as Vicar of Christ to a layman ? Not only that--if what Hume states is true --but the Adrian Bull actually permits Henry to delegate his supreme spiritual authority to "*all such godly instruments*" *as the King might select !* No matter how ignorant, vicious, immoral or heretical these disciples of King Henry might be, they could not be interfered with by Priest, Bishop, Cardinal, or even by the Pope himself ! Can any sane man calmly come to the conclusion that the Vicar of Christ ever delegated such spiritual jurisdiction to any body of unknown men ? We hope, for the honor of the intellectual enlightenment of the nineteenth century, there is not one such man to be found in the world !

No Pontiff *could* delegate such powers as the spurious Bull attributed to Pope Adrian designates. The document was gotten up by King Henry himself, aided by some of his household officials, and, as that monarch endeavored during the lifetime of St. Thomas a'Becket to be Pope of the Catholic Church in England, and caused St. Thomas to be murdered because he thwarted his ecclesiastical ambition, it was the most natural thing in the world to suggest to his amanuensis that he place in the body of the bogus Bull a clause by which the King could appoint ecclesiastics in Ireland who would carry out his intentions when he had invaded that country.

---
§ History of England, Vol. I., pp. 330, *et seq.*

This, to our mind, is very clear, and this fact goes far to prove the spurious character of the Adrian Bull.

Hume tells us that Dermot MacMorrogh, King of Leinster, appealed to King Henry when he was staying in France, to help the Irish monarch to regain his possessions. Henry promised his assistance, accepted MacMorrogh as his vassal, and, adds Hume: "gave MacMorrogh letters patent by which he empowered all his subjects to aid the Irish prince in the recovery of his dominions."

What a pity it was that Henry had not his forged Bull ready for this emergency ! This meeting between MacMorrogh and Henry took place in 1172, according to Hume; the Adrian Bull was supposed to have been issued in 1155, so that seventeen years after Pope Adrian gave Ireland over to King Henry of England, the most that King could do for the restoration of the territorial possessions of the King of Leinster was *to ask his English subjects to assist him!*

If, as some writers allege, Henry had the Adrian Bull in his possession at that period, *why did he not carry out its provisions?* Hume says Pope Adrian gave Henry "*entire right* and *authority* over the island, commanded all its inhabitants to obey him as their sovereign, and invested with full power all such godly instruments" as Henry should select to Christianize the Irish people!

Why, therefore, did not Henry delegate MacMorrogh as one of the "godly instruments," whom he had authority to select to represent the Roman Pontiff in England's new territorial acquisition ? With a copy of the Adrian Bull and Henry's letter of appointment to such an ecclesiastical position of dignity and power, MacMorrogh could have gone back to Ireland and preached from the pulpit in Armagh Cathedral—and even the Primate himself could not have prevented such a scandal !

But Henry's Bull was not yet born; so he could not avail himself of such a splendid opportunity to *gore* the Irish people in order to despoil them of life, liberty and happiness !

Hume next informs us that "Henry, jealous of the progress made by his own subjects, sent orders to recall all the English, and he made preparations *to attack Ireland in person.*" Why should King Henry "attack Ireland," if he had the Adrian Bull and that other document which is conveniently called the "confirmatory" Bull of Alexander ? The Irish people had shown no animosity toward Henry. According to Hume, the Norman and English adventurers had mowed down all the Irish that appeared before them, and when Strongbow passed through Ireland "he had no other occupation than to receive the homage of his new subjects."

It would appear, therefore, that instead of making preparations to "attack Ireland," which had—according to Hume—already been virtually conquered—the most feasible action on King Henry's part would have been to have sent a couple of "godly instruments" over to Ireland, with copies of the Adrian Bull for all the Bishops of that country, and then awaited the entire surrender of the spiritual and temporal supremacy of Ireland into his Majesty's keeping ! As Henry did not do this, it is very reasonable to conclude that the Adrian Bull was not in his stall at Winchester Castle during the ever-memorable year of our Lord, 1171.

FATHER THEBAUD'S TESTIMONY.

The eminent Jesuit whose work* we will now introduce as evidence against the genuineness of the Adrian Bull, did not enter into any extensive review of that long-controverted document. He merely alludes to it incidentally, but he was evidently convinced that the Adrian document was dictated by King Henry of England, and that Pope Adrian IV. had nothing whatever to do with it.

Alluding to the rebellion which broke out in Ireland when John Lackland went over there in order to smite the Irish to the earth by means of a glance of his English eye, Father Thébaud, says :

This solemn protest was not without effect in Europe. At the beginning of the reign of

* "The Irish Race in the Past and Present." By Rev. Augustus J. Thébaud, S. J. New York, 1873.

Richard I., Clement III., on appointing, by the King's request, William de Longchamps, Bishop of Ely, as his Legate in England, Wales and Ireland, took good care to limit the authority of this Prelate to those parts of Ireland which lay under the jurisdiction of the Earl of Moreton—that is, of John, brother to Richard. He had power to exercise his jurisdiction "*in Anglia, Wallia, et illis Hiberniæ partibus in quibus Joannes Moretonii Comes potestatem habet et dominium.*"—(*Matth. Paris*) *It would seem, then, that Clement III., knew nothing of the Bull of Adrian IV.*

Pope Clement ascended the Chair of St. Peter December 19th, 1187, nearly a third of a century after the Adrian Bull is *supposed* to have been issued, yet *he knew nothing about it!*

DR. LINGARD'S EVIDENCE.

Doctor John Lingard, the eminent Catholic divine, whose history of England is familiar to most of our readers, seems to have had a secret conviction in his soul that the Adrian Bull was spurious. Of course as an Englishman, and writing for the English people, it could never be entertained by the intolerant element among that race that Lingard should be permitted to proclaim that England's title to Ireland was based upon a bogus Bull and an unjust and brutal invasion of the country of a peaceable nation. Lingard, therefore, was compelled to keep within the bounds of mental reservation any doubts he may have had, but when he speaks of Pope Adrian "smiling" at Henry's hypocrisy, this expression clearly indicates that the historian could scarcely believe that such a Pope would grant a donation of Ireland to such a double-dyed villain as Henry the Second was in all his relations with the Catholic Church. Here is Dr. Lingard's account of the invasion of Ireland by the Norman adventurers :

> The proximity of Ireland to England, and the inferiority of the natives in the art of war, had suggested the idea of conquest to both William the Conqueror and the first Henry. * * * Within a few months after his (Henry II.'s) coronation, John of Salisbury, a learned monk, and afterwards Bishop of Chartres,† was dispatched to solicit the approbation of Pope Adrian‡ The

† *Twenty years* " afterward."
‡ Salisbury says he himself procured the Bull at " *his own request.*"

envoy was charged to assure his Holiness that Henry's principal object was to provide instruction for an ignorant people, to extirpate vice from the Lord's vineyard, and to extend to Ireland the annual payment of Peter-Pence, but that, as every Christian island was the property of the Holy See, he did not presume to make the attempt without the advice and consent of the successor of St. Peter. The Pontiff *who must have smiled at the hypocrisy of this address,* praised in his reply the piety of his dutiful son; accepted the asserted right of sovereignty which had been so liberally admitted, expressed the satisfaction with which he assented to the King's request, and exhorted him to bear in mind the conditions on which the assent had been grounded.

This is a very plausible presentation of the case from an English standpoint. Now let us see how far the statements of Dr. Lingard will serve to show the authenticity of the Adrian Bull, or, on the other hand, help in the good work of exposing this gigantic fraud of the twelfth century.

King Henry the Second of England, was crowned King at Westminster, December 19th, 1154. "*Within a few months after his coronation,*" says Dr. Lingard, John of Salisbury was dispatched to solicit the approbation of Pope Adrian to King Henry's intended invasion of Ireland. The inference is drawn from the remaining text printed above that the Pope gave John of Salisbury a letter addressed to "the King of England," but without mentioning any name. Then Dr. Lingard continues :

> ' At the following Michaelmas a great Council was held to deliberate on the enterprise; but a strong opposition was made by the Empress Mother and the barons ; other projects offered themselves to Henry's ambition, and the Papal letter was consigned to oblivion in the Archives of the Castle of Winchester.

If Lingard is correct, therefore, in saying that Pope Adrian's Bull was received by John of Salisbury, prior to Michaelmas, 1155, *that letter* could not have been *the Bull* which is printed in Maguire's bad book and dated 1156 ! This is very apparent when we come to consider that it was just as *impossible* to exhibit the Adrian Bull, bearing date 1156, before "a great Council" held in 1155, as it was to present the Alexander Bull, dated 1172, to a Synod of Irish Clergy convened in 1171 ! Yet both of these seemingly impossible feats were actually accomplished—if we are to believe English historians and their silly American copyists!

Well, indeed, may Lingard call this strange and spurious Bull of Adrian IV., a "singular negotiation," and aptly does the same writer express the sentiments of the majority of our readers when he says that "the Pope must have *smiled* at the hypocrisy of King Henry's address," when asking him for the donation of Ireland!

In a foot-note to the page from which the foregoing extracts are culled, Dr. Lingard shows that he had serious doubts regarding the genuine character of the Adrian "letter," as he remarks that "when King Louis of France, a few years later (1159), meditated a similar expedition, Pope Adrian refused his approbation unless the would-be invader first procured the consent of *the Princes, Bishops, Clergy and people of the country he contemplated invading.*"

We have said that the statements concerning the Adrian Bull made by Dr. Lingard lead to the conclusion that the spurious document dated 1156, was issued in 1155. This doubtful document itself, however, *had no date or place of publication whatever*, when it first appeared, but as a Bull without a date or place of birth would be nothing more than a nonentity in the world, several officious Englishmen have attached to it the *year in which they thought it ought to have been issued!* But John of Salisbury never received a Bull, or even a letter from Pope Adrian IV., donating Ireland to King Henry of England in the year 1155, or at any other time.

In another portion of his work, Dr. Lingard calls attention to the difference between Salisbury's statement concerning the terms of the Bull, and that document itself. Thus: Salisbury, who most assuredly should have been familiar with the tenor of a Bull which he says was given "at his request," calls that document "a concession of inheritance," but the Adrian Bull, contains no clause of any such nature.

Admitting even that Salisbury conveyed the Papal document to England, what use did King Henry make of it? That monarch made all his preparations to invade Ireland and he went there, leaving the Salisbury Bull in the secret Archives of Winchester Castle! A sovereign who was "armed" with such a document, would most assuredly have carried *his credentials* for invading a neighboring country with him, but as Henry did not do so, it is only fair to presume that the spurious Bull had not yet been concocted!

After a mock funeral and a mock burial which continued for nearly *twenty years*, the Bull (we are told by Cambrensis and his copyists) was read with great solemnity in a Council of Irish Bishops conveniently held *nowhere*, on which Lingard sarcastically remarks: "We will allow ourselves to think to what degree this document served to convince the Prelates that the King was the legitimate sovereign of Ireland."

It is clear, therefore, from Dr. Lingard's testimony, that any Pope who would be compelled to *smile* at the hypocrisy of a monarch's petition, would not be likely to grant the prayer of it. And it is also beyond belief that Pope Adrian would hand over Ireland to a foreign king, merely because a simple Priest casually made the suggestion.

TESTIMONY OF FATHER MORRIS.

In his "Life of St. Patrick," recently published, Rev. W. B. Morris, of England, in alluding to English-Irish histories of Ireland (like that of O'Halloran, alluded to above), says:

For seven hundred years England has been before the world as spokesman for Ireland. . . from the days of GIRALDUS and MATTHEW PARIS, the so-called history of Ireland as it went forth to the world, was in great part written for diplomatic purposes, and each falsehood became the parent of a brood.

The same writer, in a passing allusion to the bogus Adrian Bull, says:

The spurious Bull of Adrian IV., without name of sender or receiver, unsigned, unsealed, and undelivered, it was worthless as an ecclesiastical or political instrument. Its venom and that of other kindred forgeries lay in the motives which were supposed to influence the Popes. Those epistles, well worthy of the title of *False Decretals*, that condemned the Church and nation of SS. Celsus, Malachy, and Laurence, once entrenched in the pages of the Court historians of Henry II., became the text of honest as well as dishonest writers in subsequent centuries.

There are several other writers from whose works we also could extract testimony of the same character as that which we have given from the authorities already quoted, and all tending to show the fraudulent character of both the Adrian and Alexander Bulls, but we think the testimony already produced is sufficient to satisfy our readers on that point, hence we will introduce another aspect of this historical question in the next chapter.

CHAPTER XIV.

Intrinsic Evidence of the Fraudulent Character of the Adrian and Alexander Bulls.—An Analysis of the Text of Each.—Criticisms Proving their Fictitious Origin.—New Light on the Great Forgery of the Twelfth Century.

Now that we have presented our readers with a vast amount of extrinsic proof clearly and conclusively demonstrating the spurious character of the Adrian and Alexander Bulls, let us introduce these documents themselves in evidence, carefully analyze their contents, and thereby add additional strength to the proof already adduced against the possibility of their ever having emanated from the Popes of Rome whose names they bear.

Before doing this, however, there are a few matters of general interest concerning these documents, the knowledge of which will give our readers a fuller insight into the fact that both the Adrian and Alexander Bulls were *forged by one and the same person*. This assertion is borne out by the following somewhat singular coincidences when it is known that there are *sixteen years* difference in their dates.

Both Bulls are similar in title, and both omit the name of the person to whom they were supposed to be addressed. Both Bulls—when first published—had neither place, date nor year to designate the city from which they were promulgated, the time of their publication, or the name of the person for whom they were intended.

Both Bulls mention the "Peter-pence collection," although the Adrian Bull is supposed to be *sixteen years older* than the Alexander fabrication, and it would require more than ordinary credulity to believe that Pope Alexander would reiterate the "Peter-pence collection" in a Bull issued in 1172, when he must have been well aware that *not a cent had ever been paid* in response to a Bull supposed to have been issued somewhere about the years 1151, 1154 or 1156 by Pope Adrian the Fourth.

Both Bulls manifest a most malignant hatred towards the ever-faithful Catholic people of Ireland, a hatred which could *never* have lodged in the mind of any Prelate who ever held the supereminent position of Vicar of Christ. These spurious documents, issued in the twelfth century, speak precisely in the same strain of slander concerning the "ignorance," "rudeness," "viciousness," and "disobedience to laws" of the Irish people, as the London *Times* and all the other Irish-hating newspapers of England and elsewhere have constantly employed in portraying the "difficulty" which they experienced in the way of "settling the Irish question" during the past eighty-eight years.

The tone of both these Bulls is thoroughly anti-Catholic and British, and although Pope Adrian can be accused of being an Englishman, no such charge can be brought against Pope Alexander, yet the hatred of the Catholic people of Ireland which the *forger injected into the spurious Alexander Bull*, is even more intense, ferocious and foul than the denunciations fulminated in the fraudulent document attributed to Pope Adrian IV.

In addition to the anti-Papal tone of these documents, as well as the omission of very important features, without which no Vatican diploma can be considered complete or possessed of official ecclesiastical authority, we also desire to call the attention of our readers to the fact that in the *Bullarium Romanum* (the volume which contains the Latin text of not only the *genuine* Bulls issued by the different Popes - but also such as may have been attributed to them) —there are upwards of twenty documents which we will now proceed to classify in order to show that the spurious Bull by which King Henry and his successors on the English throne laid claim to Ireland, was fabricated deliberately for the purpose of making a false claim to that island.

From the volume of the *Bullarium Romanum* under examination we glean the following very important evidence:

All the genuine Bulls attributed to Pope Adrian IV. give the years and the date of the month, in which they were issued.

[The spurious Bull is without both].

All the genuine Bulls are attested as having been issued from some certain city or place, such as Rome, Castellana Civitas, Civita Vecchia, Benevento, Lateran, Etc.

[The doubtful "donation" Bull is entirely defective in this regard.]

All the genuine Bulls bear the proper official attestation of their ecclesiastical character thus:

Given at St. Peter's, Rome, by the hands of Roland, Cardinal Priest and Chancellor of the Holy Roman Church, on the 7th of the kalends of March, in the 3rd indiction, 1155th year since the Incarnation of the Lord, and in the first year of the Pontificate of our Lord Pope Adrian IV.

OR THUS:

Given at Civita Vecchia by the hands of Roland, Cardinal Piiest and Chancellor of the Holy Roman Church, in the year of the Incarnation of the Lord 1155, 5th indiction, 3rd of the month of October, and second year of our Lord Pope Adrian IV.

[The fictitious "donation" document, fraudulently concocted and forged by order of King Henry II. of England, contains no name whatever of Cardinal or Chancellor, no date, no month, no place, and no allusion to the year of its issuance or the era of the Pontificate of any Pope that ever succeeded St. Peter!]

All the genuine Bulls have the names of the *individuals* to whom they are addressed set forth in full after these forms:

"ADRIAN, Bishop, Servant of the Servants of God, to his venerable Brother HENRY, Patriarch of Graden, to his Canonical successors for ever."

"ADRIAN, Bishop, Servant of the Servants of God to his beloved Sons ANNUS Archpriest of the Church of Bellunus, and to his Brothers, present and to come, to be substituted according to the Canons for ever."

[The bogus Bull concocted by King Henry II. of England, *omits* entirely to name "the beloved son" to whom the spurious document was supposed to have been addressed!]

All the genuine Bulls, with the exception of four, are not only signed by Pope Adrian IV., but are also attested by several of the Cardinals as well. Some of the Consistorial Bulls have the names of six Cardinals attached and others are signed by fourteen Cardinals. The Bulls signed only by the Pope conclude thus:

"I, ADRIAN, Bishop of the Catholic Church, have subscribed." Then follows the Pope's seal, and, on the left hand corner: Given &c. &c.

[The bogus Bull King Henry concocted has neither the Pontifical signature nor the Pope's seal, nor does it pretend to have ever emanated from any special person or from any particular place!]

Among the documents in the *Bullarium Romanum*, the editor of the edition of 1739 introduces a Letter supposed to have emanated from Pope Adrian IV. to some English King, no name of said British monarch being given. The compiler of these ecclesiastical documents is careful, however, to cast off all responsibility for the genuineness of this document from his own shoulders, by printing a footnote to the page on which the spurious document is printed, in which he says that it is given only on the authority of the falsifying *Giraldus Cambrensis*, and the unreliable *Matthew of Paris*. The document in question is the bogus Bull whose defects and omissions we have already carefully defined and exposed.

Let us now turn to another volume, namely the *Patrologia* of Migne,* wherein may be consulted two hundred and forty-seven documents which are attributed to Pope Adrian IV. Of these some are fragments, and all are papers of transitory importance, the originals of which it was not necessary to preserve, whereas the so-called "Bull," which we have now under consideration, was King Henry's title-deed to an entire kingdom.

It is also to be remarked that in each and every one of these documents (with the exception of the unaddressed, unsigned and evidently spurious "Bull"), we find an intelligible, legal statement of the subject matter, with the proper names, titles and addresses of the persons concerned.

The libraries and archives of Italy, Germany, France, Spain, England, Scotland, Poland and Greece, in fact of every then Christian country, except Ireland, have delivered up their evidence to the active and powerful administration of Pope Adrian IV. for insertion in this work, and each document, whether complete or mutilated, bears the stamp of that jealous defence of the established rights of the Church which is seen in so marked a manner in all the writings of this Pontiff, and to all of which the spurious Bull fabricated by King Henry's order forms such a marked contrast.

Leaving aside and entirely out of consideration, however, any of the foregoing reasons for refusing to acknowledge the genuine character of the Adrian and Alexander Bulls, let us call the attention of our readers to the natural equity of the case under consideration, and ask: What proof has ever been adduced that these Popes ever issued these documents? *None.* What Cardinal or Roman Chancellor ever attested to these as Vatican documents? *Not one.* What Irish Prelates have admitted them to be genuine? *Not one.* Is it possible, therefore, that any Pope could issue so important a document without it being known in Rome or ever acknowledged by the Hierarchy of Ireland as the work of the Holy Father? These Bulls have been pronounced *false* by Prelates, Priests and the Irish people, and they—as the parties most interested—are the best judges in the case.

In making a critical examination of the Bull attributed to Pope Adrian IV., the first question that naturally arises is: Would King Henry II. have hesitated to perpetrate such an outrageous forgery? Let us answer this question by undoubted evidence. No man who lived contemporaneously with Henry Plantaganet knew him more intimately than Cambrensis, and this is the character this conspirator against truth gives of that master of diplomatic duplicity:

"By a certain natural inconstancy he was a *transgressor of his word,* for as often as he got into a tight place or difficulty, he preferred to repent of his word rather than of his act, and he more readily nullified his word than his act."†

The plain meaning of this extract is that beneath a deceptive exterior, there beat in Henry's breast a heart that was capable of descending to the vilest artifices, and of sporting with his honor and his veracity. No person could rely upon his word or place any confidence whatever in his promises. He justified his natural passion for duplicity by the maxim that in order to carry out his nefarious schemes it was better to break his word and sully his honor than to fail in reaching the goal of his ambition.

This double-dealing and chicanery was so marked a trait in King Henry's character that Cardinal Vivian—who knew him intimately and long—pays him this not very flattering compliment: "*I have never seen a man lie so audaciously.*"† "His anger was that of a mad man; his fury that of a wild beast."‡ The other venal traits of Henry's character have already been well described previously so now we will turn again to the forged document itself.

Having thus given our readers a general insight into some of the fatal defects of

---

* Vol. 188: C.L.XXXVIII.

† Opp. V. p.p. 304.

‡ Epist. St. Thomas, 3-6. ‡ Epist. 66. 715, Peter de Blois.

the Adrian Bull, we might stop right here and rest our case, as we have already adduced evidence sufficient to prove to every intelligent and impartial reader that Pope Adrian never saw or heard of such a document as that *forged* and fraudulently circulated by certain disreputable hirelings of the second King Henry of England. But in order that not a loop-hole may be left wherein any captious anti Catholic scribe of the future can hang a doubt, we will now place this spurious document on the MONITOR'S dissecting table and disjoint it for the edification of our readers.

THE SO-CALLED ADRIAN BULL as copied from Cambrensis by the historian Leland, that being the original copy of this doubtful document. This notorious fabrication begins with this sentence:

"ADRIAN, bishop, servant of the servants of God, to his dearest son in Christ, the illustrious king of England, greeting, and apostolic benediction."

It will be observed that this Bull is addressed to *no person in particular*. "The king of England" is an unmeaning title when the Pope calls that personage "his dearest Son in Christ," as, in the twelfth century, it took a couple of months to travel from Rome to England, and "the king" for whom the Bull was intended, might die while the Bull was in course of preparation and transition, and another king or queen even, might ascend the English throne in the interval.

Rome is far too wise to risk the occurrence of any such misapplication of so important a document as *a genuine Bull*, by omitting the name of the individual in whose interest or for whose information, guidance or instruction, it may have been promulgated. Hence, even in the very iniatory passage of the spurious document under consideration, there occurs *an omission* that, of itself, furnishes sufficient evidence that the forged instrument, which was first published by the untruthful Cambrensis, came from an evil source, was manufactured for a most malicious purpose, and was never suggested, accorded, signed, sealed nor delivered by the Pope who reigned in the See of St. Peter under the pontifical title of Adrian IV.

FIRST PARAGRAPH OF THE SPURIOUS BULL.

Full laudably and profitably hath your magnificence conceived the design of propagating your glorious renown on earth, and completing your reward of eternal happiness in heaven; while, as a Catholic prince, you are intent on enlarging the borders of the Church, teaching the truth of the Christian faith to the ignorant and rude, exterminating the roots of vice from the field of the Lord, and for the more convenient execution of this purpose, requiring the counsel and favor of the apostolic see. In which, the maturer your deliberation, and the greater the discretion of your procedure, by so much the happier we trust, will be your progress, with the assistance of the Lord; as all things are used to come to a prosperous end and issue, which take their beginning from the ardour of faith and the love of religion.

The document from which the foregoing extract is made was *supposed* to have been issued in the year 1151-4-5 or 6. Let us admit that it was written in 1156, less than two years after Henry became King, and during which time he did nothing of a beneficial nature that would entitle him to the eulogy of having achieved any "glorious renown" whatever. Later on in the reign of King Henry, when he had invaded Ireland and had defeated his enemies in Scotland, there might be some truth in saying that King Henry had gained "glorious renown," but such a laudatory phrase could never have been used by Pope Adrian in alluding to that English monarch even as long as two years after his occupancy of the English throne.

Neither Popes, Bishops nor Priests ever assume that any living man's salvation is *secure*, even though that individual may be King of England. God's *fiat* alone fixes that. Invading Ireland—even for the purpose of *reforming* "the ignorant and rude" Irish—could not add a feather's weight towards completing King Henry's "reward of eternal happiness in Heaven." Almighty God never blesses injustice, nor does the Catholic Church canonize those who perpetrate it. Hence, when the forger so forcibly asserted the saintly character of Henry, and claimed that his invasion of Ireland would "complete" that monarch's "reward of eternal happiness," he disclosed the cloven foot of King Henry's amanuensis beneath the cloak of some pretended official of the Vatican.

King Henry, we are plausibly told in the foregoing first paragraph of the fictitious Adrian Bull, was "intent on enlarging the borders of the Church" in Ireland, but how could this be possible? Pope Adrian knew full well (but the forger did *not*) that the Catholic Church *occupied all Ireland*; his Holiness was well aware that heresy had never raised its hideous head in that notable holy Island; and the Vicar of Christ had hundreds of pilgrims from Ireland to visit him every year who could tell him with truth that Ireland's heart beat constantly in unison with that of the Vicar of Christ —whether the Pontiff was called Celestine or Adrian! In the reign of Pope Adrian IV., Ireland was the daughter and Rome was the Mother, just as that lovely land of Catholic missionaries is to-day under the glorious Pontificate of Pope Leo XIII. No schism has ever separated Rome and Ireland. The golden chain of Catholic Faith whose first link was forged by St. Patrick, on Tara's historic hill, has been growing, link by link, as centuries have rolled on, until, at the present day, the chain of filial love and Catholic faith not only binds to Rome the people of Ireland, but also the tens of millions of those Irish exiles, their children and their children's children, who dwell in every continent of the world and on every island throughout the universe!

There never has been a time, therefore, when any Pope could justly commission a licentious layman with a wife and an illicit lady-love, known as Fair Rosamond, to go over to Ireland to "enlarge the borders of the Church" that was already universal on the Island, or to "exterminate the roots of vice from the field of the Lord" where no genus of the weeds of heresy or Protestantism ever prospered!

What "vices" did Henry discover in Ireland which he found it necessary to exterminate? In answering this question it is amusing to notice the "vices" which both vicious English historians and Irish writers under English pay, set forth as so many black spots on the character of the Irish people. It was only in 1152—four years before the latest date of the forged Adrian Bull—that Cardinal Paparon, as the Legate of Pope Eugenius III., had visited Ireland. *Three thousand ecclesiastics* assembled by his direction in the town of Drogheda; * four Palliums were conferred on the Archbishops of Armagh, Cashel, Dublin and Tuam; the celebration of Easter was settled in accordance with the Pontiff's desire, and all the affairs of the Church in Ireland were most amicably arranged to the entire satisfaction of both the Papal Legate and the three thousand Archbishops, Bishops, Abbots, and the great body of the Regular and Secular Clergy who met on that memorable occasion!

Are we to believe, therefore, that *in four short years*, the successor of Pope Eugenius III. could write to an English layman of immoral character that the "borders of the Church" in Ireland needed "enlarging," or that it was necessary for a layman to go over to Ireland in order to "teach the truth of the Christian faith" in a land not one-fifth of the size of California, in which there were *three thousand Catholic ecclesiastics*, and each of them in complete religious harmony with the Vicar of Christ in Rome?

When our Blessed Redeemer selected his Apostles they were laymen, but before He sent them to "teach all nations," He filled them with the grace of the Holy Ghost and consecrated them specially to His service. And again, when Pope Celestine selected St. Patrick to be the Apostle of Ireland he consecrated him a Bishop. Yet in the face of those prominent precedents, we are asked to believe that Pope Adrian selected a layman of loose morals and lax religious fervor, to "enlarge" the Catholic Church in a land where it was universal, and to "teach the true faith" to a people whose fellow-countrymen had helped to bring all Europe into the one true fold of Christ! Those persons who try to believe such a superlatively ridiculous proposition as that Pope Adrian ever commissioned King Henry to "convert" Ireland, are merely the dupes of their own ignorance or their intense hatred

---

*Leland's History of Ireland, Vol. I., p. 8.

of Ireland and the Catholic Church combined.

So far from the Church in Ireland needing "reforming" in the year 1156, there was no country in the world where it was better organized. The Archbishop of Armagh had ten Suffragan Bishops under him ; the Archbishop of Dublin had five ; the Archbishop of Cashel had twelve, and the Archbishop of Tuam had seven Suffragans. Christian O'Conarchi, Bishop of Lismore, was Pope Adrian's Irish Legate ; the saintly Gelasius (subsequently canonized) was Primate ; and in every portion of that Island of Saints the sweet breath of God's blessing rested on the religious labors of Priests, Sisters and people alike ! Abbeys and monasteries dotted every hill and valley from Antrim to Kerry and from Down to Mayo, and, when we recall the fact that neither King Henry nor one of his hireling satellites ever enlarged "the borders of the Church in Ireland' by a hair's breadth, nor "taught the truth of the Christian faith" to anybody ; nor exterminated a single "vice" from that most Roman, most Catholic and most Papal land in all the world—it is fair to conclude that Pope Adrian never sent any such message to King Henry, especially when the Church in Ireland was under the ecclesiastical jurisdiction of a Papal Legate, four Archbishops and thirty-four Bishops, assisted by 2,961 Ecclesiastics of every rank known to the Catholic Church. These facts also furnish strong evidence of the fictitious nature of the miscalled Adrian Bull.

SECOND PARAGRAPH OF THE SPURIOUS BULL.

There is indeed no doubt but that Ireland, and all the islands on which Christ the son of righteousness hath shone, and which have received the doctrines of the Christian faith, do belong to the jurisdiction of St. Peter, and of the Holy Roman Church, as your excellency also doth acknowledge. And, therefore, we are the more solicitous to propagate the righteous plantation of faith in this land, and the branch acceptable to God, as we have the secret conviction of conscience that this is more especially our bounden duty.

The English forger who concocted the foregoing extract makes Pope Adrian say something which no Pope—either before or since the Pontificate of Adrian IV.—ever uttered.

Let us now put this paragraph in the spurious Bull to the crucial test which truth possesses for all such fabrications, and the first important discovery we make discloses the fact that Christianity had no part whatever in the island possessions alluded to therein, for the potent reason that the power of Constantine, in his political relations, were precisely the same in *Pagan* islands as well as in those whose inhabitants had embraced *Christianity*. Pope Adrian of course, was well aware of this fact, hence it is an insult to his erudition, experience and well-known diplomatic genius—to assert that he ever wrote such an absurd paragraph as the above.

Again, it is well-known that Constantine had no control whatever over any islands save those that were attached to, or depended on, his Empire. Was Ireland such an island ? *Most assuredly not !* The Romans neither conquered Ireland nor is there a chart or map extant which shows it to have been within the territorial boundaries of their dominions. This very important fact must have been familiar to Constantine, who passed much of his time in insular Britain, and the fact was also equally well known to Pope Adrian, although the Englishman who forged this paragraph in the bogus Bull seems to have been not so well posted in ancient history.

And again, it is a fact easily susceptible of proof that the Popes never took advantage of the donation of Constantine for Rome, for the Italian continent, nor for the adjacent islands. Those who have any curiosity to test this assertion can do so by consulting the Letters of the *Codex Carolinus*, the authenticity of which is beyond controversy ; or they can examine the *Regesta* of St. Gregory the Great, and then they can pore over the Imperial Diplomas from the 9th to the 15th centuries.

Seeing, therefore, that preceding Popes refrained from making use of the donation of Constantine, it is not at all likely that Pope Adrian—who was well skilled in Canon Law—and very familiar with all

Pontifical documents of diplomatic character, would insert in a Bull a statement which every official in the Vatican could have at once pronounced incorrect.

We have already intimated in our criticism of other phases of this spurious Bull that the Adrian and Alexander documents were not forged until some time *after* 1172, the year in which King Henry acknowledged the feudal sovereignty of the Pope over the Kingdom of England by the oath which he took in the Cathedral at Avranches. The foregoing paragraph confirms our opinion on this point, for the reason that prior to taking the oath at Avranches King Henry could never have admitted, much less *suggested*—as the above paragraph intimates—that the Holy See had jurisdiction over "all the Islands," for the very potent reason that Henry would thereby have compromised and endangered the Kingdom of England itself! No! King Henry was too shrewd and too selfish a monarch ever to have *suggested* or acknowledged to the Holy See in the year 1154 or '55, or '56, that "all the Islands * * * do belong to the jurisdiction of St. Peter and of the Holy Roman Church." Hence it is very clear that the forgery of the fictitious Adrian Bull was not meditated until *after* King Henry had taken the oath at Avranches, when the Pontiff whose name was *forged* in the document had been dead for thirteen years! This point makes an additional link in the chain of evidence which will help to convict King Henry of having committed the great fraud of the twelfth century.

CHAPTER XV.

Intrinsic Evidence of the Fraudulent Character of the Adrian and Alexander Bulls.—An Analysis of the Text of Each.—Criticisms Proving their Fictitious Origin.—New Light on the Great Forgery of the Twelfth Century.

THIRD PARAGRAPH OF THE "ADRIAN" BULL.

You then, most dear son in Christ, have signified to us your desire to enter into the island of Ireland, in order to reduce the people to obedience unto laws, and to extirpate the plants of vice; and that you are willing to pay from each house a yearly pension of one penny to St. Peter, and that you will preserve the rights of the churches of this land whole and inviolate. We therefore, with that grace and acceptance suited to your pious and laudable design, and favorably assenting to your petition, do hold it good and acceptable, that, for extending the borders of the church, restraining the progress of vice, for the correction of manners, the planting of virtue, and the increase of religion, you enter this island, and execute therein whatever shall pertain to the honor of God and the welfare of the land; and that the people of this land receive you honorably, and reverence you as their lord: the rights of their churches still remaining sacred and inviolate; and saving to St. Peter the annual pension of one penny from every house.

The idea pervading the first sentence in the foregoing paragraph clearly intimates that Pope Adrian had received *a letter* from King Henry in which the English monarch "signified" to the reigning Pontiff his desire "to enter into the island of Ireland." The question naturally arises, therefore, as to when, where, and by whom was this letter sent to the Pope? Neither Cambrensis nor any other English chronicler record a word of its text; no Irish, English or Continental historian ever published it. The very name of the officials who carried it to the Pope (if ever such officials existed in the flesh), have never been known to a human being inside or outside of England! Was this letter a myth? It looks very much as if the English forger wanted some kind of a document apparently emanating from King Henry, whereon to base a bogus Bull, and he very conveniently inserted in the spurious document an intimation concerning a letter which had no *existence* save in his own over-vivid imagination! Thus forgery had to be supported by forgery, just as falsehood has to lean on untruth for support.

The second, or "Peter-pence" clause of the above extract we have already devoted several pages to, and our readers are no doubt satisfied already on *that point*.

LAST PARAGRAPH OF THE ADRIAN BULL.

If then you be resolved to carry the design you have conceived into effectual execution, study to form this nation to virtuous manners; and labor by yourself, and others whom you shall judge meet for this work, in faith, word, and life, that the Church may be there adorned, that the religion of the Christian faith may be planted and grow up, and that all things pertaining to the honor of God, and the salvation of souls, be so ordered by you, that you may be entitled to the fulness of eternal reward from God, and obtain a glorious renown on earth throughout all ages.

[*No date, no witnesses, no seal, and no signature*].

How the English forger must have chuckled as he put the finishing touches (in the shape of the above paragraph) to the document he wrote at King Henry's dictation! He must have fairly boiled over with British glee at the successful manner in which his Britannic Majesty had outwitted the Pope, circumvented the Irish Church, and pulled the wool over the eyes of every person in the whole Christian world!

King Henry, the gross voluptuary, the immoral sensualist, the disgusting dishonorer of his wife, was selected as the *model man* in all Europe to *form* the Irish nation to *virtuous manners!* Spirit of Christian Charity, let us bury our just indignation beneath the holy shadow of thy wings!

The world has read of "setting a thief to catch a thief," but we think this is the first instance on record where a royal rake, a licentious libertine and a noted liar was ever selected as an apostle to carry the typical palms of Catholic morality to a virtuous people! And persons pretend that the Pope of Rome, the Vicar of Christ, *did this?* Never! The tombs of the Saints of Ireland would open, and the blessed dead come forth, in order to vindicate the virtue of Ireland's sons and daughters against such a vile calumny!

And then, not satisfied with crowning himself modeler of Irish morality, King Henry had his amanuensis write that he was to act as the Pope's *substitute* in appointing other men of his own choosing to "*adorn*" the Irish Church, and to "*plant*" the Christian faith! Shade of St. Patrick, what impudent irony! Nice ornaments to "adorn" the Church in Ireland where the savage Strongbow, and the murderous crew that followed his blood-stained trail in the work of slaughtering the unarmed Irish people, pilfering their property, destroying their churches, robbing religious shrines, and pulling down the very crosses which Irish Saints had erected for the glory of God!

This English prince of putrid character became—according to the text of the forged Bull—a higher ecclesiastical dignitary than the Papal Legate in Ireland! Henry was the spiritual superior of the whole Irish Hierarchy! The 2,963 Regular and Secular priests then in Ireland, became merely puppets in the hands of this self-elected Papal Patriarch of the British Isles!

Now is it possible that human credulity is so pliable as to be stretched to that tension where people can be made to believe that any Pope of Rome ever gave a malodorous monarch such ecclesiastical powers in the Church of God? Three or four years previously *the same Pope*—who is said to have made Henry his Vice-gerent for the purpose of "planting" faith and virtue in Ireland—sent Cardinal Paparo over to that portion of the flock of Christ, for the purpose of honoring the Hierarchy by conferring the pallium of ecclesiastical jurisdiction upon four of their number! Is it not passingly strange that Pope Adrian should show such filial affection for the Irish Church in 1152, and then—three or four years later—ask a lascivious English layman to invade Ireland so that the "Island of Saints" and the "Mother of Catholic Missionaries," might be "formed to virtuous manners" and "Christian faith planted" in the land of the glorious St. Patrick, St. Columbkille, and hundreds of other saintly Irishmen who were Apostles of Christianity in every portion of the world!

It would be a vile calumny on the character of the Vicar of Christ to think for a moment that Pope Adrian IV. ever devised such a spurious document as that which contains such a transparent falsehood.

THE ALEXANDER FORGERY.

Having thoroughly dissected and analyzed the spurious Adrian Bull, let us now turn to the contemplation of the Alexander forgery, which commences thus :

"ALEXANDER, bishop, servant of the servants of God, to his most dear Son in Christ, the illustrious King of England, health and apostolic benediction."

Like its predecessor in perfidy, this document is addressed to nobody in particular, so that any King of England might claim it as addressed to him. Then this royal concoction continues :

"Forasmuch as these things, which have been on good reasons granted by our predecessors, deserve to be confirmed in the fullest manner, and considering the grant of the dominion of the realm of Ireland by the venerable Pope Adrian, we, pursuing his footsteps, do ratify and confirm the same (reserving to St. Peter, and to the Holy Roman Church as well in England as in Ireland, the yearly pension of one penny from every house), provided that the abominations of the land being removed, that barbarous people, Christians only in name, may, by your means, be reformed, and their lives and conversation mended, so that their disordered church being thus reduced to regular discipline, that nation may, with the name of Christians, be so in act and deed."

[*No date, no seal, no witness, no signature*].

In the whole range of anti-Catholic and anti-Irish literature, we know of no document more diabolical in its hatred than the foregoing. It bears the birth-marks of its British parentage upon its face. Its prominent prejudice against the faithful Catholic people of Ireland, proves at once that it must have emanated from some English hireling who hated that race.

Abbè MacGeoghegan was most assuredly right in his conjecture when he said that a comparison between these spurious bulls attributed to Popes Adrian and Alexander, with the treatise on "Ireland Conquered," issued about the same time by Giraldus Cambrensis, would indicate a *great similarity of style* between them ; and if they were not written by the same writer, it is very evident that they were concocted for the purpose of maintaining each other mutually, and thereby the more readily deceive an unsuspecting public.

DID POPE ALEXANDER GRANT THIS BULL?

Let us see ; and in order to answer this question let us take a brief retrospective glance at the relations which existed between Pope Alexander III. and King Henry, whom that Pontiff must have looked upon as more than half a heretic.

In 1164, only *eight* years prior to the date when the bogus Bull is supposed to have been issued, Roger Hoveden says that King Henry (whom Alexander is made to call "his dear son in Christ") issued a most harsh and heretical edict against the very Pontiff from whom Henry afterwards declared he procured the Bull !

In 1166, only *six* years prior to the date given to the spurious document, King Henry not only proclaimed his allegiance to the *antipope* Guido, but he also had laws enacted* by which it was strictly forbidden, under heavy penalties, to obey the Pontiff known as Pope Alexander III , or to give obedience to his commands ! Such were the *immediate* antecedents of that King who received from the Pope he cursed and condemned, a Rescript authorizing him to go over to Ireland and to "*reform* the barbarous people, in a land of abominations, whose inhabitants were Christian only in name" (!) Men who believe in the genuineness of *such* a bull, given for *such* a purpose, and to *such* a man, must be either fools that know no better or else fanatics that hate the truth and desire to persevere in their error.

MacGeoghegan quotes Baronius as alleging that King Henry "raised the waters to overwhelm not only the Bishop of Canterbury, together with the English-Catholic Church, but the entire flock of the whole Catholic Church, together with its Chief Pastor Alexander III , against whom *in particular*, he directed his machinations." Is it likely,

---

* MacGeoghegan, Hist. Ireland, p. 250.

therefore, that Pope Alexander would place such a man over the holy Hierarchy of the Church in Ireland, or authorize such an Anglican anarchist to bring "a disordered church" into discipline? No sane person can believe in such improbabilities ever having come to pass.

In 1168, only *four* years anterior to the date of the fictitious Bull, Westmonasteriensis says "King Henry, whose anger was changed into hatred of Blessed Thomas and of the Pope, in consequence of his having espoused the cause of the former, sent to the Emperor Frederick, requesting him to co-operate in removing Pope Alexander from the Papal Chair." Of course Pope Alexander III. was well aware of these different acts of schismatical insubordination on the part of Henry, and in order to properly *chastise* him therefor, he gave him an Apostolic commission to go over to Ireland in order to clean "the impurities" from the Irish Church!

In 1169, just *three* years before Pope Alexander dubbed King Henry his "most dear son in Christ," that same monarch dismissed with contempt from his court, the two Cardinals whom Pope Alexander had sent over to hold a conference with him in regard to his anti-Catholic conduct toward his Holiness and the representative ecclesiastics of the Catholic Church in England! Assuredly Pope Alexander would have proved himself a very weak and foolish Pontiff if ever he granted to King Henry any diploma authorizing him to regulate even so small a space as a rood of Christendom, much less to "reform" the Catholic Church in Ireland—the most consistent and constant in fidelity to Rome!

WAS IRELAND EVER "CHRISTIAN ONLY IN NAME?"

It seems to us to be an act bordering on an insult to the intelligence of the age to answer such a supremely ridiculous, as well as palpably false, question. Yet, inasmuch as there are persons who pose as Irish "patriots" because they have transformed themselves into anti-Catholic perverts, and who desire to impress this conviction upon the public mind, it is necessary for us—in upholding the honor of God's Church and the Catholicity of Ireland—to briefly glance at the fame Ireland had already achieved when that fraudulent document known as "the Alexander Bull," was first forged by order of King Henry II. of England.

It is not through any spirit of egotism we proclaim—without fear of contradiction—that, from the time of their conversion down to the present day, no people were ever more purely or faithfully Catholic than the Irish. Long before the Cross was acknowledged as the sign of man's redemption in many parts of Europe, Ireland was populating Heaven with saints, and thus she shone as the Sun of God's glory, whose rays penetrated far and wide, and whose Apostles carried the knowledge of God to nations then living in the darkness and shadow of death.

Ireland was the hive of holiness from the day when St. Patrick first pressed her shamrock-strewn sod with his anointed feet. From out her Monasteries, Abbeys, Cloisters and Schools went forth hundreds of holy men in order to plant the Cross in every land on the European Continent. The names of saints like Aiden, Colman, Arbogart, Maildulphus, Cuthbert, Killian, Virgilius, Fuiden, Columbanus, Brendan, Boniface, Ado, Gerard, Cormac, Celsus, Silave, Malachy, Laurence, Comgall, Cronan and hundreds of other canonized soldiers of the Church Triumphant in Heaven, all bear testimony that Ireland herself was always Christian to her heart's core, and that what she was in the early centuries, she is in the nineteenth—the garden spot wherefrom is reaped a constant harvest of Christian missionaries to plant the Cross in every section of the known world!

Could it be possible for Pope Alexander to call the people of Ireland "Christians only in name," when he had only to consult the hagiology of the Church in order to learn that in a little over two centuries—(from 432 to 664)—Ireland had no less than 350 Saints who were Bishops, 300 Saints who were Priests, and fully 200 Saints who were Anchorites, Hermits, or men whose lives justified the Church in crowning their brows with the *aureola* of superior sanctity!

In vain, then, would Pope Alexander look over the whole Christian world for a parallel among any people on a par with the holy Catholic Irish nation!

Now let us introduce some testimony from disinterested witnesses that we may show the thoroughly Christian condition of Ireland throughout the ages which followed her first joyful acceptance of the true Faith from the holy hands of St. Patrick.

SAINT BERNARD'S TESTIMONY.

The holy Abbot of Clairvaux, in his Life of the Irish St. Malachy, speaks thus of what was accomplished by a single Irish saint in the sixth century:

A most noble monastery had been founded in Bangor* by St. Comgall, which brought forth many thousand monks, and was the head of many monasteries. It was a place truly holy, pregnant with saints, and bringing forth most copious fruit to God: so much so, that one of the members of that holy congregation, Molua by name, is said to have been the founder of one hundred monasteries. Its branches overspread both Ireland and Scotland. Nor were these the only countries blessed by its religious: as bees from the parent hive, they flocked to foreign shores, and one of them, named Columbanus, proceeding to Luxieu, founded there a monastery which soon grew into a great people.

It would be strange, indeed, if the natives of a land which was so fruitful in sanctity during the sixth and seventh centuries, should be called "Christians only in name" by a Vicar of Christ.

The Irish of the seventh century were so far from being "Christians only in name," that Mirianus Scotus, under date of the year 674, makes this entry in his Chronicles: "*Ireland was filled with saints or holy men.*"

From the eighth to the tenth century Ireland was the literary lamp of Europe and her sons the Cross-bearers and Teachers throughout that continent. Two Irish missionaries went to France in 791, and so superior was their learning to those among whom they sojourned, and so attached to them did the French people become, that these saintly Irish scholars founded the first Universities in the world—Paris and Pavia.

The Venerable Bede, an Anglo-Saxon,

*County Down, Ireland.

tells us in his "Ecclesiastical History" that numbers were daily coming into Britain from the country of the Scots (Irish) preaching the Word of God with great devotion."

Eric of Auxerre, a French writer of the ninth century, in his letter to Charles the Bald, is so astounded at the immense number of saints and scholars Ireland sent at that period to the continent of Europe that he asks:

What shall I say of Ireland, which, despising the dangers of the deep, is migrating, with almost her whole train of philosophers to our coast.

Lord Littleton, in his *Life of Henry the Second*, pays this high compliment to the Irish people whom the bogus Alexander Bull declares to have been "Christians only in name":

A school was founded in Armagh, which soon became very famous. Many Irish went from thence to convert and teach other nations. Many Saxons out of England resorted thither for instruction, and brought from thence the use of letters to their ignorant countrymen.

Thierry, in his *History of the Norman Conquest*, thus speaks of Ireland during that period:

*In many things, especially in religion the Irish were enthusiasts. * * * Their island possessed a multitude of saints and learned men, venerated alike in England and in Gaul; for no country has furnished a greater number of Christian missionaries.*

A people who were "enthusiasts in religion," among whom there were such "a multitude of saints," and who had "furnished a greater number of Christian missionaries than all other nations in the world," *might* be called "Christian only in name," by some bigoted British booby hireling of King Henry II., in consequence of his ignorance and prejudice, but to insinuate that either Alexander III., or any other Pope of Rome ever gave currency to such a most unwarranted calumny upon the Catholic character of the Irish people, is one of the foulest and grossest slanders that ever soiled the literature of any age from the days of the falsifying Cambrensis down to his manikin imitator in malignancy—Judge James G. Maguire of the Superior Court of San Francisco.

TESTIMONY OF ST. COLUMBANUS.

The name of the great St. Columbanus stands high in Irish hagiology. He was the illustrious founder of Bobbio and many other monasteries. In his fourth Letter to Pope Boniface, this great Irish servant of God thus firmly and faithfully places on record the proud position Ireland then held as the truest and most loyal child of the Church of God:

> To the most lovely of all Europe, *to the Head of all the Churches*, to the Beloved Father, to the Exalted Prelate, to the Pastor of Pastors, etc.

After thus acknowledging the reigning Pontiff as "the Head of all Churches," and thus proving that Ireland was subject to Rome in all things spiritual, St. Columbanus, in the body of this Letter, continues:

> For we Irish, are disciples of St. Peter and St. Paul, and of the divinely-inspired canonical writers, *adhering constantly to the faith and Apostolic doctrine*. Among us neither Jew, heretic or schismatic can be found, but the Catholic faith, *entire and unshaken*, precisely as we have received it from you, who are the successors of the holy Apostles. For, as I have already said, we are attached to the Chair of Peter, and although Rome is great and renowned, yet with us it is great and distinguished *only on account of that Apostolic Chair*. Through the two Apostles of Christ ye are more celestial, and Rome is the head of all the Churches in the world.

What a sublime eulogy in favor of the fidelity of a great Catholic nation which only revered Rome because it contained the Chair of St. Peter! Could it be possible that such a people would ever become "Christians only in name"?

TESTIMONY OF CARDINAL NEWMAN.

We could cite a score of additional witnesses, were it necessary, in order to prove the thorough Catholic character of the Irish people throughout every century, but we feel assured that it is not necessary. So we will now conclude this portion of the defence of the Popes and the Irish people by producing the testimony of Cardinal Newman and a few other modern writers, in order to show the fidelity of the Irish people to the Church of Rome *throughout all ages.* Here is the eulogy which the great English Cardinal, John Henry Newman, passes upon the Catholicity of the Irish people:

> "I look towards a land both old and young — *old in its Christianity*, young in its promise of the future; a nation which received grace long before the Saxon came to Britain, *and which has never questioned it*; a Church which comprehends in its history the rise and fall of Canterbury and York, which Augustine and Paulinus found, and Pole and Fisher left behind them.

Cardinal Newman evidently never harbored the thought that there ever was an epoch in the history of Ireland, when the false and foul charge of being "Christian only in name," could be successfully brought against that nation of Virgins, Anchorites, Confessors, Martyrs and Apostles of the Church of God!

TESTIMONY OF ARCHDEACON LYNCH.

Dr. Lynch, the learned Archdeacon of Killala, whose historical work wherein he refutes the ribald calumnies of Cambrensis, we have already alluded to, thus depicts the close and constant intimacy which existed throughout all ages between Rome and Ireland:

> If I allowed myself to detail at length the intercourse of the Irish with Rome in former ages, my page would swell to unreasonable limits, and exhaust my power of language, though not the subject itself. To sum up then in a few words: No dissension on religious matters ever arose in Ireland which was not referred to Rome. From Rome Ireland had her precepts of morality, and her oracles of faith. Rome was the mother; Ireland the daughter; Rome the head, Ireland the member. From Rome, the fountain-source of Religion, Ireland undoubtedly derived, and with her whole soul imbibed, her faith. In doubtful matters the Pope was the arbiter of the Irish; in things certain their master; in ecclesiastical matters their head; in temporals, their defender; in all things their judge, in everything their adviser; their oracle in doubt, their bulwark in the hour of danger. Some hastened to Rome to indulge their fervor at the tomb of the Apostles; others to lay their homage at the feet of the Pope, and others to obtain the necessary sanction of his authority for the discharge of their functions.*

TESTIMONY OF HISTORIAN GORRES.

The learned Gorres, the eminent German

---

*Cambrensis Eversus, vol. ii., p. 633.

historian, thus depicts the monasteries of Ireland and the prolific faith which proceeded from them:

When we look into the ecclesiastical life of the Irish people, we are almost tempted to believe that some potent spirit had transported over the sea the cells of the valley of the Nile, with all their hermits—its monasteries with all their inmates, and settled them down in this Western Island; an island which, in three centuries, gave *eight hundred and eighty saints to the Church*, won over to Christianity the North of Britain and a large part of Germany, and while it devoted the utmost attention to the sciences, cultivated with especial care the mystical contemplation in her communities, *as well as in the saints which they produced.*

The German Gorres, evidently never harbored in his mind the horrible idea that Ireland was even for a second of time "Christian only in name."

REV. A. COGAN'S TESTIMONY.

In his "History of the Diocese of Meath," Rev. Anthony Cogan, Curate of Navan, thus beautifully portrays the enduring fidelity of Ireland's faith throughout all past Christian ages:

Insula Sancta! Missionary Island! Ever faithful and ever true! In the long night of thy bondage, when thy enemies were drunk with the blood of thy saints, when thy soil was purpled with the blood of martyrs, when thy temples were desecrated, thy shrines plundered, thy virgins banished, thy Priests were struck down on the very steps of thy altars; when the Mysteries of that saving Faith for which you sacrificed all in this world, were celebrated in the lone glen or in the fastnesses of the mountain, as well as in the days of thy greatness and glory, when admiring Europe hailed thee as the *Insula Sanctorum et Doctorum*. Holy Island! Through the gloom of thy chequered and mournful history, *true hast thou been to thy sacred trust!* †

† "Diocese of Meath, Ancient and Modern." Dublin, 1862.

We are firmly convinced that nothing more need be said on our part in order to prove most conclusively the constant, unswerving Catholic character of Ireland in every age of her long Christian career. We will close this chapter, therefore, by asking those few people who believe the Alexander Bull to be genuine, why it is that neither Pope Alexander III., nor any Pontiff since the year 1172, ever stopped the missionary spirit of the Irish people? Most assuredly a people who were "Christians only in name," were not the proper material from whence to procure Apostles to carry the true faith all over the world! If Pope Alexander harbored such an idea, he should have *forbidden* the Irish priests from penetrating into other lands to plant the Cross therein! But did Irishmen ever evince a single trace of being Christians only in name? Look at England, look at Scotland, look at America, look at Australia, look at New Zealand, look at every portion of the whole world which has been brought under the sweet yoke of Christ in recent centuries by means of Irish missionaries, and wherein Irish Priests and Irish Bishops predominate to day, and what man—be he heretic or a hater of Irish Catholics—who will dare to say that the immutable and eternal Faith which they have transplanted from Ireland, bears the faintest shadow of "Christianity only in name"?

It is clear, therefore, that Pope Alexander never had act or part in perpetrating the foul calumnies against the Irish Catholic people which make up the forgery which men like Judge Maguire delight in digging up from its reeking rottenness in order to fling the foul mess with the hands of apostates into the faces of the ever-faithful Irish people!

CHAPTER XVI.

John of Salisbury Dissected.—How King Henry II. Concocted the "Adrian" Bull.—Salisbury's "Metalogicus."—Who Wrote the 42nd Chapter?—Proof that it was not the Work of John of Salisbury.

It was impossible that any false Bull attributed to Pope Adrian IV., and concerning Ireland, could have been successfully promulgated during the lifetime of King Louis VII. of France, for the cogent reason that the fraud would at once have been discovered in consequence of the King of France having in his possession the Letter which Pope Adrian IV, sent to him, in which that Pontiff flatly refused to give his sanction to any attempt at invading Ireland, which that Prince in conjunction with King Henry II. had planned, and which Louis VII. had presented to Adrian IV. for his approval.

It is for this potent reason, therefore, that not a single trace of the bogus Adrian bull is to be found in any document issued in England prior to the year 1180, which was the year in which King Louis VII. died. This incident will appear all the more singular when we bring to mind the fact that a number of occasions occurred when King Henry could have made good use of a *genuine* Bull—had he possessed one—during the *many years* which transpired between the spurious date of the fictitious Adrian Bull, and the year when it first appeared in print by means of the instrumentality of that champion historical falsifier of the twelfth century—Giraldus Cambrensis.

If the Bull of Pope Adrian was *genuine*, why is it that such a document was secretly concealed for upwards of *twenty years* after the death of Pope Adrian? Nor was it until King Louis of France had been for some time in his tomb, that Cambrensis injected into his "*Topographia Hibernica*," for the first time, the dubious document falsely supposed to have been issued by that Pontiff.

The answer to this question is very simple. When Pope Adrian was dead, and King Louis was entombed also, the two main witnesses who had the power and knowledge which would enable them to discover and expose the fraud, could no longer offer any opposition; hence there was no risk to run by first injecting the forged document into the "Conquest of Ireland," by Cambrensis, so as to prepare the minds of those who perused the work of Giraldus, for the belief that such a Bull actually existed in the archives of England.

Cambrensis says that the Adrian Bull was procured by John of Salisbury, and that personage says so himself. We have already exposed the calumnies and the falsehoods with which Cambrensis filled his book entitled the "Conquest of Ireland," and now let us pass the testimony of John of Salisbury through the crucible of truth, in order to discover if that priest was *particeps criminis* with Cambrensis, or was he merely made the *means* by which the evil intentions of Henry II. were consummated.

The first question to be answered is: Did John of Salisbury make any mention of the Adrian Bull? It is true that there is an allusion to that document in the last chapter of his work entitled "*Metalogicus,*" forty-one chapters of which are devoted to a defence of Logic, Metaphysics, Dialectics, the Categories of Aristotle, and the philosophers themselves—both the peripathetics and the Platonics—against the assaults of ignorant adversaries. These themes are consecutively continued with great perspicuity and erudition throughout every chapter written by Salisbury, and the work closes with a suitable peroration at the end of the forty-first chapter, when the different difficult subjects treated of have been diffusively and exhaustively explained and elucidated. In fact it would be almost impossible to add another chapter congenial to the themes discussed—and say anything new.

But, *presto, change!* The forty-second chapter reads just as appropriate as would the addition of Mark Twain's "Innocents Abroad" if added to Burke's work on "The Sublime and the Beautiful"!

There is neither autonomy, coincidence, consistency or connection with the text of the previous forty-one chapters, and the themes therein explained, nor has the last chapter a single broken link even to bind an idea or an occurrence in it with the deep and metaphysical subjects which are handled in such a masterly manner by the author in all the previous sections of his erudite production.

We now intend to introduce to our readers the contents of the forty-second chapter of the "*Metalogicus*," but before doing so we again desire to bring vividly before their minds the fact that the book to which it was added, was devoted to the exposition of the intricacies of Logic, guiding tyros in knowledge through the mazes of Metaphysics, diagnosing the difficulties of Dialectics, explaining the Questions of Aristotle, and separating the dross from the pure metal in Philosophical treatises. Now to forty-one chapters on these abstrusive, deep and difficult subjects even for scholars themselves, we find the work in which they are expounded with marvellous skill, closed with this specimen of literature, which is not only laughable from the very ridiculous attitude it occupies, but also *darkly suspicious* from the falsehoods with which it is embellished in order to strengthen the forged Bull which is attributed to Pope Adrian the Fourth.

Following is the text of the dubious chapter which we present to our readers as it has been translated from the French of the editor of the *Analecta Juris Pontificii*, of Paris, who translated the document from the original Latin. Here is what John of Salisbury is made to say in the last chapter of his work on *Logic*:

"I have just finished (the "*Metalogicus*"). The present time is to be devoted to weeping rather than writing. I am taught by sensible experience that the whole world is subject to vanity. We looked for peace, but alas! the storm has burst upon the inhabitants of Toulouse, and it has stirred up all around the French and the English kings that formerly lived in harmony, as we can bear testimony, now relentlessly with each other. Furthermore, the death of our Lord Pope Adrian, has brought grief to all Christendom, but especially to England, the land of his birth. All good people deplore his loss, but no one should weep for him more than I. Indeed, though he had a mother, and a brother, *he loved me more than he loved them.* He declared, both publicly and privately, that he loved me better than he did any one else in the whole world. He had such an opinion of me that he felt pleasure in opening his heart and his conscience to me whenever an opportunity presented itself. Though Roman Pontiff, he was pleased to have me as his guest at his table, and, notwithstanding my opposition, he would have it that we should use together *the same plate and glass* At my request he conceded and gave to the illustrious king of England, Henry II., Ireland, to be possessed by him, by hereditary right, as Adrian's Letters, which are preserved to this day, plainly show. For all the islands, by virtue of an ancient right, are regarded as belonging to the Roman Church. Besides, Pope Adrian sent through me a gold ring adorned with a ruby of great value, for the king's right of investure in Ireland, and that ring is, according to order, preserved in the public archives of the Court.

I would never get through if I attempted to mention all the virtues of the illustrious Pontiff. But what deeply afflicts all hearts, is the schism which, in punishment of our sins, desolates, just after the death of the Pope, the Church. Besides the public grief which affects all, I endure a personal affliction which is not less oppressive. Indeed, my Father and Lord, who is also yours, the venerable Theobald, Archbishop of Canterbury, is seriously sick, and we cannot yet tell what will be the result of this infirmity. Being no longer able to attend to business, as was his wont, he has imposed on me a very severe duty, a very heavy burden, by confiding to me the care of all the ecclesiastics. My mind meets everywhere but afflictions and sufferings, and I feel that I am incapable of expressing the torments that I endure. There remains to me no other support than to pray to the God-Man, the Son of the stainless Virgin."

This strange document—says the editor of the *Analecta*—calls for some very serious observations, which we shall divide into sections, so as to throw all the light possible on the subject.

—I.—

"The passage in the document which refers to the Siege of Toulouse, is copied from the preface of the "*Polycraticus.*" If John of Salisbury entered, about that period, into the service of A'Becket, could he be, at the same time, the Chancellor and Secretary of Archbishop Theobald?

— II. —

In the preface to the *"Metalogicus"* Salisbury speaks of functions which he performed by order of his Lord, in regard to the ecclesiastical causes of all England; but he does not name the Archbishop; he does not say that he is speaking of Theobald. Here is the passage of the preface referred to:

"Scarcely any more time was taken from my necessary occupations than what was needed for my meals and sleep, for, at the command of my Lord, which I was faithful in obeying, the care of all England, with regard to ecclesiastical causes, devolved on me."

Now all this harmonizes well enough with the early period of A'Becket; with the period anterior to the conflict with Henry II. It follows then that the *"Metalogicus"* must have been composed about this period.

We cannot see what motive prompted the author to repeat in the 42nd chapter what he had already said in the preface, to wit: That he was completely absorbed by business; by the labors that his office superinduced. What is clear in the preface becomes amphibological in the 42nd chapter. The preface thus reads: "The care of all England with regard to ecclesiastical causes." This reading denotes the exercise of Metropolitan or Primatial jurisdiction. In the 42nd chapter, on the contrary, there is no longer question of the affairs of all England; he speaks only of ecclesiastics, which reading certainly points out only persons of a special class—*omnium ecclesiasticorum sollicitudo*. It might be that Salisbury was a simple superintendent of the moral conduct of the clergy!

What is truly new in the suspected chapter, is the name of Theobald, which is not in the preface. As it is extremely doubtful whether Salisbury was ever in the service of Theobald, this circumstance greatly aggravates the suspicion against the 42nd chapter of the *"Metalogicus"*

What the writer relates about the familiarity with which Pope Adrian treated him, is, beyond all question, unworthy of the Papal majesty. Salisbury expressed himself far more modestly in the *"Polycraticus"*:

"I remember that I set out for Apulia with the intention of visiting our Lord Pope Adrian IV., who admitted me to close familiarity with him. I remained near him at Beneventum for about three months. As we often spoke on different topics, as is the custom among friends, and as he questioned me familiarly and carefully about what men thought of him and the Roman Church, I took the liberty of declaring plainly to him what I had learned in the different provinces." (*Polycraticus, lib. 6. chap. 24*).

What mortal will believe that Pope Adrian ever said, publicly or privately, that he "loved Salisbury better than he loved any other person in the world, better even than he loved his own mother and his brother!" If there ever was "bosh," there it is.

Now we know that the Pope eats alone. The Roman Ceremonials of the twelfth century point out the days on which the Cardinals were invited to the Papal table. It would be already a sufficiently strange story that Salisbury was an habitual guest of the Pope for nearly three months, but that the Pope himself should have arranged matters in such a way that he and Salisbury should *eat from the same plate and drink from the same glass*, is an enormity which ought to have been, from the beginning, sufficient to reject the document under consideration as truly apocryphal. There was only one thing more needed to be said by Salisbury to render this document supremely ridiculous, to wit: that he and the Pope *slept in the same bed!* It seems *incomprehensible* how the forger did not see that his ridiculous exaggeration would take away, beforehand, all faith in what he was going to say about Ireland.

— IV. —

If it is true that Pope Adrian gave Ireland to the King of England, at the request of Salisbury (*ad preces meas*), that naturally signifies that King Henry II. did not solicit this donation, which was spontaneous on the part of the Pope. But this circumstance is contradicted by the apocryphal Bull, which mentions the Letter of the King. In any case, it is a very strange thing that the donation of a kingdom should have been obtained by an individual who had no official character. The pseudo-Salisbury of the 42nd. chapter does not even hint that Henry II., had charged him with the mission of soliciting, in his name, the authority to invade the land of Ireland, and to force its inhabitants to acknowledge him as their lord and master. On the other hand the apocryphal Bull does not name Salisbury, nor does it designate any ambassador who solicited the gift in the name of the King. One would be inclined to think that the whole affair was managed and concluded by epistolary correspondence!

—V.—

Salisbury designates in the *Polycraticus* the period of his interview with Adrian IV. by saying that he saw him at Benevento. Adrian IV. sojourned at Beneventum more than seven months, viz: from the 21st of November, 1155, to the 10th of July, 1156. If the concession of Ireland was made during the three months that Salisbury remained at Beneventum, how explain the silence he observed in regard to the Bull in his *Polycraticus*, which was published three years afterwards, viz : in 1159?

And, on the other hand, if the donation of Ireland occurred during another visit made by Salisbury, the author of the 42nd. chapter should have for so much the more reason designated the epoch of the Bull's issuance, as the apocryphal Bull is without date in the works of Giraldus Cambrensis, who was the first to publish it.

Other historians or compilers have added *Datum Romæ*, etc. According to that the Bull could not have been issued during the sojourn of Adrian at Beneventum. Nor can it be connected with the visit of John of Salisbury, described in the *Polycraticus*.

—VI—

The author of the 42nd. chapter of *Metalogicus* tells of a Letter of Adrian IV., in relation to Ireland; but he certainly did not know the tenor of it, and he never saw it. Had he known its tenor or seen it, he would not have stated that the Pope gave Ireland to the King of England and to his successors *to be possessed by them by hereditary right.* "*Ad preces meas illustri Anglorum regi Henrico secundo concessit et dedit Hiberniam Jure hæreditario possidendam, sicut litteræ ipsius testantur in hodiernum diem.*"

What a misfortune that the writer did not give the date of the *hodiernus dies!* In the apocryphal Bull, on the contrary, there is no question of investiture, and still less of perpetual investiture, which passes to the heirs and successors without the obligation of having it renewed at every change of government. The apocryphal Bull simply announces a *personal* concession to Henry II. given to him for the purpose of reforming morals and repressing vices. It was only for the accomplishment of this temporary mission—exclusively religious and moral—that the Pope urged the people of Ireland to receive with honor the king, and to revere him as their lord.

"We therefore," (it is the apocryphal Bull that is speaking) "with approving and favorable views commend thy pious and laudable desire, and, to aid thy undertaking, we give to thy petition our grateful and willing consent, that for extending the boundaries of the Church, the restraining the prevalence of vice, the improvement of morals the implanting of virtue, the propagation of the Christian religion, thou enter that island and pursue those things which shall tend to the honor of God, and the salvation of His people, and that they may receive thee with honor, and revere thee as their lord."

Now all this differs essentially from feudal investiture!

—VII.—

The sending of a ring as a sign of investiture, *is unparalleled in history*, unless the Pope designates at the same time a delegate charged with performing publicly the ceremony of the giving of the ring. The pseudo-Salisbury says, in all seriousness, that "Pope Adrian sent a gold ring adorned with a ruby of great value, by which the right of investiture would be made, and that the very same ring was preserved, according to orders given, in the public Archives." We are looking all around to see who the Papal Delegate was who performed the ceremony? But we cannot make out who it was. It certainly was not Salisbury, who was only a simple priest. *It was no one!* The apocryphal Bull does not say a word about a ring, nor investiture. We nowhere find a vestige of the ring save in Giraldus Cambrensis—and in the pseudo-Salisbury !

— VIII —

There is not a single case of hereditary investiture to be found in the Papal diplomatics of the twelfth century. The Popes who permitted the investiture to pass to heirs and successors, required a renewal and confirmation of it at every change of government and Pontificate. The Normans of Naples and Sicily were subject to the common law. The Diplomas may be seen all through Baronius' Annals and other works. According to the pseudo-Salisbury Adrian IV. treated the Normans of England with more consideration than their brethren elsewhere, and arranged that their investiture should continue perpetually--through the magical influences of a ring kept in the royal Archives of Winchester !

— IX —

Salisbury was by far too well instructed to say that the Emperor Constantine *founded* the Roman Church. Its foundation dates from JESUS CHRIST, and the days of the Apostles. It is not even quite true that the Emperor endowed the Roman Church, for even during the persecutions, the Church possessed goods which, being confiscated under Diocletian, were restored by order of Constantine.

If John of Salisbury wrote in 1160 that all the islands belonged to the Holy See, it is clear that he did not reflect that he was, by his very words, putting the island of England under the Holy See ! We meet with the same inconsistency in the false Bull. In a word the whole 42nd. chapter of the *Metalogicus* is a tissue of blunders, inconsistencies and inaccuracies. Our remarks entirely relieve John of Salisbury of its fathership—it is certainly the work of a pseudo-Salisbury and very bunglingly gotten up !"

SALISBURY'S CONNECTION WITH HENRY II.

For the better understanding of this important historical question, it may not be out of place to give our readers an idea of the close intimacy which existed between the King who caused both the Adrian and Alexander Bulls to be forged, and the ecclesiastic in whose work the statement was made that Pope Adrian gave—at his simple request—Ireland to King Henry II.

John of Salisbury spent a number of years on the Continent, until in the year 1160, the publication of his *Polycraticus* gained for him such public attention that Thomas a'Becket, at that time Chancellor of England, sent for him and attached him to his service.

Among the voluminous correspondence which Salisbury left behind him, there have been discovered a number of letters to Pope A., written by him as Secretary of Archbishop T., but unfortunately these initials are just as well adapted to Pope Alexander and Archbishop Thomas, as they are to Pope Adrian and Archbishop Theobald.

Here the question naturally arises : Could Salisbury be in the service of Archbishop Theobald, and, at the same time, act as Secretary to St. Thomas ? In answer to this interrogatory the only solution is presented by the last and *interpolated* chapter of the *Metalogicus*, which most undoubtedly was written by *some person* whose interest it was to circulate the rumor that during the last years of the life of Archbishop Theobald, viz : in the year 1160, or the year following, Pope Adrian donated Ireland to King Henry II. of England. Did Salisbury add this chapter, or was it forged and appended to his work by other hands ? Let us probe deeper into this problem.

Salisbury's secretaryship to St. Thomas is admitted, because he volunteers his own testimony that he was constantly on the alert to *restrain the zeal of St. Thomas*, in order to prevent any breach of friendship between King Henry and that Prelate. From his officious intervention, it would seem that Salisbury was more favorable to the King of England than he was to the Primate of Canterbury who employed him, yet we must do him the justice to say that he shared the exile of St. Thomas when Henry's threats and turbulence drove that holy Prelate over to France. And when St. Thomas returned to England, Salisbury came over also and resumed his position as the Archbishop's secretary, an office he occupied up to the fatal hour when the saintly form of Thomas a'Becket was struck down by the hands of his murderers.

After the death of St. Thomas, Salisbury continued to be attached to the Cathedral of Canterbury as a simple priest, up to the year 1176, when he was nominated to the See of Chartres in France *through the influence of King Henry*. It is true, however, that Salisbury was e'ected to that See by the canonical mode then in custom, and moreover it is of record that King Louis of France sent him an epistle advising him to accept the See. These circumstances may look plausible enough on the surface, but nevertheless we are justified in suspecting conspiracy and dissimulation in all such mat ers where the secret influence of King Henry is apparent.

Why did King Henry originate the movement to make Salisbury the Bishop of a French See? Did the King expect some great favor in return, or had he bargained beforehand for such a requisite return for his royal condescension? In a word, was the See of Chartres the price of Salisbury's treason to truth, and was that benefice the *quid pro quo* for Salisbury's kindness to the King by adding the forty second chapter to his *Metalogicus, in which alone appears any allusion to Adrian, Henry or the bogus Bull, throughout the whole work?*

The priestly character of John of Salisbury compels us to reject the idea that he ever entered into any bargain whatever with King Henry II., relative to the bogus Bull. But from what our readers already know of the cunning and unscrupulous character of King Henry, it requires no stretch of the imagination to suppose that monarch capable of carrying out any nefarious scheme that he deemed necessary for the gratification of his passion, his aggrandisement or his ambition.

It is supposed by several authorities that John of Salisbury wrote his *Metalogicus* in 1176, previous to his elevation to the See of Chartres, nor is it unlikely that he left the manuscript of his work with King Henry, *who caused the forty-second chapter to be added thereto after the author's death.*

CHAPTER XVII.

Further Criticisms on the Fictitious Chapter in Salisbury's "Metalogicus."—Professor Jungmann's Judgment.—King Henry's Oath at Avranches.—An Insight into the Characters of the two Popes to whom the Spurious Bulls are Attributed.—Finding the Matrix from which Papal Seals were Forged.

In the last chapter we gave the very exhaustive and caustic criticism of the Adrian Bull, as well as the added chapter to the "*Metalogicus*" of John of Salisbury, which Victor Palmé, the learned editor of the *Analecta Juris Pontificii*, published some six years ago in Paris. But in order that our readers may fully understand that the subject is by no means entirely exhausted, we now produce the testimony of other writers on the spurious character of two documents which are at last beginning to have the light of historical truth turned upon them, in order to prove beyond controversy that they were purposely *forged* by a licentious English King, in order to give him a false claim—under cover of which he hoped to invade Ireland and to rob that people of their liberty and their property.

CONSIDERATIONS ON POPE ADRIAN'S CHARACTER.

In the apocryphal chapter of the "*Metalogicus*," by John of Salisbury, which has already been published, occurs the following brief but rather singular account of how Ireland was supposed to have been taken from its rightful owners and handed over to King Henry II. of England, without that King ever going to the trouble of making such a request! Here is what the "*Metalogicus*" is made to say on that subject:

"*At my request* he (Pope Adrian IV.,) ceded

and gave to the illustrious King of England, Henry II, Ireland, to be possessed by him, by hereditary right."

If we are to believe the above extract from the "*Metalogicus*," Pope Adrian gave Ireland to King Henry at the mere *request* of John of Salisbury! The folly of such a donation being given at the request of a simple priest without courtly influence or kingly credentials, is too preposterous to be worthy of any consideration!

Are we to believe that the same Pontiff who refused the kiss of peace to the Emperor Frederick Barbarossa, because the German conqueror declined to hold the Pope's stirrup while his Holiness mounted his horse, gave away an Island with a million of inhabitants, 3,000 Catholic ecclesiastics and hundreds of churches, convents, monasteries and abbeys—at the *simple request of a visiting priest* without official character or credential of any kind?

Are we to believe that the Pope who refused to surrender a single town in Italy to the German Emperor, backed by a hundred thousand German spears, could hand over the independent Irish nation to an English monarch at the *after-dinner request* of John of Salisbury?

Is it not past human credence to suppose that the Pope who for years defied Arnold of Brescia, and finally vanquished him by the power of the spiritual sword, would think so lightly of the lives, liberties and happiness of the Irish Catholic nation, as to barter them all away without once asking that people if they desired such a change?

Could it be possible that the sagacious and courageous Pontiff who boldly told Frederick of Barbarossa that "the rights, the possessions, and the liberties of the Roman Church would be maintained *at any cost*," would prove so inconsistent to all his former actions as to bestow Ireland upon King Henry as a *personal favor* to a *transitory visitor?*

Pope Adrian's life—to use his own exact words—had been passed "between the anvil and the hammer." He had been compelled to flee from Rome by the violent assaults of the vicious enemies of the Church, and more than one-half of the years of his Pontificate were spent in exile battling against the persecutions and antagonism of armed allies who desired to crush the Papacy and to rob the Church of her temporal possessions. Is it possible, therefore, that the Pope who so persistently, and at such personal sacrifice, defended the temporal possessions of the See of Rome from the hands of vandal Emperors, would surrender so quietly, so unjustly and so ridiculously, the whole people and the land of Erin into the keeping of a foreign king who had no more right to Ireland than he had to the Chair of St. Peter or the tiara of the Pope himself?

Pope Adrian was *not* the Pontiff to act in the foolish and unjust manner John of Salisbury is supposed to depict him, and few people there are who will believe that such a "donation" was ever bestowed upon the mere *request* of a friendly visitor whose description of his life in Boneventum, places the stamp of "doubt" upon his whole narrative.

PROFESSOR JUNGMANN'S JUDGMENT.

Professor Jungmann, from whose "Historical Lectures" we are about to quote, has been for several years Professor of History in the University of Louvain, and as this justly celebrated Belgian historian is entirely devoid of any prejudice which might be attributed to an English or an Irish writer, thereby preventing them from giving impartial testimony in the case, we claim that Professor Jungmann's evidence adds much additional weight to the volume of testimony which we have already produced in order to show clearly, explicitly and conclusively, that the spurious Adrian Bull was manufactured in England.

Professor Jungmann says there are grave reasons for considering the Adrian Bull to be spurious, "as it is well known from history that everywhere towards the close of the twelfth century—forged or corrupted Papal Letters or Diplomas *were not uncommon* ‖ That such was the case in England

‖ The Anglo Norman adventurers, who entertained the design of invading Ireland even as early as 1155, fortunately left behind them the evidence of their guilt in the shape of *a matrix which was used for forging the Papal seal*, which was found some years ago in the ruins of one of

is susceptible of proof from the Letters of John Sarisbiensis and of others.*

"Richard, Archbishop of Canterbury, the successor of Thomas A'Becket, commanded all the Bishops to promulgate in all their churches the severe punishment of excommunication against the public pest of forgery, so common had this crime become in the twelfth century†. In the time of Pope Innocent III., also, various statutes were enacted against this abominable crime, which was becoming daily more widespread and dangerous.‡

"In view of these facts," says Jungmann, "it is not at all to be wondered at if some forged document attributed to Pope Adrian IV., should be produced and circulated. Moreover, the document attributed to Pope Adrian, which has no place, day or year whereby to locate it, must necessarily be ascribed to the year 1155 or 1156, that being the time when it is said John of Salisbury visited the Pope at Beneventum. But down to the year 1175, there is not a vestige of proof that the so-called bull of Adrian was shown or published by King Henry of England, although it was of the highest importance that it should be made known, since there was question of the submission of Ireland."

"It is true," continues Professor Jungmann, "that Sylvester Malone, in his Church history of Ireland, states that the Letter of Adrian was shown and its purport made known to the bishops and princes of Ireland in 1172, at a synod said to have been held in Cashel, and that, therefore, we can readily understand the cause of the ready submission of Ireland to King Henry II. "But," remarks Jungmann, "there is no mention whatever of the Adrian document found, and the submission of a portion of the Irish people to the English King is explained sufficiently well from far different circumstances."

---

the earliest Anglo-Norman monasteries founded by De Courcy, and which is now preserved in the Royal Irish Academy.—"Froude's Slanders on Ireland and Irishmen," by Col. James E. McGee. New York : 1872.

* Cfr. epp 83, 89, 120, in Epist 120 petit ab Alexandro III. : "Nobis si placet, rescribite qua animadversione feriendi sunt corruptores literarum vestrarum."

† Peter Bleus, ep. 53.

‡ Phillip, K. R. B. III.—§ 154 168.

"Even Pope Alexander III., the immediate successor in the Papal Chair of Pope Adrian IV., makes no mention in his own genuine epistles of such a concession ever having been made by his predecessor in the Papacy, nor does he allude to the donation, or to any Bull granting such a right to the King of England.

There are three genuine epistles of Pope Alexander III.,* which relate to the submission of Ireland. One dated Tusculani, September 20th, 1172, to King Henry II., to the kings and princes of Ireland, and also to Christian, Archbishop of Lismore, Legate of the Apostolic See. There is another, which was first published by Giraldus Cambrensis, and is said to have been issued from Rome in the year 1172, but this is held to be a *forgery*, for the reason that Pope Alexander was not in the Eternal City during that year, and also because the style of the document is widely different from that known to be Pope Alexander's.

In the *forged* document of 1172 alone is found any mention of the supposed "donation" of Pope Adrian IV., and Cambrensis himself, in his little work entitled, "*De Principis Institutione*," which was re-published in 1846, makes this confession concerning this *forged* Bull of Pope Alexander III :

"*Sicut a quibusdam impetratum asseritur aut confingitur : ab aliis autem unquam impetratum esse negatur.*"

Malone lays considerable stress on the genuineness of this document to which is attached the name of Alexander III., but

---

*Concerning the authenticity of these letters there is a diversity of opinion. Victor Palmé, in his valuable historical essay published in the *Analecta*, says of them : "There is no need to discuss the authenticity of these three letters. They have come to us only as copies and have seen the light of day only after 555 years from their date, and they contain invectives against the Irish people such as are never found in the Acts of the Holy See—at least as to expression and form. They announce things that are evidently false and fabricated, and which would cause us to believe that surreptition and obreption had a great deal to do with them, even if we could suppose that their authenticity was positively certain. We will assume that they are authentic, but we will on that very account, infer an argument that will demonstrate that the false Bull of Adrian had even yet remained unknown : *Now none of the three letters mention the Bull of Adrian, nor does any one of them make the slightest allusion to it.*"

the most erudite critics reject it as apochryphal, nor did Jaffé include it among the *Regesta* of that Pontiff's Rescripts, hence, concludes Jungmann, the statements of Malone are not correct."

"Whether the epistle of Adrian IV., was published, proclaimed or made known in the year 1175 (or in 1177) in some synod that was held in Waterford, is very doubtful. For Giraldus Cambrensis, who asserts that it was, is very inaccurate in his relation of historical facts, nor can much faith be placed in his statements. It is well known, however, that it was not until towards the close of the twelfth century that the so-called Bull of Pope Adrian IV. was first made known, as may be proved by Giraldus himself, who at that period published his "*Hiberniæ Expugnatio*," in which it first appeared. From the first introduction by Cambrensis, the document supposed to have been given to King Henry by Pope Adrian, was nowhere published until the year 1175, although there were frequent opportunities for publishing it, hence it follows that this document must have been purposely kept secret, and that there were other reasons besides domestic ones, for keeping the supposed "donation" document locked up.

THE "METALOGICUS" OF JOHN OF SALISBURY was completed by its author in 1159 or 1160, for he speaks therein of matters that clearly refer to that period as being the time when his work saw the light of day. If, therefore, John of Salisbury could speak so positively of the "donation" made by Pope Adrian IV. to King Henry, how does it happen that although the books of Sarisberensis were known, there was no mention made of the aforesaid "donation" until the year 1175? Several authors maintain that the forty-second chapter—that being the portion of the work in which the "donation" of Ireland to King Henry is narrated—*is an interpolation* The context of the book reads correctly even if the 42nd chapter was omitted altogether.

"*Ad preces meas illustri regi Anglorum Henrico II., dedit Hiberniam jure hereditario possidendam, sicut literæ testautur* IN HODIERNUM DIEM."

The expression, "*in hodiernum diem*," suggests *per se* the idea that there was a series of years (a long interval) between the issuance of the Adrian Bull and the publication of the work of Sarisberensis. Such language is never used to express short intervals when there is question of historical fact. Yet, only three or four years intervened (from 1156 to 1159 or 1160) between the issuing of the supposed Adrian Bull and the completion of the "*Metalogicus.*" There can be little doubt, therefore, that *some person*—for a purpose only known to themselves—but which we of the nineteenth century may surmise from surrounding circumstances—inserted the words used in the above Latin extract, without giving due consideration to the proper difference of expression when designating a long or a short time.

John of Sarisberensis died in 1180, and there are many critics who believe that the whole 42nd chapter—which is entirely foreign to the work—*was added in time.*"

KING HENRY'S OATH AT AVRANCHES.

All readers of the events of the twelfth century are familiar with the fact that in order to clear himself from the charge of being *the instigator* of the murder of St. Thomas A'Becket, it became necessary for King Henry of England to make oath that he was guiltless of that fearful crime.

Some writers assert that Henry went to Ireland in order to escape from being served with the notice of excommunication which Pope Alexander III. had promulgated against him, and, after waiting in that country for several months—whilst his representatives were pleading his cause before the Papal authorities—he at length received a favorable report from his friends and then hastened at once over to Avranches, in France, in which country Pope Alexander then was, in order to swear on the Holy Gospels, in the Cathedral of that city, in the presence of the Pope's Legate, the Cardinals, Prelates and the people there assembled, that he was not guilty of any crime which deserved excommunication.

Here is the oath which King Henry took on that memorable occasion, as given by both Baronius and Muratori, and which they copied from the Vatican documents:

I, Henry, swear on these Holy Gospels that I did not premeditate the murder of St. Thomas; that I did not know that it was going to take place, and that I did not command it to be done; that on hearing the account of this crime, I felt grief as intense as if I had heard of the murder of my own son. But there is a point that I cannot excuse myself in regard to, viz: that he was put to death in consequence of the anger and resentment I conceived against him. I appeared then to have given the occasion for his death. For this fault I will send at my own expense, and without delay, two hundred cavaliers to Jerusalem, for the defense of Christianity, and I will maintain them there during the year. I will myself take the Cross for three years, and I will set out in person for the Holy Land, unless the Sovereign Pontiff dispenses me in this matter.

All the illicit customs that I introduced during my reign into my country, I will remove entirely, and forbid them to be practiced hereafter. I will guarantee full liberty to make appeals to the Apostolic See, and I will not interfere with any person in this matter. Furthermore, I, King, and my beloved son, swear that we will receive or hold the Kingdom of England from our Lord Pope Alexander and from his successors for ever, and we will not regard ourselves as the true Kings of England until the Pope or Popes look upon us as Catholic Kings.

The silence observed by King Henry concerning *Ireland* in this oath, shows most conclusively that Pope Adrian did not bestow that nation upon the English monarch. It also proves that the bogus Bull had not as yet been evolved from the inventive brain of whoever forged it. Assuredly King Henry would never have thought of placing *England alone* under the jurisdiction of the Holy See, if he possessed any right to Ireland, especially when we consider that the *double* offering would have materially assisted him in becoming reconciled to the Holy Father, in gaining absolution for his admitted participation in the murder of St. Thomas, and also in regaining the prestige which he had temporarily lost by the grave charge brought against him.

Again, it is of record that King Henry wrote to the Pope at the end of the same year in which he took the above oath, asking the assistance of his Holiness in a war which his eldest son was then waging against him. In that letter he again declares that England is under the jurisdiction of the Pope, but makes no mention whatever of Ireland occupying a similar position.

Now if any Pope had bestowed Ireland upon King Henry, and if that monarch was feudatory of the Holy See in that island, would he have neglected to ask the protection of the Pope against the Irish "rebels" as they were called, especially when at that juncture the English monarch had lost nearly every portion of the land usurped by the Norman invaders? These points are additional links in the chain which serve to prove that the Adrian Bull was forged for the purpose of procuring a fraudulent title to Ireland.

POPE ALEXANDER NOT IN ROME IN 1172.

The Bull which is attributed to Pope Alexander III., concludes thus in Judge Maguire's bad book:

Given at Rome in the year of Salvation, 1172

Now let us briefly trace the career of Alexander III., in order to *prove beyond doubt* that the fictitious Bull was never issued from Rome in the year designated in that spurious document.

Pope Alexander was crowned at a place called Cisterna, midway between Velletri and Terracina, in Italy, on Sunday, September 20th, A. D., 1159. The Holy Father then fixed his residence at Terracina, thence he went to the following places in the years designated. The Pope was in Tusculum in 1172; in Segni in 1173; in Anagni in 1176, in Monte Gargano in 1177, then to Venice, from whence he did not reach Rome until 1178.

The *impossibility*, therefore, of this Bull ever having emanated from Rome is fully established, and its *forgery* clearly and successfully proved!

Aside, even from the irrefutable facts we have furnished, we feel quite positive that the illiberal, untruthful and even un-Christian document, miscalled the Alexander Bull, never could have emanated from a Pontiff who is thus eulogized by the Protestant critic Bower:

"Most of the contemporary writers speak of him (Alexander) as a man of *great prudence and discretion.* * * * He is said to have been *the most learned* of all the Popes that for the space of a hundred years have presided in that See, and better acquainted than any of them with the Canon Laws and Decrees of the Roman Church."

Dr. Miley, the distinguished author of "The Papal States," says of Pope Alexander III. :—"After a protracted reign of three and twenty years, during which he piloted the bark of Peter with such singular wisdom, skill, moderation and energy, as to secure for it peace the most profound and glorious, after all sorts of storms and dangers—this great High Priest of the Church and author of Italian liberty, Alexander III , was called to his reward, on the 30th of August, A. D., 1181."

That a Pope possessing such superior prudence, discretion, learning, wisdom, skill, energy, moderation and experience, could not subscribe to such a scurrilous concoction as the forgery said to have been issued from Rome in the year 1172, must therefore be a foregone conclusion in the mind of every intelligent reader, regardless alike of all previous prejudices or anti-Catholic bias.

CHAPTER XVIII.

An Able Article Proving the Adrain and Alexander Bulls to be Forgeries.—Father F. A. Gasquet's Learned Contribution to the "Dublin Review."—Severe Strictures on the Spurious Chapter Attributed to John of Salisbury.—The Genuine Letter of Pope Adrain from which the Bogus Bull was Compiled.

One of the main objects we had in view when we undertook the task of proving both the Adrian and Alexander Bulls to be forgeries, was to compile under one cover the different contributions of learned men who have hitherto written wisely and well upon this subject. Already we have placed within reach of our readers the scholarly essay of Cardinal Moran, as well as the exhaustive criticism of Professors Palmö and Jungmann, and now we introduce the more important portions of the very interesting article which Rev. Francis Aiden Gasquet, O. S. B., of St. Gregory's, Downside, Bath, England, contributed to the *Dublin Review* in July 1883, omitting only those paragraphs which treat of facts that have already been introduced in evidence in these pages.

Father Gasquet prints the text of the spurious Adrian Bull, and then he thus clearly and caustically criticises the bogus Bull itself as well as the different persons who were in any way connected with its construction or publication.

FATHER GASQUET'S TESTIMONY.

"This document," [the Adrian Bull] says Father Gasquet, " is not dated, but John of Salisbury, who claims to have been the ambassador who obtained it for Henry II., gives the year 1155 as the date when it was granted. There are however, grave, *if not overwhelming, reasons for questioning the value of this testimony*, since the biography of Salisbury makes it exceedingly improbable that he was ever entrusted with such a mission to Rome. Educated out of England, which he left in 1137, John of Salisbury did not return to his native country until 1149, and then only for a very short time, as he can be proved to have returned almost immediately to the Continent, where he became occupied in teaching at Paris. It is hard to believe that Henry would have made choice of *an unknown and untried man* to conduct so important and difficult a piece of diplomacy as negotiating with the Pope about the expedition to Ireland. This much is certain, indeed, that Henry did, at the beginning of his reign, send ambassadors to Adrian, who was then almost at the close of his pontificate; but this mission was given to three bishops and an abbot—namely, Rotrodus,* Bishop of Evreux, of whom we shall have more to

* "Gallia Christiana," tom. ii. pp. 557 and 776.

say; Arnold, Bishop of Lisieux; the Bishop of Mans; and Robert, Abbot of St. Albans. John of Salisbury, if he were with this embassy, could not have played the important part he claims to have done, but would have gone only in the capacity of a simple clerical retainer. It is a curious fact that the date of this mission to the Pope from Henry is the same as that claimed by Salis'ury for his visit, A. D. 1155; and it is most unlikely that the English king would have sent two different embassies at the same time. The old Chronicles give as the object of the visit of these prelates to Rome at this time, the wish of Henry to obtain from Adrian absolution from an oath made by him to his father Geoffrey. Apparently other English business was treated of at the same time, as we judge from a letter bearing the date of February 27, 1155, written by Adrian to the Scotch bishops. Nothing whatever appears as to the proposed expedition to Ireland.

Other circumstances *also tend to throw discredit* upon the account given by John of Salisbury. When he finished his work called "Polycraticus," he dedicated it to Thomas, afterwards S. Thomas A'Becket, then Chancellor of England, who at that time was with his royal master at the siege of Toulouse. This was in the year A. D. 1159; and in that year, apparently for the first time, Salisbury was presented to Henry by St. Thomas. If, as we may suppose from this fact, he had been up to this time unknown to the king, *it is most improbab'e that four years previously the same monarch had entrusted him with so private and confidential a mission to Rome.*

Moreover, although Salisbury speaks in the "Polycraticus" of his having passed three months at Beneventum with Pope Adrian—*a fact itself rendered most unlikely* by reason of the details he gives of the extraordinary familiarity with which the Pope treated him—he makes no mention whatever in that work of the important grant of Ireland accorded to his petition. Such an omission is all the more curious because the work in question was intended by its author as a means of securing the favor and patronage of the Chancellor; and had Salisbury been the means of obtaining for England so signal a favor, this mere fact would have been a certain pass to the countenance and protection, not alone of St. Thomas, but of King Henry himself. This omission is sufficient to make us suspect either that the chapter in Salisbury's subsequent work, the "Metalogicus," in which mention is made of Adrian's grant, *is not his work at all*; or *that the grant was inserted by him at the instance of the king, and to gain his favor.*

* * * * * * *

It is undeniable that the forty second chapter of the work has absolutely *nothing to do with the rest*, which had for its object the defence of the study of logic and metaphysics. The forty-first chapter finishes this subject in a natural and Christian manner by a quotation from the Book of Wisdom, and it is a strange contrast in the next chapter (forty-second) to come upon a lament over the siege of Toulouse and the evils likely to arise out of the quarrel of the two kings, oddly mixed up with records of a most unlikely familiarity existing between himself (Salisbury) and Pope Adrian. The Pontiff is represented as insisting on eating off the same plate with him and drinking from the same cup, while he is supposed to have declared publicly that he loved Salisbury more than his own mother and brother. *These curious details* are immediately followed by the declaration of Adrian's gift of Ireland, to which is added a repetition of what he had said in the prologue about his occupation as chancellor and secretary to the Archbishop of Canterbury. The whole chapter is thus *so strange in itself, so different in style* to the other writings of John of Salisbury, and so oddly tacked on to a work on philosophy, that it is highly probable *it was not his work at all.* This probability is increased by the fact that the circumstances of the interview with Pope Adrian described in the "Metalogicus" differ so much from those in the "Polycraticus," where no mention is made of Adrian's donation; nor of the "fine emerald ring" sent from the Pope to Henry to convey some strange sort of investiture. Moreover, *the hand of the impostor* is betrayed by one or two expressions such as "*usque in hodiernum diem'* and "*jure hæreditario possidendum.*" Lastly, if the last chapter of the "Metalogicus" is genuine, it was written about the year 1159, since the illness of Archbishop Theobald, who died in 1161, is mentioned. At latest the date of the work is 1160; while it is a matter beyond dispute that no mention whatever was made by Henry of this "grant" of Ireland by the Pope till at earliest A. D. 1175,† or fifteen years after it was published in the "Metalogicus." *This is inexplicable*, except on the ground that the chapter is *a subsequent interpolation* in order to give color to Henry's claim on Ireland. We must here note that the possession of such a "Bull" would have been most useful to Henry in 1167, when his followers first joined Dearmaid, in order to justify English interference; it was of vital importance when he went over to receive the homage of the Irish, and could never have been withheld or concealed at the Council of Cashel in 1172, at which the Papal legate presided. Such silence can only mean that *the "Bull" did not exist, and as yet Henry was unable to forge it* for a reason which will be obvious later.

* * * * * * * *

We may here note a strong confirmation of our doubts as to the authentic character of Pope Adrian's "grant," even if the subsequent "Bull" of Alexander is not also affected. Directly the murder of St. Thomas became known, Henry crossed over to Ireland with the object apparently of preventing the anger of the Pope finding him out by letters of excommunication or interdict. For five months a strict watch was kept on all vessels coming from the Continent, and not a ship was allowed to reach the Irish coast, even from England, without the king's knowing that it was not conveying any Papal letters. Directly a favorable message was brought to him at Wexford he set out at once, and, crossing England, passed over into Normandy. There, in the cathedral of Avranches, on the Sunday before the Assumption, 1172, Henry swore on the Gospels, in the presence of the legates, bishops, barons and people, that he was not guilty of the murder of the Archbishop. This oath, taken under such solemn circumstances, included the placing of the kingdom of England under the Pope, and the oath of fealty for it to Alexander.‡ Had Ireland at this time been really given to England by the Holy See, under such circumstances as these *it would have been mentioned*. This, however, is not the case. "Prœterea ego," runs the oath, "et major filius meus rex juramus, quod a Domno Alexandro Papa, et ejus Catholicis successoribus recipiemus et tenebimus *regnum Angliæ*, et nos et nostri successores in perpetuum non reputabimus nos *Angliæ* veros reges donec ipse nos Catholicos reges tenuerint." In the following year Henry wrote to Pope Alexander by his secretary, Peter of Blois, and referred to his holding *England* as a fief under the Holy See, but neither in this is there any mention of Ireland.§ These two facts are *strong confirmation* of any suspicions of the genuineness of Pope Adrian's Bull.

We have shown that the evidence in favor of the authentic character of the Papal grant of Ireland to the English Crown must be accepted with extreme *caution*, if not with *positive suspicion*. The authorities upon which it has been so long received by English historians as a strange but true fact, prove, on examination, to be hardly reliable sources of information. Many external circumstances, as well as the inherent, intrinsic improbability of the "grant," confirm the impartial mind in objecting to receive it as undoubted history. Moreover, the labors of the editor of the *Analecta* have now made it possible to show with reason that Adrian IV., so far from giving any encouragement to Henry in his designs on Ireland, in reality *refused*, when asked, to be a party to the enterprise, and pointed out the injustice of it. The idea of effecting the conquest of the island had suggested itself to the Conqueror and to Henry I., and it was but natural that the project should revive in the restless mind of Henry II. It must have been evident, however,

---

† "Cambrensis Eversus," vol. ii. p. 440, note.

‡ The clause in the oath is not found in John of Salisbury's account; but Baronius inserts it as found in the Vatican Archives. Also Muratorio, "Rerum Italicarum Scriptores," tom. iii. 463.

§ Lingard, vol. ii. p. 191, note.

that an *English Pope would of necessity be cautious* in favoring any pretensions of his own countrymen against a neighboring country. The knowledge that Adrian's approval would in all probability be withheld, if the idea was started as an English scheme, seems to have obliged Henry to look for some other sovereign to help him in obtaining the authorization of the Pontiff for his design, and Louis VII. of France was clearly the only prince in a position to render him this service. On the theory that for this purpose Henry wanted to make *a tool* of Louis, we can explain a fact that has appeared to puzzle annalists—namely, why it was that these two kings, who had been for a long time avowed enemies, suddenly, and by the advances of Henry, became fast friends, just at this very period, A. D., 1158. After many years of war and contention Henry met Louis at Rouen, and not only made peace, but espoused his son to the infant daughter of the French King. The Pope wrote to the Chancellor of Louis to convey his congratulations to the two sovereigns on their complete reconciliation. The two proceeded together to Paris, and afterwards made a joint pilgrimage to Mount St. Michael's in Normandy.* So complete was their reconciliation that at this time they despatched a joint mission to Rome to ask Adrian's *blessing* and *approval* of a *hostile expedition* they were intending to make together. The choice of an Englishman as an ambassador seems to point to the fact that the projected enterprise was of more importance to the English than to the French King. Rotrodus, the envoy selected,† was at that time (A. D. 1158) Bishop of Evreux, and had been one of the witnesses of the reconciliation between the two kings ‡ He was much attached to the interests of the English King, and had, from the time of his coronation, at which he assisted, been employed in several missions for his royal master. Amongst others, as we have noted before, he was in the embassy despatched to Rome by Henry in 1155. It was thus a courtier of Henry who was sent on this joint mission from the two monarchs.

*Migne, "Patrol." tom. clx. p. 484.
† "Gallia Christiana," tom. ii. p. 776. See also the Pope's letter in reply.
‡ "Gallia Christiana," tom. iv. p. 633.

"Rotrodus arrived in Rome at the close of the year 1158. or the beginning of the following year, and informed the Pope of the project entertained by Henry and Louis. What this project was does not absolutely appear, but there can be little doubt that it was really *the invasion of Ireland* upon which the mind of Henry was intent. In order to give color to the pretensions it was necessary to represent it as being intended in reality as a crusade in favor of religion. The Pope, however, would not enter into the designs of the two kings, and *refused to be a party to such an injustice*. He not only *refused* the request of Bishop Rotrodus, but wrote to Louis at some length to point out the reasons that compelled him to take this course. On this letter can be based many arguments to show that the attitude of Adrian towards the proposals of the English King as regards Ireland was one of *strong disapproval*, and that granting that this letter refers to Ireland, it would be *impossible* for Adrian to have issued, very much about the same time, the "Bull" of donation at the request of John of Salisbury.

"In the first place, the Pope's letter shows clearly enough that his consent had been asked solely on the ground that the expedition had a religious character, and the fact of the reply being addressed to Louis would probably only prove that Henry had taken care not to be too prominent in the business for fear that *the real motive* might become too apparent to the English Pope. Adrian proceeds to say that *he could not give consent* to any project of such a nature, unless he were certain that *the people and clergy of the country wanted foreign interference.* This, be it remarked, is a very different sentiment to that with which the same Pope is credited in the alleged "Bull." The various dangers which Louis is likely to run are then pointed out to him by the Pope, and for every reason he concludes not to give him any "Bull" encouraging the project until such time as *he has warned the people of the kingdom* of the intention of the two kings, in order to see whether they will co-operate with them. In conclusion the Pontiff begs the king to reflect well on the matter, and not to undertake the enterprise before consulting the Bishops and clergy of the country

"It is well at once to declare that the great difficulty in fixing the reference of this letter to the design of invading Ireland is the fact that the country is not mentioned by name. Unfortunately, it was a common custom in the transcription of documents to write only the initial letter of proper names. Thus, in this letter the envoy is called "R." Bishop of Evreux, and the country the two kings were anxious to obtain the Pope's approval to invade is only "H," which may stand equally well for "Hispania" and "Hibernia." We are thus left to the internal evidence of the document itself to determine to which of these two countries it has reference. Dr. Lingard was apparently aware of the existence of the letter,§ but it did not suggest itself so his mind that it had any reference to Ireland. He says: "When Louis a few years later (1159) meditated a similar expedition into *Spain*, and for that purpose requested the "consilium et favorem Romanæ Ecclesiæ," the answer was very different. Adrian dissuaded him because it was "inconsulta ecclesia et populo terræ illius."

"It is, however, clearly shown in the *Analecta* that it is impossible that this letter of Adrian, addressed to the two kings, can have any reference to Spain, while every circumstance in it tending to fix the special country, gives weight to the opinion that it was Ireland about which the Pope wrote. It the first place, the document refers not to a kingdom (*regnum*) but to a country (*terra*). Now Ireland was not recognized as a kingdom officially till the sixteenth century, and in all formal papers before that time it is constantly spoken of as a country (*terra*) merely. Spain, on the other hand, was at this time divided into three kingdoms —Castile, Aragon and Galicia; and the most powerful, the King of Castile, had the title of Emperor. King Louis of France had only a year or two before the date of the letter (1155) made a pilgrimage to St. James, and was well received by his father-in-law the Emperor of Castile.|| Hence, not only have we the official title of Spain to be a kingdom at the time when Adrian wrote, but it is impossible to suppose that Louis could have been so ignorant of the feelings of a country in which he had not long before been journeying, and over which his own father-in-law reigned as Emperor.

"Again, the country referred to in Adrian's letter clearly had many princes or chiefs, which was quite true of Ireland but not of Spain, about the state of which the Pope could not be ignorant. It also, undoubtedly, must have possessed its own episcopal hierarchy, capable of free deliberation; for Adrian advises Louis and Henry to consult the *Bishops and Clergy* as to their wish to receive foreign intervention in their affairs. The Church in that part of Spain, at this time overrun by the Moors, had almost disappeared, and for the rest it would have been quite unnecessary to ask the advice of the Spanish Bishops as to punishing their oppressors. On the other hand, the Holy See must have been well acquainted with the flourishing state of the Church in Ireland at this period. During the hundred and fifty years which preceded the reign of Henry II., numerous and well-attended Councils had been held for the maintaince of discipline and regulation of morals. Only a few years before Henry made his first attempt on the country, several great and renowned Irish saints occupied Sees in the country, and a great Council was held at Athboy at which 13,000 representatives of the nation attended to hear what the Church commanded. That Adrian must have known the state of the Church is rendered all the more likely since he had studied in Paris under a celebrated Irish professor, Marianus, afterwards a monk of Ratisbon, for whom he conceived a great affection. It was only to be expected, therefore, that if he had this knowledge of the Irish Church, *he should require that the Bishops and Clergy be consulted* as to the propriety of such an invasion as the French and English kings contemplated.

"It must be remembered, also, that Adrian desires that *the people* of the country be consulted, a thing impossible in the portions of Spain in possession of the Saracens. He also, throughout, repeats his

---
§ "History," vol. ii. p. 178, 5th ed., note.
|| Robertus de Monte. Migne, "Patrol." tom. clx. p. 478.

doubts as to the utility and necessity of the enterprise proposed by the kings, which would certainly not have been the case had their wish been merely to drive the infidel out of Spain. It is obvious that Adrian, like all his predecessors, would have been only too glad to grant protection to the kingdoms of France and England, had the wish of the kings been merely to fight against the Moors in Spain.

"Lastly, *a comparison of the alleged* "Bull" of Adrian and the authentic letter brings out one or two strange facts. In the first place, the document, as given by Giraldus, does not express the name or even the initial of the prince to whom it was granted: "Adrianus episcopus servus servorum Dei, carissimo in Christi filio illustri anglorum regi salutem." Next, the preamble of the "Bull" is almost word for word the same as that of the letter written to Louis VII., in 1159, and although it might happen that a few words of the two official documents would be the same, *there is no other example* of such a singular similarity, extending, as it does, over ten or fifteen lines. As this curious fact is the basis of a theory we shall state in brief, to account for the forgery of the "Bull" of Adrian, it is worth reproducing the two documents in order that our readers may judge for themselves.

ADRIAN'S LETTER TO LOUIS VII.	"BULL" TO HENRY II.
Satis laudabiliter et fructuose de Christiano nomine propagando in terris, et æternæ beatitudinis præmio tibi cumulando in cœlis, tua videtur magnificentia cogitare, dum ad dilatandos terminos populi Christiani, ad paganorum, barbariem debellandum et ad gentes apostatrices, et quæ catholicæ fidei refugiunt nec recipiunt veritatem, Christianorum jugo et ditioni subdendas, simul cum charissimo filio nostro Henrico illustri Anglorum regi, in H. properare intendis, et studes assidue (ut opus hoc felicem exitum sortiatur) exercitum ut quæ sunt itineri necessaria congregare. Atque ad id convenientius exsequendum, matris tuæ sacrosanctæ Romanæ Ecclesiæ consilium exigis et favorem. Quod quidem propositum tanto magis gratum acceptumque tenemus, et amplius sicut commendandum est, commendamus, quanto de sinceriore charitatis radice talem intentionem et votum tam laudabile processum credimus, ac de majori ardore fidei et religionis amore propositum et desiderium tuum principium habuerunt.	Laudabiliter satis et fructuose de glorioso nomine propagando, in terris, et æternæ felicitatis præmio cumulando in cœlis, tua magnificentia cogitat; dum ad dilatandos Ecclesiæ terminos ad declarandum indoctis et rudibus populis Christianæ fidei veritatem et vitiorum, plantaria de agro Dominico extirpanda, sicut catholicus princeps intendis; et ad id convenientius exsequendum consilium Apostolicæ sedis exigis, et favorem. In quo facto, quanto altiori consilio et majori discretione procedis, tanto in eo feliciorem progressum te, præstante Domino, confidimus habiturum; eo quod ad bonum exitum semper et finem solent attingere, quæ de ardore fidei et religionis amore, principium acceperunt, etc. Significasti siquidem nobis, fili in Christo carissime, te Hiberniæ insulam. ad subdendum illum populum legibus et vitiorum plantaria inde extirpanda, velle intrare, etc. Nos itaque, pium et laudabile desiderium tuum cum favore congruo prosequentes, et petitioni bonæ benignum impendentes assensum, gratum et acceptum habemus, ut pro dilatandis Ecclesiæ terminis, pro vitiorum restringendo decursu, pro corrigendis moribus, et virtutibus inserendis, pro Christianæ religionis augmento, insulam illam ingrediaris.

"It is almost impossible to compare the two documents here given without coming to the conclusion that the similarity is not the result of a mere accident. The idea consequently suggests itself as possible that *the text of Adrian's actual refusal*, as conveyed to the kings in the letter brought back by Rotrodus to Louis, *was made to serve as the basis of the forged "Bull."* What is certain about the matter is, that Louis and Henry having applied to the Pope for his approbation of a proposed invasion of a country called by its initial letter "H." the Holy Father *refused* to grant any such approbation, and grounded his refusal upon reasons similar to those by which he is supposed, about the same time, to have been induced to grant permission to Henry to invade Ireland. *The two documents are strangely like in form and expression,* and every circumstance, by which the country referred to by the letter "H" may be identified, points to the conclusion that it also was meant to refer to the proposed Irish expedition. Of course, had Adrian really refused the permission asked for, as he clearly did in his letter to Louis, the French king would have known that any pretended permission was *a forgery;* and had the refusal been intended to prevent any expedition to Ireland, the "Bull" which is supposed to have sanctioned it, *could never have been produced during the lifetime of the French king.* A reference to dates will show that this is so, and that all mention of the existence of the document was carefully avoided before the year A. D. 1180, when Louis died.* The silence which was kept for so many years about so important a document, and one which would have been so useful to Henry, has often been remarked upon as suspicious, and has puzzled many historians to explain. May it not be accounted for by the knowledge that *such a forgery* would be at once detected by Louis?

"In fact, although the secret of the negotiations of Rotrodus with Adrian in behalf of Henry and Louis was kept so well, that the text of the Pope's refusal was until lately almost unknown, still the annalist of Anchin, who continued the chronicle of Sigebert, appears to have had some suspicion of the fact. Speaking of the year A. D. 1171, about the preparations made by Henry for the invasion of Ireland, he says:† —"Henry, King of England, puffed up with pride, *and usurping things not conceded;* striving for things he had no business to do, prepared ships and called together the soldiers of his kingdom to conquer Ireland."

"Whether this theory as to the origin of the "Bull" be correct or not, it can safely be said that the evidence upon which the authenticity of the document has so long been held *is at best very doubtful and should be accepted with extreme caution.* A careful examination will, we believe, induce most inquires to *reject* the "Bull" as *an undoubted forgery,* and to consider it more than probable that Pope Adrian IV., so far from granting any approbation to Henry in his designs on Ireland or making any donation of that country to the English crown, *in reality positively refused to be a party to such an injustice.*"

---

*In A. D. 1177, Henry was chosen to arbitrate between two Spanish kings. In this office he styled himself "King of England, Duke of Normandy and Aquitaine, and Count of Anjou." *No mention is made of Ireland* (Rymer, tom. i).

†Migne, "Patrologie," tome clx. p. 307.

CHAPTER XIX.

English Translation of Pope Adrian's Letter to King Louis VII. of France.—The Pope's Refusal to allow Ireland to be Invaded.—A Comparison Between the Wording of the Letter and the Text of the Spurious Bull.—Reasons why the Fraud was not Exposed in Past Centuries.

The portion of the Latin text of the Letter which Pope Adrian IV. sent to King Louis VII. of France, which we have already laid before our readers, will reveal at once the corner-stone upon which the fraudulent Bull, falsely attributed to Pope Adrian IV. was founded.

On this point there can be no doubt whatever, as the Latin text which we published in last week's issue clearly shows the close copying of the forger of the fraudulent document from the original text of the Letter which was *purposely*, and with malice aforethought, *concealed* by King Henry in the secret archives of Winchester Castle.

The genuine Letter which Pope Adrian sent to King Louis VII. of France is given by Mansi as well as by Migne, and as the history of that important document will throw considerable light upon the forged Bull, we append it for the better understanding of the question at issue.

It is most likely that it was on the occasion of the alliance between the two royal families of France and England, and at the meeting in Paris in the year 1158, of the two monarchs—Louis VII. of France and Henry II. of England—that these two ambitious rulers came to the determination that the invasion of Ireland would not only give congenial employment to a vast number of restless men of martial mien in both kingdoms, but that such an enterprise would also redound to the renown of the allied monarchs, for the reason that hitherto Ireland, though often invaded, had never been conquered.

Both kings had in their respective dominions large numbers of knights and veterans whose only trade was war, and who were becoming restless for want of an opportunity to prove their prowess upon some battlefield, either as invaders of some foreign shore or as adventurers in extending the possessions of the respective monarchies under whose flag they gloried in fighting.

It was necessary, therefore, to find some congenial employment for these martial spirits, many of whom had accompanied King Louis himself, when, in 1145, that monarch in conjunction with Conrad III., of Germany, undertook to aid in capturing Jerusalem from the Mussulmans, but were ingloriously defeated through the treachery of the Greeks, at the loss of four-fifths of their forces.

In all probability the suggestion for the invasion of Ireland was made by King Henry, as such a scheme seems to have been brooding in his brain for years previously. So when King Louis heard the proposition, he discovered at once a military enterprise which would furnish occupation for the thousands of restless military heroes who were compelled to idleness through peace.

King Louis, therefore, commenced at once to call together his troops, to procure munitions of war, prepare vessels for the voyage, and to make all necessary preparations for invading Ireland. In order, however, to conform to the custom of the age, Louis deemed it right and proper to address a diplomatic document to Pope Adrian IV., in order to acquaint him with the contemplated project, as well as to ask the reigning Pontiff to extend his paternal blessing upon the enterprise, and to issue a Bull of Indulgences similar to those applied to the Crusaders, so that the martial valor of the French military forces might be aroused, and success crown the dual scheme of the French and English plotters against the peace of the Irish people.

Pope Adrian replied to the letter of King Louis, but not in the affirmative manner that monarch anticipated. So far from encouraging and blessing the enterprise, the Holy Father *forbade such a contemplated act of injustice against the Irish people.*

After proving to the King of France, by a very apt illustration, that an act or project, in order to be acceptable to Almighty God, and beneficial to those who might successfully accomplish such a scheme, should be *good in every respect,* and that any deviation from the line marked out by Heaven for its justice and propriety—would render such acts and such projects unfit to be offered to God. The same teaching is expressed by all theologians in this maxim: "*Bonum enim ex integra causa;* malum vero ex quolibet defectu."

The just and holy Pontiff defines the King's duty as a Catholic prince, and then Adrian the Just gives this sage counsel to the French King:

"Furthermore, it appears to be neither wise nor safe to enter for the object named into a territory belonging to other people, without first consulting *the wishes of the princes and people* of that territory. But you, as We have been informed, have all arrangements made, and are most eager to make the journey, without having consulted the Church or the princes of the country that you are so anxious to enter. *Under no consideration* should you attempt anything of the kind until the necessity for so doing is made manifest to you by the *princes of the country,* and until you are *invited by them* for the purpose specified.

Because We love with all the intensity of Our heart your honor and exaltation, it is Our wish that you *enter into no such project* unless a reasonable cause exists for so doing, and through this Letter We urge your Excellency to find out from the *Princes of the country* if there be a necessity for carrying out this project of yours, and also to enquire diligently what are the wishes not only of the princes but also of *the Church and the people of the country* in regard to the journey you are contemplating, and to be directed—*as is just*—by *their wishes.**

"After you shall have done all that We urge to be done in this matter," continues the Pope, "if you should find that there is a necessity for the journey, that is, that the Church of the country *advises you to undertake it,* and the princes call on you for help, and unite their counsel to that of the Church for the *same purpose,* you may, under such circumstances, proceed to act and carry out your laudable intention, and God's blessing shall accompany your efforts."†

"But should you enter the country *under any other circumstances,* it would be to be feared that your journey would be unfruitful, and would not lead to the end desired. The princes themselves, and the people of the country, would be *annoyed and oppressed* by such an entrance as your project implies, if there were no necessity for its execution, and We Ourselves might be regarded, for many reasons, as being rather capricious in the matter. For, your Excellency ought to consider, and remember how, on another occasion, when both Conrad of happy memory, formerly King of the Romans, and yourself, unwisely undertook—*without consulting the people of the country*—the Jerusalem project, you both failed to reap the advantages you looked for, and what detriment and injury came upon the Church of God, and the whole Christian people, from that expedition. Indeed, the Holy See suffered not a little from its having advised and helped you in that business, and all cried out with much indignation against it, declaring that it was the cause of the whole calamity.

"In fine, follow in the matter before us for consideration, that counsel which you know should be observed according to the dictates of right reason."

The wise and just Pontiff concludes his

---

*"Unde quia nos honorem et incrementum tuum tota mentis intentione diligimus et nihil tale aggredi, nisi ratiouabili causa exigente vellemus, sublimitati tuae praesentibus suademus ut prius necessitatem terrae per principes illius regni inspicias, et consideres, et tam illius ecclesiae quam principum et populi voluntatem diligenter inquiras, et ab eis consilium sicut decet, accipias.'

†"Quo facto, si et necessitatem terrae videris imminere et ecclesiae consilium fuerit, ipsi etiam terrae principes tuae sublimitatis auxilium postulaverint, et consilium dederint, juxta postulationem et consultum eorum poteris postea in facto ipso procedere et laudabile votum tuum, divino comitante praesidio adimp'ere."

Letter by warning King Louis to receive the words of Rotrodus, Bishop of Evreux, as if they came directly from the Vicar of Christ, and he eulogizes in the highest degree the prudence and virtue of that great Bishop.

This Letter is dated from the Lateran, 12 kalend. Maii, apparently 1159.‡

The sources from which the Letter of Pope Adrian IV. to King Louis VII. of France, has been procured, renders that most important document thoroughly genuine beyond a shadow of doubt. People do not forge documents containing refusals, and, moreover, the Letter itself is as much in keeping with the undeviating principles and implicit rectitude of Pope Adrian IV., as the spurious Bull is diametrically antagonistic thereto.

Inasmuch as some of our readers might resurrect the now obsolete objection that the letter "H" in the document which Pope Adrian IV., sent to King Louis VII., of France, referred to Spain, it is well to anticipate such an objection by fortifying what we have already said upon this matter, through the introduction of additional testimony which will show plainly to every discerning mind that by the letter "H" the Holy Father meant *Hibernia*, Ireland, and not *Hispania*, Spain.

Before proceeding with our additional proofs, however, we will state the fact that the first person to assert that the letter "H" in Pope Adrian's missive to King Louis alluded to *Hispania*, Spain, was a Calvinist, named James Bongars, born at Orleans, in France, in the year 1546, and who afterwards became the counsellor and steward of the French King Henry IV., and was also employed by that prince as his Ambassador at the Court of Germany. During his official career he came into possession of a large number of manuscripts belonging to the Library of Saint Benoit-sur-Loire, which were scattered in consequence of that abbey having been pillaged by the Calvinists. In addition to these valuable documents, Bongars also procured by purchase a great many important manuscripts which were originally a portion of the valuable collection stored in the Library of the Cathedral of Strasbourg.

Bongars died at Paris, in the year 1612, the year following the publication of a work known as the *Gesta Dei per Francos*—a volume which has become very valuable in the great question under debate.

The letter of Pope Adrian IV., to King Louis VII., of France, which we have already presented to our readers, first appeared in the *Gesta Dei per Francos*,** where it is catalogued as the 28th. among the missives written to King Louis VII, by Kings, Princes and Prelates. Twenty-seven of these letters were borrowed from the valuable collection of manuscripts in the library of President Pótau, but Bongars does not mention the source from which he procured the 28th. letter, viz : the missive sent by Adrian IV., to King Louis VII. It is not unlikely, however, that all these letters were originally the property of the Abbey Saint Benoit sui-Loire, and it is not improbable that Bongars had given them all —with the exception of the Adrian-Louis missive—to President Petau, retaining the latter document in his own possession until after the death of the editor or collector of these letters.

Thirty years later a French bibliophile, found these valuable documents in the possession of Alexander Petau, Senator or Counsellor of the French Assembly. They appeared in the 4th. tome of a work entitled *Rerum Franciccarum Scriptores*, published in the year 1041, shortly after the death of the editor.

The compiler tells us that the manuscript of these letters is ancient.†† As already stated, the volume did not appear until af er the demise of Andrew Duschene, but this learned man doubtless was aware of the fact that Bongars had previously published these letters.

The Abbey of St. Victor, in Paris, pos-

---

‡ Bougars, *Gesta Dei per Francos*, pag. 1174. Andre Duschesne, *Rerum Franciscarum Scriptores*, Tom. lv. pag. 557. Dom. Bouquet. *Recueil des historiens*, Tom. 15. Migne, *Patrologie*, Tom. 188. Col. 1615.

**P. 1174, Hanoviæ 1611.
††Epistorarum volumen, quas *Pontifices* Romani, etc., ad Ludovicum VII. Scripserunt, ex veteri codice MSS. viri clar. Alexandri Petavii Senatoris Parisiensis nunc primum editum 1041.

seased another manuscript copy of these valuable letters, a fact borne out by the testimony of the editor of the Duschene volume, in these words: "Whence it can easily be conjectured that this collection of letters was made by some Abbot or Canon of the Monastery of Saint Victor, in Paris."‡‡

The manuscripts owned by President Pètau were considered so extremely valuable that they were ultimately purchased for their weight in gold by Queen Christina of Sweden, who presented them to the Vatican Library, and thus greatly enriched that vast storehouse of historical lore, and also saved to the world valuable testimony on the present historical question.

Bongars was the first to interpret the initial "H" in the letter of Pope Adrian IV. to King Louis VII., as meaning *Hispania*, Spain. And, when it is taken into consideration that this man was a Calvinist at a time when that persecuting sect was most bitterly waging a blood-thirsty persecution against the Church, it is easy to surmize that such an arbitrary decision was not altogether undesigned on the part of Bongars.

Like the numerous errors, calumnies and falsehoods of Cambrensis, this wrong interpretation of the letter "H" by Bongars, has led subsequent writers into erroneous conclusions, simply because they did not stop to consider the prejudiced *source* from whence this opinion came.

Right here this important question will no doubt suggest itself to the minds of many of our readers: "Did the Calvinist Bongars have any peculiar sectarian interest in keeping the world in ignorance of the fact that Pope Adrian IV.,—so far from having authorized the iniquitous invasion of Ireland—had, on the contrary, formally dissuaded the Kings of both England and France from any such scheme, *and openly refused his consent to any such expedition ?*"

One thing is certain, that the publication of Pope Adrian's letter to the French King, if published in the year 1611, and made known to the English-speaking world, would have subsequently exercised a wonderful influence in thwarting the pretensions of England in proclaiming its supremacy over Ireland by authority of any Bull or other Papal document.

Another question which naturally suggests itself in this connection is this: Could it be possible for a Calvinist to so denude himself of his determined and diabolical hatred of both Popes and Popery, as—by any act of his—to let a single beam of the light of truth fall upon the falsely-sullied character of a Pope whose memory, for so many centuries, had been clouded by a calumnious charge coated with the blackest odium? The answer to this question will suggest itself to every mind enlightened by the knowledge of the black-hearted bigotry which has constantly been demonstrated by Calvinists against the Catholic Church.

Now let us return to the consideration of the letter "H" in Pope Adrian's letter, so as to adduce a few more proofs in substantiation of what we have already asserted *i. e.* that the letter of Pope Adrian to Louis VII., could not possibly have referred to Spain, and that it necessarily alluded to Ireland alone.

Aside from all other reasons why "H" could not mean *Hispania*, it would appear perfectly ridiculous for the King of France to ask permission of the Pope to help the King of Castile, who was his own father-in-law. Again, if Spain was the objective point against which the English and French monarchs desired to move in martial array, why select the Englishman, Rotrodus, Bishop of Warwick, to undertake negotiations therefor with the Holy Father?

And again, let us look at the text of the Adrian letter and ask any impartial reader if by any remote possibility even, these words could apply to Moorish Spain:

"The Clergy, the Princes and the people must be consulted, and their wishes with respect to intervention must be followed."

It is entirely unnecessary to dilate on this point, as every reader of history knows that Pope Adrian could never intend such an allusion to refer to a country many of whose inhabitants were at that period Mos-

---

‡‡Fuit et simile olim exemplar in Bibliotheca Canonicorum Regularium Sancti Victoris, Paris. —Not : 11, 22. Rerum Franciccarum Tom. IV, pag 557.

lem enemies of the Church, and who were consequently at direct enmity with the Spanish Clergy and the Christian rulers of a portion of Spain. In order, however, to meet any captious critic who may adopt the Calvinistic interpretation of the letter "H" as inspired by Bongars, let us suppose that Pope Adrian's letter had no reference— either remote or immediate—to Ireland. Would such an admission, *even if true*, militate against our defence of Pope Adrian IV.? By no means! The sterling sentiments of that grand Pontiff—no matter what country they allude to—stand as a triumphant refutation of the moss-covered calumny which has clouded his memory during the past seven centuries.

Pope Adrian's letter expresses the Christian grandeur and integrity of his soul; his sublime nobility of character, and his unflinching integrity in defending the rights of an inoffensive people about to be assailed in their own land!

With pride then, we ask: Could a Pope who gave such divine, such heaven-born instructions as are found in Pope Adrian's letter to King Louis, ever be capable of concocting the vile, unchristian document which the hireling Cambrensis ushered into the world as King Henry's title to a land which has ever since been crucified on the Calvary of British injustice?

These points add still another link to the chain of cumulative evidence which clearly proves that neither Pope Adrian IV., nor Alexander III., ever issued the diabolical documents attributed to them, and which, by the way, neither Bongars nor Duschene met with among all the 12th century manuscripts they investigated.

Now let us call the particular attention of the reader to some very interesting points of peculiar similarity between the *genuine* Letter and the *spurious* Bull, so as to convince every candid reader that King Henry II. of England forged the Bull by which he is said to have acquired Ireland through Pope Adrian IV.

In the *genuine* Letter of Pope Adrian IV. it is said that King Louis VII. of France had gathered an army and provided munitions of war and all other things necessary for making both a journey by land as well as a voyage by sea: "Studes assidue . . . exercitum, et quæ sunt itineri necessaria congregare." It is scarcely necessary to say that a military expedition on land required nothing more than a well-equipped army, and thus we discern that the expedition regarding which Louis VII. of France, and Henry II. of England, sent a joint letter to the Pope, consulting him regarding the project, alluded to Ireland, and not to Spain, as some writers erroneously assert.

The true Letter reads thus: "*In H. properare intendis*," and in the Apocryphal Bull: *Significasti nobis, te Hiberniæ insulam . . . . velle intrare . . . . Gratum habemus ut . . . . insulam illam ingrediaris.*" These expressions seem to indicate that there is question of *penetrating* into the interior of Ireland, and, moreover, they plainly indicate that the King of England occupied some points on the Irish sea coast, while the fact is that it was about *ten years* after the death of Pope Adrian IV. that the Norman invaders and King Henry took possession of Waterford and Dublin. This latter fact, alone, clearly shows the utter *impossibility* of the bogus Bull ever having emanated from Pope Adrian, ever having being sent to King Henry from Rome or from any other place in Europe whose soil was ever pressed by the foot-prints of a successor of St. Peter!

The forgers who fabricated the fraudulent Bull were evidently ignorant of the very important fact that all Bulls of concession of investiture were Consistorial acts which required the *signatures of the Cardinals*. But inasmuch as many members of the College of Cardinals who flourished during the pontificate of Pope Adrian were still alive when the bogus Bull was under the stylus of some British caligrapher, it would never do to sign the names of any Cardinals to such a fraudulent document, hence the name of Adrian IV. was made to do duty solitary and alone, and the owner of that name having died about thirty years previously, the forger had little to fear that Pope Adrian IV. would discover the fraud!

Finally, the forgery of both the so-called

Adrian and Alexander Bulls is so palpable it is actually amazing that the transparent fraud had not long ages ago aroused the suspicions of historians who could have penetrated into the vitals of the vicious documents and dissected the diabolical inventions for the enlightenment of the whole world.

That such a discovery was not made several centuries ago, can be accounted for only on the hypothesis that no historical writer took the time or trouble to compare the documents before him, to analyze their language, or to subject the dates, facts and circumstances set forth to that scrutiny which has resulted in such a triumph for truth and justice, and gained such a glorious victory for the Popes so long maligned by ignorant and designing men, and also for that Church which has been the recipient of the calumny of even some of her own children, but of whom she can with great truth say: "Father, forgive them, for they know not what they do."

Among the multitude of facts which we have brought forward to prove the spurious character of the forged Papal documents under consideration, there is still another circumstance which will add strength to all that has already been said on this subject, and that is the instinct (which to us appears to have been super-human), by which every Pope prudently refrained from making any direct official reference to the fraudulent document falsely attributed to Pope Adrian IV. even upon important occasions when it might seem judicious to allude to it casually or to mention it directly.

This fact comes forcibly before us in the action of the Cardinals who officiated at Avranches, when King Henry swore that he had no intention to be accessory to the murder of St. Thomas A'Becket, as well as in the case of such Pontiffs as Innocent III., John XXII., Paul IV., and St. Pius V., in his Bull against Elizabeth; Gregory XIII. and Clement VIII., all of whom had frequent occasion to mention both the Adrian and the Alexander "Bulls," when treating of subject matters relating to Ireland. But no doubt these Pontiffs had no faith in the forged diplomas, and thus they ignored them altogether as entirely unworthy of their notice.

CHAPTER XX.

The Papal Court of the Fourteenth Century had no Knowledge Concerning the Bogus Adrian Bull.—The Letter Sent by King Edward of England to Pope John XXII. Reply of that Pontiff.—Letter from O'Neil, King of Ulster, to Pope John XXII. Comments thereon Proving that the Spurious Adrian Bull never Originated in Rome, nor was its Genuine Character ever admitted by the Irish People.

In the year 1316, a short time after the election of Pope John XXII., King Edward of England sent three plenipotentiaries to Rome in order to place in the hands of the Holy Father the tribute of one thousand pounds sterling promised by John Lackland, and to offer the excuses of his Majesty for the tardiness of payment, there being then about twenty-four annuities in arrears. The annalist who succeeded Baronius publishes the King's Letter in which Edward makes no mention of any portion of the same as coming from Ireland. If Pope John XXII. had any knowledge of the existence of the Adrian and Alexander Bulls, he must have entertained a very peculiar idea of King Edward's honesty when that monarch informed him that there were twenty four years indebtedness of Peter Pence due from a nation that had first promised to pay it in 1156 under the supposed Bull of Pope Adrian! From 1156 to 1316 is one hundred and sixty years, and Pope John would certainly have reminded King Edward of this fact in their financial agreement, if such a Bull could be discovered *anywhere in the Papal archives!*

Pope John XXII. was one of those Pontiffs who took deep interest in all matters that concerned the welfare of the Holy See, and no doubt he gave this question of the Adrian Bull a rigid investigation. Besides, his Holiness was assisted in such secular concerns by a staff of saintly, able and erudite men—such as the eminent Dominican Bernard Guido and others. Yet, after all the scrutiny devoted to the search for the Adrian and Alexander Bulls, by these archivists and officers of the Vatican, *not a solitary trace of either of these documents could be discovered!*

The annals of the Church kept in Rome failed to reveal a particle of evidence that would throw any light upon the two English documents. The Cardinals had never heard of them, common rumor had never mentioned them, and thus the bogus Bulls of both Adrian and Alexander were as unknown to the Pope of Rome in the year 1316, as any other document could be *that never had a legitimate existence!*

The Pope wrote a reply to King Edward, in answer to the epistle which he sent by his equerries, and therein he tells Edward that John Lackland delivered up his kingdom, with its rights and dependencies, to the Pope of Rome; that the English King promised—for himself and his successors—that he and they would render proper homage, and pay the annual tribute, under pain of forfeiture. "All this," says the Pope, "is known both by rumor and from the Chronicles.*

It follows, therefore, in the most logical manner, that neither the officials around the Pontifical court, nor Pope John himself, had ever heard of the existence of these bogus Bulls.

Let us suppose, however, that the annals of Giraldus Cambrensis, Raoul de Diceto, Mathew Paris, Roger of Wendover, and all the other Englishmen who who had compiled Chronicles for more than a century previous, were entirely unknown in Rome, would the Pope have rested satisfied? Certainly not. His Holiness would have applied to the text of the official *Regesta*, then the *Bullarium* would have been tried, and when that failed, the Vicar of Christ would have referred to public rumor (*fama notificat*) in order to ascertain some information concerning the existence of such ecclesiastical compacts with two English Kings.

So certain is it that the Pontifical Court

* "Prout haec omnia fama notificat, et chronicarum inspectio manifestat."

had no knowledge of the Adrian and Alexander Bulls, that the Irish people, when they felt themselves constrained to send a long letter of complaint to Pope John XXII., enclosed a copy of the spurious Adrian Bull to the Holy Father and to the Cardinal Legates.

In his reply to the complaint of the Irish petitioners, Pope John spoke precisely as any person would who harbored grave doubts as to the genuineness of the documents sent to him.

In reference to the bogus Adrian Bull his Holiness wrote: "Quas (litteras) praedictus Adrianus Praedecessor noster eidem regi Angliae de terra Hiberniae Concessisse dicitur," the translation of which is: Which letter the aforesaid Adrian, our predecessor, *is said to have conceded* to the same Henry King of England, in reference to the country of Ireland."

This is plain and positive proof that the first intimation Pope John XXII. ever had that such a document as Pope Adrian's Bull to King Henry of England had any existence, was when he received it from the people of Ireland who used it as an *argumentum ad hominem* against the cruelties and injustice which the King of England's minions in Ireland were then subjecting them to.

The chiefs and the Irish people of the Province of Ulster, being no longer able or willing to undergo the robbery, rapine, cruelty and injustice heaped upon them by their British tyrants, broke out in rebellion and called to their assistance Edward Bruce, brother of the celebrated hero Robert Bruce, King of Scotland. In order that their rebellion might be justified in the estimation of the then reigning Pontiff and the Catholic princes of the whole world, the Irish sent couriers to the two Cardinal Legates, Joscelin and Fieschi, then living in Scotland, enclosing a copy of the so-called Adrian Bull for the purpose of pointing out the fact that its conditions having been ignored by the English monarchs— the whole document was void in consequence of such violations.

When Pope John XXII. received the Letter of complaint from the Irish people, he caused a Brief to be addressed to King Edward, fo which the following is a *correct* translation, there being in existence several *false* translations which were purposely made through English influence, in order to make it appear that the Pope sent to the King of England a transcript of the Adrian Bull as he found it in the Vatican archives:

> JOHN, Bishop, Servant of the Servants of God, to Edward, Illustrious King of England, Health and Apostolic Benediction.

The earnest exhortations which We address to you, Dearly Beloved Son, in order to move you to do what is pleasing to the truly just Judge, to preserve peace in the countries and among the subjects of your kingdom; to provide for all that can contribute to your renown and glory, emanate from a paternal heart which desires the exaltation of your Excellency. You ought then to receive them with affection, and show yourself prompt and docile in fulfilling them.

We have received a Letter which the Rulers and people of Ireland sent some time ago to our Dear Sons Joscelin, Cardinal Priest of the titles of SS. Peter and Marcellinus, and Luke Fieschi, Cardinal Deacon, of the title of St. Mary *Inviolata*, Nuncios of the Apostolic See. This Letter these same Cardinals have transmitted enclosed in their own Letter to Us.

In these Letters from the Irish, among other things, we have read that Pope Adrian, our predecessor of happy memory, having, under a certain manner and form expressed in the Apostolic Letters drawn up for that purpose, conceded the domain of Ireland to your ancestor King Henry II. of illustrious memory. That Prince and his successors the kings of England until this day, far from observing the aforesaid manner and form, have, on the contrary, transgressed against all rule, and by cruel vexations, unheard of oppressions, unsupportable servitude and most inhuman tyranny, crushed the Irish in a manner so much the more unfortunate and unsupportable as that tyranny has lasted so long, and no one until this day has repaired the wrongs done, nor put a stop to the disorders. No one has had compassion on their misfortunes, although they have many times addressed their complaints to you, and although the cry of the oppressed had reached your ears. These are the reasons why, not being any longer able to support their condition, they have been constrained to withdraw themselves from your house and to call in another prince to govern them.

If these complaints are well founded, dearly beloved Son, they affect us so much the more intensely, as we are most anxious that all your affairs may turn out well and prosperously for you. You should exert all your care to remedy the evils, and act with promptness in striving to please your Creator in this matter. Beware of doing anything that may provoke God Himself —the Lord of vengeance—against you. Him who does not despise even one of the sighs of those who are unjustly treated, and Who, as a punishment for injustices, rejected His chosen people, and transferred from them His kingdom —as we learn from the Holy Scriptures.

At a period so disturbed as this is, We desire most earnestly also that you will adopt the measures that will bring back to yourself the affection and submission of the people complaining, and that you avoid everything that can detach them from your service.

As it is to your highest interest to arrest new charges, and to remedy at once the trouble which may increase and become irremediable, We seriously solicit your Royal Excellency, and prudently counsel you to reflect wisely and to act promptly, through ways and means that are suitable, in order that you may put a stop to the complaints, and that you may effect reforms which will arrest movements that are so dangerous. You can in this way please Him by whom you rule, and by fulfilling faithfully your duty you will put an end to all complaints.

Then there will be room for hoping that the Irish, being inspired with better counsels, will submit to your authority, or even, if they wish to persist in the rebellion inaugurated (which may God forbid) they will transform their cause into a flagrant injustice, and you wil stand excused before God and man.

In order that you may thoroughly understand the griefs and complaints upon which the Irish lay stress, we enclose in the present Letter, the one which they had transmitted through the undersigned Cardinals to Us, and We join with it the one which, *it is said*, Our predecessor Adrian granted to said Henry, King of England, in regard to the land of Ireland.

Given in the 3rd Kalends of July—29th of June.

It is scarcely necessary to call particular attention to the severity with which Pope John XXII. lashes the oppressions condemned by the divine law and conscience, nor to point out in any extended remarks how that Pontiff informs the King that the cause of the Irish will be entirely just if he does not speedily put an end to the iniquities perpetrated against the Irish people for so long a period.

This language is not such as would be used by Pope John XXII., if he had the slightest notion that his predecessor Adrian IV. had donated Ireland to an English King. Again : If Pope Innocent III. had accepted the suzerainty of Ireland which King John offered to him at the same time that he offered England, would Pope John XXII. have omitted all mention of such an important diplomatic transaction? Would he have confined his counsel to the King within the limits of "justice and conscience"? Would he not rather have charged his Legates to have the case of Ireland's complaint against the English King brought before them, who would then give judgment in the case between the Papal feudatory King and his Irish vassals who would also have become the vassals of the Church of Rome? Moreover, he would have written direct to the representatives of the Irish people, in order to assure them of redress for their grievances, and to put an end to the wrongs that were perpetrated in their land. As Pope John XXII. did not act thus, we claim his failure to carry out such a line of duty, as another proof against the authenticity of the so-called Adrian Bull.

We have said that *false translations* have been made of the letter of Pope John XXII., by biased British writers, and here is a brief explanation of the crime thus committed. According to the continuator of Baronius, who collated the original *Regesta*, Pope John XXII. expressed himself doubtingly on the subject of the so-called Adrian Bull, when he used the words "*concessisse dicitur*," but the British copyists, with the desire to falsify the Pope's expression of doubt, have made the passage read thus: "*Adrianus Henrico regi Angliae de terra Iberniæ concessit.*" According to that false rendering, the Pontiff would have admitted without dispute the authenticity of the Bull of Adrian, and thus falsehood and fraud would have triumphed over truth and justice.

So cleverly was this mistranslation effected that some Irish writers themselves, not suspecting such sinful scheming on the part of prejudiced English historians, have, in many cases, copied the English "*concessit.*" Thus, Peter Lombard, Archbishop of Armagh, representing the Irish people at Rome during the Pontificate of Pope Clement VIII., followed the interpolated text in his work, "Annals of Ireland."*

Abbé MacGeoghegan, who published his history at Paris in 1758, copied from Lombard, but he would have discovered the fraud had he consulted "Baronius' Annals," which gave the true text in these words:

"Ut autem de praedictis gravaminibus et querelis quibus praedicti innituntur Ibernici, tuis sensibus innotescat ad plenum praedictas litteras missas Cardinalibus antedictis, tum formam litterarum quas praedictus Adrianus praedecessor noster eidem Henrico Regi Angliæ de terra Hibernae *concessisse dicitur*, tuae magnitudini mittimus praesentibus interclusas."†

The remarkable circumspection of Pope John XXII., in quietly repudiating the Bull manufactured by King Henry II. in Pope Adrian's name, is increased several degrees when it is known that the representatives of the Irish people who sent the letter of complaint against King Edward to that Pontiff, seemed to imagine that the Adrian forgery was a genuine Papal document which, they alleged, was obtained by fraud.‡

On the other hand it is well known to all persons familiar with Irish history, that the vast majority of the people of Ireland, constantly and persistently rejected the so called "Bull" falsely attributed to Pope Adrian as spurious, false and apocryphal. This fact is susceptible of proof in many ways, but we will give a single instance

* Page 260, Louvain edition, 1632.

† Annal. Baron. Ami. 1317, N. 43. [Judge Maguire, in his bad book. asks this question: "Where did Pope John XXII., get the copy of Adrian's Bull which he sent to the King of England, if the Bull itself was not in Rome?" This question is answered above. The Ulster Irish sent a copy of the false Bull to that Pope, and John XXII, transmitted the same copy to the English King, as he had neither use for it nor faith in its authenticity.]

‡ Vide MacGeoghegan Hist. Ireland, p 33.

which will serve to furnish sufficient evidence to justify our assertion.

The Library Barberini, of Rome, contains a fourteenth century manuscript comprising numerous original documents relating to the Pontificate of Pope John XXII., and embracing events which occurred during the period of which we are at present treating. Among the manuscripts is a letter from the Royal Council of Dublin, accusing the Irish of various misdemeanors displeasing to their English appointed rulers, and among the most heinous crimes charged against them is their treasonable and unpardonable custom of perpetually declaring that King Henry II. of England, and his successors, employed *fraud and spurious Papal Bulls in order to support their pretended dominion over Ireland*.§

Writers who desire to prejudice the reading public against the Popes, and who have some particular reason for spreading falsehood so as to divorce the Irish Catholic people from their allegiance to the Vicar of Christ, falsely assert that the document which we have laid before our readers represented the sentiments of the Irish people, whereas the letter in question was sent by O'Neill, King of Ulster, who took to himself the title of heirship of all Ireland, but such a very violent presumption by no means proves that the admissions made in that letter concerning the so-called Adrian "Bull" should be set down as the unanimous opinion of the whole people of Ireland, the great majority of whom had neither hand, act nor part in concocting the O'Neill letter to Pope John XXII., nor did they place any reliance whatever upon the British made "Bulls" under which King Henry claimed authority to unjustly invade, rob and ruin both the temporal and the spiritual rights of the Irish people.

§ "Asserrentes etiam Dominum regem Augliæ ex falsa suggestione et ex falsis Bullis terram Hiberniae impetrasse, *ac communiter hos tenentes.*"

CHAPTER XXI.

The Erection of Ireland into a Kingdom by Pope Paul IV.—How English Fraud Accomplished that Object.—Comments on Certain Expressions in the Letter of Pope John XXII.—Rome's Equal and Exact Justice Exemplified.—England's Vicious Methods Illustrated.

Up to the year 1555, Ireland was known in all public acts and official documents as "The Land of Ireland." Anterior to that date the word "Kingdom," never meant Ireland, except in the bogus Bull attributed to Pope Adrian, when the forger forgot this fact and inscribed the wrong word in that spurious document.

In all official mention of the Kings of England, from the time of the invasion, these monarchs were known as Lords of Ireland, nothing more. "Land of Ireland" was the appellation used in all the Bulls, Rescripts and Encyclicals from Rome. Of this fact we have sufficient proof in the genuine Letter of Pope Adrian IV. to King Louis VII. of France, wherein that Pontiff invariably makes use of the same term to designate the country which the Kings of England and France designed to invade.

King John offered to surrender to Pope Innocent III. the "kingdom of Ireland," but the Sovereign Pontiff was sufficiently wise to avoid using the word "kingdom" in relation to Ireland, because he knew the country was not known under such an appellation. King Henry VIII., in writing to Pope Leo X., did not style himself "King," but merely "Lord of Ireland," as he also well knew that Ireland was not styled a kingdom.

The Protestant Parliament which was held in Dublin, erected Ireland into a kingdom, and Edward VI. took for himself the pompous title of "King of England, France and Ireland." This example was followed by Queen Mary, who succeeded her brother Edward in 1553. When she married Philip of Spain, son of Charles V., the proclamations and ordinances of the royal titles mentioned, among others, that of "King and Queen of Ireland," On this historical point Dr. Lingard says:

"Cardinal Pole understood that difficulties might arise from the taking of this title by Philip and Mary, and for this reason he asked the Sovereign Pontiff to erect Ireland into a kingdom before the arrival of the ambassadors at Rome. But the death of Julius III. following closely upon that of Marcellus II., had prevented these Pontiffs from carrying out the Cardinal's suggestion. The urgency of the matter therefore suggested itself to Pope Paul IV., and immediately upon his coronation that Pontiff published a Bull by which, at the request of Philip and Mary, he erected the seignory of Ireland into a kingdom."

Pope Paul IV., in the Bull by which Ireland was erected into a kingdom, makes no allusion whatever to any Bulls concerning that country issued by Popes Adrian IV., Alexander III., or any other of his predecessors. Had this Pontiff known of such documents, most assuredly he would have mentioned them, instead of making a vague allusion to the fact that the Kings of England had acquired the sovereignty of Ireland by or through the Apostolic See. It is very apparent, therefore, that—down to the year 1555—the Apostolic See had no knowledge of any such Bulls ever having been issued by any Pontiff who had previously occupied the Chair of Peter. In this connection it may be well to state that it was not until half a century later that Baronius, the Papal ecclesiastical chronicler, accidently came across the Adrian forgery in the works of Mathew of Paris (who had copied it from Cambrensis) and entered it in the Bullarium, at the same time throwing discredit upon its authenticity.

In the Letter which Pope John XXII. sent to King Edward II., that Pontiff alludes to the Bull attributed to Pope Adrian IV., and it may be well to consider the reasons which impelled that Pontiff to forward to the English monarch the copy of the English forgery which he had received from O'Neill and the other petitioners of Ulster. The reason, it is plain enough, was for no other purpose than to inform the Prince that the Pope had no official knowledge of any such document having ever existed.

The Bull of Pope Paul IV., passes over in silence the agreement entered into in the year 1213 between Pope Innocent III. and King John of England. It is a matter of historical certainty that the King offered the "kingdom of Ireland" to the Pope, the language used being, "*totum regnum Hiberniae*" ("the whole kingdom of Ireland,") but it is equally certain that the Pope did not receive the proffered donation.

As the Latin proverb runneth: "*Nemo dat quod non habets;*" "No one can give what he has not got," and thus it was with King John, who, possessing by force and fraud only a small portion of the sea coast of Ireland, consequently he could not donate "the whole kingdom." It must also be borne in mind that no Pontiff would ever think of accepting such a trust in the case of Ireland, as no such "kingdom" had any status in the diplomatic circles of the whole world. In point of fact, in order to accept the suzerainty of Ireland, it would be necessary for the Holy Father first to raise Ireland to the dignity of a kingdom, but as it is nowhere stated that the Pope conferred the investiture of Ireland on King John or his successors, Pope Paul IV., knowingly and prudently, kept silent on the subject.

Inasmuch as neither the spurious "Bull" attributed to Pope Adrian, nor the diploma of Pope Alexander III., furnishes a foundation for a title to Ireland, it will doubtless puzzle our readers to account for the expression which Pope Paul IV. used when he alluded to the Kings of England as having acquired the sovereignty of Ireland through the Holy See.

But this expression of the Pope is easily accounted for. In the meantime, however, we desire to remind our readers that King John, at the beginning of his reign, took to himself the illicit title of Lord of Ireland, a title which had no foundation whatever, as—even admitting the spurious Adrian Bull to be authentic—that document conferred no such hereditary right upon any of the descendants of King Henry II. And as it was Henry II., who created, by his own usurped and valueless authority, John Lord of Ireland, his claim to such a title was just as spurious as that of the "Bull" by which that royal robber, his father, made to himself a "donation" of Ireland under the seal of a forged Papal document.

What did the Popes do in this matter? Mark the prudence and justice of the Vicars of Christ even in this seemingly small matter of diplomatic etiquette. The Popes, so far from acknowledging King John's title as "Lord of Ireland," styled him merely "Count de Mortagne," the distinctive title he owned prior to his father's mock ceremony by which he was put in illegal possession of a small part of Ireland.

After the death of King Henry II., and when England had passed under the control of Richard the Lion-hearted, Pope Clement III., having occasion to speak of Ireland and of John Lackland, addressed that prince by the title of Count de Mortagne, entirely ignoring the spurious appellation of "Lord of Ireland."

From these facts it may easily be understood that there is no historical co-relation between the unjust adoption of King John's title and any concession whatsoever of English sovereignty in Ireland by the Apostolic See. All that need be said, therefore, on this phase of the question, is that the compiler of the Bull of Pope Paul IV., *transcribed the request of Philip and Mary*—and herein lies the whole explanation.

England has always studiously endeavored to impress upon the minds of every succeeding generation of the Irish people since the twelfth century, that British rule in Ireland originated with the Pope, and that the Irish people should look upon the Holy Father as the Lord Suzerain of that land. But notwithstanding England's anxiety to impress this falsehood upon the minds of the Irish people, the natives of that land continued incredulous, and their incredulity on this point grew stronger with each succeeding generation. In order, however, to apply the seal of Papal approval to that usurped title, Philip and Mary had representations made to the Papal Court during the reign of Pope Paul IV., that the King of England had acquired the sovereignty of Ireland by concession of the Apostolic See. But had the ambassadors of the English monarchs not stated a wilful untruth for the special purpose of deceiving the Pope, Paul IV. would never have acceded to their request.

Rome is guided by justice in all her actions. The Holy Father may be deceived by designing conspirators filled with falsehood in order to accomplish a diplomatic scheme, but in all decisions emanating from Rome, religion, sound reason and rigid justice are indelibly stamped thereon. It is a fundamental principle at the Roman Chancellor's office, that concessions on request are eminently conditional and depend altogether on the intentional and objective veracity of the statement of the facts in each case. But when untruth and fraud are resorted to, the foundation of such a case gives way, and all rights conferred through such misrepresentation crumbles into useless and valueless atoms.

In no matter that comes before it for adjudication is the Holy See more particularly scrutinizing and just than in the preservation of the rights of others. This is clear in the Bull of Pope Paul IV., wherein that Pontiff throws this guard around the rights of the Irish people: "*Sine prejudicio jurium ipsius Romanæ Ecclesiæ, et cujuscumque alterius in illa (insula) vel ad illam jus habere prætendentis.*"

The Consistorial Decree contains the same reservation, and this consideration on the part of the Pontiff for the reserved rights of the Irish people, did not only include their present peaceable possession (*jus in re,*) but also their future right or disputed right (*jus ad rem.*)

The Irish people inhabiting twenty-one counties possessed full and peaceable possession of their lands and property, and the Holy Father had no intention whatever of altering their condition in favor of the English invaders. Rome, therefore, left to the Irish people the right to win back the territory possessed by the invaders, as well as to hold intact that portion of Ireland which had then held out against the English enemy. Neither investiture nor donation are alluded to in any way, nor did the English usurpers of Irish rights acquire an iota of authority over that people by reason of the Bull of Pope Paul IV., elevating Ireland into a kingdom.

In treating of the Bull of Pope Paul IV., Bzovius relates the private conversation that Pontiff held with the ambassadors of Queen Mary. At this private audience, says Bzovius, the Pope complained that the ecclesiastical goods pillaged by the English invaders from the Irish churches, monasteries and abbeys, had not been restored, and he reminded them that the restitution should be full and absolute on the part of the pilfering usurpers. The Holy Father reminded them that the English ought to know that such sacrilegious robberies would draw down upon their perpetrators the maledictions of Almighty God. The Pope, therefore, urged the ambassadors to write to their monarchs on this matter and to counsel them to make full and immediate restitution. But to England's shame be it said, the pilfering and sacrilege of the fourteenth century was continued down to the nineteenth century, regardless alike of the sacred rights of God or the natural rights of the Irish people

CHAPTER XXII.

A New and Important Witness to the Fraudulent Character of the Adrian and Alexander Bulls.—Selections from the Celebrated Historical Work "Cambrensis Eversus," by Dr. John Lynch.—Seventeenth Century Evidence Against both the Spurious Documents.

In the first portion of this volume we made a passing allusion to a celebrated work on Ireland entitled *Cambrensis Eversus*,* by Dr. John Lynch, and expressed our regret that the work was so rare that not a copy of it could be found on the Pacific coast. Fortunately, however, through the great kindness of friends, a copy was purchased in London, and now we are enabled to lay before our readers some very important evidence which hitherto has been completely hidden from public gaze both in consequence of the high price of Dr. John Lynch's invaluable work, as well as from the fact that but very few copies of this historical work are for sale in any portion of the world.

Cambrensis Eversus consists of a general history of Ireland from the earliest ages, and from the amount of historical matter to be found in this vast store-house of Irish lore, we are surprised that so little attention has been given to the exhaustive work of an author whom we look upon as certainly the most truthful, polished and learned among all the men who have ever attempted to write on Ireland.

Dr. Lynch devotes but a few chapters to the consideration of the bogus Bull attributed to Popes Adrian and Alexander, but—as our readers will discern further on—in that brief space, he has furnished such proof of the spuriousness of these documents that not a doubt can remain in the mind of any impartial reader.

The forger of the falsely-called Adrian Bull, our readers will remember, insinuates in that document that the Catholic population of Ireland in the twelfth century was steeped in vice both morally and intellectually. In order to show the falsity of the forged document, and also to overthrow the aspersions made by Giraldus Cambrensis upon the moral character of the faithful Irish Catholic people, Dr. Lynch, in the work before us, devotes three chapters of the second volume to that disputed point, and although we have touched upon that aspect of the question under consideration already, in a brief way, we feel that Dr. Lynch's evidence will not only add to the share of useful knowledge which every Catholic should possess, but it will also re-affirm the fact that neither in the twelfth century, nor at any time anterior or subsequent, were the morals, customs or habits of the Irish people in that state of degradation set forth by the notorious Giraldus Cambrensis, the English falsifier, whose untruths were so numerous as to gain for him the very doubtful honor of being distinguished from all other historical writers as the man who "could not tell the truth except by accident."

Alluding to the charge made against the piety and morality of the Irish people by Giraldus Cambrensis, Dr. Lynch says :†

St ll adhering to his original error, our author here gives Muircheartach the title of king of Ireland, though our annalists make him only successor to his father on the throne of Munster, and assign his death to 1167. Perhaps it may be Muircheartach Mac Lochlinn, who was proclaimed king of Ireland in the year of our Lord 1157, and reigned to his death in 1166. If all other circumstances concurred, we may consistently with chronology, maintain that he was the king referred to in the chronicle; for Pope Adrian

---

* The full title of the work is, "Cambrensis Eversus; or Refutation of the Authority of Giraldus Cambrensis on the History of Ireland. By Dr. John Lynch (1662), with some account of the affairs of that kingdom during his own and former times. Edited, with translation and copious notes, by the Rev. Matthew Kelly, Royal College of St. Patrick, Maynooth. Published in Dublin by the Celtic Society, during the years 1849-50 and 1851."

† Vol. II., chap. xxi., page 403, *et seq.*

breathed his last in 1159. Now, as these journeys which took place in his day evidently prove that Irish kings at home and Irish ecclesiastics abroad were zealous in good works, is it not impossible to believe that Pope Adrian would solemnly have charged the Irish with depravity of morals? Would not the fear alone of being denounced as ungrateful have deterred him from maligning them? It is utterly abhorrent to reason, that the only mark of his gratitude for the service of his Irish preceptor Marianus, should be to transmit to posterity a defamatory character of that preceptor's native country; especially when he must have seen Irishmen rising in foreign countries to such eminence in learning and piety, as to be selected for the arduous honor of instructing others.

Every person who has even a slight knowledge of the Christian religion, is very well aware that it would be a crime to desert one's country, when it is plunged in savage depravity and universal ignorance of the rudiments of faith, and to go plant an abundant harvest of virtue and religion on a foreign soil, while barrenness and aridity wastes the whole extent of his native land. The men who were so eminent for all other virtues, assuredly cannot be supposed deficient in charity, which requires that its fruits should begin at home, with ourselves and our friends, before it extends its beneficence to others. St. Paul desired to become an anathema for his brethren according to the flesh, nor would those Irish have gone out in "crowds," as our author says, "to instruct foreign nations in virtue and learning, if there was not abundance of public instructors left after them at home."

The Pope, after duly weighing those facts, would certainly have come to the conclusion that the Irish could not teach abroad what they had not learned at home. He must have known, that either immediately before or during his pontificate, Dionysius, Isaac, Gervas, Conrad, his preceptor Marianus, Christian and Gregorius at Ratisbon, Maurus and twelve other monks, in the monastery of Maniurgghen, and Macarius, with his twelve associates at Wurzburg, were celebrated for their sanctity and learning.

At home in Ireland every diocese had its Bishop, every parish its priest, old monasteries were repaired, new ones were built, and all abundantly supplied with monks. The written catalogues of Sees and monasteries prove the uninterrupted succession of bishops and monks. So great was the number of priests in Ireland, that 500 of them assembled in council in 1143, with twelve bishops and Muireadach O'Dubhthaich, Archbishop of Tuam. Catholicus, Archbishop of the same See, a prudent and a learned man (for his age), was accompanied to the Council of Lateran, 1179, by Lorcan, Archbishop of Dublin, Conn of Kill-da-lua, Bric of Limerick, Augustine of Waterford, and Felix of Lismore. If their flocks were plunged in that hideous barbarism charged against all the Irish by some writers, how could they be worthy of being called to a distant place to sit in council on the important interests of the Catholic world; men who either could not or would not heal the infirmities of those whom they were bound by duty to protect? That Pope, at all events, would not summon them, who is said to have made over the dominion of Ireland to King Henry to improve the morality of the Irish. This fact alone justifies a strong suspicion that the Bull attributed to Pope Alexander is as spurious or at least as surreptitious, as that by which Pope Adrian is said to have annexed Ireland to the dominions of King Henry. Neither could it ever be reported that St. Lorcan, Archbishop of Dublin, had, in his patriotic zeal, obtained some privileges from Pope Alexander, derogatory to the dignity of the crown if the authority of the same Alexander had already armed Henry for the conquest of Ireland. The Pope would never have made St. Lorcan his legate, who he knew had taken the field against Henry at the siege of Dublin, and encouraged others to take arms. The Pope could not have been guilty of such inconsistencies. Nor could St. Lorcan himself, a Prelate so eminent for his piety, and so obedient to the Supreme Pastor of the Church, ever have so openly resisted by his letters, his council, and his arms, those bulls of the Pope, had they really existed. There are most abundant reasons, therefore, for believing that those bulls, which I am about to produce, were never issued by the Popes.

In the following chapter Dr. Lynch gives the text of the spurious Adrian Bull, and comments on it at some length, but as we have already included in the evidence presented, several of the points dwelt upon in the pages of *Cambrensis Eversus*, we will extract only those portions which will introduce new testimony in proof of the fraudulent character of the papal documents forged in England.

After citing the names of numerous Irish ecclesiastics famous for their apostolic zeal and rich in every Christian virtue, Dr. Lynch says:

We know from Colgan that Muircheartach, Marianus, Clement, John, Isaac, Candidus, Magnoald, and many others went over to Ratisbon about this period, and refreshed the inhabitants of that city and its environs with the salutary waters of piety and learning. No person can imagine for a moment that these holy men were so lost to the feelings of humanity as to renounce that love which all men bear to the land of their birth; if they had not well known that Ireland was abundantly supplied with teachers, to conduct her in the ways of salvation and civilized institutions, they would have been more mindful of the duties of well-regulated charity, and devoted themselves to the instruction of their countrymen at home, rather than of strangers abroad. Our Saviour Himself first began by instructing His own countrymen, the Jews, and then proceeded to conduct the Gentiles from the darkness of ignorance. Who ever watered another man's field, when his own was parched with drought? Do not the laws themselves declare that it is severe and akin to cruelty to turn a water-course from your own estate, for the use of others, to the injury of your neighbors, and while your own fields are parched? I beg of any person who reads this to consider for a moment how many kings of Ireland and princes as I have proved, by the testimony even of foreign writers, nobly discharged their duties as kings? How many monasteries were erected as great nurseries of literature and piety? How many retreats of anchorites? How many facilities were afforded for the acquisition of learning? Masters in all branches of science being ready to instruct all comers in the cathedrals, the colleges and the monasteries. The man must either have no conscience, or not be in his right senses, who would hand over the government of such a people to a foreign prince, on the sole grounds of reforming their morals.

This bull, therefore, must be a forgery of some unknown impostor, and not the decree of Adrian, He was raised to the purple by Eugene the Third, and was colleague in that great dignity with Eugene's legate, John Papyro, a man of the strictest integrity, and praised in the highest terms by St. Bernard in his Epistles. Adrian could have easily ascertained that during the legatine mission of his colleague, Papyro, all the disorders of Ireland had been rectified. Moreover, he must have heard, if he had not actually seen with his eyes, the great works accomplished by St. Maelmaedhog; for it is natural to suppose that as both were members of the same Order of Canons Regular, the surviving brother would make some inquiries into the life of one who had but recently departed.

When the devils appear in the form of angels of light, to deceive men, they are always betrayed by the cloven foot or some other mark. The forgers of documents, in the same way, let something unwittingly escape them, which reveals the fraud. I have already given one instance. Here follows another, given by the concoctor of the bull.

Dr. Lynch then alludes to the Peter Pence clauses of the spurious Bull, and also to the allusion in the fictitious Bull concerning the supposed right conferred on the Pope over Ireland by reason of the alleged donation of Constantine, but as we have already alluded to both these phases of the question, we will pass on to where Dr. Lynch mentions the reasons which impelled King Henry II. to conceal the forged Bull for seventeen years:

But there are still more powerful objections against this bull than any of those which have been mentioned. And first, Baronius assures us that no date either of day or year is given in it, a circumstance which, of itself alone, is a certain ground of suspecting any document as a forgery, and which authorizes us to reject it as such. "A rescript (says Masuerus) which does not give its date, the day, the consul, and the year of our Lord, is invalid."

Moreover, this bull, when obtained by secret solicitations, was for a long time suppressed, for the writers state that it was given in 1155, but not published before the year 1172, as if the imprudence of obtaining it were to be prudently remedied by suppressing it. For second thoughts are best. Stolen goods are not exhibited publicly very soon. But Nicholas Trivetus, A. D., 1155, says that the Bull was not produced, because when "King Henry, in a parliament at Windsor, was deliberating with his barons on the conquest of Ireland, his mother, the empress, was opposed to the project, and its execution was therefore deferred to another time." So that it would appear this noble and virtuous lady, more humane than the king who demanded, more just than the Bishop who received, more merciful than the Pope who granted the bull, abhorred the execrable design; but when an opportunity offered after her death, the project was revived and the expedition undertaken. But as "a rescript is null, if the petitioner do not avail himself of it within a year," of what service could this grant be to king Henry who concealed it during seventeen years, without even availing himself of the rights which it corferred upon him?

Moreover, the author of the bull unconsciously represents a most virtuous Pope as trampling on the law of nature, on the laws of nations, and on all the laws of justice. For is it not a violation of all the dictates of all laws, to rob, not one man, but a whole nation, not of some trifling right, but of their country, their fortunes, and their lives, without hearing one word in their defence? Does the humblest official that administers justice, presume to adjudicate on a case without having heard the statements of both parties? Whoever decides after hearing one side only, "is unjust, though his judgment should be just."

The judge, who is influenced by favor and not by equity in his judgments, is not only branded among men with the foulest stigma of disgrace, but incurs, moreover, the damnation of his immortal soul. God himself says, "judge that which is just, whether he be one of your country or a foreigner." For who can look upon himself as the friend, when he assumes the character of the judge? Liberty is the dearest right of man; and whoever deprives him of it, and unjustly hands over princes, prelates and people to a foreign yoke, is excessively temerarious, and (to use the mildest phrase) unjust.

The concoctor of this bull, therefore, merits the most hearty execration for representing the character of a Pope in so odious a light. He represents him in the first place as having no title to be called an honest man; next, as a man who was swayed by his own interests, not by justice; then as condemning the innocent without a hearing; again as subverting that kingdom of Ireland, which had never before owned any foreign power; moreover, as the credulous dupe of whispering slanderers, the violator of the rights of immemorial possessions; the enemy of all laws; the most profligate scoffer at all religions; finally, the firebrand of execrable war, and the most odious propagator of burning hatred. See the load of ignominy which this vile scribe would heap upon the head of a Pontiff whose virtues were not a disgrace to his high station; calumniously representing him as trampling upon every principle of justice to make his prince sovereign lord of Ireland. He cared not in what odious colors this lying bull exhibited the Pope, if he attained his object, and gave the king of England some shadow of title to the Irish crown. He forgets the maxims of positive law, "That rescripts are invalid, which were either obtained on false grounds, or are opposed to the Divine law, to human positive law, or to the public good;" and also "that a rescript of the Pope, obtained by a layman, on any matter regarding the secular forum, can have no effect;" finally, "that a rescript is invalid, if obtained to the injury of a third person." After this exposure of the base arts by which this treacherous villian attempts to blast the character of an excellent Pontiff, we proceed to refute all his other quibbling.

But to clothe the nakedness of this story: Matthew of Westminster, who lived about 200 years later, borrowed some false plumage from his own imagination, for he was the first who said that a solemn embassy was dispatched by order of king Henry to Pope Adrian, then lately elected, to obtain this bull. Such is the general lot of stories, circulated among the vulgar; the farther they travel, the greater bulk and consistency they acquire. Matthew, seeing that this flagrantly fictitious bull had lived to so respectable an age, could not think of allowing it to go farther on its journey without giving it a retinue; and accordingly, without any warrant from the bull itself, or from any preceding writer, he draws upon his own creative powers. A common courier, bearing the bull from Adrian to Henry, was too vulgar a picture for the page of history, and accordingly Matthew metamorphoses him into a solemn embassy; but with his kind permission, the interval of so many centuries cannot be so easily bridged over by his mere authority, that we must credulously believe his word, without the support of a single writer from our own day, to the supposed date of the bull.

Dr. Lynch next alludes to the fabulous stories attributed to John of Salisbury in the interpolated chapter of his *Polycraticus*, which we have already reviewed extensively, so we will pass on to where the learned author of *Cambrensis Eversus* exposes in a most thorough manner the errors of Matthew of Paris:

Still drawing on his imagination, Matthew asserts "that the Pope empowered king Henry to enter Ireland by force of arms and subjugate it," though the bull expressly orders the reverse, "that the people of that land should receive Henry with honor, and venerate him as their lord." Thus, with consummate treachery, the Pope would publicly command the Irish to obey the Englishman, and encourage him privately to cut their throats. So with heartless barbarity he would order the Irish to embrace with open arms the man who pointed his sword at their heart; with horrible rigor he would rob of their native land a people guilty of none, or at least of trifling offences, and punish with the excruciating scourge a fault that at worst deserved the whip; in fine, he would repeal that law of nature, which tells a man to repel force by force. That law is not written, but born with us; we have not learned nor received it from others, nor read it in books; it is the dictate, the impulse, the cry of nature, to which we have not been schooled, but created, not influenced by others, but inspired: if your life is in danger from treachery, or from violence, whether of robbers or of enemies, all means of defence are justifiable. It is intolerable that Matthew should exhibit the Pope in colors of such varied malignity, and deprive Irishmen of the right even of the slave. What slave could brook those edicts of a Manlius or Phalaris, even from his master? Were he ordered, for no crime, to hold his throat for the murderer, would he not infallibly resist with all his might?

Tyranny of that kind was never known, under the mild government of the Popes, whose pious and learned delegates employed gentle and persevering persuasions, not violence and platoons, to civilize the hearts of men, lighting by admonition the path for voluntary obedience, not goading them against their will at the point of the sword. When the Apostles went forth to propagate the Faith, they were not allowed to carry even a staff; and can it be lawful for their successors in that sacred duty to force by arms some nameless sort of reformation on men eminently instructed in religion? Arms rather barbarize than civilize man; war destroys learning and law; levels cities, burns houses, devastates land, tramples the corn fields, begets murder, adultery, incest, rapes, and rapine; in a word, throws everything into disorder. A most contemptible fool the man must be, who first invented the story of the adoption by the Apostolic See of so preposterous a mode of reforming the morals of any nation: Christ addressing His Apostles said to them: "if they do not receive you, going forth, shake off the dust of your feet" at them. He does not say, gird on your swords, brandish your daggers, cast your javelins, in a word, make war on them.

St. Bernard addressed a work *De Consideratione*, to Pope Eugene, which Adrian no doubt perused attentively; it was then a new book and of course was eagerly sought for and read with avidity, especially as coming from so illustrious a man, and proposing to admonish Pope Eugene of the duties of his office, a point on which Adrian himself, as Harpsfeld informs us, was extremely solicitous. Adrian, moreover, had a singular respect for Eugene, by whom he had been raised to the episcopacy and appointed legate, and elevated to the College of the Cardinals; and moreover, Eugene had occupied the same Apostolic chair, immediately before Anastasius, Adrian's predecessor. Now, in this book, which must have had so many irresistible attractions for Adrian, he could read that "it is not domination, but Apostleship over the world that becomes the Vicars of Christ:" and also St. Leo, "that (Rome) held more extensive sway by the Divine religion than by earthly empire." Could he then allow himself to be carried so far from the line of his duty, as to let loose an army for the massacre of the Irish, at the very moment that his legates were laboriously and successfully discharging their duty in Ireland? Would he present an antidote in one hand, and the poisoned cup in the other? The virtuous Pope could not so far contemn the laws of prudence and justice as to arrogate to himself a power never claimed by any of his predecessors. Whenever nations were contaminated with any horrible crimes, the censures of the Church were always used before an appeal to arms, that they might be induced to repent by prayers and threats, rather than compelled by the eloquence of the sword. The charges of the accusers were heard in one ear; the defence of the accused in the other; both were not open to the former, both were not closed to the latter. Punishment was invariably preceded by admonition; nor were blemishes of a lighter nature ever punished by the ruin of a whole nation. The Apostles permitted the Jews to use those peculiar customs which were only gradually and insensibly eradicated. St. Gregorious writes to St. Augustinus, the Apostle of England, "what cannot be easily reformed must be tolerated; the Church must purge away some things by her fervor, tolerate others by her mildness, and overlook others by her prudence." St. Augustinus also asserts "that the very change of a custom however beneficial in itself, causes disorder by its novelty;" and St. Gregorius tells us "that they who wish to propagate the faith by severe methods, show that they love their own cause more than the cause of God." The forger of the bull intimates very plainly either that the Pope's understanding was wrapt in such a night of ignorance as not to know these things, or that his will was steeled by such depravity, that he knowingly and willingly dishonored his name, and damned his conscience by so execrable a crime. History and common sense clearly attest the falseness of such an inference. And hence, a bull which is vulnerable in so many points, evidently cannot have any authority. What has been already said appears of itself sufficient to refute it.

CHAPTER XXIII.

More Proofs of the Spurious Character of the Adrian and Alexander Bulls, from the "Cambrensis Eversus" of Dr. John Lynch.—That Eminent Scholar's Criticisms on the Alexander Forgery.

In the twenty-third chapter of his great work entitled *Cambrensis Eversus*, Dr. Lynch passes under review the singularly-worded document falsely attributed by some writers to Pope Alexander III. After giving the text of the document in question, the scholarly author we quote from says:

This Bull, which is grounded on the former, is, most undoubtedly, *equally devoid of authority*. I have many reasons for asserting that *both were forged by the same hand*, though, like the sources of the Nile, their paternity is yet a mystery. Be it observed in the first place, that of all the arguments already advanced against the former Bull, there is not one which does not apply with equal force to this, so that if anything appear incomplete in my reasoning here, its defects can be supplied from the preceding chapter. * * * * *

Can any man in his senses believe, that the Supreme pastor of the church would entrust the moral regeneration of Ireland, and the amelioration of her ecclesiastical discipline, to a king who surpassed William Rufus, Henry I., and King Stephen (immoral men, all, as I have shown), nay, all his predecessors and successors, by intemperately cherishing his great power, to assail and destroy and disgrace the dignity of the Church? A man who stood forth prominently as *the enemy of the Pope*, and strained all his might to nullify the laws and destroy the authority of the Apostolic See; who sacrilegiously ordered the ecclesiastical Orders of his kingdom to be dragged before lay tribunals, and exerted all his power to destroy every vestige of the ancient immunities of the ecclesiastical body?

Take up, one by one, his crimes against the Church, and with their proofs. The first sparks of his fury against her, burst forth in his burning hatred of St. Thomas, Archbishop of Canterbury. This was the black source of the evil. Taking the others in order, you have in the year 1163, the foundations of the contests laid at Westminster, the king fiercely insisting on the enactment of some unjust laws, most oppressive to the ecclesiastical Order, though introduced under the imposing title of ancient customs, which St. Thomas firmly resisted. In the year 1164, King Henry, according to Hoveden, issued a severe and execrable edict against Pope Alexander III., for it was in this year that he carried the constitutions of Clarendon, prohibiting obedience to the commands of the Roman Pontiff, and declaring all censures issued by him or St. Thomas, null and void, and entailing severe penalties. Baronius truly sketches the character of this king: "Henry excited a storm to overwhelm not only the Primate of Canterbury and the whole English Church, but to destroy the Holy Catholic Church herself, with Alexander her chief pastor, *who was the special object of his machinations.*"

What better witness could you have of the wickedness of King Henry than the Pope himself? He held the authority of the Apostolic See in such sovereign contempt, that he told the Cardinals sent to him by Alexander III, in 1169, "I care not for you or your excommunications; I value them no more than a single egg." To such a pitch of frenzy did he ascend at last, that he stands charged with the murder of St. Thomas, A. D. 1171, and became so odious to the Pope, "that the Pope would neither see nor hear the ambassadors whom he sent twice to clear himself of the murder of the martyr, Thomas, Archbishop of Canterbury. But the whole court of Rome cried out to the ambassadors, 'stop, stop, as if the very name of King Henry, their master, was an abomination in the ears of our Lord the Pope. So our Lord the Pope had immutably made up his mind, with the unanimous consent of his brethren, to issue a sentence of interdict on King Henry by name, and on his lands at this side of the sea, and to confirm that which had been issued against the Bishops."

But the ambassadors having sworn before the Pope and the Consistory, that the king would submit to whatever he decided in this matter, the Pope abstained from mentioning King Henry's name in the sentence, which however excommunicated those who aided, assisted or abetted the assassination.

Can any man imagine that the Pope who thus tacitly excommunicates King Henry, would publicly load him with his favors? Who could expect a foreign nation to be brought under the authority of the Pope, by a king who withdrew his own kingdom from that same authority? that he would make foreigners observe a law against which he himself had rebelled? that the seeds of virtue would be planted in a foreign soil by one who profligately abandoned himself to vice at home? In truth, the king indulged in loathsome excesses; he profaned the holiness of the marriage bed, by intercourse with paramours and abandoned women; but, far beyond all his excesses of this kind, was his unchaste solicitation some say, his violation of Adela, sister to Philip, King of France, and betrothed wife of his own son Richard. Nay, was it not believed that, after his divorce from his lawful wife, he intended to marry Adelaide, and if he had issue, to bastardize and disinherit the children of the former marriage! Certain it is, that by tergiversation and negotiation he deferred so long the marriage of his son Richard, that the Frenchman declared war against him, and that Richard conceived such an aversion for Adela, on account of that sinister suspicion, that he refused her hand, and married Berengaria, daughter to the King of Navarre."

Moreover, he allowed "his kinswoman Mary, daughter to King Stephen, the Abbess of the Nuns of Ramsey, to live as wife with Matthew, Count of Boulogne—a horrible precedent for posterity." Oaths were always on his lips. Nothing more common than to hear him swear "by the eyes of God." He is even charged with perjury more than once, "for having violated the last will of his father, Geoffrey, to which he had sworn, and another oath, thrice repeated, of going to the crusades." * * * * *

The forger of this Bull must have been deranged when he represented the Pope entrusting the moral reformation of any nation to a man blasted with such vices. The Pope could not so far forget himself as to give a remedy which would propagate rather than cure the disease, and make the cicatrized wounds gape afresh more hideously. A master of that character, instead of cleansing the blemishes of those placed under his tuition, would blacken them with his own hues As well might you entrust him with the office of moral reformer as fit a saddle on an ox. * * * * *

Would not Henry be a fitter instrument for alienating the Irish from the Pontiff, and preventing them from embracing his laws, than for winning them over to the Pope, and subduing them to his authority? *Had not himself rebelled against the Pope*, and trampled on his most solemn decisions? Were his unparalleled contumacy and dogged obstinacy to be rewarded, not punished, by the Pope? When the King applied for the honor of such an office, well may we address him in the words of Horatius:

"The courser asks a plough, the ox a saddle."

Or reproach him with Ovidius:

"Phaeton, great thy desires, and far beyond
Thy strength, the office which you seek."

The Popes never before commissioned, even persons who wore the royal diadem, to reform the savage morals of men, if they were not eminent for piety and virtue as well as for rank. And whoever undertook the responsibility, did not trust to an army to subdue the people whom they were to instruct, but used persuasion to conciliate them. Henry's services to the Church were not so signal as to excite the Pontiff to grant him a novel and unprecedented favor. On the contrary, the most rigorous ecclesiastical penalties were inflicted on him for his *injuries to the Church*, and especially for shedding *the innocent blood of St. Thomas*, which excited the indignation of the Pope more than of all the others. "For the first announcement of that murder struck such deep and bitter grief into the Pope's heart, that for eight days he never spoke even to his domestics; and strictly ordered that no Englishman should be admitted to his presence." Henry, no doubt, most bitterly repented the perpetration of this murder, but he does not appear to have ever so far recovered the good graces of the Pope as to get a grant of such extraordinary importance. The Pope "was a prudent man, eloquent, subtle, and profoundly learned in the sacred Scriptures, and in Divine and human laws. Very few of his predecessors were equal to him in learning," according to a contemporary author. Such a man, knowing well that the King's daily delinquencies must have engendered a propensity to evil, *would never confide to him the moral reformation of a whole nation.*

Of all the Bishops of England, Thomas alone adhered to the Pope; all consented publicly or tacitly to the iniquitous constitutions of Henry against the liberty of the Church. "So low were they fallen, that with the exception of the Archbishop, none openly opposed " How could the Pope find among such Prelates a person fit to bring any nation to the head of the Church, from which they were themselves cut off?

But an attempt to bind the Irish more firmly to the Pope was superfluous, because *they never separated from him.* All Orders in Ireland, lay and ecclesiastical, were unanimous in their zealous protestations of obedience, and in all things submissive to his will; his legates were promptly, unreservedly obeyed; the liberties of the Church were extended and confirmed by law, and the preservation of *all the rights of the Pope, whole and entire,* was the chief concern of the nation. Therefore, they that are in health need not a physician but they that are ill."

If a lawsuit arise regarding some little estate, or any property, however trifling, a judgment is never pronounced until both the claimants come forward and state their arguments, or, at least, through their own fault do not appear. This rule, invariably followed in matters of minor interest, should it be denied to the Irish in the most momentous of all? Liberty is "a thing beyond all price," the dearest treasure of man; so dear, that there is no evil, however great, which they would not encounter to preserve it. Yet this judgment annihilates the liberty of Irishmen, who are not aware of their trial, nor even summoned. They are doomed to be slaves in their own soil, before they are afforded an opportunity of confronting and refuting their accusers. War itself is more just in its rules; for an enemy sends a declaration of war before he draws the sword, and would deem himself disgraced if slaughter, burnings, devastation, and the other evils of war, were the first notification he sent to his surprised antagonist to meet him in the field.

In this judicial proceeding *the Irish were condemned without evidence*. For, contrary to the law of God and man, the enemy was sole witness and accuser. "In the mouth of two or three witnesses, every word may stand;" and therefore the laws decide that one witness is to be valued as if there were no witnesses. The laws also exclude from giving evidence a person of known partiality for one party. But all, save the wilfully blind, must perceive that *the author of the Bull was a partisan of his own countrymen, and a furious enemy to ours.*

Finally, every form and principle of law is violated by this judgment, which, by a heinous injustice, deprives the Irish of their kingdom, their liberty, and their property. In their case the maxims of law and right were set aside; their ruin was doomed to be consummated by force, and could they be blamed, if they strained all the energies of body and soul to resist it? "This has reason prescribed to the learned, and necessity to the barbarians, and custom to nations, and nature herself to the wild beast, that they should at all times, by all means, repel all violence from their body, from their head, from their life." For when argument is not a sufficient protection, there can be no injustice to appeal to arms. Such is the express doctrine of Cicero. "As there are two kinds of dispute one by argument, another by force, and as the former is peculiar to man, the latter to beasts, we must appeal to the latter if we cannot use the former. Ulpianus also approves the maxim of Cassius, "that it is lawful to repel force by force, and that the right is founded in nature." The same is expressed by Ovidius:

"Arms against arms to take all laws allow."

These Bulls, therefore, have no authority, because "whatever is done, contrary to law, ought to be regarded as null." * * *

The author of the Bull must therefore have been under some malignant influence when he sent forth this document as a trumpet blast to inflame men to rage, rapine, conflagration, devastation, murder, and the other ills of war, and to stimulate them, as Tertullianus says, "to treachery, savageness, injustice, the peculiar business of war." To make war on a people in order to give them laws, is the same as to use inhumanity and ferocity to produce humanity and gentleness. Law is silenced by the clash of arms. Antigonus senior, when storming some cities, laughed at a man who presented to him a treatise on justice, and Marius protested that, amidst the din of War, he could not hear the voice of Law. Even Pompeius himself, generally so modest, dared to say, "How can I think of law while I am in arms?"

Noble instruments, truly, for introducing virtue and more refined manners among any nation. Henry II., a man black with crime, and his armed followers, ferocious by nature, and by the example of their leader!

"The morals of our king infect us all.
Pliant as soldiers at the trumpet's call."

If rank shoots of immorality disfigured the Irish character, they should be lopped off by the pruning knife of erudition, not cloven down with the battle-axes of those savage sons of Mars.

The forger of this Bull, which has been put forth under the name of Pope Alexander, represents the character of the Irish in a more horrid light than they appear in the Bull attributed to Pope Adrian. The latter rather insinuates than directly asserts that some Irish customs were barbarous; the former styles them "Christians in name, but barbarians in reality," though it is a most undoubted fact that at this very period the efforts to reclaim and civilize them were never more zealous and successful." * * *

But now, to set before my reader what I have already frequently proved, in various places, how, I ask, could that nation be deficient in refinement of manners, where there was not a single extensive territory that had not several monasteries, and where every respective monastery had at least one learned man publicly dispensing the treasures of his knowledge? Each cathedral had its school open to all who wished to avail themselves of it; at this day there are thirty-one such churches in Ireland, and formerly the number was much greater. Moreover, there was at all times an immense concourse of scholars to the University of Ardmacha, and so great was it at one period, according to Florence McCarthy, that they reached the number of 7,000.

Thus we need not found the glory of Ireland exclusively on her primitive ages, "when she was the rich and verdant land of scholars—when her pastures, if I may so speak, were gemmed with the living flowers of learning, thick as the starry coruscations of the twinkling orbs around the pole ! ! !" Whence Eadfrid "imbibed Ambrosia ; where three times, in the course of about two years, he drank of the rich cream of wisdom, and feasted on the gemmed honeycomb of Irish learning : for great crowds and fleets of Britons went over to Ireland," as Adelm testifies in his letter to Eadfrid, the 13th in Ussher's Sylloge. Camden, page 730, adopts their authority: "In those days," he says, "our Anglo-Saxons flocked from all sides to Ireland as the mart of useful learning. Hence nothing is more common in our histories of the lives of holy men than "he was sent to Ireland for his education." And in the life of Sulgen, who flourished 600 years ago, we read, "Inspired with a love for study, he went, after the example of his fathers, to the Irish, so illustrious for their wonderful learning. From the Irish, the old English, our ancestors appear to have derived the form of our letters, which are the very same as those used in Ireland at the present day. Thus was Ireland abundantly stocked with eminent saints and brilliant scholars, at a time when the culture of useful learning was neglected and unknown throughout the Christian world." May we not justly apply to Ireland the lines of Buchanan :

"Thither, when war convulsed the Roman world,
The muses in their flight their wings unfurled;
Their only home ; whence to the shores of Gaul
Doctors and learned guides of youth recall
The oracles of Greek and Latin lore,"

CHAPTER XXIV.

Further Extracts from Father Lynch's "Cambrensis Eversus."—Ireland Always Loyal to Rome—Additional Testimony proving the Adrian and Alexander Bulls to be Entirely Spurious.

In his great work, "Cambrensis Eversus," Dr. Lynch makes the following important allusion to the forcible historical fact that —unlike England—Ireland never revolted against the dogmas of the Church or opposed the lawful Pontiff of Rome. On this point Dr. Lynch says:

"But let me resume once more the train of my argument. England has revolted more than once to anti-Popes ; Ireland has always faithfully clung to the true Pope. In England the clergy were sullied with the loathsome stain of impurity ; in Ireland they were pre-eminently distinguished for chastity. In England ecclesiastical discipline was shaken by the violent dissensions of the Bishops amongst themselves, and their disobedience to the higher authority, which compelled St. Thomas to launch against them the anathemas of the Church ; but in Ireland the discipline of the Church was strictly observed, the second order of the clergy assiduously attending the churches, both in reciting the divine offices, and observing the most rigid abstinence, while the Bishops held numerous synods, meeting and consulting together on the canons most conducive to the spiritual interests of their flocks, but never deciding on the affairs of greater moment without the authority of the Legate. To him, if to any man, must be attributed the refinement of morals which was wrought in Ireland, and not to King Henry, whom Cambrensis flatters in the following strain : "He was appointed by Heaven, King and Lord of Ireland. To that glorious King, the Church and kingdom of Ireland owe whatever peace or religious improvement they have yet enjoyed. For, before his arrival in Ireland, multifarious evils had constantly luxuriated there in all ages back, until his power and agency extirpated them for ever."

One would imagine, heaven save us, that this Henry was a god that dropped down from the clouds, with a "divine" commission, to reform the morals of Ireland by the mere breath of his spirit, and to fight the battles of the Lord like another Gideon or Baruc, or Sampson, or Jeptha, or David, or Samuel, or the Machabees. But Giraldus must allow us to remark, among a great many others, one very striking difference between Henry and these holy men ; that they "by faith conquered kingdoms," while he attempted to subdue Ireland by "the force of his own arm." They, placing their confidence in God alone, believed "that the success of war is not in the multitude of the army, but strength cometh from heaven." He, relying on his own strength, burst upon Ireland with the whole weight of his power: he landed in Ireland with 400 large ships, freighted with warlike men, and horses, and arms, and provisions—an estimate which is given by Walter of Coventry, not in numerals, but in express words, "the King," he says, "went with four hundred ships, full of armed men, to Ireland."

Nothing but loathsome flattery could have extolled, beyond all measure, and attributed even to God himself, an enterprise reeking with such ferocity; "but flatterers forget even the common meaning of words; make a present of another man's goods, it is liberality; be obstinate in wickedness, it is fortitude." In the same way, cowards, and loons, and misers, and wicked men of all sorts, are metamorphosed into heroes, and great souls, and generous hearts, and models of all virtue. So far from having a commission from heaven to oppress Ireland, he had none even from earth—that is, no human power had given to him any extraordinary authority to make war upon Ireland. That spurious Bull of Pope Adrian never saw the light, until it was shown to the Irish in the synod of Waterford many years after its supposed date, and, according to the English writers themselves, Henry had invaded Ireland before he obtained the Bull from Pope Alexander.

Both Bulls, I contend, must be pronounced spurious, for many reasons; but above all, because they condemned the Irish without a hearing, to forfeit their liberty and the homes of their fathers. No mortal man has a right to condemn any one without a hearing: the law of nature declares, "that innocence, if brought to trial, can be acquitted, but that guilt cannot be condemned without a trial." God himself appears to have revealed that law, for, when Adam and Eve had committed a manifest crime, He did not condemn them unheard. Neither did he wish to punish severely the notorious horrors of the inhabitants of Gomorrah, until he had witnessed them himself. "For," he says, "the cry of Sodom and Gomorrah is multiplied, and their sin has become exceedingly grievous. I will go down and see whether they have done according to the cry that is come to me, or whether it be not so, that I may know." Hence the first admonition of the Council of Lateran to judges is that they should not hastily hearken to accusations, but that after the example of God Himself, they should carefully examine them, before they pronounce the doom of the accused.

When the Pope had resolved to introduce solid reformation into Ireland, could he have so far forgotten the rules of prudence as to entrust the establishment of religious rites to a layman, rather than to some member of the ecclesiastical body whom he could select for the task? Is the helm of the ship entrusted to a ploughman, or the plough to the cobbler? No, let all men work at their own trade. It is the excellent advice of Horatius:

"The landsman fears the helm to guide;
  health's rules
Physicians teach; each trade knows its own
  tools."

He, forsooth, is to prescribe the best rules for celebrating or hearing Mass, "who, even during the short hour of the Sacrifice of the Sacred Host, was so oppressed by cares of state and of his crown, that even that short time was spent more in conversation and deliberation than in devotion." Surely, he was not sufficiently grounded in piety to undertake the religious reformation of others. I have clearly proved that he was so deeply tainted with vice, that you might as well expect to gather grapes from thorns, or figs from briars, as learn virtue from him. It is not my intention now to return to that subject, because stale repetition is always disagreeable. But if the Irish were delivered over to his care to be cleansed from their iniquities, it would be, to use a common saying, only throwing them from the limekiln into the coalpit.

There is no cleansing Giraldus from the guilt of flattery, when he said, "that the Church of Ireland owed to Henry alone whatever perfection it had attained." But more outrageous still was his assertion, "that whatever peace Ireland enjoyed was to be attributed to that King;" for, what is this but to say plainly that a man who convulsed a kingdom by the blast, or rather the tempests of war, had breathed over it the gentle zephyrs of peace. May we not apply here, with strict propriety, the words of Isaias: "Woe to you that call evil good, and good evil; that put darkness for light, and light for darkness; that put bitter for sweet, and sweet for bitter." Such is the natural bent of flatterers, to call the scoffer an agreeable man; the obscene talker, a jovial companion; the hot-tempered, brave; the miser, an economist; the spendthrift, munificent; the obstinate, persevering; in a word, dazzled by the false lustre of evil deeds, they veil their hideousness under the name of virtues. Though Henry were admirably qualified in every other respect, to confer on Ireland such vast blessings, both in religion and in peace, he had neither time nor leisure for the work, as he spent no more than six months in Ireland, and was employed more in evoking ferocious passions by his arms, than in instructing the nation.

For Diarmuid, King of Leinster, being guilty of adultery and rebellion, the Irish, in order to enforce the legal penalties of those crimes, took up arms against him, when all other means of repressing his audacity had failed. King Henry then came forward as the determined patron of adultery and rebellion, and did not only not crush the insolence of a man who trampled on the laws and spurned his lawful superiors, but even goaded him on in his career of vice by sending an army to his support. Is it not, then, plain that Henry inculcated no virtue in Ireland, but rather sowed vice broadcast; he established no new laws, but labored with all his might to abolish the good old laws of the land. Truly, it amazes me, that any man could have ever imagined Henry had the Pope's authority for such proceedings.

Though the proofs already advanced are more than sufficient to show that the Bulls of Adrian and Alexander are spurious, there remains yet one argument, which, in my humble judgment, places the question beyond the possibility of doubt. "Now John De Courcey," says Newbrigensis, gathering a valiant band of horse and foot, resolved to invade the province of Ireland, which was separated from Scotland by a narrow channel, and is called Ulster. But it so happened that Vivian, a very eloquent man, and Degate of the Apostolic See, had landed there from Scotland, and was received with every mark of respect, by the Kings and Bishops of that province. While he was stopping at Dun (Down), a city on the sea shore, news came to the Irish of the advance of the hostile army. They consulted the Legate as to what they should do in such a conjuncture, and he told them that they should fight for their country, and he gave them his blessing with hearty prayers for their success." But they were defeated, "and the city of Dun was taken." The Roman Legate, with his attendants, took refuge in a church that was famed for its relics of the saints; for he was a prudent man, and had procured letters from the King of the English to his governors in Ireland, to aid him by their authority in the discharge of his legatine functions among the barbarians. On the security of those letters he passed unmolested to Dublin, and by virtue of a commission, either from the King of England or our Lord the Pope, held a general council of the Irish Bishops and Abbots. But wishing to enforce too violently the observance of Roman custom, in a church of barbarian simplicity, the King's governors ordered him either to depart or to take part with them in the war. He did depart, loaded with Irish gold, which had been the grand object of his wishes."

Can any man imagine that such a minister either knew not or despised the orders of his master? Would he have come to Ireland without the order of the Pope, and utterly ignorant of the duties he was bound to inculcate among the Irish? If the Pope had appointed Henry Lord of Ireland, as the Papal Letter had ordered the Irish to obey Henry, why were not the Irish ordered to obey the words of his Legate, especially as Cardinal Vivian was the first Papal Legate that came to Ireland after the supreme dominion of Ireland had been conferred on Henry by the Pope. It was notorious that the Irish not only did not acknowledge, but opposed by arms, Henry's claims to their kingdom; and hence the principal duty of the Legate should have been to produce the Pope's Bull, and to restrain them within the bounds of duty, and curb their impetuosity by his exhortations. If the short interval of five years from the supposed Papal grant of the Crown of Ireland to King Henry had obliterated the Bull from his memory, it is amazing that the strife of arms did not rouse him from his lethargy and remind him of that important document. Would not so singular and unprecedented a power, conferred on a foreign prince without the knowledge of the victims themselves, challenge attention and excite wonder? This fact alone proves to demonstration that the Bull never existed; it was not produced at a conjuncture when there was not only occasion but even necessity for it; does the soldier let his sword rust in the scabbard when the army is on him?

* * * * * * * *

At all events, it is certain that King Henry either did not believe in the authenticity of the Bulls of Adrian and Alexander, or the validity of the claim which they purported to give to the sovereignty of Ireland. For we find him distrusting them, and laboring to extort from Pope Lucius, the Third, successor of Alexander, a grant similar to the preceding. Yet, though he had deserved well of Pope Lucius, and sent him a large sum of money in 1188, he was disappointed in his expectations. The Pope refused the request, probably, as well as we can conjecture, because, after an attentive examination of the whole affair, he discovered either that the Bulls had never been issued or that they were fraudulently obtained. Hence we find Henry still restless, from the conviction, perhaps, that the preceding Bulls had been unjustly procured, and were therefore invalid. Again, he applies to Urban III., the successor of Pope Lucius, and begs a new grant of the kingdom of Ireland. In the year 1185, Henry, King of England, sent his ambassadors to

Urban and obtained many favors, which had been sternly refused by Pope Lucius. One of the concessions was that he was empowered to have any of his sons crowned King of Ireland, and the Pope confirmed that right to him by a Bull, and sent to him, as a token of his will and approbation, a crown of peacock feathers wreathed with gold." As merchants of slender means cannot get goods on credit, but must pay down ready money, even so this writer has no more claims to the assent of his readers than what his authorities can command. Would it, I ask, have been more troublesome to give a copy of that Bull than to make this passing notice of it? Can there be any possible reason for suppressing it, but the conviction that it had not really been granted by the Pope? In the first year of his pontificate, before he was under the least obligation to Henry, could Urban be so indecorous, so flexible, as to grant thus readily what neither the most pressing solicitation nor the choicest favors could extract from his predecessor? Surely he could not take such liberty with the property of others, as to make a present of a whole kingdom to a foreigner, without even communicating his designs to the inhabitants or hearing their defense. Surely he would send some more respectable pledge of his liberality than a hunting cap of peacock's feathers, which would gird, with more propriety, the temples of some stage king in a theatre, than the head of a true and real monarch.

But what is the substance of this grant of the Pope? Henry is authorized to select any of his sons and have him crowned King of Ireland. Now the author himself assures us that Henry had already actually usurped that power. In the year 1177, "the King came to Oxford, and in a general assembly appointed his son John King of Ireland, with permission and authority of Pope Alexander." When the business was concluded, it was an odd time to ask permission to have it done. It was a mockery of authority. But such was Henry's habit, first to seize upon a territory and then to beg a grant of the same from the Pope. Thus he lands in Ireland at the head of an army, *before he published the Bull of Adrian, or obtained the Bull of Alexander;* proceeding in an inverted order, beginning where he should end. When war is over, succor is too late and useless; when a possession is secured, a grant of it is needless, a petition for the grant is a mockery. What crime more revolting than to make another man bear the infamy of your crime while you enjoy its fruit? To ask another to staunch the wound which your own hands have torn open, and load him with the execration due to your own guilt?

One of the most powerful arguments, perhaps, against the authenticity of these Bulls of Adrian and Alexander is, that the editors, who have used all possible diligence to give a complete edition of the Bulls, *passed them over with contempt, and never inserted them in their collections*. They could not dream of registering such spurious bantlings, so unbecoming the solemn dignity of the Pope among the legitimate emanations from the Apostolical See. These editors were like the eagles which are said to know their young by the following ordeal: The parent bird takes the fledgling in its talons and holds it against the rays of the sun. If the eaglet gazes at it steadily it is acknowledged legitimate, but if the eye blenches, "the talon opens and the spurious pretender is dropped to the earth." Another excellent reason for doubting the authenticity of the same Bulls, is the confession of Giraldus himself, who appears to doubt their validity, by introducing other princes to make good by their assent the Papal grant of the sovereignty of Ireland to Henry II. "There was, moreover," he falsely says, "the authoritative sanction of the Popes and of all the princes and primates of Christendom." Thus the power of giving a ruler to Ireland, which Giraldus had at first represented as the exclusive prerogative of the Pope, is now divided among the emperor and foreign kings and primates. Wretched, indeed, must have been the condition of the Irish, who had as many masters to obey as there were princes and primates in Europe, though "no man can serve two masters, for he will either hate the one and love the other, or sustain the one and despise the other."

But what friendship could foreign princes have for Henry when his own sons hated and took up arms against him, and if they had no friendship for him how could they delegate to him their authority over Ireland? I am at loss to know what inducements primates could have to bestow any favor on a man who had murdered one of their own Order, the primate of England, St. Thomas, Archbishop of Canterbury. Could foreigners expect favors from him who was savagely cruel to his countrymen? It was a silly dream of Giraldus to give so many colleagues to the Pope in the supreme dominion of Ireland. The greater the number of colleagues in that supreme dominion the less the power of the Pope, because the princes and primates of all Christendom are represented as coequal in power to the Pope in disposing of the sovereignty of Ireland. Nay, this very attempt to strengthen Henry's authority over Ireland utterly destroys it, for as the princes or primates never claimed the least power over Ireland, their colleague the Pope ought not to have assumed it.

But I ask, in the first place, did these princes and primates of all Christendom assemble in general conclave to make a present of the kingdom of Ireland to King Henry? Or were they solicited individually to ratify this grant to King Henry? Synodical act, or private letters of the kind I have never been able to discover, and the word of Giraldus, if not supported by authorities, is not a very safe ground of certainty. Moreover, Maurice Regan, retainer and interpreter of Diarmaid, King of Leinster, who first brought the English to Ireland, has left us a detailed account of the events of his own time, but never makes any allusion to those supposed bulls of Adrian and Alexander. Now, a man of ordinary judgment must find it very difficult to believe that a writer who has given minute details of comparatively trifling matters would have passed over in silence an affair of momentous interest, when the intrinsic importance of the documents and even the very names of the Popes should have been a powerful inducement to bring their bulls from their obscurity into the light of day. Such documents could not escape the notice of a writer even of ordinary diligence, who undertook to record the current events of Irish history.

The forgery of the two Bulls was considerably facilitated by the previous exploits of others in the same work of deception. Thus, the Bull of Pope Honorius, purporting to be a grant made to Cambridge, is considered by many to be apocryphal. Harpsfield gives the following opinion regarding it: " Without presuming to pronounce a positive decision, or dispue the wiser judgment of others, I cannot extricate myself fully from doubts of various kinds, arising from chronological difficulties. It is, if not impossible, at least exceedingly difficult to reconcile these statements, with a history of undoubted authority, and composed nearly at the same time by the venerable Beda, who states that after this period a school for boys was founded by Sigebert at East Anglia on the Kentish model, and that masters and professors were brought there from Kent; but above all, I cannot reconcile it with the chronology and events of the reign of Honorius. For, can any one believe that theological studies were so flourishing, or that either Archbishops or Bishops had any authority in a territory then governed by Pagan Saxons! Or that Honorius himself and the said son of Petronius, of consular rank, could have studied in Cambridge in those days? I need not observe, moreover, that the words, "when I was in the University in minor orders, were, if I do not mistake, unknown in that sense during that century. I omit other questions which perplex me on this intricate and slippery topic. Others I fervently hope may at length, perhaps succeed, in clearing them up." This Bull is published in the "Antiquities of Cambridge" (lib. 1, p. 75); but it is impugned by Brienne Twine and completely refuted. The Bulls of Eugene IV. and Sergius I. to the same Cambridge are admitted to be spurious also. Twine refutes both of them. Spelman also proves, conclusively, that a Bull purporting to be a grant of certain privileges to the monks of Canterbury, by St. Augustine of Canterbury, is spurious. Again, Gervase, at the year 1181, writes "that the Augustinian monks brought forward several rare and suspicious documents." Thus, if the author of the forged Bulls of Adrian and Alexander can be defended by precedent, it were easy to collect and scrape together a great number of forged and surreptitious Bulls, to mitigate, in some measure, the pain of his guilt.

CHAPTER XXV.

Profound Reverence of the Irish People for the Vicar of Christ. — Nearly Every Nation in Europe placed under the Ban of the Church except Ireland.

In continuing his argument in order to prove the spurious character of the Adrian and Alexander Bulls, Dr. Lynch thus brings forth the stern fact that so far from Ireland being in a state of insubordination alluded to by the fictitious Bull attributed to Pope Alexander III., that Island of Saints was the only nation in Europe which was faithful to the Holy Father and loyal to the Catholic faith in the dark days which tried men's souls:

It has ever been the custom of Holy Mother Church to admonish her offending children before she subjects them to any severe penalty, and to endeavor to deter them by threats from the commission of crime, before she applied severe remedies. Thus Adrian II. threatened Charles the Bald with excommunication for attempting to deprive Louis, son of the deceased Emperor Lothaire, of his crown; and in the same way John VII. threatened Charles the Fat, if he did not restore the property of a certain monastery. When Alphonsus, King of Spain, was about to marry the relation of his wife, Gregorius VII. ordered a threat of excommunication to be pronounced against him, Many similar examples of the lenity of Popes in punishing the guilty could be produced, but I omit them at present for brevity's sake.

Is it possible that so kind a mother would have departed from her constant course of mercy to crush Ireland by her severity, and involve the innocent in ruin, without the slightest intimation of the impending woes? The horrors of the punishment would press heavily on Ireland if she had been openly convicted of some heinous crimes. The just punishment of crime must be borne with cheerfulness and fortitude.

"Pain on the guiltless to inflict is pain."

But how excruciating must have been the agony of being condemned, absent and unheard, when the Roman laws themselves enacted that no sentence should be pronounced on any person in his absence, and that if pronounced it should be invalid. The senate even decreed that no judgment should be pronounced on King Phillippus in his absence. In fine, St. Augustinus reproves Secundus, Primate of Tigisitan, for not preventing persons from being condemned in their absence.

That Ireland was never degraded by crimes of an atrocious die appears from this single fact, that while all other Catholic kingdoms were, at some time or other, laid under excommunication or interdict by the Pope, according to the nature of their offences, Ireland alone never incurred his ecclesiastical censures.

Let us begin with Scotland, as it is the nearest neighbor of Ireland. In the year 1186, William, King of Scotland, obstinately opposed Pope Alexander III., by not only preventing John, the lawfully appointed Bishop of St. Andrews, from taking possession of his See, but even by expelling him from his kingdom. He appointed his own chaplain, Hugh, and then placed him by force of arms in the See of St. Andrews, whereby the Pope was so deeply offended that he excommunicated the King and laid his kingdom under an interdict. Again, in the year 1216, "Swalo, the Pope's legate, launched the final bolts of the Church against Alexander II., and laid the kingdom of Scotland under interdict until the injuries inflicted on England were repaired, and Carlisle restored to the English, from whom it had lately been taken." In the year 1318, "the Cardinal legates fulminated the thunders of the Church against Robert, King of Scotland, and laid his whole kingdom under interdict, because he violated his treaties and waged forbidden war against Edward, King of England."

Passing now to England, we find it more than once visited with the same punishment. "Thus, about the year 905, the Roman Pontiff laid an interdict on Edward the Elder, on account of some flagrant disorders in ecclesiastical discipline in the western parts of the kingdom. And Eugenius III., quashing every obstacle from appeal, ordered the sentence of interdict to be pronounced, by the authority of the Pope, on the land of King Stephen." Innocent III. visited King John with a similar punishment, so that all England was under an interdict during six years and fourteen weeks, the conventual churches alone being allowed to have the sacred mysteries celebrated once only in the week, and even then with doors closed. During that time "the bodies of the dead were carried out from the cities and towns and buried like dogs in the bye-ways and ditches, without prayers or the ministry of the clergy."

Let us go now from England to Germany, where Lothaire, Emperor and King, was excommunicated by Nicolas the First for associating Veldreda, a concubine, with his lawful wife Therberga. King Robert also was excommunicated by Gregorius V. for marrying a relative of his mother, within the degrees of affinity. So completely was he abandoned by all his friends, that only two poor slaves remained with him to serve his table; and yet so loathsome was even that simple duty, that they burned all the vessels in which the king's meat and drink was served up. When Philippus the First repudiated his lawful wife Bertha, and took Bertrada his concubine to wife, he was excommunicated by Pope Urban II. Ivo, Cardinal legate of Innocent II., laid the kingdom of France under interdict, because Rudolph, Count of Verdun, divorced his wife and married a sister of the Queen, and because Louis VII. contumaciously opposed the orders of the Sovereign Pontiff. These examples, however, were not sufficient to deter Philippus Augustus from repudiating his lawful Queen Gereberga, and forming a criminal connection with Agnes; but to punish that crime, "the whole territory of the King of France," says Baronius. "was laid under the strictest interdict, so that all the churches were closed and the bodies of the dead were never buried in cemeteries, but left rotting in all quarters of the earth." France lay during eight months under this interdict, and then, as had already happened, under Philippus the First, all the public documents and deeds were dated, as I have heard, in the reign of Christ.

Spain itself has not been exempt from these visitations. When Innocent III. was informed that the King of Leon had married his cousin, the daughter of the King of Portugal, he excommunicated the incestuous couple and the King of Portugal himself, and laid their kingdoms under an interdict. Again, Sanchez, King of Portugal, having married his daughter Tarsia to his nephew Adelphonso, King of Gallicia, Celestinus III., excommunicated Adelphonsus, and laid his kingdom under interdict until after a lapse of five years, during which three sons were born to him; he at last dismissed her. Portugal was under an interdict during full twelve years for no other reason than the repudiation of his wife by King Alphonsus, and his cohabiting with a concubine. The kingdom of Navarre, also, was interdicted during one year by Pope Julius II.

Poland also suffered under these penalties. Gregorius VII. placed the whole province of Gneson, the metropolitan of Cracow, under a general interdict on account of the murder of St. Stanislaus, and deprived King Boleslaus of all regal honors and authority. Celestinus III. also anathematized Leopold, Duke of Austria, for disobedience and subjected his territory to interdict. Need I mention the Emperors of Germany, Henry III., Henry IV., Frederic II., and Henry V., who were often smitten with the thunders of the Church, and Henry III. and Frederic, who were, moreover, deposed from their Imperial thrones by the Popes, and beheld all their subjects absolved from that oath of allegiance which had once bound the people religously to their masters.

Even in Italy the city of Naples was laid under anathema by Adrian II. Rome herself, the head of cities, suffered a similar punishment for wounding a Cardinal; and Florence, also, for hanging a Bishop. Rome was punished by Alexander III.; Florence by Sixtus IV. But long before that period St. Catherine of Sienna had prevailed upon Gregorius XI. to relieve the Florentines from the sentence of interdict. Thus, to sum up in one word, every country in Europe was punished by those scourges for some heinous crime. Ireland alone never compelled the Pope to wield the spiritual sword against her, for she has at all times devotedly persisted in her obedience to him, and never raised her own rebellious will against his authority. Neither were her kings ever contaminated by crimes heinous enough to excite the indignation of the Pope to excommunicate them and to absolve their subjects from the oath of allegiance. * * * * *

When heresy first acquired its political ascendancy in Ireland there was no point of Catholic doctrine for which the Irish were more persecuted than for their constant profession that the Pope was the Supreme Visible Ruler of the Church Militant, and for their unflinching refusal to take the oath of the King's ecclesiastical supremacy, though the heretics exhausted all the appliances of force and persuasion to compel them to renounce the authority of the Pope.

In Ireland, the cities and municipalities were authorized by an ancient privilege conferred on them by the King, to elect from among their citizens or burgesses a magistrate to watch over the common interests. But if he presumed to enter on his office without having previously taken the oath of supremacy he was carried off to Dublin and lodged in prison, and when he persisted that the Pope was the Supreme Visible Head of the Church Militant, he was detained in prison until he abdicated his office and was condemned to a fine, which generally was greater than all his wealth.

Students of our common law, after great labor and enormous expense incurred in the study of law, were not only debarred from ever sitting as judges in the courts and tribunals, but were, moreover, prevented from pleading even in civil or criminal cases, because they firmly refused to renounce the Pope and take the oath of the King's ecclesiastical supremacy. This unanimity in maintaining the supremacy of the Pope had long since taken firm hold of the souls of the Irish. Even at the very birth of the English heresy, when King Henry VIII. first revolted from the authority of the Pope, John Travers, an Irishman and Doctor of Divinity, published a work strenuously advocating the supremacy of the Pope over the Church. When asked by his judges who was the author of the book, he held out the thumb, index and middle finger of his right hand before the judges, "these fingers," he nobly avowed, "wrote that book, and I shall never forget the labor it cost me." For this heroic deed his unjust judges ordered his right hand to be cut off and cast into the fire, but the three fingers were taken out unhurt from the flames and persevered afterwards by the Catholics with religious veneration.

What need of more ? Of all the countries in Europe subject to heretical kings, there is not one in which a greater number of subjects have preserved in the old faith, and in obedience to the Sovereign Pontiff, than in Ireland. Cardinal Bentivoglio has truly observed, "that the Irish would seem to have sucked in the Catholic faith with their mother's milk." In other countries smitten with heresy the majority followed the example of the King or other governing power of the state and renounced the old faith and the supremacy of the Pope. But in Ireland, I do not hesitate to assert, that not the tenth, nor the hundredth, no nor the thousandth part revolted from the faith of their fathers to the camp of the heretics. Orlandinus might say, with perfect truth, "that the Irish had preserved in heart and soul the Catholic faith in all its integrity, and the most devoted obedience to the Roman Pontiff." And Bozius also, "as far as we can judge from history, not one of all the northern nations has been more constant in the profession of the one faith." May I not then apply to the Irish what Virgilius sang regarding the Romans :

"Let others better mould the running mass
Of metals, and inform the breathing brass ;
And soften into flesh a marble face ;
Plead better at the bar : describe the skies,
And when the stars descend, and when they rise.
But, Erin, be it thine, mark well ! I pray,
Thy faith to hold, Christ's vicar to obey."

The following passage of the author of the Analecta may be appropriately introduced here. "Though the authority of the Pope has been long since proscribed and condemned by all the public authorities and tribunals, and by the laws of the land, no violence could extinguish, nor fear obliterate, the ardent attachment to the Vicar of Christ, which is deeply imprinted on the hearts of these people. Laws, discipline, and forms of government have been changed, but wherever they interfered with religion no violence or artifice could induce the people to adopt them. Knavery was employed to deceive, seduction to allure, insult to provoke, intrigue to solicit, threats to terrify, rewards to conciliate. They oppress and they promise, they chalk out their approach and seize on the avenues ; they work both the mine and the battery ; all machines are plied, but all in vain ; they do not advance one inch ; we gain more on them than they on us."

Truly hath Andrew Thevet asserted "that the people of Ireland have maintained the Christian religion in all its integrity in despite of the English, who exerted all their strength to prevent and involve them in their own execrable sect. When the supreme council of the Catholics of Ireland refused obedience to the censures of the Pope's Nuncio in the year 1648, the vast majority of the Irish adhered to him and left but few supporters to the council. The common people were inflamed with so ardent a love of the Pope, that they deemed it an inexplicable crime not to obey the orders of his minister. Tumults frequently burst forth like a torrent in all quarters, and contentions were rife in public and private. The chief men of the confederate Catholics themselves maintained the principle, for they appealed to the Pope himself. Thus all orders have been at all times unanimous in Ireland in their profound reverence and obedience to the supreme authority of the Pope.

CHAPTER XXVI.

Ireland's Aid to Rome in the Propagation of the Faith.—Irish Saints and Apostolic Missionaries who Helped to Spread Christianity Throughout Europe.

In order to illustrate the unity which existed between Rome and Ireland throughout all ages, from the time of St. Patrick down to the twelfth century, Dr. Lynch presented the following important historical facts to his readers, and as the glory of Ireland is one of the greatest objects of this work, we present the following pages from *Cambrensis Eversus* as valuable testimony that both Rome and Ireland were a unit in the true Faith, notwithstanding the slurs cast upon Ireland by the English forger of the Adrian and Alexander Bulls. On this interesting historical subject Father Lynch says:

But it was not in our times alone, and in those of our fathers and grandfathers, that the Irish clung with invincible fidelity to the Pope; they evinced, in ancient times, the same devoted attachment to the Catholic faith and to the head of the Church. "The reverence of the Irish," says Lombard, "for the authority of the Apostolic See, so far transcends their reverence for all other powers and dignities, that they bow to its authority, not only in ecclesiastical but even in temporal affairs." If what Polydorous relates be true, "the Irish subjected themselves and all their rights to the dominion of the Apostolic See, and invariably professed that the Pope was their sole Lord from the time that the Christian religion was first established among them." Sanders repeats the same assertion in nearly the same words, "that they never admitted any other supreme Lord but the Pope." Keating refers this acknowledgment of the temporal sovereignty of the Pope to a later period, when Donnchadh O'Briain, son of Brian Borumha, and King of Ireland according to him, but of Munster only according to all others, and even deposed from that throne in 1604, went on a pilgrimage to Rome, and, with the consent of all his chieftains, surrendered the supreme dominion of Ireland into the hands of the Pope.

Though there are strong reasons to doubt the accuracy of those statements of Polydorous, Sanders and Keating, and powerful arguments to prove that the Irish never surrendered the political supremacy of their country to the Pope, it is an undoubted an incontrovertible fact that, from the moment the Irish received the faith, all their principles in religious affairs were subordinate to the power of the Pope; and the great pillars of our Church in all ages and conjunctures sought in Rome direction and authority for all their arrangements in ecclesiastical concerns. On the first dawn of the Christian faith, St. Mansuetus, an Irishman, went to Rome in the year 66, and met St. Peter, Prince of the Apostles, by whom, according to Saussaye, "he was baptized in the saving waters, and renouncing his old Gentile name, with the old man, took the name Mansuetus, as a type of the lamblike gentleness of his character. He was then sent by St. Peter to enlighten with the rays of divine faith the city of Tulle in Lorrain." St. Kiaran, Bishop of Saighir, having heard in the year 382 of the fame of the Christian religion in Rome, left Ireland and went to that city, where he was baptized and instructed in the faith of Christ, and remained there twenty years studying the Sacred Scriptures, collecting its different books, and acquiring a full knowledge of all the details of ecclesiastical discipline, until he was consecrated Bishop."

Again, "St. Hilarius, seeing the great holiness of St. Ailbhe, sent him to our Lord the Pope to be consecrated Bishop. He was most graciously welcomed by the Holy Pontiff, and remained with him one year and fifty days." Now, there came at the same time 50 other holy men after St. Ailbhe from Ireland to Rome, and when they met the Pope and St. Ailbhe, the Pope appointed a monastery for themselves and placed them under the government of St. Ailbhe. Many of them were homonymous; thus, 12 Colmanns, 12 Caoimhghins, 12 Fintans." This residence of St. Ailbhe and his associates at Rome is referred by Ussher to the year 397.

About the same time, also, St. Declan, as his life informs us, conceived the design of going to Rome to learn the Canons of the Church and to receive permission from the Apostolic See to preach, and also to introduce the Ritual and rules of the Roman Church. Now, when he and his holy companions arrived in Rome, the Pope received him with great demonstrations of joy and proclaimed to the Roman people his high descent and his great virtue, so that the holy deacon was exceedingly honored and beloved by the clergy and people of Rome.

St. Scizin also attended the scripture schools in Rome in the year 435, and was afterwards consecrated Bishop by the apostolical authority of Celestinus the First, and appointed to accompany St. Patrick in his Irish mission.

St. Ibar afterwards went to Rome, accompanied by his disciple St. Abban, who, on three subsequent occasions, made the same pilgrimage in honor of Christ. St. Enda also went to Rome about the year 461, and Scothin, a disciple of St. David (who died in the year 550) having, on one occasion, some urgent business to be settled at Rome, is said to have journeyed, or rather to have been translated thither, in one day from Ireland, and after dispatching all his business, to have returned to Ireland in the next.

St. Cassan, a Bishop, who flourished about the year 465, took some companions with him to Rome, "to imbibe true learning and piety at the fountain head."

St. Mochta, a Bishop, "was engaged in his sacred studies in Rome in the year 480. He was a favorite of God and man, every day surpassing himself in wisdom and edifying others by word and example. Disciples crowded around him, who imbibed from his holy soul the salutary waters of wisdom, and became perfect men in faith, word and work. His extensive erudition, adorned as it was by a life of unsullied purity, having induced the Pope to exalt him to the episcopal rank, he returned to his own country with the authority and blessing of the Pontiff, accompanied by twelve associates "

In the year 522, St. Nennidh, went to Rome to visit the tombs of the apostles, and during his pilgrimage great was his fasting, and greater still his abstinence from all sin. St. Senanus also, who by some is supposed to be the Archbishop of Ardmacha, " went to Rome to visit the tombs of the apostles. He flourished about the year 544. Nearly at the same period St. Carthac the Elder also visited Rome."

St. Barr, Bishop, with twelve companions, amongst whom were St. Eulogius and St. Maidoc, of Fearna-mor (Ferna), having gone on a pilgrimage about this time to Britain, proceeded thence accompanied by St. David of Menavia, "on a pilgrimage to Rome to visit the tomb of the apostles.".

St. Fridian or Finnan, "visited the tomb of the apostles in 555." His learning and piety, his high rank and singular beauty of person, secured for him an honorable reception from Pope Pelagius with whom he remained during three months, having in that short space of time made himself perfect master of the ecclesiastical and apostolical discipline: for he was a man of brilliant genius. Having received, according to the usual custom, the Pope's blessing, he returned to his own country.

About the year 599, St. Dagan, Abbot, but afterwards Bishop, "going on a pilgrimage to Rome, brought with him the rule which St. Molua had prescribed and dictated for his monks. When Pope St. Gregorius read that rule he said before all present. 'the Saint that composed that rule made a bulwark around his monks that raised them to heaven.' So Pope St. Gregorius sent his prayers and his blessing to St. Molua."

In the year 628, St. Laisrean "went to Rome with fifty holy men, where he was ordained and consecrated Bishop by the Pope and appointed apostolical legate on his return to Ireland." For when the Paschal controversy was discussed in the synod of Leith-ghlinn (Leighlin), and could not easily be decided, " it was decreed,' as Cumin relates, " by our seniors, according to the command, that if any difference arise between cause and cause, and opinions vary between leprosy and no leprosy, they should go to the place which the Lord hath chosen ;" and if the cause was one of the *causæ majores*, that it should be referred to the head of cities according to the synodical canon.' We, accordingly, sent men of tried wisdom and humility, who, by the favor of God, had a prosperous journey. and some of them arriving in the city of Rome, returned thence to us in the third year." St. Laisrean was the principal of those legates. About the year 630, St. Caidoc renounced, with St. Richarius, the vanity of the world and retired to Rome. St. Monon retired thither also about the same period. In the year 648, "the Pope earnestly entreated St. Fursa to remain at Rome and consent to be enrolled among the lords of the Roman court (to use the old words of the legend) that is, the College of Cardinals. But no importunities could induce him to accept the offer. The Pope then invested him with all his authority, and gave him different relics of saints and a pastoral staff, resembling in shape the pilgrim's staff, which had been used by several Popes before himself, and also consecrated him and St. Foilan Bishops." Molanus also records of St. Foilan, "that he went to Rome to obtain the blessing of the Pope for the conversion of the infidels."

St. Indracht, son of the King of Ireland, "went to Rome with nine companions, but returning thence in the year 678, was martyred. St. Kilian also abstained from preaching the Word of God until he had presented himself to Pope Conon in Rome in the year 686, in order to receive from the See of Rome the entire deposit of Christian doctrine and authority to preach it."

If I allowed myself to detail at length the intercourse of the Irish with Rome in former ages, my page would swell to unreasonable limits and exhaust my power of language, though not the subject itself. Such prolixity would also, no doubt, weary the patience of my reader. To sum up then in a few words ; no dissension on religious matters ever arose in Ireland which was not instantly referred to Rome for adjudication. From Rome Ireland had her precepts of morality and her oracles of faith. Rome was the mother, Ireland the daughter; Rome the head, Ireland the member. From Rome the fountain head of religion, Ireland undoubtedly derived, and with her whole soul imbibed her faith. In doubtful matters the Pope was ever the arbiter of the Irish; in things certain, their master ; in ecclesiastical matters, their head ; in temporals, their defender; in all things their judge ; in every thing their adviser ; their oracle in doubt, their bulwark in the hour of danger. Some hastened to Rome to indulge their fervor at the tomb of the apostles ; others to lay their homage at the feet of the Pope, and others to obtain the necessary sanction of his authority for the discharge of their functions. * * *

All the world knows that the Irish went over, not one by one, in crowds, to Britain, to Gaul, to Belgium, and to Germany, to convert the inhabitants of those regions to the Christian religion, and bring them under the obedience of the Roman Pontiff. A signal testimony to this fact is found in the letter of Eric of Auxerre to Charles the Bald. "Need I mention Ireland ; she, despising the dangers of the deep, emigrates to our shores, with almost the entire host of her philosophers; the most eminent amongst them become voluntary exiles, to minister to the wishes of our most wise Solomon." Such, also, is the testimony of St. Bernard, "from Ireland, as from an overflowing stream, crowds of holy men descended on foreign nations." Walfridus Strabo says, "that the habit of emigrating had become a second nature to the Scoti," namely, the Irish, as I have already proved ; hence the just observation of Osborne, that the habit of emigrating "had taken the strongest hold of the Irish. For what the piety of other nations has made a habit, they have changed from habit into nature." Those holy emigrants of the Irish were distinguished by a peculiarity, never, or but very seldom found among other nations.

As soon as it became known that any eminent Monk had resolved to undertake one of these sacred expeditions, twelve men of the same order placed themselves under his command, and were selected to accompany him ; a custom probably introduced by St. Patrick, who had been ably supported by twelve chosen associates in converting the Irish from the darkness of paganism to the light of the true Faith. St. Rioch, nephew of St. Patrick, and walking in his footsteps, was attended in his sacred mission to foreign tribes and regions by twelve colleagues of his own order ; and when St. Rupert, who had been baptized by a nephew of St. Patrick, apostle of Ireland, departed to draw down the fertilizing dews of true religion on pagan Bavaria, twelve faithful companions shared the perils and labors of his journey and mission. St. Finnian, Bishop of Cluain-irard, selected twelve from the thronged college of his disciples, to devote them, in a special manner, to establish and to animate the principles of the Christian religion among the Irish ; and Columba was accompanied in his apostolic mission to Scotland by twelve Monks. Twelve followed St. Finnbar in his pilgrimage beyond the seas, and twelve St. Maidoc, Bishop of Fearna-mor, in one of his foreign missions. St. Colman Finn was never seen without his college of twelve disciples. When the ceaseless eruptions of foreign enemies, or the negligence of the Bishops had well nigh extinguished the virtue of religion in Gaul, and left nothing but the Christian faith—when the medicine of penance and the love of mortification were found nowhere, or but with a few, "then," says Jonas, "St. Columbanus descended on Gaul, supported by twelve associates, to arouse her from her torpor, and to enlighten her sons with the beams of the most exalted piety." Twelve disciples followed St. Eloquius from Ireland to illumine the Belgians with the rays of faith ; twelve accompanied St. Willibrord from Ireland to Germany, the pilgrimage and labors of St. Farannan, in Belgium, were shared by twelve faithful Brothers of the cowl ; and the same number were fellow-exiles with St. Maccallann. Perhaps the reason, why the Irish clung with such invincible attachment to this custom, was the number of the apostles chosen by our Saviour, and the same number of disciples appointed by the Apostolic See to accompany Palladius to Ireland.

But it was not in companies of twelve, alone, that great men went forth from Ireland to plant or to revive sound doctrine and discipline in foreign lands. Bodies, far more numerous, are also mentioned. St. Albert was accompanied by nineteen disciples. Sixty accompanied St. Brendan in his voyage in search of the land of promise. St. Guigner, son of the King of Ireland, passed over to Britain, with a noble band of 777 associates; and St. Blaithmac, son of the King of Ireland, was followed thither by a good number of Monks. St Donnanus led away from his country fifty-two associates. Twenty-four disciples of St. Ailbhe were sent by him to propagate the faith in Iceland. St. Emilius brought to the aid of St. Fursa at Lagny, a large body of their countrymen, and gave him wonderful aid in instilling the grace of God into the souls of men. St. Sezin was accompanied by seventy disciples to Bretagne, and Alsace welcomed St. Florentius, with Arbogastus, Theodatus, and Hildulph. Irish Saints are also found toiling in strange lands, in smaller numbers, and fertilizing them abundantly with the dew of their faith and of their virtues. In Italy there were Donatus of Fiesole, Andrew, and his sister, St. Brighid of Opaca; in Picardy, SS. Caidoc and Fricorius, otherwise Adrian; at Rhemess, SS. Gibrian, Tressan, Helen, Abram, German, Veran, Petroan, Promptia, Possenna, and Truda; at Paris, hence they were styled by posterity the twelve apostles of Ireland. St. Claude, Clement, and John; among the Morini (of Boulogne), SS. Vulgan, Kilian, and Obod; in the territory of Beauvais, SS. Maura and Brighid, virgins and martyrs, and their brothers Hyspad; at Fusciria, SS. Mathilda, virgin, and her brother Alexander. In Kleggon, a district in Germany, St. Northberga, with Sista, and nine others of her children. At Ratisbon, SS. Marian, John, Candidus, Clement, Murcherdach, Magnoald, and Isaac. In Austrasia, SS. Kilian, Cohonatus, and Totnan; and St. Cathro and his associates at Walcedor. These devoted their lives to the instruction of the people, and were celebrated for the miraculous favors obtained by their intercession.

Though it would be too tedious to mention, in detail, the great number of our countrymen who were distinguished on the continent for their marvellous works, and for the sanctity of their lives, it would be unpardonable to omit them altogether. Not taking into account those who were canonized in Britain, nor those who went over to the continent in large bodies, we have in Italy, St. Cathaldus, patron of Tarentum, St. Donatus, patron of Fiesole, St. Emilian, patron of Faventum, and St. Frigidian of Lucca. Pavia honors John Albinus as the founder of her University; and St. Cumean is, above all other Irish saints, the favorite patron of Bobio.

In Gaul, St. Mansuetus is patron of Tulle; St. Finlag, Abbot of St. Simphorian, patron of Metz; and St. Præcordius of Corbie, situate between Amiens and Peronne. Amiens honors St. Forcenaius and Poitiers, St. Fridolinus, Abbot of the monastery of St. Hilarius. St. Elias is patron of Angouleme. St. Anatolius of Besancon, St. Fiacre of Meaux, St. Fursa of Peronne, and St. Laurence of Eu. Liege honors St. Momo, and Strasburgh SS. Florentius and Arbogastus. In Bretagne, SS. Origin, Joava, Tenan, Gildas, Brioc, and many others are revered as patrons. In Rhemes and the surrounding district; SS. Gibrian, Heran, German, Veran, Abran, Petran, and three sisters, Frauda, Tompa and Passima, are held in the highest veneration. In Burgundy, the vineyard of the Lord yielded an abundant harvest to the zeal of St. Columbanus, who founded there a great number of monasteries and colleges of Monks, restored the true service of God, and left there after him Deicolus, Columbinus, and Anatolius. In Burgundy, also, St. Maimbod is honored as a martyr.

In Belgium you have in Barbant, SS. Rumold, Fredegand, Himelin, Dynipna, and Gerebernus. In Flanders, SS. Levin, Guthagon, Columbanus; in Artois, SS. Liugluio, Liuglianus, Kilian, Vulgan-Fursa, and Obodius; in Hainault, SS. Etto, Adalgisus, Abel, Wasnulph, and Mombolus; in Namur, SS. Farannan and Eloquius; in Liege, SS. Ultan, Foillan, and Bertuin; in Gueldres, SS. Wiro, Plechelm, and Othger; in Holland, St. Hiero; in Friesland, SS. Suitbert and Acca.

But Germany, especially, was the most flourishing vineyard of our saints. St. Albuin, or Witta is honored as apostle in Thuringia; St. Disibode, at Treves; St. Erhard, in Alsace and Bavaria; St. Fridolin, in the Grisons of Switzerland; St. Gall, among the Suabians, Swiss, and Rhœtians; St John, in Mecklenburg; St. Virgil, at Saltzburg; St. Kilian, in Franconia; St. Rupert, in part of Bavaria: From these saints, these different places received the grace of faith, and the sacred discipline of Christian virtue, and afterwards honored the memory of their benefactors, as the apostles of their nation. But these are not the only saints to whom the Germans send up their filial prayers; equal honors are paid by them to some other of our countrymen. St. Albert is honored at Ratisbon, SS. Deicola and Fintan at Constance, and St. Eusebius in Coire. The town and canton of St. Gall took their names from our countryman, St. Gall. "This monastery," says Munster, "was the school of the noble and of the peasant, and the nursery of a great number of learned men; at one period it contained no less than one hundred and fifty students and Brothers." Ireland was, therefore, both the athenæum of learning, and the temple of holiness, supplying the world with literati, and heaven with saints. Truly doth she appear the academy of the earth, and the colony of heaven. Was ever panegyric more appropriate than the words of Eric of Auxerre? "Need I mention Ireland, who, despising the dangers of the deep, emigrates to our shores, with almost the whole host of her philosophers: the most eminent amongst them become voluntary exiles to minister to the tastes of our most wise Solomon?'

Accordingly, the Popes have frequently evinced their affectionate solicitude for the Irish, in a remarkable degree, when they found them fervent in receiving the faith, faithful in observing, constant in preserving, and zealous in extending it to others, and, above all, so convinced in their hearts of this principle, never to allow themselves to be separated from the visible head of the Church; lest, if the life sap of religion and of true piety should not circulate constantly amongst them, they should shrivel up and wither, and be at length cut off, and cast into eternal flames. They never dreamed of building on any foundation but on that which was laid by Jesus Christ himself, who said to Peter, and, in him, to all his successors, "Thou art Peter, and upon this rock I will build my Church, and the gates of hell shall not prevail against it: and I will give to thee the keys of the kingdom of heaven; and whatsoever thou shalt bind on earth, shall be bound in heaven; and whatsoever thou shall loose on earth, shall be loosed in heaven."

Whenever occasion required, the Popes were, therefore, ever ready to bestow their choicest favors on the Irish. For, as the greatest of all blessings and favors is to point out the most certain path to salvation by substituting religion for superstition, truth for falsehood, faith for error, and light for darkness, so the greatest of all benefits was conferred on the Irish by the Popes, who commissioned many others to feed the lamp of true faith amongst them, in addition to those many illustrious men, whom we have already described as laboring in the same noble work.

CHAPTER XXVII.

The Irish Church under the Popes.—How the Holy Union was kept Intact.—List of Legates Sent from Rome.—Historical Errors Corrected by Dr. Lynch.— His Concluding Remarks in which he shows up Cambrensis in the Garb of a Notorious Calumniator of Both the Catholic Church and the Irish People.

In the third volume of his very valuable work, which has proved such a mine of historical lore, and which has thrown so much light on the subject under consideration, Dr. Lynch introduces the following well-authenticated evidence in proof of the fact that it would be impossible for any Bulls such as those attributed to Popes Adrian and Alexander, to originate in Rome, for the reason that both Popes were too well informed concerning the excellent condition of the Catholic Church and the fidelity of the Irish people to the See of St. Peter, to use the harsh, unjust and untruthful language in which both these Bulls are couched. On this and similar points Dr. Lynch says:

The labor of those Popes (Honorius and John), in extirpating the Pelagian heresy, and establishing the canonical observance of paschal time in Ireland, were crowned with such perfect success, that the Irish Church was now without a blemish and attained the summit of perfection. Under the care of the Popes, "she was presented as a glorious Church, not having spot or wrinkle, but holy and immaculate." The Irish, therefore, owe the whole glory of their Church to the Popes; and as eternal salvation is the greatest of all blessings, boundless should be their gratitude to the Popes who pointed out to them the right road to heaven, nay, conferred, in a certain sense, everlasting happiness itself by showing how it could be attained. But when the Popes beheld the Irish Church radiant with such surpassing splendor, they relaxed for a considerable time their ancient solicitude for the Irish, sending neither legates nor letters, lest they might be said to be holding up a lamp to the sun, but they employed an immense number of pious and holy Irishmen in instructing other nations in morality and religion. The catalogue of those apostles I omit inserting at present, because I have given it in different parts of the work, not indeed full and complete (for that would require an enormous volume), but such as the occasion required.

But as sorrow often follows on the footsteps of joy, so the ferocity of the Danes almost extinguished the glory of the Irish Church. During full two hundred years. the lives and fortunes of the Irish, laity and clergy, were at the mercy of their relentless rage ; palaces and temples were burned, the country laid waste, the people massacred, and the clergy sacrificed to their atrocious fury, doomed, wherever they were taken, either to a dungeon and chains or to a death of excruciating torture. But when the gentle breath of peace once more succeeded the horrid tempest of war, the ancient light of piety and learning burst forth afresh ; not only could Ireland boast of having a high name in literature and piety at home, but she also sent forth many (as you see from other parts of this work) who revived literature and piety in foreign nations.

The torrent, however, which had so long deluged Ireland, left some of its slime and weeds on the national fame. To remove them the Popes exerted all their pastoral solicitude, by sending legates in uninterrupted succession to Ireland, who left no source untried to repair the lost splendor of her religious fame. Gilbert, Bishop of Limerick, was the first of those legates. He was an honor to his country, and devoted his life exclusively to re-establishing good institutions. St. Mael-maedhog succeeded. On his departure from Rome he had received a stole and episcopal mitre from Pope Innocent II. Christian, Bishop of Lismore, was next appointed by Eugenius III. St. Laurentius succeeded under the pontificate of Alexander III.; and Matthew, or Maurice, Archbishop of Caiseal, was the next. They were all Irishmen, and therefore better qualified than any others to inflame their countrymen with a love of virtue, to censure their vices with severity and to stimulate their progress in learning. The Irish, who were so very remote from the court of Rome, would never have been entrusted to the care of those legates if the Popes had not been convinced that they were eminently qualified for the teaching of nations.

The zeal of the Popes for the reformation of Ireland appears more manifest still in the appointment of subsidiary and extraordinary legates, to aid the preaching of the former in Ireland. Three Cardinals were ordered by the Pope to visit Ireland : John Paparo, Cardinal priest in Damaso, Vivian Tomasius, and John of Salernum. Three thousand bishops, priests, monks and canons, met in council at Keannanus under Paparo, ; the legatine labors of Vivian, Cardinal priest of St. Stephen, in the Cælian Mount, are set forth in another part of this work. John of Salernum. who was also Cardinal priest of St. Stephen, on the Cælian Mount, held two councils in the year 1202, one at Dublin, the other at Athluain, and in both enacted salutary canons. From the office of the translation of St. Patrick, Brighid, and Columba, we learn that the same Cardinal, " with all due veneration and solemnity, translated the said relics in the church of St. Patrick at Dun, from the place where they were buried. At this ceremony of translation there were present, with the legate in St. Patrick's Church, fifteen bishops, together with abbots, dignitaries, deans, archdeacons, and an immense number of faithful believers."

Ussher believed that this legate's name was Vivian, but this grievous error arose, probably, from the fact that both were Cardinals of the same title. After the death of Vivian, John was promoted to the same office, a circumstance which led Ussher, though generally correct, into the mistake. Cardinal Bellarminus certainly states that there were several Cardinals of the title of St. Stephen in Mount Cæli about that period. While John resided as legate in Ireland, he received letters from Innocent III., and our annals also record that James, the Pope's penitentiary or chaplain, was exercising legatine authority in Ireland about the year 1220." I had almost forgotten the Italian Giraldus, an ecclesiastic of the Church of Rome, " who was sent over to those parts with legatine powers." according to Cambrensis. Cardinal Othobon was also legate in Ireland, for he celebrated at London a great council of all the prelates of England, Wales, Scotland and Ireland in 1268

In consequence of the negligence of historians, we have fewer records of legates in Ireland in succeding ages. Matthew of Westminster states that Peter de Sufflein was legate in Ireland in 1240 and John Rufus in 1247. Stanihurst also records in his English history of Ireland, that a great quarrel having arisen between the citizens of Dublin and the retainers of the Earl of Ormonde, the citizens burst in a body into St. Patrick's Cathedral, where the Earl had taken refuge, and attempted to kill him. They cast their javelins against the images of the saints, threw down the statues, desecrated the relics, and most profanely violated the holy place. Ormonde appealed to the Holy See to punish this sacrilege, and a legate was immediately sent over to punish the delinquents according to their deserts. But at the earnest request of Walter Fitzsimon, Archbishop of Dublin, and other prelates, the citizens were pardoned on this condition, that the " Mayor of the city, as a perpetual commemoration of the thing, should walk barefooted every year in the solemn procession on Corpus Christi." And that was faithfully observed until the

Catholic religion was abolished by law. After the death of Henry VIII. and Edward VI., the Church recovered her former power and splendor under the reign of Queen Mary. Cardinal Pole was then appointed legate, both for England and Ireland (as appears from the letters of the King and Queen in Reymer), but he never entered Ireland; but when Elizabeth succeeded to the throne of both kingdoms the Church was once more deprived of power and almost totally destroyed, whence there were but few legates in Ireland during her reign. Alphonsus Salmero, of the Society of Jesus, was, however, a nuncio apostolic in Ireland, according to Ribadeneira's "Writers of the Society of Jesus," I also saw a dispensation granted by David Wolf, of Limerick, to Richard Lynch, a citizen of Galway, grandfather to Nicholas Lynch, provincial of the Irish Dominicans, who died at Rome about twenty years ago, deeply regretted by his friends. The dispensation was signed by David Wolf, apostolic nuncio. Orlandinus speaks of him in his history of the Society of Jesus. I have learned that he was a man of extraordinary piety who fearlessly denounced crime whenever it was committed. When the whole country was embroiled in war he took refuge in the castle of Clunoan, on the borders of Thomond and of the county of Galway, but when he heard that its occupants lived by plunder, he believed it a sin to take any nourishment from them, and sickened and died.

The relentless cruelty of Elizabeth against all ecclesiastics could not deter that great man, Nicholas Sanders, from nobly discharging the legatine functions in Ireland. He not only devoted himself to the punctual discharge of his duties, but even sacrificed his life as himself had anticipated. Thadæus Egan succeeded him as legate. He was assassinated while he was in the act of exhorting the soldiers on the day of battle to fight bravely for the Catholic religion. After a long interval, Father Francis Scarampi, a man of noble rank and great virtue, a priest of the Oratory, came to Ireland by order of Urban VIII. Some time after John Baptist Rinnucinni, Archbishop and Prince of Fermo, came as extraordinary legate to Ireland from Innocent X., and was received with transports of joy by the Irish. He spared neither labor nor expense to raise Ireland from her prostrate condition, but the evil genius of the land blasted his exertions and the fond hopes of the Irish.

Moreover, while heresy in its rampant atrocity was clouding the splendor of the true faith, all the Popes for the time being sent over many learned men as lamps to dispel that great darkness; and if they removed not altogether those clouds of error, they at least succeeded happily in preventing them from remaining on the minds of most of the natives. And that the Popes should leave no means untried that could be desired for sustaining the Catholic religion in Ireland, Innocent X. sent over, in our own days, a large quantity of money for the restoration of the faith, as Gregorius XIII. had, in our fathers' time, sent over an army raised at great expense, to assist the Irish, and save religion from the total destruction to which it was then exposed.

But what need of more? There were only two archbishoprics in England and two in Scotland, that is four in Great Britain, established by the Popes, though Great Britain, according to Cæsar's estimate, is twice as large as Ireland. Religious worth, not extent of territory, made them place Ireland on a level with a country so far superior in extent. For the same reasons the Popes have not appointed Bishops to the Episcopal Sees of England, Scotland, Denmark, Sweden, Norway, and other kingdoms which revolted against the Church and the papal authority; though an almost uninterrupted succession of illustrious Bishops has been appointed in almost all Irish Sees, even while the government was exclusively in the hands of the heretics.

If, then, St. Gregorius has been justly styled by Beda the Apostle of England, because he commissioned Augustinus and his companions to emancipate the English from the darkness of paganism, how great and powerful are the bonds between the Irish and those Popes, who not only labored strenuously in pouring out on them the full light of faith, but also in preserving, at all times, that faith when once planted, and rooting it deeply in their hearts, and diffusing it more and more, sometimes by the public ministry of papal delegates, more frequently by the secret missions of learned men, and at times by military aid to assist their righteous resistance to the destruction which threatened the country. To the Popes, therefore, Ireland owes not only the ornaments of her dignity, but much more, the elements of her constancy.

Should it be objected that I was seduced by a false love of country to assert, without grounds, that Ireland was never visited by the censures of the Pope, I answer that if the documents produced against me be submitted to a serious examination, it will clearly appear that the thunders of the Church were never launched against Ireland: "It is evident," they say, "from the letters of St. Gregorius and the life of St. Kilian, that Ireland was often cut off from the Church by censures." But let us examine both assertions separately; and commencin with St. Gregorius, I maintain his two letters were not directed to the Irish, but to the Iberians, a people of Asia. between Albania and Colchis, and at present a part of western Georgia. The MMS. copy of the second letter in the Vatican library reads "Iberia," not "Hibernia." By the negligence of transcribers one letter was added and afterwards printed; and thus the affairs of two distant nations, having no connection with each other, were jumbled and confounded. This circumstance, and other arguments which I am about to adduce, leave no doubt on my mind that both the letters were addressed to the Iberians, and not to the Irish.

An error, similar to that in St. Gregorius's, has also crept into the writings of others. Thus, Rufinus relates that a servant maid, a Christian, converted the King of Iberia, and then his whole people, from the darkness of paganism to the light of Christian faith. The fact is thus recorded in the Roman Martyrology: "In Iberia, beyond the Euxine Sea, the festival of a holy Christian maid, who, by her miraculous powers, converted that nation to the faith of Christ in the time of Constantinus." But preceding writers, by a gross blunder, apply to the Irish Church the establishment of Christianity among the Iberians. Philippus of Bergamo says "that an humble Christian woman, being carried a slave into Ireland, established the faith of Christ in that country." He adds, however, that "those Iberians are called Gregorions at present, and form but one province or territory with the Armenians and Colchians." Thus, though he writes the word Hibernia, he gives us clearly to understand that he means Iberia. Is it surprising, then, that Sabellicus, who adopts this history on the authority of Philipius, should have applied it to Ireland. Hector Boethius copies not only the facts, but the very words of Sabellicus, but makes one little addition of his own, namely, that this woman, of whose country the others are silent, was a Pict. He appeals for that circumstance "to the Scotic annals, but Dempster grounds it on Irish tradition." The discrepancy in their testimony proves that vague rumor, which the credulous always exaggerate, was the sole ground for their statements.

Arnold Pontanus must have also been misled by confounding those names, when he writes, "that the Iberians were converted to the faith of Christ by the preaching of St. Patrick." Again, in the words of St. Hieronimus, "he won over Iberia to Christ." Iberia is read by some Hibernia, as Erasmus observed. Hence arose the error of Arnold Merriman, grounded on the common editions of Eusebius, that Galba had extended his empire to Ireland; and again, in the life of St. Firmin, Pampeluna, a city of Iberia or Spain, is set down as being in Ireland; Vincent also, misled by confounding the words Hibernia and Iberia, as Ussher thinks, "states that St. James visited the coasts of Ireland." But as in the last copy of the last epistle of St. Gregorius, the word is written "Iberia," and as the first was certainly directed to the same country, both were evidently sent, not to the Irish, but to the Iberians.

In the concluding chapter of the fourth volume of his *Cambrensis Eversus*, Dr. Lynch gives a brief summary of the principal points contained in this valuable work, and then he thus scores the slanderous Giraldus Cambrensis for the foulness of the falsehoods which he either fabricated himself in order to gratify his anti-Irish venom, or which he heard from the traductive tongues of some hirelings like himself, who deemed it an honor to fulminate falsehood, because thereby they could calumniate the Irish people and damage the reputation of the greatest and most loyal Catholic nation the world has ever witnessed.

The object of my labor has, I think, been now obtained. Truth, which can often defend herself without aid against the craft and ingenuity of man, has been brought to light from under the hoar of centuries which enveloped her. She cannot be crushed by the might of calumny, nor overwhelmed by the length of time, nor extinguished by all the efforts of violence; the more vehemently and bitterly she is assailed, the more majestically does she rise, like the palm the which has been weighed to the ground. In vain has Giraldus endeavored to defile her with his bitter calumnies; these dissertations have removed all his foul colorings, and she rises on our view with more than her pristine brilliancy. "Great is the power of truth, which can easily and without aid defend herself against all the intellect and craft, and cunning and concocted conspiracies of men." The very title of his first work—"Topography," was a lie. Through the whole course of his work there is not even a shadowy sketch of the subjects signified by that title.

He had the audacity to commit a similar disgraceful error in entitling that work of his "The Conquest of Ireland," the book itself not containing the least realization of what its title promises. The conquest of Ireland was not completed for several hundred years after the death of Giraldus. Thus he sticks in the very port which portends certain shipwreck, when he launches out into the great ocean of Irish history, especially when he was not well provided with those aids which would enable him to construct his projected fabric. Chronology he neglected; and where its cynosure is wanting, there can be but blind sailing on the deep of history. For some persons maintain that accurate chronology is the only eye of history; and as that eye is wanting in the history of Cambrensis, it must be "a horrid, shapeless, and sightless monster." An evident proof of the defectiveness of his chronology is, that he makes "St. Columba and St. Brigid contemporaries of St. Patrick," though he had previously stated that St. Patrick had rested in the Lord in 458 (which Colgan proves ought to be 493), that St. Columba, who died in or near the year 496, was not born before the year 519 and that St Brigid departed to heaven about the year 523. What could be expected from a stranger who knew nothing of Irish affairs nor the Irish language, without which a knowledge of the records of Ireland could not be acquired, and who spent only two years in collecting the materials for his work, without visiting, in the meantime, hardly one-third of the island? The only witnesses cited as his authorities were generally his own countrymen, the principal of whom were overwhelmed in debt at home, and had broken faith with their creditors, and therefore may be fairly pronounced unworthy of much credit abroad. Many of the statements in his book were taken from a different class of his countrymen, namely, sailors, common soldiers, robbers, incendiaries, debauchees, and murderers, and, in fine, from the dregs and refuse of the people, the outcasts and disgrace of human society. He caught up with greedy ears the rumors of lying report, and proposed them to the belief of mankind as gravely as if they had been pronounced by oracles. Other facts he records, to which he says he was himself an eye witness. He culled the most discreditable facts from the Irish annals, and suppressed those that eminently deserved to be recorded—like the leech which sucks out corruption, but leaves the sound humors untouched. Is not a work raised on such frail foundations obviously tottering to ruin? especially when he who attempted to raise the structure was turbulent and quarrelsome, and a diviner, and crediting dreams and auguries, shamefully parading his own panegyric, and immoderate in his eulogy of his friends, as he was merciless in vituperating his enemies, and contradicting himself as well as others, and never recited with praise by any respectable author, and the most vapid enemy of the Irish. What calm sense could be expected from a firebrand, or fair statement from a litigant, or consistency from a diviner, or solidity from a dreamer?—what but visionary folly and insincerity from a soothsayer and a boaster?—what truth could be expected from the slave of prejudice—what consistency from the fickle—what worth from the contemptible—what justice from an enemy—a man who labored to patch up his case with variegated shreds of equity, like seasonings of rancid meat? When bulrush columns support a marble palace, then you may expect a fair history from a man blasted by such defects! If the vanity of dreams and the divinations of augurs can command the implicit belief of an historian, must not everyone suspect that a similar weakness destroys all the credit of his narratives?

But these are not the only blemishes which exclude him from the rank of creditable historians. Historians are bound as strictly not to suppress things worthy of record as not to state falsehoods in their history. Now Giraldus, after promising a complete history of Ireland, suppressed not trifles merely or inconsiderable events, but the most capital points of history. He has suppressed not only the deeds but even the names of the kings of Ireland. It would not suit his purpose to have even the names of kings glittering in the pages of a work, which was intended to be filled with the filthy and discreditable practices of the Irish; his sole object being to collect from all quarters into one mass whatever was disgraceful to them, and to find matter for calumny in their soil, and sea and climate, asserting falsely that the climate was excessively severe, the sea torn by eternal tempests, and the land swamped by extraordinary humidity. So inveterate was his lust for calumny, that he should reproach us with the small size of our cattle, and the black color of our sheep. * * * * The bulls of Adrian IV. and Alexander III. he falsely imagined gave grounds for his calumnies, those bulls being either entirely spurious or surreptitiously obtained by the fradulent and secret machinations of the calumniators. The filthy practices falsely imputed to the Irish in these bulls were exaggerated and multiplied by Giraldus, who magnified flies into elephants, and atoms into mountains; but he was building on sand when he labored to rear the fabric of his own calumnies on those false documents, the bulls being one tissue of unfounded stories, utterly at variance with truth, and, if attentively examined, outrageously opposed to the laws both of God and man, because they condemned the innocent without a hearing to the most frightful punishment, and were full of many other intolerable defects.

* * * * * * *

I appeal now to the judgment of every candid reader, whether I have not established, that no credit can be given to the writings of a man who was morose and quarrelsome, a diviner and a believer in soothsayers, a flatterer, and vainglorious panegyrist of himself and his friends: who consulted his prejudices and not truth in his writings; who recorded what should have been suppressed, and suppressed what should have been recorded; who was opprobrious to his adversaries and calumnious against his enemies; who reconciles impossibilities, publishes falsehoods, and has often concealed the truth; who disgorged his filthy calumnies against the whole Irish people, sparing neither the tender years of the child, nor the sex of the woman; ridiculed the commonalty, libelled the noble, insolently despised the princes and kings, carped at the clergy, lacerated the prelates, aimed a mortal blow at the Church Militant herself, and hurled his calumnies, even to the court of heaven, against the saints of Ireland. Such, alas! is the fate of all things; when they once begin to totter, there is no stay to their fall till they sink to the lowest depths of ruin.

CHAPTER XXVIII.

Further Historical Proofs Concerning the Letter which Pope Adrain IV., sent to King Louis VII.—Evidence Showing the Letter to have Alluded to Ireland and not to Spain, as Claimed by Anti-Catholic Writers.

Having now given the evidence of the celebrated Dr. Lynch, as recorded in preceding chapters, we will turn again to the *Analecta Juris Pontificii* of Victor Palmè, in order to adduce some additional testimony from the fruitful pen of this most recent—and, we may add, most successful, writer of modern days among all who have attempted to treat of this intricate historical question.

M. Palmè, in his *Adrian IV. and Ireland*,* has left nothing unsaid on this subject. He has viewed this long-disputed historical question from every standpoint, and he has advanced arguments and presented documents which throw new light upon the subject and which cannot fail to convince every candid-minded reader that the Bulls in question were most assuredly forged. In the introductory remarks to his exhaustive essay M. Palmè says:

We know of no historical document which has evoked so many controversies as the Letter of Pope Adrian IV., authorizing, it is said, Henry II., King of England, to undertake the conquest of Ireland, and ordering the Irish to submit to that prince as their legitimate master.

For seven hundred years the Irish have questioned the authenticity of the Papal Letter. They could not be persuaded into the belief that the common Father of Christendom had, without consulting the clergy and the people of the country, without being informed as to whether the intervention of the English prince was solicited or desired by the parties most concerned, condemned—on an incomplete and inexact statement of affairs—a nation distinguished for its attachment to Christianity, to forfeit its independence and to become the prey of the covetous and ferocious Anglo-Normans.

This train of thought has been developed with a great deal of warmth and bitterness by Abbe MacGeoghegan, as the following words show:

The above (the letter of Pope Adrian IV.) was an edict pronounced against Ireland, by which the rights of men and the most sacred laws were violated, under the specious pretext of religion and the reformation of morals. The Irish were no longer to possess a country. That people who had never bent under a foreign yoke (*nunquam externae subjacuit ditioni*) were condemned to lose their liberty without even being heard. * * * * It may be well affirmed that no Pope, either before or since Adrian IV., ever punished a nation so severely without cause. We have seen instances of Popes making use of their spiritual authority in opposition to crowned heads; we have known them to

---

* Published in the year 1882 in the *Analecta* in Paris, of which M. Palmé is the distinguished editor.

excommunicate emperors and kings, and to place their States under an interdict, for crimes of heresy or other causes; but we here behold innocent Ireland given up to tyrants, without having been summoned before any tribunal, or convicted of any crime."†

Furthermore, Irish writers have at all times laid particular stress upon the fact that *the original diploma of Pope Adrian has never been seen or produced by anybody*; that it was not seen or exhibited by anybody at the period when it was first mentioned or referred to, that is, towards the close of the twelfth century, and that no annalist or historian—from that time forwards—*has been able to say that he saw the original document or quoted from it.* So true is all this that Rymer, who took the greatest care with regard to every document of the *Fœdera*, to cite on the margin the autographs *ex Turre Londonensi*, or from some other official Registry, found himself compelled, in respect to this Letter of Adrian IV., to cite as a guarantee only Matthew Paris, *who lived about a century after Adrian.*

It is true that Cardinal Baronius has inserted in his Ecclesiastical Annals the Letter attributed to Pope Adrian; but the manner in which the learned annalist expresses himself shows conclusively that he had not before him the original document, and, consequently, that *it did not exist in the archives of the Vatican at the time of Baronius.* In fact Baronius does not give date, year, nor day of the Letter. Other writers have dated it from Rome, whilst it is proved that at the period in question Adrian IV. was at Benevento, where he dwelt for a considerable period of time. But would Baronius have neglected to affix the name of the place, the year and the day of the Letter (conditions so essential, especially to an important document) if he had before him *the official Regestum* of Adrian IV., or, at least, an *authentic transcript* of the Letter? From this it is clear that he had in his possession, or under his control, only *a private copy which was destitute of every mark of authenticity.*

The defenders of the authenticity of the spurious Adrian document agree in saying

† MacGeoghegan's *History of Ireland,* p. 246.

that it was written in 1155, a few months after the election of Pope Adrian IV. Baronius, on the contrary, places the document at the *end* of the pontificate of the Pope, and *declines to assume any responsibility with regard to its date.* It was not because Baronius attached any importance to the document that he inserted it in his Annals, but simply because he did not wish to leave out anything that was even attributed to so illustrious a Pontiff. "Moreover,' he says, in alluding to this doubtful diploma, "for fear that anything should perish that belongs to the memory of so great a Pontiff, we here transcribe from a manuscript of the Vatican, the diploma given to Henry, King of England, relating to the affairs of Ireland, restored to a better condition in respect to religion "§

So then, Baronius refrained from remarking on the political character of the Letter which has been for so long regarded by many as the act of donation of Ireland to the English king; the annalist preferring, on the contrary, to call attention only to the amelioration of the religious status of the country.

The defenders of the apocryphal Letter attributed to Pope Adrian IV., imagine, no doubt, that all the manuscripts which are kept in the vast library of the Vatican, are *original diplomas* and official collections. They also pretend that it was from the Vatican itself, and from a Vatican manuscript (*ex codice Vaticano*) that Baronius took the document in question. But these champions of the authenticity of Adrian's Letter are, evidently, not aware that the Vatican Library contains thousands of manuscripts, which, beyond a doubt, *have no official or authentic character.* The original *Regesta* of the Popes are preserved, not in the Library, but in the archives of the Vatican. Furthermore, the series of the *Regesta* commenced only in the year 1198, that is, *forty years after*

§ Ad hæc insuper, ne quid excidat de tanti pontificis memoria, hic describimus ex codice Vaticano diploma datum ad Henricum Anglorum regem de rebus Hiberniæ in meliorem statum religionis restitutis, sed quoto sui pontificatus anno, incertum. Baronius, *Annales Ecclesiastici,* tom. 12, page 531. Moguntiæ, 1608.

the death of *Pope Adrian IV.* What, then, is the *Codex Vaticanus* in which Baronius found the Letter attributed to Pope Adrian the Fourth? It is nothing more than *a copy of the work of Matthew Paris.*

In 1872 an interesting and truthful article on Pope Adrian IV., and his pretended donation of Ireland to Henry II, appeared in the *Irish Ecclesiastical Record,* wherein the author states that during a sojourn of several years in Rome he made it his business to ascertain what the manuscript of the Vatican (*codex Vaticanus*) from which was taken the copy of Adrian's Letter, amounted to. The Archivist of the Vatican, after long and earnest investigation in the universal Library, attested that Baronius had absolutely *nothing* as a foundation for the Letter in the Annals, *save the "Major Historia" of Matthew Paris.*

It follows then, that the testimony of the *Codex Vaticanus,* and that of Baronius himself who used it, are precisely one and the same with that of Matthew Paris, that is, the testimony of a historian who never saw the original of the Letter, and who wrote about *a century after Adrian's time.* Here, then, we have another confirmation of the fact that Cardinal Baronius discovered nowhere in the Vatican the *original Letter of Adrian IV.,* with its date and other marks of authenticity.

It now remains for us to answer an objection arising from the fact that the Diploma attributed to Pope Adrian has been inserted in some of the editions of the *Bullarium Romanum.*

The learned know that the collection called the *Bullarium Romanum* was a *private* and individual undertaking *whose authenticity the Popes have not guaranteed.* It was quite possible, then, for apocryphal documents to gain admittance therein.

When, in 1234, Pope Gregory IX. published the Decretals, he placed at their head a Papal Diploma authenticating the collection.

Popes Boniface VIII. and Clement V. did the same in regard to other Canonical codes. Subsequently, Leo X. declared authentic the Acts of the Fifth Council of Lateran. Pius IV. did the same in respect to the Decrees of the Council of Trent, an edition of which was brought out in Rome in 1564. Some years afterwards, Gregory XIII. authenticated, in like manner, the Roman edition of the *Corpus juris Canonici.* Under the pontificate of Pope Paul V., the great editions of the General Councils was brought out at Rome, but it was clearly expressed in the Preface that the work laid no claim to official and judical authenticity.

The Holy See has *never assumed the responsibility* of the contents of the different editions of the *Bullarium Romanum,* which have, at various periods, been published; hence the Bulls|| and Briefs‡ inserted therein have legal value only in so much as they are copies or transcripts in the authentic form *and with all the other requisites.*

The four volumes of the *Bullarium* of Pope Benedict XIV. *alone* form an exception to the rule just stated, because that Supreme Pontiff authenticated them by a Diploma placed at the head of the collection¶.

¶ Remigius Maschat, Cl. Reg. S. P., lays down the same doctrine, and in it clearly voices the sentiment of the learned, in his *Institutiones Canonicæ* vol. 2 part 1 mo., pag 126. No. 20.

|| "*An magnum Bullarium continens Constitutiones Pontificias habeat auctoritatem juris?'* R. *Negative,* nisi certo, saltem moraliter, constet, quod dicrm Constitutiones *rite sint promulgatæ usu receptae et per omnia conformes suo originali.* Hinc ʀtante dubio in judicio non probant, *nisi producantur in forma authentica,* et quidem in Curia R mana sub Sigillo Cancellarii, vel Camerarii, Auditoris, extra vero sub plumbo cum consueta subscriptione. Si *Breve* seu *Diploma* apostolicum est, plerumque constat brevi Scriptura in papyro, cera rubra, et annulo piscatoris sigillata, ac signo secretarii notata, et subscripta. Si *Bulla* est, scribitur plerumque in membrana plumbo e funibus pendente munita, salutationem cum narratione, et concessione Parræ continens."

‡ "BULLS, so called from the seal, whether of gold, silver or lead, which is appended to them, begin thus: LEO (or the name of the reigning Pontiff), *Episcopus, Servus Servorum Dei.*

BRIEFS begin with a superscription, having the name of the reigning Pontiff thus: LEO P. P. XIII. Formerly Bulls had appended, on a silken or hempen cord, a leaden (sometimes silver or even gold) seal, and were, moreover, written upon thick, coarse and somewhat dark parchment, in old style or Teutonic letters, and without any punctuation. At present, according to a *motus proprius* of Pope Leo XIII., now happily reigning, issued December 29th, 1878,

CHAPTER XXIX.

Criticism on the True Letter of Pope Adrian IV., and the False Bull.—Reasons Why the Letter "H" alludes to *Hibernia* and could not mean *Hispania*.

In the concluding summary of his exhaustive criticism on the Letter written by Pope Adrian IV., to King Louis VII., of France and Henry II , of England, M. Palmè thus epitomizes the reasons which impelled him to believe that Letter to have alluded to Ireland and not to Spain.

THE TRUE LETTER AND THE FALSE BULL.

1.—Adrian IV., *never* conceded to the King of England authorization to invade Ireland. On the contrary, he positively *refused* to have anything to do with the undertaking, the danger and injustice of which he pointed out in a most signal manner.

2 —The Letter commonly attributed to Pope Adrian is *spurious* or *apocryphal*. This conclusion follows necessarily from the foregoing, independently of all reasons that concur to prove the spuriousness of that document.

3.—The *true Letter of Adrian*, in which he peremptorily *refused* to allow Ireland to be invaded, *is not lost*; it has been preserved by safe, authorized and irrefutable witnesses.

4.—The tenor of the *true Letter* itself does not allow a shadow of suspicion to fall on its authenticity, whilst the extrinsic proofs combine to render wonderfully clear and potent the intrinsic.

5.—This *true Letter* of Pope Adrian IV., by itself furnishes *the key* to the proper understanding of a great number of facts

the use of the Teutonic characters is entirely abolished, and the ordinary Latin mode of writing is substituted. The use of the leaden seal is restricted to the more important Bulls. The other Bulls, like Briefs, have a red seal impressed, and are written on fine white parchment. The new red seal of Bulls—as prescribed by Pope Leo XIII.—bears on its face the images of SS. Peter and Paul, surrounded by the name of the reigning Pope."—*Smith's Ecc. Law*, vol. I., chap. 3 , art. 5, no. 48.

See also Konings *Theologia Moralis*, S. Alphonsi Comp. pt. 2; No. 175; pp. 73–4. Ferraris, verbum, *Cancellaria*.

Consult especially Devoti's *Institutionum Canonicarum*. Tom. 1. cap. vii §§ xcv–cli., but particularly §§ xcviii. and xcix. pp. 88–9.

that have hitherto remained dark, inexplicable and enigmatical. It unveils the motive of the mysterious silence that was kept *for more than twenty years* on the existence of a supposed act of Adrian IV. relating to Ireland It explains why Henry II. caused that country to be attacked first by adventurers; for the *refusal* of the Pope to concur in his scheme at once *blocked every direct and open invasion of the country*.

6.—The *spurious* Le ter *was forged on the true* one. Henry II. preserved in the apocryphal Bull *the preamble of the true Letter*, but he completely changed the enacting part. In place of the *refusal* on the part of the Pope to have anything to do with the scheme of the invasion of Ireland, *he inserted the donation of Ireland*, and an exhortation to the Irish to recognize the King of England as their Lord and Master. The falsification is flagrant.

7 — Not one of the successors of Adrian IV., in the Papacy, *confirmed his pretended donation*. It is true that in the treatise of Giraldus Cambrensis, entitled *Expugnatio Hiberniæ*, we find a Brief attributed to Alexander III., but that historian *acknowledged* in good faith, in a subsequent work, that the Brief just referred to *had been purposely forged*.

THE LETTER "H" MEANS HIBERNIA.

In the Middle Ages the Chancellors who transcribed Papal Diplomas, had the habit —sometimes very annoying to modern writers—of giving simply the *initials* of proper names. This habit may be constantly noticed in the very *Regesta* preserved in the Archives of the Vatican.

The ancient manuscripts which have preserved to us Pope Adrian's Letter (which we have already placed before our readers) does not designate the country to which it has reference, except by the initial "H." But the tenor itself of this important document clearly points out marks by which we are enabled to recognize at once, and beyond all doubt, the country to which it relates. I say that the Letter of Pope Adrian IV., relates to Ireland (*Hibernia*) whose conquest Louis VII., and Henry II., wished to bring about, and that *it it not possible to app'y that document to any other country, nor to any other affair than its conquest.*

The following marks, clearly designated in the Papal Letter, show that it is *Ireland alone* of which there is question in that document.

1.—The country of which there is question is not *a kingdom*, a political society which is in the possession of that eminent dignity. Adrian IV., constantly calls it by the name of *country*. Mark his expressions: 'The princes of that *country*;' 'The population of the same *country*,' etc. Such was the official title that Ireland bore throughout all antiquity, and kept until the 16th century, when it was erected into a kingdom.*

3.—This same *country* (referred to in Adrian's Letter) possessed a Church of its own, that is, an Episcopal Hierarchy regularly constituted, and free to enter into common deliberations. Adrian IV., recommends that that Church be consulted, and its decision be obtained in regard to foreign intervention. This action of the Pope plainly points out that the Church alluded to did not by any means exist *under a hostile domination* which might or could interfere with its assemblies It is clear, too, that the Church of which he speaks in his Letter, exercised a preponderating influence even in political questions; for the Pope required that it should be *consulted* in regard to the projected intervention.

3.—The country that Pope Adrian wished to preserve from foreign intervention did not depend on only one chief, or on only one king. His words designate *several princes* who governed, independently of one another, their respective districts. How can it be doubted that Ireland is the country in question? Adrian IV. recommends that the princes *be consulted* and their consent be obtained, before intervention can be employed; but he does not name those princes neither by their personal appellation nor by the title of the districts they governed. Indeed at that period the interior situation of Ireland was but little known on the Continent. Rome knew well enough of the Episcopal Hierarchy, which had been re-constituted in Ireland about a decade of years before, but it had only imperfect information in respect to the political divisions of the country and the names of the reigning chiefs and princes. The English themselves were not much better informed on these points, although living in such close proximity to Erin.

4.—Adrian IV, wished that the people should be *consulted*, and that they should freely express their opinion about intervention. The conduct of the Pope clearly supposes that the people of the country of which he is speaking, instead of being oppressed by tyrants, enjoyed such liberty as it was necessary for them to have, in order to assemble together, deliberate in common, take part in general interests, and also in political affairs. A Christian people bowed down under the yoke of Infidels, would not have the power to express their opinion in regard to an expedition projected for their deliverance from servitude. It follows then, in the plainest manner possible, from the Papal Letter, that the people of that country of which he is speaking, instead of being plunged in barbarism, possessed, on the contrary, a certain culture and civilization. *No one is ever obliged to consult barbarians or brutes!*

5.—The great majority of the inhabitants professed Christianity; if it were otherwise the Pope would not make use of the term 'Church of the country,' but by so doing he gives us clearly to understand that the Ecclesiastical Hierarchy comprises the whole country. There were still some pagans there; but they were not in such force as to constitute a body, society or government possessing whole districts. There were there too some bad Christians, who behaved as apostates, and who denied by their irregularities the faith that they had once professed. This situation explains and justifies the terms employed in the preamble of the Papal Letter; but these expressions do not imply that there is question of a country ruled over by Infidels against whom a crusade should be preached.

6.—No doubt could be for a moment entertained about the necessity of an expedition to expel Infidels cruelly oppressing Christian provinces; all that was to be done in such a case was to count and measure the forces which the Christians could employ against their enemies. But here Pope Adrian constantly doubts of the opportuneness, utility and necessity of the undertaking, although two powerful kings proposed to unite all the forces of France and England for the undertaking. It is very clear, therefore, that the country referred to in the Papal Letter was not one of those oppressed by the Moors or other Infidels.

7.—*There is no example in all history* where the Pope refused to take under his protection, and to defend against every at-

---

* Among the many proofs that could be adduced to substantiate this statement, consult the collection of the *Fœdera* of Rymer, in which, on almost every page, the reader will find Ireland alluded to by the term *country*.

tack, the kingdom of a prince starting out on a Crusade against Infidels. In the present case Adrian IV. *refused* the Bull of protection which Louis VII.. entreated him to issue, and he did not permit the Crusade to be preached.

HISPANIA NOT MEANT BY THE LETTER "H."

We have designated *seven marks* which Pope Adrian specified in his Letter as belonging to the country which was the object of his epistle. But not one of these marks can be applied to Spain (*Hispania*). It would be absurd, therefore, to maintain that the Papal Letter concerned an expedition which Louis VII. and Henry II. wished to undertake together against the Moors who oppressed a part of that peninsula.

1.—Adrian speaks of a *country*. Spain, on the contrary, enjoyed in the twelfth century the dignity and title of *kingdom* Indeed, it embraced three kingdoms Castile, Aragon, and Galicia. As the King of Castile was the most powerful of the three kings, he bore the title of *Emperor*. Robert de Mont, the continuator of Sigebert relates (1153) that Louis VII., King of France, having repudiated Eleonora of Guyenne, married Constancia, the daughter of Alphonsus, King of the Spains. The annalist says that Toledo was the capital of the *kingdom;* and as the King of Castile was far above the *petit* kings of Aragon and Galicia, he was called the Emperor of the Spains Louis VII. having made a pilgrimage in 1154 to St. James of Galicia, was well received by his *father-in-law*, the Emperor of the Spains "†

In 1170 the Emperor of Spain married Eleonora, the daughter of Henry II., King of England. On that occasion again Robert de Mont remarked that Toledo was the capital of Castile. As the Prince was then but fifteen years old, he was persecuted by the kings of Galicia and Navarre, who were, however, his near relatives. If the expedition proposed to Pope Adrian IV., had reference to Spain (*Hispania*), would Louis VII. have omitted to speak of the Emperor of Castile, his father-in-law, who demanded his assistance? Would not a Castilian ambassador have accompanied Rotrodus to Rome for the purpose of smoothing over matters there?

2.'—The country of which Adrian IV. speaks in his Letter, had a Church, and an Episcopate, and the Pope demanded that it should be consulted in reference to the projected expedition. But Spain was at that time divided into two camps. In the part under the possession of the Moors there was no Church nor Bishops; or, at least. it would have been passably absurd to exact that the sentiment of these Bishops should be taken in regard to an expedition that was prepared against their tyrants.

3. – If the Papal Letter concerned Spain, Adrian IV. would have undoubtedly said that there should be concert of action with the Emperor of Castile and with the kings of Aragon, Navarre and Galicia, who were each well-known throughout all Europe.

4.—As to the population; it is useless to speak of the Moors who occupied the country. But could the unfortunate Christians who were subject to their yoke, find the ghost of a chance to express their opinion in regard to an expedition which had for its object their deliverance from bondage? To apply to Spain the Letter in which the Pope says *the people should be consulted* and express their sentiments with respect to foreign intervention, is to make Pope Adrian IV guilty of the greatest folly.

5.—The fifth mark does not suit Spain any better than do the first four. The Moors, after having massacred the most of the Christians, resided principally in the provinces which they reserved for themselves On the other hand, not being idolators. did they present the quality of pagans (*pagani*) of which Pope Adrian speaks in the preamble of his Letter. And where do we find in Spain the apostates, whom Louis VII. and Henry II. wished to bring under the Christian yoke?

6.—Adrian, certainly, would not have exhibited so much hesitation if there was really a question of an expedition against the Moors of Spain.

7.—Finally, he would not have refused to have the Crusade preached, and he would have readily received the kingdom of France under the care of the Holy See during all the time the expedition lasted, if the expedition was destined for operations in Spain.

† Robertus de Monte in "Patrologia de Migne," Tom. 160, pag. 478. *Ibid* 511.

CHAPTER XXX.

What the Popes Have Done for Ireland.—Help Extended to the Irish People.—Important Historical Facts.—Correspondence Between Pope Pius IX. and the Irish in Rome.—Cardinal Manning's Tribute.

Having now completely refuted the assertion that the Adrian and Alexander Bulls are genuine, and having shown from irrefutable evidence why and wherefore these long-disputed documents were purposely forged, we return again to Judge Maguire's malicious book in order to complete our task by exposing and refuting the other falsehoods with which he filled the pages of his publication.

Speaking of the unfriendly attitude which he claims the Popes always manifested towards Ireland and the Irish people throughout their numerous struggles for national independence, Judge Maguire says:

"Consistency thou art a jewel," but surely Rome cannot be charged with inconsistency in dealing with the Irish. She has been consistently and constantly unjust and insulting to them. She has found them confiding and obedient, while she has spurned and spat upon them, and she has spurned and spat upon them incessantly apparently for no other reason than that she has found them *still* confiding and obedient, and that their humiliation pleased and conciliated a more independent power.*

Fortunately for the cause of the Catholic Church, the Popes, and the people of Ireland, History is an open book to every person in search of facts wherewith to refute such falsehoods as the above fabrications, and within whose pages we hope to find proofs which ought to put to blush even apostates who bear false witness against the long line of Popes who have succeeded the much-maligned Adrian IV. and the equally slandered Alexander III.

We are told in the work before us that the Roman Pontiffs have "*spurned and spat upon*" the Irish people incessantly, and, furthermore, that Rome has been "consistently and constantly *unjust and insulting* to the people of Ireland." Can such an allegation have even an atom of truth in its whole formation? Let us turn to the records of the past and from the pages of history again convict Judge Maguire of being a wanton calumniator of the Pontiffs of the Catholic Church.

Before doing so, however, it may be well to call the attention of our readers to the fact that *Rome has done more to help Ireland, both in her spiritual and temporal concerns, than she has done for any other country in the world.*

It is the fashion of certain fallen Catholic Pope-haters—who are heretics at heart—to harp upon the assertion that Rome never helped Ireland in her struggles for constitutional liberty, or when she was struggling in the throes of religious persecution. But it must be borne in mind that the Vicar of Christ is not a military Major-General; the College of Cardinals is not composed of martial officers; St. Peter's is not a powder magazine; the Vatican is not an arsenal, nor are the Roman Basillicas barracks in which a vast army of soldiers are housed. The Pope has neither an army nor a navy to resist assaults upon his own territory, much less to help other nations either to defend or to win their freedom. There exists no treasury in Rome from whence can be drawn funds wherewith to furnish the munitions of war to foreign nations engaged in revolution, or in the defence of their lives and property against the assaults of persecuting tyrants.

What folly, then, on the part of demagogues and quasi-Catholics who are a disgrace to the Church that made them Christians, to upbraid the Popes with having been "consistently and constantly unjust and insulting" to the Irish people, because

---

*Ireland and the Pope pp. 29-30.

Rome did not furnish firearms which she had not, powder which she did not possess, and soldiers which she knew not of—in order to help in every effort which Erin has made in the past to shake off the English yoke.

We have already declared that Rome did more for Ireland than she has ever done for any other nation under the sun, and, in order to illustrate the truth of this assertion, we will briefly run over a few events as they crop out in Irish history, showing how Rome drew the temporal sword in Ireland's behalf on many occasions, although Judge Maguire says that Rome has "spurned and spat upon the Irish people *incessantly*"—that is *constantly and without cessation*.

Now let us discover what Irish history reveals regarding this important subject:

1. During the reign of Queen Elizabeth, when the Plantation of Ulster was inaugurated in order to replace the Catholic Irish with Protestant English, "letters were intercepted from Rome, addressed to the Irish natives, wherein the Pope earnestly exhorted them to persevere in their opposition to the Queen's government, *with assurance of being supplied with money and troops*," as well as with spiritual favors. This financial and martial help was tendered to Ireland about the year 1574-5.†

2. A short time subsequently, during the reign of the same Queen, and in accordance with the previous promise of the predecessor of Pope Gregory XIII., a ship of war was furnished, *six hundred well-disciplined soldiers* were supplied, and *three thousand stand of arms* were contributed by the Papal influence to help the Irish to defend their homes against the minions of the English Queen. These munitions of war were furnished by Rome about the year 1580.‡

3. Speaking of the Confederation of Kilkenny, which met on the 10th of May, 1642, the Nun of Kenmare says: "Envoys were arriving from foreign courts, and Pope Urban VIII., had sent Father Scarampi with indulgences *and a purse of $30,000 collected by Father Wadding*.§

4. "The terrible rising of 1641, was the commencement of a war of eleven years, ending with the surrender of Galway, in 1652. Innocent X., sent the Archbishop of Fermo (Rinuccini), as his Nuncio to Ireland, in the autumn of 1645, with *considerable supplies of arms and money*. This war was for complete religious freedom and national independence."‖

5. About the year 1688, 72,000 francs a year were supplied by Rome for the support of the *Irish secular clergy and laity*. In 1699 the Pope sent to King James II., at St. Germain's *fifty-eight thousand francs* for the Irish Ecclesiastics exiled that year. From about 1750 to 1800 the Popes sent the Irish Bishops *a hundred Roman crowns a year* in aid of the Catholic poor schools. ¶

6. "The Roman Pontiffs, as Rulers of the Papal States; the Emperors of Germany, as heads of the German Empire; and the Kings of Spain and France, always covertly and sometimes openly received the envoys of O'Neill, Desmond and O'Donnell, and *openly dispatched troops and fleets* to assist the Irish in their struggle for their *de facto* independence. All this was in perfect accordance, not merely with the authority which Catholic powers still recognized in the Sovereign Pontiff, but even with the new order of things which Protestantism had introduced into Western Europe, and which England, as henceforth a leading Protestant power, had accepted and eagerly embraced. By the rejection of the supreme arbitration of the Popes on the part of the new heretics, Europe lost its unity as Christendom, and naturally formed itself into two leagues, the Catholic and the Protestant. An oppressed Catholic nationality, above all a weak and powerless one, had therefore the right of appeal to the great Catholic powers for help against oppression. And the pretension of England to the possession of Ireland was the very essence of oppression and tyranny in itself, doubly aggravated

---

† Leland's History of Ireland, vol. II, p. 311.
‡ Lingard's History of England, vol. VI., pp. 157-8.
§ History of Ireland, p. 488.
‖ Cath. Dict. Art. *Irish Church*, p. 461.
¶ Catholic Dictionary, Art. *Irish Church*, p. 461.

by the fact of an apostate and vicious king or queen making it treason for a people, utterly separate and distinct from theirs, to hold fast to its ancient and revered religion. Who can say, then, that Gregory XIII. was guilty of injustice and of abetting rebellion when, in 1578, *he furnished James Fitzmaurice, the great Geraldine, with a fleet and army to fight against Elizabeth?* The authority greatest in Catholic eyes, and most worthy of respect in the eyes of all impartial men—the Pope—*thus endorsed the patent fact that Ireland was an independent nation, and could wage war against her oppressors.* Here we have a stand point from which to argue the question for future times."=

The foregoing selections, culled hurriedly from Irish and English writers, prove beyond cavil that when Judge Maguire asserted that Rome had "constantly and consistently spurned and spat upon" the Irish people, he was only carrying out the programme of calumny against the Popes and the Catholic Church which defiles every page of his falsifying, malicious and misleading publication. Nor was it for the cause of religion alone that the Popes assisted the Irish people, as untruthfully asserted in the work under review; on the contrary, the Pontiffs who succeeded Adrian IV., and Alexander III., well knew that Ireland was *an independent nation,* and was, therefore, perfectly free to wage war against England or any other power which tried to enslave that valorous people. On these grounds, therefore, the Popes assisted Ireland in several of the uprisings of her people, sending ships, soldiers and munitions of war to help the Irish to win back their national independence.

It has ever been the aim of the enemies of the Popes—both inside and outside the Church—to make capital for themselves by calumniating the Sovereign Pontiffs. This fact is patent to all readers of Church History. In the same way there are certain men of the present day, who, although born of Catholic parents and baptized in the Catholic Faith, are blatant in their bold denunciation of the Pope because he refuses to endorse every hair brained attempt made by irrepressible and inexperienced mock patriots for the purpose of gaining Ireland's freedom through means that are neither pleasing to Almighty God, nor acceptable to Irishmen with common sense and Christian principles.

These men pose as "patriots" whose ideas are far in advance of those peace policy Irishmen who prefer to live under unjust laws a little longer, rather than to abbreviate their time of enslavement beneath the iniquitous laws of England even a single minute—by having recourse to midnight meetings of sworn associates where murder is plotted and where the vengeance of God is invoked upon the cause of Ireland by means of the Satanic blood stained bond which binds these misguided men who leave a foul stain upon the fair character of their suffering country.

The Vicars of Christ have ever been the champions of liberty in every age and for every land. Why, then, will men strive to impress upon their fellow-men the false idea that the Popes, who have been the means of striking the shackles from millions of slaves and of emancipating woman from her long bondage of serfdom, should desire that Ireland—of all countries in the world—should remain a languishing slave chained by the unjust laws of England and slowly dying of destitution and decay?

There is no country in the world which the Popes would sooner see numbered among the nations of the earth than Ireland. Any why? Because she has—as she deserves to have—the deep sympathy of every reigning Pontiff in consequence of the fidelity with which Erin's sons and daughters have "fought the good fight," "kept the faith," and planted the Cross upon nearly every island and continent of the known world!

Already we have shown what some of the Popes did for Ireland in the earlier centuries, let us now turn to our own times and learn from the lips of the saintly Pope Pius IX., and his successor now gloriously reigning what sentiments they enunciated in behalf of Ireland's right to self govern-

=Father Thebaud, *The Irish Race,* p. 210.

ment even in the very hour when their calumniators were crying vengeance against the Vatican so as to make themselves conspicuous and thus gain questionable celebrity among the bitterest enemies of both the Pope and the Irish people.

The sea of trouble which lashed around the Chair of Peter in the year 1860, drew from the Catholic body in every country in the world expressions of deep sympathy for the sad state in which the Vicar of Christ was placed, surrounded as he was, by both foreign and domestic enemies. On the 11th of March in that year, the Irish residents of Rome met in conference on the condition of the Holy See, and determined at once to proclaim to the world their fealty to the Holy Father Pope Pius IX., as a grateful return for the love he ever manifested for the Irish people, and also to place themselves on record as protesting against the diabolical diplomacy practiced by the Italian Government, by which the Holy Father was despoiled of the property of the Church and deprived of his personal liberty.

The Address presented on that memorable occasion will stand on record for all ages as a durable refutation of the false ideas promulgated by certain anti Papal "patriots" who strive to win both fame and fortune by endeavoring to persuade the world that the love which the Irish people once had for the Holy Father has vanished from the hearts of that Catholic people, and that the Irish have no grateful memories of the past to recur to in their connection with Rome. The following address is presented to our readers in order that they may understand the grateful feelings which welled up in the hearts of the Irish residents in Rome, in return for the many favors bestowed by the Popes on Ireland during by-gone centuries.

ADDRESS PRESENTED TO POPE PIUS IX., BY THE IRISH RESIDENTS OF ROME, ON SUNDAY, MARCH 11TH, 1860.

Most Holy Father:—Whilst the Irish nation from one extremity to the other is moved at the sight of the indignities offered to the Vicar of Christ in the august person of your Holiness, we, your devoted children of the same country, are gathered around your throne to share in their sentiments of unbounded devotion to the Chair of St. Peter, and to give expression to our most deep felt sympathy and filial love towards your Holiness. Most Holy Father, it will ever remain a true glory to our country that when some unworthy few of your subjects. stimulated by foreign enemies to your throne, prepared so severe an ordeal for the Vicar of Christ, Ireland should be the first nation whose heart throbbed with affectionate sympathy and inaugurated the great Catholic movement, which, spreading through the universe, now fills with dismay the enemies of our holy religion and displays the ever enduring vitality of the Catholic faith. Most Holy Father, Ireland has many special reasons for approaching your Holiness in the hour of trial. Long has she deemed it her happy privilege to be assailed by every storm that was raised against the Bark of Peter; for more than two centuries and a half her children gladly suffered confiscation of their property, exile, imprisonment and the gibbet, rather than sever the sweet bonds that united her with Rome, and, even at the present day, it is our glory to share with the Holy See the assaults of the enemies to all order and religion. But, Most Holy Father, persecution could not overcome the fealty of our hearts for the Vicar of Christ; and even those children who were torn from the bosom of Ireland and compelled to seek a home in other lands, became, in the hands of God, harbingers of the glad tidings of faith, and, true to the tradition of their fathers. The churches that they founded in England, and Scotland, and Australia, and India, and the United States and the many British possessions in the Old and New Worlds, some of whose representatives have the honor of approaching to-day the feet of your Holiness, re-echo still the same sentiments of unalterable attachment to the Chair of St. Peter. Therefore, Most Holy Father, as Irishmen, who are indebted, after the grace of God, to your glorious predecessors for the blessings of faith which they now enjoy—for it was a Roman Pontiff that sent St. Patrick to the shores of Ireland—it was Rome that, in the centuries of her persecution and desolation, watched by her side, sharing her trials and her sorrows, pouring into her bosom words of consolation and sweet hope, and inviting the nations of the earth to alleviate her sufferings; and it is, moreover, to the constant and inviolate attachment of the Irish nation to the successors of St. Peter that she owes, after Heaven, her having ever preserved undiminished, by any native heresy, or schism, the most glorious title of "Island of Saints"—as ministers of the sanctuary, who deem it a special privilege to apply to the study of sacred knowledge, under the shadow of the Chair of Peter, in this city of holy shrines, the new Jerusalem of Christ, the central See of the Church of God—as Catholics who contemplate, in the monuments of the Eternal City, the triumph of the Church over the powers of the world, and who, moreover, are witnesses (some of us for many years) of the mild and paternal sway of your Holiness in your temporal dominions, we deem it our duty to approach the throne of our beloved Father, to tender the tribute of our affection and sympathy, and to present to him the homage of all that we possess, as well as of our devotion and love. At the same time, Most Holy Father, we wish to record our protest against every violation of your territorial rights, and to declare, in unison with the whole Catholic world, that we will ever look upon any usurpation or political infringement on the temporal sovereignty of the Holy See as a deep wound inflicted on the whole Catholic Church of God Yes, Most Holy Father, in the political independence of the successors of St Peter we recognize a providential disposition of that Divine Spirit which vivifies and directs the Catholic Church—for it is yours to watch over the spiritual interests, not alone of one province, or of one kingdom, but of all the kingdoms of the universe that are illumined by the rays of heavenly faith. It is yours to uphold the eternal laws of justice, the indissolubility of the marriage bond, the discipline of the Church, and to vindicate their infraction by the proper penalties, no matter who may be the offender, whether rich or poor, potentate or subject; and hence it has been recognized for centuries by the jurisprudence of all nations that the common Father of all should be subject to none. Most Holy Father, if your sorrows have been great, they have been only portionate to the glory with which you have adorned the Catholic Church. Too many were the bulwarks raised by your hands around the mystic edifice of the House of God—too happy were the efforts of your zeal in invigorating sacred discipline, as well as in extending the tents of Israel, and gathering new nations to the fold of Christ, not to provoke the special rage of Satan, and render your sacred person the special object of his fiercest assaults. But be consoled, Most Holy Father, for whilst the voice of History attests that every hand raised against the Vicar of Christ has withered, each era of glory in the Church of God has been marked by the fierce storms which assailed the Bark of Peter The Immaculate Virgin, whose brow you have decked with a peerless crown, shall once more crush with a virginal foot the infernal the head of enemy that assails you. And when it was asked in the words of the Psalmist: "Why do nations rage and people devise vain things?" the Divine assurance will be verified in reply, "He that ruleth in the Heavens shall laugh at them, the Lord shall deride them." Most Holy Father, at your sacred feet we ask for ourselves, our Bishops, our families, and our whole nation, your Apostolic Benediction.

REPLY OF POPE PIUS IX.

The reply of the Holy Father was to the following effect:

No one could have doubted that faithful and Catholic Ireland, which in every age has given such signal proofs of its attachment to the successors of St Peter, and so zealously guarded the only true treasure on earth, the Catholic faith, would be found amongst the first to manifest its sympathy in the present afflicting circumstances and sufferings of the Vicar of Christ, of the Head of the Church, or, rather, of the Church itself For it is certain that all the schemes and plotting of the revolutionists of the present day have for their chief object to assail our Catholic faith and destroy the Church of God. Nor is it without pleasure that I reflect that the words of the Gospel of this day: "*Omne Regnum in seipsum divisum deso'abitur*,"* cannot be applied to you. Union is the secret of strength, and it was your union in past ages, as at the present day, that enabled you to preserve the faith and strike with terror the enemies of God. I recommend to you this holy union - union of faith, union of sentiments union of charity, union of prayer; for prayer is our support in every tribulation Let this union be ever inviolate, and you may rest assured of Heaven's aid. I enjoin you to exhort all to maintain it, whilst at the same time you will communicate my blessing to the thousands and millions of your countrymen who so fearlessly and efficaciously display their sympathy, and by words and deeds sustain the rights of the Holy See. Whilst you are thus gathered around the threshold of the House of God —of that sacred edifice in which are divinely deposited the blessings and the riches of faith, the powers of hell cannot overcome you. This is the threshold that opens on the path of salvation, and ever bear in mind that through it alone can man hope to enter the fold of Christ I exhort you, therefore, to cherish this sacred threshold, and to be vigilant in its defence, especially by prayer. Prayer has always been our refuge; let your prayers never cease to be offered up to God, Who, in His own time, will make known His power to the nations

---

*"Every kingdom divided against itself shall be made desolate."—ST. MATTHEW, xii., 25.

that now "rage against the Most High," and endeavor to destroy the work of His right hand. Powerful, indeed, are the enemies that assail us; but God's omnipotent arm will crush and discomfit them. However, let it be our prayer that the majesty and power of God may be displayed, not in the chastisements which proceed from His divine justice, but in the fullness and depths of His infinite mercy. With sentiments of the liveliest gratitude, I leave you now, imparting to you my blessing, and I pray the Almighty to shower down the plentitude of His benediction upon you, that it may accompany you on your journey, be communicated to your families and relatives, and to the whole "Island of Saints." In return pray to God for me; pray to Him to grant me a spirit of patience and resignation to the Divine will, as well as of courage and fortitude amidst the difficulties which now encompass me. Pray to Him especially through that Saint, your glorious Apostle, St. Patrick, whose festival and memory you will celebrate in a few days. That great Saint so deeply rooted the plant of divine faith in Ireland, that the continual assaults and persecution to which your country was subjected could never destroy the practice of all Christian virtues for which your island is renowned, or weaken its devotedness and reverence to the Vicar of Christ. Pray to him now that he is seated near the Throne of God, that he may obtain for you the greatest of all heavenly blessings—which no creature can merit—the gift of final perseverance. I impart to you now my blessing in the Name of Jesus Christ, in the Name of the Most Holy Trinity, of the Father, the Son, and the Holy Ghost; may these Names be ever on your lips during life; in the name of Mary the Immaculate Virgin, who is our hope and our consolation; and may you utter them with your dying breath when about to be freed from all earthly sufferings, and admitted to the joys of the Lord.

In the foregoing magnificent tribute to the Irish people, Pope Pius IX., arises up in the nineteenth century to give his testimony concerning the fidelity of the Irish people to the Chair of St. Peter, and thereby to vindicate that consistent Catholic race from the aspersions cast upon their Christian character by the forged Bulls falsely attributed to his predecessors Adrian IV., and Alexander III.

Speaking of the fidelity of the Irish people to Rome Pope Pius IX., uses these words which welled up from the deep gratitude he felt in his heart for "faithful and Catholic Ireland, which, *in every age*, has given such *signal proofs of its attachment to the successors of St. Peter*, and so zealously guarded the only true treasure on earth." It follows, therefore, that the language used in the two Bulls under criticism was purposely invented by some enemy of the Church, the Irish people, and of truth.

———

In connection with the exalted eulogy which Pope Pius IX., bestowed upon the Irish people for their fidelity to the Vicar of Christ—*throughout all ages*—it may be well to annex the following beautiful tribute from Cardinal Manning on the same point. The sentiments of both these exalted Church dignitaries demonstrate beyond cavil that they were fully conscious that the calumnies against the Catholic character, fidelity and consistency of the Irish people injected into the Adrian and Alexander Bulls, were founded only in the malicious misrepresentations of the miserable hireling who concocted them, and that neither of the Popes mentioned ever saw the diabolical documents in which they appeared.

Speaking of Ireland's fidelity to the Holy Roman See, his Eminence Cardinal Manning made use of these glowing words of admiration for the sufferings of the Irish people for the true Faith.

"For 300 years the Catholic Church in England lay desolate. For 300 years there was no hierarchy uniting it with the hierarchy of the Church throughout the world; for 300 years there were scattered faithful who preserved their religion at the peril of their lives; there were scattered Priests who ministered to them in secret; but there was no Catholic Church in England in the full perfection of its structure and authority. It had fallen from being a province in the Empire of Our Divine Master to be a wilderness. The greater part of those who hear me are the children of a Church which was never wrecked, and though trodden down and persecuted, never lay desolate. It never lost its Bishops. They were martyred, but others rose in their stead. It never lost its Priesthood. They were martyred; they were deprived; they were exiled; they were driven away; but when one left his post vacant, another took his place. The Episcopate and Priesthood of Ireland have never failed. Pius

IX. had no need to do in Ireland what he had need to do in England. No Pontiff had been called to restore the work of St. Patrick; and yet, the children of the Church in Ireland have gone throughout the wide world, and wheresoever you have been scattered you have carried with you the holy Catholic faith. Not so with us. And therefore I call on you by that greater benediction which you have never lost, to work together with us, in union of gratitude and charity, to enable the Catholic Church in England to spread among heathen nations that faith which has cost you so dear and which you have loved better than your life."

CHAPTER XXXI.

The Paternal Love of Pope Leo XIII. for the Irish People.—How Public Opinion was Prejudiced against the Holy Father.—Calumnies cabled around the World.—The Pope presented in his True Character as the Consistent Friend of the People of Ireland in their struggle for National Independence by rightful means.

Among the long line of successors of St. Peter, few Popes have been more maligned and misrepresented through the public press than Leo XIII., at present gloriously reigning. Since the very day of his election, eleven years ago, the enemies of the Church in Italy, France and England, have been untiring in their efforts to prejudice public opinion against him in every portion of the world. A coterie of Jews and infidels have the management of the cable dispatches sent from Rome, and, in a hundred instances at least, some of the most malignant and baseless misrepresentations of both the public and private acts of the Holy Father, have been furnished to the reading world for no other purpose, seemingly, than to arouse the antipathy of all nations against the innocent victim of their diabolical slanders.

Realizing the unity of Faith and of love which exists between the Vicar of Christ and the glorious Catholic race of Ireland, the enemies of God's Supreme representative on earth have labored with might and main to break that adamantine chain of consistent loyalty which unites the hearts of the Irish people in every land with the Head of Christ's Church. For this purpose Pope Leo XIII. had to be accused of holding opinions adverse to the national aspirations of the Irish people. Fabulous charges were concocted by an Italian coterie of conspirators against truth, and then circulated by cable to all parts of the world. The Holy Father was accused of being hostile to Home Rule; of being opposed to any redress for Ireland's political wrongs through public agitation; and of being in league with the English Ministry to keep the Irish people plunged in the sea of misery which has marred their progress ever since English law became supreme in that misruled Island.

These calumniating charges were kept up so constantly and repeated so often that they had a direful effect in many instances. Falsehood flies with lightning speed, whilst the stride of truth is slow but sure. Before, however, the truth could reach the public ear in distant lands, even some Catholics had come to the conclusion that Pope Leo XIII. was not the friend of the Irish people. How groundless and erroneous was that opinion thus precipitately and passionately formed, is best known now to many once guilty of rash judgment against the Vicar of Christ.

The best test by which to judge Pope Leo XIII., in his connection with the affairs of Ireland, is to place before the reading world his words and his acts concerning Irish affairs, and when these have been presented in the garb of truth, it will be clear to every impartial reader that the hatred which Pope Leo XIII. is said to have manifested towards the cause of national independence in Ireland, was merely the malicious invention of mendacious allies of anti-Christ, whilst the love which His Holiness manifested in every instance toward the Irish people was the love of a Father for his children—whose temporal and spiritual happiness pervaded every pulsation of his heart.

Let us, therefore, pass under review the acts and expressions of Pope Leo XIII. during the past eleven years, so as to exhibit the Holy Father in the true light in which he stands now—and will stand for ever—in the estimation of all just-minded men. This is the more necessary because prejudice and passion have forced false conclusions upon the minds of some Catholics who have seen the reigning Pontiff only through the haze which hatred has cast around his august presence for the purpose of antagonizing the children of the Church of God against their spiritual Father.

Monsignor O'Rielly, in his "Life of Leo XIII.," informs us that shortly after the election of his Holiness, one of the first missions entrusted by the Holy Father to Cardinal Franchi, Secretary of State, was to visit Ireland for the purpose of gaining personal knowledge of the true condition of that unhappy country.

"Certain it is," says the author in question, "that Leo XIII. had a clear conception of *the just claims of Ireland to self-government* and to a full and practical religious liberty, and that his efforts thenceforward aimed at keeping the Irish Catholics and the National party within the strict bounds of constitutional agitation, legal, orderly, and peaceful methods, while seeking for the justice which so many Englishmen acknowledge to be due them."*

Thus we see that even in the very first years of his pontificate Pope Leo XIII. was a firm believer in the justice of Ireland's claims to self-government, and as the Chief Shepherd of Christ's flock, he was determined that as far as his counsel and influence could go, the Irish cause should never be crimsoned with crime against the supreme laws of God or the Christian ethics of His Church. No Catholic can gainsay these precautionary methods of the Holy Father—who is the guardian of God's Faith.

In March, 1878, the Mayor and municipal officers of the city of Cork sent an address of congratulation and filial homage to the Holy Father on his election to the pontifical throne In response thereto Pope Leo XIII. expressed his deep sense of gratitude for their filial affection and constant love. In concluding, his Holiness said: "To you therefore, beloved sons, we gladly express in this letter our gratitude and affection; and, ready as we are ever *to give you every proof of our fatherly love*, we pray God from our heart to be evermore your protector and helper, and so to inspire your counsels that your labors may procure His glory as well as *the welfare and prosperity of your fellow-citizens.*"

Such language coming from the pen of a great Pontiff, proves beyond cavil that every pulse of his heart beat in unison with the aspirations of the Irish people for Home Rule and national prosperity.

It is asserted by designing demagogues of low degree and of little conscience that Pope Leo XIII. wrote two Letters to the Irish Bishops in the years 1882 and 1883, in which he unreservedly condemned the Irish Land League and the National League which succeeded it, and which subsists to this day. How far such an assertion is from the truth may best be ascertained by a candid perusal of the Letters themselves, copious extracts from which we append in order that truth may triumph over falsehood in such an important historical matter.

The Letters in question which Pope Leo XIII. addressed to the Hierarchy of Ireland in reply to several missives sent by them to him, as well as to Pastorals issued by the Irish Bishops concerning agrarian outrages then becoming prevalent, were dated August 1st, 1882, and January 1st, 1883, respectively, and the sentiments they contained partook far more of Fatherly love than of the passionate condemnation so falsely attributed to the present Pontiff.

"The kindly affection which we have cherished toward Irishmen," says the Holy

---

* Life of Pope Leo XIII., p. 343.

Father in his Letter dated August 1st, 1882, "and which seems to increase with their present sufferings, forces us to follow the course of events in your island with the deep concern of a fatherly heart. From their consideration, however, we derive more of anxiety than of comfort, seeing that the condition of the people is not what we wish it to be, one of peace and prosperity.

"There still remain many sources of grievance; conflicting party passions incite many persons to violent courses; some even have stained themselves with fearful murders, as if a nation's welfare could be procured by dishonor and crime!

"This state of things is to you as well as to us a cause of serious alarm, as we had evidence of ere now, and as we have just noticed by the resolutions adopted in your meeting at Dublin Fearful as you were, for the salvation of your people, you have clearly shown them what they have to refrain from in the present critical conjuncture and in the very midst of the national struggle.

"In this you have discharged the duty imposed alike by your episcopal office and *your love of country.* At no time do a people more need the advice of their Bishops than when, carried away by some powerful passion, they see before them deceptive prospects of bettering their condition. It is when impelled to commit *what is criminal and disgraceful* that the multitude need the voice and the hand of the Bishop to keep them back from doing wrong, and to recall them by timely exhortation to moderation and self-control. Most timely, therefore, was your advice to your people, reminding them of the Saviour's injunction, 'Seek ye first the kingdom of God and His justice.' For all Christians are therein commanded to keep their thoughts fixed, in their ordinary conduct as well as in their political acts, on the goal of their eternal salvation, and to hold all things subordinate *to the fulfilment of their duty to God.*

"If Irishmen will only keep to these rules of conduct they will be free to seek to rise from the state of misery into which they have fallen. *They surely have a right to claim the lawful redress of their wrongs. For no one can maintain that Irishmen cannot do what is lawful for all other peoples to do.*

"Nevertheless, even the public welfare must be regulated by the principles of honesty and righteousness. It is a matter for serious thought that the most righteous cause is dishonored by being *promoted by iniquitous means.* Justice is inconsistent not only with all violence, but especially so with any participation in *the deeds of unlawful societies,* which, under the fair pretext of righting wrong, bring all communities *to the very verge of ruin.* Just as our predecessors have taught that all right-minded men should carefully *shun these dark associations,* even so you have added your timely admonition to the same effect.

"As, however, these same dangers may recur, it will become your watchful care to renew these admonitions, beseeching all Irishmen by their reverence for the Catholic name, and *by their very love for their native land, to have nothing to do with these secret societies.* These can in no way help a nation to obtain redress for its grievances; and, all too frequently, they madly impel those whom they have ensared to commit crimes.

"*Irishmen take a just pride in being called Catholics*—an appellation which, according to St. Augustine, means *the guardians of all honor and uprightness, the followers of all equity and justice.* Let them fulfill by their acts all that this word *Catholic* implies; and let them, while vindicating their own just rights, endeavor to be indeed all that their name suggests. Let them remember that '*the highest liberty consists in being free from all crime;*' and let no one among them, so long as he lives, have to undergo lawful punishment '*as a murderer, or a thief, or a slanderer, or one who has coveted other people's property.*'"

" . . . We deem what you have decreed concerning your young priests to be proper and timely. For if ever there were circumstances when priests should be zealous and energetic in maintaining public order amid popular excitement, such are the present circumstances with you. And just as the estimation in which one is held by the public is the measure of his influence over others, even so should priests endeavor to win this public esteem by self-respect, firmness, and temperate word and deed. They should do nothing that prudence could condemn, nothing that can fan the flame of party strife. . . . .

"In this way, and by following such rules of conduct, *we do believe that Ireland shall yet attain to the prosperity which she seeks, and that, too, without wronging any one*. As we have already declared to you, we trust still that the government will conclude *to grant satisfaction to the just claims of Irishmen*. This we are led to believe from their acquaintance with the true state of things and from their statesmanlike wisdom; for there can be no question that on the safety of Ireland depends the tranquility of the whole empire.

"Meanwhile, sustained by this hope, we shall lose no opportunity of helping the Irish people by our advice, pouring forth to God for them prayers filled with the warmest zeal and love, beseeching God to look down with kindness on a nation made illustrious by the practice of so many virtues, to appease the present storm of political passion, and to reward them at length with peace and prosperity."

Breathes there a Catholic so dead to Divine Faith and so disloyal to the justice of Ireland's holy cause, as to condemn Pope Leo XIII. for a single expression contained in the above love-laden epistle to the Irish Episcopate? The Holy Father counsels Christian justice and he condemns the commission of crime. What true Irish patriot desires to ignore God's laws in order to gain liberty for his native land? "Let them remember," says the paternal Pontiff, "*that the highest liberty consists in being free from all crime*," and in thus keeping the Irish Land League free from the stain of crime, the Holy Father became at once the most powerful as well as the most prominent friend of the Irish people in the whole world. The Popes never condemned constitutional agitation as a political remedy for political wrongs, but when misguided men go outside God's law and the moral law in order to find, through secret and illegal sources, remedies for political injustice—then it is the duty of not only Popes, Bishops and priests, to condemn their course, but even the humblest Catholic layman should raise his voice to warn his fellow-countrymen against becoming the willing victims of such vicious men, who seek only self-aggrandizement by betraying their dupes, and earning the wages of sin by turning State's evidence against the very men they have drawn into their meshes.

The cruel operation of the Coercion Act in Ireland, in the year 1882, was the cause of much turmoil, excitement and crime in that sad country during that year. Accordingly, the Hierarchy appealed to the Holy Father for light, counsel and guidance in the hour of their country's trial, and in replying to their appeals Pope Leo XIII. wrote thus:

"Your letter," he says in reply, ' is a new proof of your respect and affection, as it is an evidence of the gratitude you and they feel toward us for our concern in the welfare of Ireland, and for the counsels given in our letter of August 1st, last.

" . . . We cannot help congratulating you . . . on the zeal displayed in calming the existing agitation. . . . We also congratulate these children of the Church, who have listened so obediently to your admonitions, and who, enduring with holy Christian fortitude the sufferings of adversity, knew how to keep their sense of wrong *within the bounds imposed by duty and religion*.

"Still, although Irish Catholics continue to give splendid proofs of their zeal for religion and of obedience to the Supreme Pastor, the condition of public affairs requires that they should bear in mind the rules of conduct which our affectionate solicitude for them induced us to lay down for their direction. *The secret societies*, as we have learned with pain during these last months, always persist in putting their hope *in the commission of crime*, in kindling into fury popular passions, in seeking for the national grievances remedies worse than the grievances themselves, and in pursuing a path which will lead *to ruin instead of to prosperity.*

"It is, therefore, imperative that you inculcate deeply into the minds of your beloved people, as we have already said that *there is but one rule for what is right and for what is useful;* that the just cause of their country must be kept separate from the aims, the plots, the deeds of criminal associations; *that it is both right and lawful for all who suffer wrong to seek redress by all lawful means, but that it is neither right nor lawful to have recourse to crime for redress;* that Divine Providence enables the just to reap at last a joyful harvest from their patient waiting and their virtuous deeds, whereas the evil doers, having run their dark course to no purpose, *incur the severe condemnation of both God and man.*

"While we remind you of all these truths, impel'ed to do so by our ardent desire to secure some solace, quiet and prosperity for Ireland, we are also filled with confidence that you, acting in concert and bound together by brotherly love, will continue to bestow your best care in preventing your faithful people from having anything to do with men who, carried away by their own passions, think they are doing their country service *when they commit the worst crimes,* and who, by urging others to like wickedness, bring shame and dishonor on the cause of the people."

Neither in the above extracts nor in those copied from the preceding Letter, do we find a single word of condemnation against the Land League, although this was openly charged against the Pope in the press of the period. The Holy Father commends a peaceful solution of Ireland's difficulties, and the only objects against which he hurls the anathemas of the Church is *crime and secret societies* - two fatuitous factors which have worked ruin in Ireland to every cause with which they were allied. Here, again it is self-evident that Pope Leo XIII. had the cause of Ireland close at heart when he sent these Letters to the Bishops of Ireland, and every friend of Home Rule will bless him for his paternal solicitude.

Commenting on the fatherly counsel which the Vicar of Christ imparted to the Irish people in order that even their aspirations for freedom for their native land might be in full accord with the justice of God, Monsignor O'Rielly, from whose biography we quote, says:

"It was worthy of the great heart of the Pontiff, tried as he was then by many sorrows, and burdened by an intolerable load of care, to utter his sentiments regarding Ireland with such solemn emphasis and such fatherly tenderness, while the struggle in Ireland was growing in intensity, and every effort to coerce only increased tenfold the power of resistance, and intensified in the same measure the hatred of laws, law-givers, and law-courts, wh'ch to the people meant only the administration of injustice.

"No doubt the words of Leo XIII., repeated and commended from every pulpit in Ireland, went far to assuage the public resentment at the passing and enforcement of the 'Crimes Act,' and still further to prevent many from joining the dark societies which always spring from national misery and thrive on national discord.

"The Land League was suppressed and its members imprisoned by the hundred; but this repression only left the secret societies a free field to work, and murders and outrages increased apace. The prison-doors were opened by the government, and it became at once apparent that the Land League, instead of being a source of agitation outrage, and crime, was the only effective barrier against them.

"Then arose the National League, which grew and grew until it counted among its members or its fellow-workers the whole body of the clergy, nine-tenths of the Catholic laity, and not a few of the most enlightened and influential among Protestant clergymen and laymen.

"An incident occurred soon after this which chilled for the moment the warm feelings of gratitude and veneration felt in Ireland and among Irishmen everywhere for the Holy Father. We allude to the famous Propaganda circular. But the See of Dublin becoming vacant in February, 1885, by the death of Cardinal McCabe, the Sovereign Pontiff reserved to himself to confirm the choice made of Very Rev. Dr.

Walsh, President of St. Patrick's College, Maynooth, to succeed to the deceased Cardinal.

"The election of this distinguished man was in itself remarkable, as indicating among the clergy of the metropolis an almost unanimous impulse to join the national movement and thus reverse the policy followed by the two last Archbishops. The intrigues, authorized or unauthorized, which thereafter occurred, to have the nomination of Dr. Walsh set aside by Rome, proved ineffectual. The Irish Hierarchy had been summoned to Rome before the death of Cardinal McCabe. They repaired thither in May. The Sovereign Pontiff had, therefore, ample opportunity to ascertain the wishes of the Irish Episcopate on the subject of this important election, and to be made acquainted with the true significance of the national movement.

"In June Dr. Walsh's nomination was confirmed. Thenceforward this Prelate was both the organ of his brother-Bishops in all public and national matters and the spokesman of his fellow-countrymen. From that moment, too, there was a unity of thought, purpose, and action between the clergy and the Parliamentary party.

"The passing cloud which had in the Propaganda circular for a moment darkened and chilled the Irish Catholic heart was now forgotten, and Leo XIII., became to Ireland and her sons the *Lumen in Cœlo* of their own St. Malachy.

"In dealing with the British cabinet the Pope, while considering the interests of the Catholic subjects in Great Britain and in Ireland, as well as throughout the colonies, had also to have a regard for the feelings of the Irish race both inside and outside the British dominions. As the settled gloom on the material prospects of the Emerald Isle deepened with every decade that passed, leaving the Irish agriculturist less of resources and hope, and Irish labor no remunerative field or market within the compass of the Irish seas, the best and most religious men in the nation found increasing difficulty in restraining the outbursts of mingled despair and righteous wrath arising from wrongs easy of redress, but to which the Government only applied homœopathic doses of relief, coupled with intolerable coercion.

"English statesmanship, Orange fanaticism, and hatred of race cried aloud: Let them starve or emigrate! What could the religious guides or the wise political leaders of a starving and oppressed people say or do to prevent an armed uprising, which would have justified the accusations and the demands of the exterminators? And what could the fatherly heart and the unpurchasable justice of the Roman Pontiff do to save the sufferers, to inspire the misgoverning with a sense of equity and humanity, to refuse to the oppressor a sanction of any of his schemes for redressing the wrong, but what, in the preceding pages, as we can judge from his own letter, he has done?

"He has set the seal of his sanction on the justice and righteousness of Irish claims for self-government; he has recommended to the nation and its leaders, churchmen and laymen, obedience to the laws, peaceful and constitutional methods, and he has expressed his hope and uttered his prayer *that justice may be done to Ireland.*"

CHAPTER XXXII.

Further Manifestations of the Love of Pope Leo XIII., for the Irish People.—Address of His Holiness to the Irish Pilgrims in Rome.—The Papal Rescript of 1888 Explained.—Archbishop Walsh's Views.—Addresses of his Grace on the Sympathy of the Holy Father for Ireland. Opinions of Cardinal Pecci, Cardinal Moran, Bishop Keane and Monsignor O'Rielly.

We now come down to the eventful year of 1888, during which the personal character of his Holiness Pope Leo XIII. was made a prominent target for traducement at the hands of both the avowed enemies of the Church as well as by hot-headed politicians who—taking their cue from anti-Irish and anti-Catholic authority—condemned the Pontiff at present gloriously reigning, even before they knew the truth or the falsehood of the charges brought against him concerning his sentiments on the Irish question.

The first important event which took place during the year 1888, in which the Irish people were interested, was the visit of the Irish pilgrims to the Eternal City. Whilst visiting the shrines of the Apostles the Irish pilgrims had an audience with the Sovereign Pontiff, during which an address of fealty to the Holy See and also to the Successor of St. Peter was presented, and in reply thereto his Holiness—after alluding to other matters—said:

"We accept heartily the assurance you give Us of the great joy with which both you and your fellow-countrymen commemorate Our Sacerdotal Jubilee. On Our side We desire that you should have no doubt as to Our reciprocating your affection.

"Yes, indeed, Our mind was turned to Ireland from the very beginning of Our Pontificate with a true fatherly solicitude. For Ireland, commended herself to Us on many grounds, above all for the integrity of her faith, upheld by the triumphant courage of your ancestors, after the good seed had been sown among them by the labors and virtues of St. Patrick—a faith which Ireland has handed down to you as a deposit to be sacredly guarded.

"Nor is it without good reason that you firmly rely on Our affection. We shall never cease to treat the Irish people with the love which We justly owe them; and We shall therefore continue to watch over their peace and prosperity in a way to convince everybody that We have always responded to the trust you have reposed in Us.

"Of this kindly disposition towards you, you have at this moment a striking evidence in the fact that We have, at the present juncture of your affairs, sent to Ireland on a specific Mission, Our Venerable Brother, the Archbishop of Damietta, in order to make it possible for Ourselves to gather from his report, information about the condition of things there, and what is best suited to you.

"But, inasmuch as your difficulties are most urgent you must in your conduct, adopt the rule laid down in the Letters addressed by Us some years ago to the Archbishop of Dublin. This is what your religion requires of you, that religion in which the Irish nation chiefly glories; it is also what is demanded by the common good of the people, since it never can serve the common good to violate justice—the foundation of order and all prosperity."

The most hypocritical heretic can find nothing in this address to turn to the Holy Father's disadvantage, or in any way to lessen his right to the gratitude of all the Irish people, as one of their best friends and their most reliable counsellors

The feast of St. Agatha, (Feb. 5th, 1888,) was celebrated with great pomp, ceremony and joy in the Eternal City, and after the religious exercises of the day had been brought to a close, a banquet was given at the Irish College, at which the toast of the Holy Father Pope Leo XIII., was given and responded to by his Eminence Cardinal Schiaffino, who thus portrayed the feelings of love which welled up in the Holy Father's heart for the Irish people and the lovely land for whose liberty they were struggling. His Eminence made this allusion to the Irish question, which is another proof in contradiction to the angry aspersions cast upon the Holy Father by both open and secret enemies:

"Although every Catholic rejoices when he hears the Holy Father named, the special ties which bind the Irish Catholics to the Pope are more holy and indissoluble, because united by the sacred title of martyrdom. For three hundred years, gentlemen, you have struggled to maintain your faith, to uphold the prerogatives of St. Peter and the right of the Holy Roman See. While defending that Primacy and those inalienable rights you have spared no sacrifice, and have freely given up the dearest things of the earth. The sad history of your country has won for you the love of the Pope. The green flag of Ireland has always been pure and stainless, and as that flag has waved in your own glorious land, you need not fear to unfurl it in the Vatican, where you have just offered to Leo XIII. the homage of your love and faith. You are passing through difficult times, and if you only keep away from dangerous enemies, *if you will give no ear to societies condemned by the Pope, your triumph cannot be long delayed.*"

Here again we find in the words of Cardinal Schiaffino, a reverberation of the language of the Holy Father addressed to the Irish people: "If you will give no ear to societies condemned by the Pope, your triumph cannot be long delayed." The Holy Father has no condemnation to hurl at the legitimate struggles of the Irish people for the attainment of their liberties, his condemnation including only acts of violation of God's law and the moral order— which acts were caused by the secret societies which were so justly condemned by not only the Pontiff and the Cardinals, but also by every Bishop in Ireland as well as by Charles Stewart Parnell and the Catholic members of the Irish movement.

In April, 1888, a Rescript was issued in Rome which caused a great sensation throughout the whole world. The excitement at the time was both intense and vindictive beyond consistency—even among Catholics themselves. The Holy Father was assailed by the Press of Europe as the foe of freedom, and even in Ireland he was ranked among the staunchest allies of England in her efforts to keep Ireland under the galling yoke of slavery.

But now that the clouds which obscured the vision of thousands of well-meaning Irish Catholics have become dissipated, let us look at this doubly-denounced Rescript dispassionately, and we shall soon learn how illogical and indiscreet were those Catholics who considered Pope Leo XIII. Ireland's worst enemy because a Roman Congregation had certain questions in morals proposed to them and the Cardinals gave their decisions based upon the questions as they were put before them.

It is now nearly a year since this document was issued, and there is not on record a single case where it has operated to the injury of the Irish National cause. Why is this? Simply because the advice of the Holy Father was hearkened to by the Hierarchy, the priests and the people of Ireland, and the constitutional agitation of the Irish question has not since been sullied by the commission of any act at variance with the rules for its regulation as laid down by Pope Leo XIII.

On May 24th, 1888, when the excitement regarding the Rescript was yet at white heat, Archbishop Walsh of Dublin was on the eve of leaving Rome for Ireland, when he was favored with a long interview by the Holy Father, and he afterwards stated publicly that—so far as the Irish question was concerned—it was of a "*most satisfactory character.*"

The Rome correspondent of the Boston *Pilot*, cabled about the same time to the effect that "the Irish cause" had "nothing to fear from Leo XIII.," and also that "papal interference in Irish politics is impossible."

Immediately after the departure of Archbishop Walsh from Rome, the correspondent of the Liverpool *Catholic Times* in that city wrote an account of the interview between the Pope and the Prelate, in which he thus described the nature of the document which was the innocent cause of such excitement for the time being:

"The Archbishop had an audience with his Holiness a few days before he left, which lasted more than an hour, and the result of it leaves his Grace full of hope.

He takes with him to the Irish people a message of encouragement from the Holy Father in reference to the National movement which will dispel a good deal of misunderstanding, and will calm the fears of many. The message, I am sure, will leave no doubt on the minds of the people about the sympathy of the Holy Father with both the present object of the National movement and with the movement itself. No persons are more dissatisfied with the recent Decree than those who tried every means, fair and foul, to obtain it — and no persons have more reason. What they worked for was the condemnation of the movement itself, or, at least, of the National League. Their misrepresentations and calumnies have been nailed, and they themselves have been found out. It is hardly possible to give you an adequate idea of all that has been said and done to deceive the authorities in Rome and that by those from whom ought to be expected more respect for the Holy See and more regard for the Decalogue which they so zealously preach to others. That Ireland has not been placed under an *interdict* as the effect of their falsehoods, ought to be a clear indication to those malicious busybodies that the authorities here suspected them even without any refutation of their tales. Certainly, if all they said were believed, nothing less could be done.

But the Archbishop of Dublin has nailed every calumny, and I believe that the very near future will give the well known clique cause to regret their action much more than their present disappointment causes them to regret it now. It may be said that they believed that they were doing a duty. That may be. But, however, a sense of duty may urge them to carry their tales to the authorities, it is hard to see how it could make them go about the shops and private houses here, trying to poison the minds of every one."

These facts so succinctly set forth by the correspondent in question also serve to show how inconsiderate and uncalled-for was all the malicious misrepresentation circulated at that time, and fanned into flame by designing men for the sole purpose of making a breach in the bond of unity which has always bound Ireland to Rome, and which has been an eye-sore to all the enemies of the Church throughout the past fourteen centuries.

When Archbishop Walsh arrived in Dublin he was accorded a reception by the Dean and Chapter of his Archdiocese, at which an address of welcome was presented to him, and as the Archbishop's response thereto will serve still further to show that the Rescript which caused so much rancor was never intended to interfere with the legitimate actions of the Irish people in their agitation for Home Rule, we print the following extracts therefrom:

I beg to thank you, Monsignor, and you, my lord, and all the members of the venerable Chapter of Dublin, for the warmhearted welcome with which you have greeted me on my return from Rome. It is, I believe, without precedent in the annals of this ancient See — at all events since the close of the era of persecution — that its Archbishop should have been absent from it so long as I have been. But I think I am safe in saying that at no time in all those centuries could an Archbishop of Dublin have had the satisfaction of feeling that he was engaged in a work more directly tending to the advancement of the best interests of the diocese and of its people than that in which it was my privilege to be engaged, in compliance with the wishes of the Sovereign Pontiff himself, during the months of my recent absence in Rome.

"That absence, I have learned, was at times, and especially at one most critical moment, a source of anxiety to you, and to the clergy and people of the diocese at large. If I use strong language in referring to those things that gave rise to your anxiety, I only borrow the words of your address. No other ground for it existed than that 'unbroken series' of 'perversions' and, indeed, of 'absolute falsehoods,' which were poured forth from day to day by men whose Pharisaical zeal for the observance of one of the commandments seems absolutely to have blinded them to the existence of another that stands by its side.

"It was their policy, it would seem, to set in circulation such rumors as they deemed most likely to serve their purpose in shaking that firm foundation of Irish Catholicity, the confidence of our people in the Holy See. Viewing it merely as a policy, we cannot deny that it was in some sense a skillfully devised one. But it labored under one serious drawback. The course that it could run could, at the best, be but a short one. They could hardly hope that its period of usefulness to them could be measured by months, or indeed by many weeks. How short-lived it would be must have been as well known to its authors as it was to me, or to the great Pontiff whose venerable name and whose august dignity they treated with such painful levity in presuming day after day to make him figure in their foolish tales. From the very nature of the case, the mere fact of my return to my post of duty would manifestly be sufficient to overturn the whole fabric of their misrepresentations. Knowing all this, they must have been sadly astray in their estimate of the firmness and constancy of the attachment of our people to the See of Peter when they so foolishly thought that any harm could come to it from so frail an engine of attack.

* * * * *

"To these, and to the other matters of interest referred to in the latter portion of your address, I shall doubtless again have occasion to refer. But I do not wish to leave unused the opportunity which you have to-day afforded me, of saying at all events this—that the Holy Father was no less anxious to learn the truth about Ireland that I was to make the freest use of the occasion which he so graciously extended to me, of putting before him in the fullest detail the true character of the claims and aspirations of our people. Whether as regards the movement for national autonomy, or as regards the national struggle for the redress of all that cruel injustice which, notwithstanding the adoption of so many measures of reform, still oppresses the agricultural tenants of Ireland; all those claims and aspirations are now most fully in his possession. He has grasped them in all their bearings and, whilst of course we must remember that in matters purely of politics it is not for him to interfere, it is well for us to know, and it is my privilege to be authorized to make it known to the people of Ireland, *that in every legitimate effort for the attainment of that for which they strive, our people may count upon the fullest sympathy.*

"Wherever else the foolish fiction may have had its way, that the legislation of recent years has done justice to the people of Ireland, or to the Irish tenant, that fiction finds no footing at all events in the Vatican. Unfortunately indeed for Ireland and her people, and unfortunately, most of all, for that cruelly-oppressed section of her people to which I have just now referred, the revolutionary changes of modern times have left but little of political influence in the hands of the Sovereign Pontiff. *That influence, if it existed, would to-day be freely and unreservedly placed at our disposal.*

"Of some incidents of our recent history, as they occurred during my absence from Ireland, I do not wish to speak in detail. Some words of mine have already been published in which I spoke of the pain they had brought to the heart of the Holy Father. To those who know, as I have reason to know, the warmth of his paternal feeling for his Irish children, it will not come as a surprise to hear that during the months of anxiety through which we have recently passed, the thought which brought to him perhaps the heaviest load of sorrow was that of *the injustice which seemed to be done to him* by some, whose words appeared to indicate a want of confidence in the sincerity and earnestness of his desire for the welfare of our people. Of all this I had, before leaving Rome, an assurance from his own lips. I hold in my hands to-day an assurance of it in a more enduring form, in a letter to the Irish Bishops.

"In this most important document, whilst enforcing with all the weight of his supreme pastoral authority the unlawfulness, as well as the short-sighted policy of allowing the banner that is uplifted in so good a cause to be darkened by even the faintest shadow of moral guilt, his Holiness assures the Bishops of Ireland, and through them the Irish people, that there is not one, even of ourselves, who feels more intensely than he does the miseries under which our country still suffers. Not satisfied even with this, he assures us in words of solemn emphasis of the earnestness of his desire that our distracted country may speedily receive the blessing of a lasting peace, a peace based upon that which alone can be regarded as a solid or secure foundation—the attainment of that prosperity which Ireland, by the heroic steadfastness of her faith through centuries of persecution, has so nobly earned."

It is hardly necessary to point out to the reader the sterling sentiments which the Holy Father advances for Ireland's temporal and spiritual prosperity in the foregoing extracts from the addresses and correspondence of Pope Leo XIII., but, as a fitting climax to the triumphant vindication of this great Pontiff, we append the Letter which the Holy Father addressed to the Bishops of Ireland at the close of his Jubilee year, and which entirely exonerates the Vicar of Christ—at once and forever— from the foul aspersions of antagonism to Ireland's best interests which his enemies have so unjustly and iniquitously hurled at the Head of the Church of God on earth.

Following is the text of a document which removes every stigma with which slander may have smirched the saintly character of Pope Leo XIII.

"*Venerable Brother* :—Health and Apostolic Benediction.

"Whilst we embrace with a father's love every member of the fold of Christ, which He has entrusted to Our keeping, Our most special care, and the first place in Our thoughts, are reserved for those whom We know to be sufferers from misfortune. For

We are moved by that instinct which nature has implanted in the heart of every parent to love and cherish beyond all the rest, those of their children who have been stricken by any calamity. For this reason, We have always held in a special feeling of affection, the Catholics of Ireland, long and sorely tried by so many afflictions. And We have ever cherished them with a love all the more intense, for their marvellous fortitude under those sufferings and for their hereditary attachment to their religion, which no pressure of misfortune has ever been able to destroy or weaken.

"As to the counsels that We have given them from time to time, and in Our recent decree, We were moved in these things not only by the consideration of what is conformable to truth and justice, but also by the desire of advancing your interests. For such is Our affection for you that it does not suffer Us to allow the cause in which Ireland is struggling to be weakened by the introduction of anything that could justly be brought in reproach against it.

"And that Our affection towards the people of Ireland, may now be specially manifested, we send to you a number of gifts. Among them there are vestments, sacred vessels and ornaments of various kinds for the furnishing of the altar. These, for the greater splendor of the house of God and of His worship, We present to the Cathedral churches of Ireland. There are also other gifts of less value. These We have specially blessed. They will serve to promote the piety of the persons to whom We wish them to be given, in accordance with the directions that will be sent to you.

"We are confident that even from this it will be most clearly seen that *Our paternal love for the people of Ireland has undergone no change.* And upon this, Our love for them, they will have ever stronger and stronger claims if they continue to receive Our teaching with docility, trusting in Us, and keeping on their guard against the deceits of those who do not shrink from putting a false construction upon Our counsels in the hope of uprooting, if it were possible, that renowned fidelity to the Catholic Church, which holds so high a place amongst the virtues of the people of Ireland, and which has come to them from their forefathers as their chief and richest inheritance.

"With a fervent prayer that Our Apostolic Benediction may bring with it the richest gifts and graces of Heaven, We most lovingly bestow it upon you, venerable brother, upon the clergy and faithful of your charge, and upon all Ireland.

"Given at Rome, at St. Peter's, on the 21st day of December, in the year of Our Lord, 1888, the eleventh year of Our Pontificate.

"LEO XIII., Pope."

CARDINAL PECCI'S SENTIMENTS.

It will be gratifying to every Catholic reader to know that the deep interest felt by the Holy Father in the welfare of Ireland, both religiously and politically, is ardently shared in by the brother of His Holiness, His Eminence Cardinal Joseph Pecci, whose Titular Church is that of St. Agatha in Rome, whose feast is kept with imposing solemnity every year by the faculty and students of the Irish College in the Eternal City.

His Eminence was duly installed in his titular Church on December 27th, 1879, and on that occasion Mgr. Kirby, President of the Irish College, delivered an address, in which, after congratulating his Eminence on the dignity that had been conferred on him, he said:

"Our church, Most Rev. Eminence, which was dedicated to St. Agatha, Virgin and Martyr, erected in time of Constantine, and constituted a Cardinal's title by Honorius III., lays aside to-day her mourning garb of widowhood to receive, with joyful exultation, your Eminence as her new titular. The great heart of Daniel O'Connell, which reposes near your throne, must rejoice when it feels that the brother of our glorious Pontiff, Leo XIII., is titular of the National Church of the Irish in Rome, the Church of that country for whose faith and for whose emancipation O'Connell, for half a century, and armed only with the weapons of reason, truth and legality, fought and conquered. Your Eminence is not merely a golden support (*cardine*), which will aid and dignify the Church, but also a model of Christian and ecclesiastical virtues for our students to copy, and a brilliant torch of profound science to kindle in the breast of our young Levites a vivid desire to gain by prayer and study the treasures of learning, and to imitate, even at a long distance, their sainted ancestors and fellow-countrymen, such as St. Fregidianus, Archbishop of Lucca; St. Cataldus, Archbishop of Tarento; St. Donatus, Bishop of Fiesoli; St. Columbanus, founder of Bobbio Monastery, who was styled by Bellarmine the luminary of his century; and many other illustrious Irishmen who left their native shores, and poured themselves, as St. Bernard says, like an inundation over all the countries of Europe, watering them with the sweat of apostolic toil, and adorning them with examples of doctrine and piety. The crown is put to our rejoicing when we reflect that in your Eminence we possess a lively image of Leo XIII., who was given as a light in the heaven of the Church Militant, to dispel the dark errors of the lurid and lying philosophy which in those days has invaded the minds of so many foolish and corrupt men, perverting or concealing the most essential truths of natural as well as of revealed religion. In your Eminence we recognize a near resemblance of the lofty wisdom and integrity of heart of this great Pontiff, whom we thank for his exceeding kindness in giving us his brother to be Titular of this church and our own Cardinal-Deacon, entitled to our love and veneration. We invoke the invincible martyr to whom this temple is sacred, and the Apostle of Ireland, protector of our college, to grant to you length of days and felicity of every kind, spiritual and temporal. The same blessing we implore for the Pontiff, your brother. Tell to him that we Irish, devoted like our fathers even to the shedding of our blood for the cause of the Holy See, desire to behold his triumph, as once in times of old these walls witnessed the triumph of Gregory the Great, when, after the profanations of the Arians, he consecrated this Church of St. Agatha, amid the prodigies of heaven and the applause of the Romans."

The reply made by Cardinal Pecci to this speech of Mgr. Kirby was an elaborate and magnificent oration, delivered in the Italian language, with the utmost fluency and grace. The Pope, it is well known, was attracted in an especial manner, when a young student to the history of Ireland, and probably owed to his elder brother, Giuseppe, his interest in the trials of the Irish nation. For this reason, the language used by Cardinal Pecci in the Church of the Irish College, may be taken to represent the sentiments of the Holy Father, and that language was truly remarkable. After alluding to the cruel and excruciating tortures so nobly and triumpnantly endured by St. Agatha, in defence of the faith of Christ, his Eminence observed that St. Patrick, the Apostle of Ireland, knew how to infuse into the hearts of his Irish children the spirit and fortitude of the virgin saint. He traced with a master hand the extraordinary courage and endurance displayed by the Irish in defence of the Catholic Church during long centuries of persecution, entering into elaborate and minute details of confiscations, torments and deaths under various shapes during the reigns of Henry VIII., Elizabeth, James, Anne and the Georges. To the sanguinary persecution succeeded another, which the Cardinal styled a continuous and slow assassination, tending to depopulate the country by the fabrication of the most inhuman and unjust laws the world had ever seen. He quoted the words of Edmund Burke, characterizing in fit terms this singularly subtle code of legislation, formed for the purpose of driving the Catholic nation into exile or compelling them to deny their faith and embrace the Anglican heresy. He described in glowing expressions of commendation the obstinate and successful resistance of the Irish to these anti-Catholic enactments, and *their steadfast attachment to the creed of their fathers and to the Holy See, in spite of all allurements and temptations to apostasy.* The Irish, he said, knew how to suffer and to die for their religion; but they, thanks to the spirit inherited from St. Patrick, were *incapable of betraying their conscience or becoming apostates.* The Cardinal did not omit the services of O'Connell, but went over every stage of his career, alluding most touchingly to his final attempt to lay in person before the Roman Pontiff the trophies of his exertions, and to attest with his dying breath his unsullied loyalty to the Chair of Peter. But, said his Eminence, God did not think fit to gratify his last desire. He died at Genoa, on his way to the tomb of the Prince of the Apostles, and bequeathed his heart to Rome. The throbbings of that heart vibrate in every Catholic breast. Finally, Cardinal Pecci concluded an oration, which was heard with rapt attention, by a well-deserved compliment to the zeal and piety of the students of the Irish College.

CARDINAL MORAN'S SENTIMENTS.

In the beginning of the present year Cardinal Moran returned to his affectionate flock in Sydney from his visit to the Holy Father. His Eminence was received with a most unanimous enthusiastic welcome and addresses were presented to him by both the Priests and the laity. In the course of his reply to the sterling sentiments of veneration for the Vicar of Christ which was voiced by the Catholics of his See, Cardinal Moran attested to the love which he well and intimately knew possessed the heart of the Sovereign Pontiff for the Irish people in general and the cause of Home Rule in particular:

"Whilst I was in Rome," said Cardinal Moran, "I received from the Pontiff's hands the 'Encyclical on Christian Liberty,' which I commend to every one who has at heart that important subject, so vital to society at the present day. It lays down the rules and principles which alone can rescue social order from shipwreck, whilst, at the same time, it does not conceal the great truth, so often ignored by statesmen in modern times, that it will not suffice to engrave the sacred name of Liberty on our chains, to give us the heaven-born blessing of true liberty. It is no breach of confidence to say that the Holy Father was in a particular manner pained by the misrepresentations which, for awhile, caused such anguish to millions of Irish hearts at home and abroad, as if his views were in opposition to his Irish children in the struggle for national life in which they are now engaged. *Nothing could be more unfounded than such a supposition.* I do not know that in the long line of Sovereign Pontiffs there has been even one to love Ireland with greater affection than does the present illustrious Pope. He has sympathized with her in her sorrows and rejoiced with her in her triumphs, and at the present moment his best wishes are with her devoted sons, who, through good repute and through evil repute, are endeavoring to assert her rights and redress her wrongs. And when the cause of truth and justice shall have triumphed, and the Empire shall decree to Ireland the laurel wreath of national freedom, none shall more lovingly rejoice with her in victory than Leo XIII."

BISHOP JOHN J. KEANE'S TESTIMONY.

In the course of his instructive and interesting lecture on "The Providential Mission of Leo XIII.," Rt. Rev. John J. Keane, then Bishop of Richmond, but now Rector of the Catholic University, thus delineates the fidelity with which the Holy Father clung to the cause of Ireland's national aspirations, even when every species of English diplomacy was brought into sway in order to induce him to cast the weight of his powerful and extensive influence on the side of the English Government:

"While," says Bishop Keane, "the Holy Father was thus busy foiling the fierce assault of mail-clad Germany, he had to withstand another attack of Cæsarism from another quarter. This time, however, it came in a very different guise. It was not Cæsar trying to coerce the Church or to crush her; it was Cæsar cunningly seeking to cajole the Church and to use her as a cat's-paw for his own selfish ends. This tells plainly enough whence the attempt emanated. With stealthy overtures of friendliness on the one hand, and insinuated threats of hostility upon the other, *England sought to win the Pope to the unworthy task of restraining poor Ireland's aspirations after just government and rightful freedom, of holding her submissive to the chains of centuries, from which the spirit of our era is delivering her.* But here, too, Leo XIII. *was found impregnable.* Calmly but firmly, heeding neither promises nor threats, *he threw his sympathy and his influence on the side of justice and humanity.* Poor, down-trodden, long-suffering Ireland felt that she had indeed in him a *Father and a friend,* when, in spite of the bitterest opposition and the most wily influences, he appointed to the See of Dublin the patriot Priest who was the choice of the Irish hierarchy and the darling of the Irish people. Few men have a more difficult position than that held by Archbishop Walsh. Compelled by his providential situation to be not only the spiritual guide but also the temporal adviser of a down-trodden, generous-hearted, and impulsive people, who, asking only the barest justice, are exasperated by taunts and goaded by coercion; forced, on the one hand, to assert his people's right, and, on the other, to restrain their honest indignation and hold them in the wise and safe paths of peace; constantly maligned by his country's enemies, and often misunderstood and misrepresented by those who ought to be her friends; he must indeed have many a sad and weary hour. But *his chief comfort, next to his trust in the God of truth and justice, is the loving sympathy of Leo XIII.*"

MONSIGNOR O'RIELLY'S TESTIMONY.

The name of Monsignor O'Rielly is well-known to the majority of our readers through the numerous letters which he has written for the American press upon Irish affairs. In one of these contributions published in February, of this year, this distinguished Irish ecclesiastic passes this well-deserved eulogy upon Pope Leo XIII., for the fortitude and friendship which he manifested in Ireland's favor, even when every avenue to the Vatican was crowded with the representatives of England and the paid emissaries of English power in Ireland.

Alluding to the Letter which the Holy Father sent to the Irish Bishops on December 28th, 1888, Monsignor O'Rielly says:

"It is, then, with unspeakable satisfaction, after all the efforts made and the intrigues set on foot to obtain from Leo XIII. a condemnation of the Irish national cause, that we hail his Letter to the Irish Bishops. No more explicit or formal indorsement of the cause pursued by the immense majority of the Irish people, their clergy, and their representatives in Parliament could be given by the supreme authority in the Church. than is contained in this most opportune document. "Venerable brothers," the letter begins, "although embracing in one fatherly love all individuals composing the flock confided to our care, we reserve our most special solicitude and the first place in our thoughts for those who are tried by affliction. We are impelled by an instinct which nature has given to the heart of every father to love and cherish above all others such of their children as misfortune has stricken. For this reason we have always entertained a sentiment of particular affection for the Catholics of Ireland, so long and so cruelly tried by many afflictions. We have cherished towards them a most intense love because of their marvellous fortitude in bearing with their sufferings, and of their attachment to their religion, which no ill fortune has ever been able to destroy or weaken." This, surely, is an outspoken profession of generous love worthy of the heart of the Pontiff, and worthy of the much-tried nation for whom he cherishes such deserved and honorable predilection. But in no manner can the love of a father for his dearest ones be shown more convincingly than by counselling them in danger and warding off from the cause with which their honor and their happiness are identified any temptation, any peril, any element of a nature to threaten seriously the one or the other It is a knowledge of this rule of fatherly love and care which will enable us to judge aright the next paragraph. "In what relates," he says, " to the advice which We have occasionally given you, and Our recent decree, they have been inspired not alone by considerations based on truth and justice, but by a desire to advance your cause. For Our affection for you is such that it will not permit the cause for which Ireland is struggling to be weakened by mixing it with anything that may bring on it just reproach." I do not believe that a Pope placed in the delicate and difficult position in which Leo XIII. finds himself with respect to the great powers of Christendom could express himself more undisguisedly in favor of the cause of a nation heroically struggling for the attainment of her just rights. Even where the Pontiff's counsel or decree might seem at first sight, to wound the national sentiment, or to be adverse to the policy pursued by the people and their guides, Leo. XIII. affirms that what he advised and what he did were intended solely to advance the cause of Ireland. That sacred cause, he adds, was so just in his eyes, so dear to his heart, that he could not bear to see its success marred, its justice or its honor tainted by any proceeding that could deserve condemnation in the public opinion of Christendom, which he is so anxious to conciliate in favor of our struggling people. Statesmen, public men of long experience and ripe wisdom, will say that no proof of love in a parent, in a ruler, is greater than when he has the courage to advise those who are dear to him to prefer the eternal principles of honor and justice to the results of a questionable and short-lived expediency. I have reason to know that, had the crops failed in Ireland last summer, as it was very much feared at one time they would, the affection of Leo XIII., for the suffering people of Ireland would have been further demonstrated by generous deeds. As it is he will not allow his jubilee year to close without sending to every diocese in the Green Isle, for distribution, gifts which will remain to speak of his fatherly love during many a coming year. "In order," he continues, "that Our affection for the people of Ireland should be especially shown at the present time We send you a goodly number of presents, among which you will find vestments, sacred vessels and ornaments of various kinds for the service of the altar. We offer them to the cathedral churches of Ireland to enhance the splendor of God's house and of His worship. There are also gifts of less value. These We have blessed in a special manner. They will serve to stimulate the piety of the persons We desire them to be given to, in conformity with the special instructions which shall be sent to you. We trust that it will be clearly seen that Our fatherly love for the Irish has undergone no change. On this love they shall have still greater and greater claims if they continue to receive Our teaching with docility, to have confidence in Us, and to be on their guard against the wily dealings of men who do not fear to give a false meaning to Our words of advice, in the hope of plucking up by the roots that far-famed fidelity to the Church which holds a foremost place among the virtues of the Irish people, a fidelity handed down from their ancestors as their richest inheritance. Praying fervently that Our Apostolic Benediction may bring you the richest gifts and graces from on high, We lovingly bestow it on you, venerable brothers, on your clergy, on the faithful of your diocese, and on all Ireland. Given at Rome from St. Peter's, the 21st day of December, in the year of our Lord, 1888, the eleventh of our Pontificate. Leo XIII., Pope." It is with feelings of an indescribable joy that I write you this letter. If religion is to count in the present struggle in Ireland, as it has ever counted in the past, as one of the mighty forces which sustained the nation at every new crisis in its existence, it is now more than ever important that this force be not weakened—that it be, on the contrary, like the core in the Transatlantic cables, the life centre through which the Irish people shall feel every pulsation of their undivided and increased national energies."

With this extract we close this chapter, in the full belief that no impartial man of any nationality who has read the preceding pages, can retain for a moment the false impression that Pope Leo XIII. ever harbored for an instant a single sentiment adverse to the legitimate struggle of the Irish people for their political emancipation from the slavery which England has imposed upon them.

CHAPTER XXXIII.

Refutation of Miscellaneous Historical Errors which are the Cause of Unjust Censure upon the Roman Pontiffs.

Having thus traced the conduct of the Popes towards Ireland down through many centuries, and proved by the force of impartial and incontestible evidence that there was not a single successor in the See of St. Peter who can be named as an enemy of Ireland, let us conclude this labor of love by exposing the remaining fallacies in the work before us, and thus bring to an end a review and a refutation of historical errors which, it is earnestly to be hoped, will not fail to convince all who peruse these pages that the Pontiffs of Rome were by no means possessed of the prejudice against Ireland which their enemies assert.

The first question which we propose to answer is this:

DID POPE JOHN XXII., EXCOMMUNICATE EDWARD BRUCE AND HIS ADHERENTS?

In seeking for slanders by which to stain the character of the Popes, so as to arouse the angry passions of the Irish people of the nineteenth century against the whole line of Pontiffs, the author of the book under review extracts a large portion of his false history from the pages of a work which we have thoroughly exposed already under the caption of the O'Halloran-Dolby Anglo-Irish History.*

From this source of English-fabricated falsehoods against both the Popes and the Catholic religion, any enemy of the Catholic Church can draw comfort and consolation, as, like his infamous predecessor and fellow-countryman Cambrensis, Dolby delights in depicting both the Popes and the religion of the Irish people in the darkest colors that arose in his anti-Irish imagination.

We are not much surprised, therefore, to read in the book under review—upon the authority of the fallacious Dolby—that Pope John XXII., pronounced sentence of excommunication against Edward Bruce and all his Irish adherents, and thereby caused the national cause to be defeated in consequence of the Irish people imagining they were under "*the curse of the Church*—the blighting breath of Roman curses."

It is a fact well known to all readers of

*See pages 79-80.

history that since the fatal day when the basilisk eyes of a British king were first fixed upon Ireland as a suitable country for invasion, every English Protestant writer who wrote on Irish subjects, did so under the inspiration of the Father of Lies. From calumniating Cambrensis down to the Cockney Dolby—at the end of nearly every link in the chain of English writers on Irish subjects there stand the names of Englishmen whose minds generated falsehood and whose pens diffused poison against both the Popes and the Irish people.

Pope John XXII, against whom this charge is brought, was the Pontiff to whom Donnell or Donald O Neil addressed the letter on the sufferings of the natives of Ireland under their English and Norman invaders—to which we have already devoted a chapter,† and a perusal of that Pontiff's Letter in reply to the petition of the Irish princes will satisfy every impartial reader that Pope John XXII., never hurled the anathemas of excommunication against a people whom he styles "*the Rulers and the people of Ireland*," thereby acknowledging their *national independence* and their *legitimate right* to drive out of their country the English, Norman or other invaders.

What did Pope John XXII., do in the case of the Scotch, when, in 1318, they besieged and captured several English border towns belonging of right to King Edward of England? Did he excommunicate the Scotch for this act of reprisal? No. The Pontiff acceded to the request of the Scotch rulers and people; he sent a letter to King Edward (precisely as he did in the case of Ireland) asking him to conclude an honorable peace.‡ Why, therefore, should Pope John XXII., excommunicate Edward Bruce and his Irish followers, for defending Ireland against foreign invaders, when he merely recommended the English king to make an honorable peace with those Scotch invaders who captured and burned many English towns in revenge for wrongs which that people had suffered at the hands of the English.

Pope John was one of those Pontiffs who will be honored by the Catholic world throughout all generations. His Pontificate was a model of *prudent, firm, and well-regulated* administration§ and until there is more reliable authority than the detracting Dolby, Catholics will refuse to believe that any Pontiff ever excommunicated any portion of a people who were attempting to drive out of their country foreign invaders, who—as said by O'Neil in his letter to the Pope—"oblige us by open force to give up our houses and our lands, and to seek shelter like the wild beasts upon the mountains, in woods, marshes and caves." After specifying in detail the proofs of these and other general charges, the eloquent prince concludes by uttering this memorable vow that the Irish "will not cease to fight against and among their invaders until the day when they themselves, for want of power, shall have ceased to do us harm, and that a Supreme Judge shall have taken just vengeance on their crimes, which, we firmly hope, will sooner or later come to pass."‖

WAS MAYNOOTH COLLEGE FOUNDED IN ORDER TO EDUCATE IRISH PRIESTS IN THE INTERESTS OF ENGLAND?

In the work under review we find the following fallacious remarks concerning the origin and objects of the foundation of Maynooth College, an educational institution in Ireland which has given to the Church many of her most learned and patriotic Priests and Prelates:

"In the year 1795 a most extraordinary, but keen, far-sighted and statesmanlike change was made by the English government in the matter of governing the restless, liberty-craving Irish. * * * * Edmund Burke, Wm. Pitt, Lord Granville, J. Fox and other English statesmen resolved upon a plan, acceptable to the Vatican, and also to the Irish Bishops and representatives, by which the great influence of the Irish Priesthood might be made, at least negatively, to serve the purposes of the English Government. This plan was no less than the establishment of a royal college for the education of Irish Catholic Priests at the expense of the English Protestant Government."

The above extract is false from beginning to end, and as the history of the manner in which Maynooth College was founded, and the names of the celebrated Irishmen

---

† Lingard's *England*, under date 1316-18.
‡ Abbe Darras' *Church History*.

§ See pages 120 to 123.
‖ McGee's *Ireland*, Vol. I. pp. 219-20.

who originated the idea, are but little known, the best way to refute the foregoing fallacious assertions is to give the details concerning Maynooth College, which, in brief, are as follows:

In the year 1794 Archbishop Troy, of Dublin. presented a memorial to the Earl of Westmoreland, then Lord Lieutenant of Ireland, on behalf of himself and other Catholic Prelates of that Island. In this memorial, after referring to the destruction of the Ecclesiastical colleges in France, and representing the absolute necessity for places of education in Ireland for young men intending to reinforce the ranks of the Catholic clergy, the memoralists stated that they were induced to undertake the establishment of proper places for the education of the clerical youth of their communion, and prayed a royal license for the endowment of academies and seminaries for educating and preparing young men to discharge the duties of Priests in Ireland under Superiors of their own communion.

The result of the petition of Archbishop Troy and the other Irish Prelates was the enactment of a law by the *Irish* Parliament which did not expressly ordain the foundation of Maynooth College or any particular institution for the education of Priests in Ireland, but which provided facilities for the foundation of a Catholic College which the then existing state of the laws affecting Catholic education did not allow.

The Act in question, set forth the fact that by the laws then in force in the Kingdom of Ireland, it was not lawful to endow any college or seminary intended exclusively for the education of Catholics. It required a special Act of Parliament, therefore, to entitle Catholics to educate their children, and when the measure passed into a law, the then Lord Chief Justice of the Queen's Bench, the Chief Justice of the Common Pleas, the Chief Baron of the Exchequer, six Catholic laymen, namely, the then Earl of Fingall, Viscount Gormanstown, Viscount Kenmare, Sir Edward Bellew, Richard Stronge, Sir Thomas French, and the four Irish Catholic Archbishops, and seven other Catholic Ecclesiastics, were appointed trustees for the purpose of establishing, endowing and maintaining one academy for the education solely of persons professing the Roman Catholic Religion.

Such was the origin of the foundation of Maynooth College, and the object for which it was founded. The idea first originated with Dr. Troy, Archbishop of Dublin; it was then taken up by the Bishops of Ireland; the Act was passed by the *Irish* Parliament, and by referring to the document itself (36 George III., C. 21, A. D. 1795) the reader will find therein *not a word authorizing the education of Roman Catholic ecclesiastics.*

The College was founded, as already related in 1795, and an annual Parliamentary grant of about £8,000 was given towards its maintenance. Rev. Thomas Hussey was the first President. The College contained about a hundred students in 1798, when the notable rebellion broke out in Ireland, and it was publicly proclaimed that *the Maynooth Priests were at the bottom of the new insurrection against England!* Evidently the people nearest Maynooth in those days did not consider that the Irish Priests could be turned into English tools by the curriculum of the College!

The number of students in Maynooth continued to increase as the reputation of the College became known, until fully four hundred and fifty students found educational facilities within its hospitable walls. With the increase of students the Government very justly increased the annual pension, thus in 1813 Maynooth received a grant of £9,673 per year, and again in 1845 the Government allowance was increased owing to the strenuous efforts of the Irish Bishops, backed by the arguments and influence of such eminent men as Thomas Babington Macaulay, whose memorable speech on the Maynooth Grant, when before Parliament in 1845, contains this beautiful passage:

In the debate on the Maynooth grant in 1845, Macaulay spoke in no measured words on the gross injustice done to Catholics by those who had appropriated their property and granted a pitiful return.

"When I consider," said Mr Macaulay, "with what magnificence religion and science are endowed in our Universities; when I call to mind their long streets of palaces, their venerable cloisters, their trim gardens, their chapels, with organs, altar-pieces, and stained windows; when I remember their schools, libraries, museums, and galleries of art; when I remember, too, all the solid comforts provided in those places, both for instructors and pupils; the stately dwellings of the principals, the commodious apartments of the fellows and scholars; when I remember that the very sizars and servitors are lodged far better than you propose to lodge those priests who are to teach the whole people of Ireland; when I think of the halls, the common-rooms, the bowling-greens, even the stabling of Oxford and Cambridge—the display of old plate on the tables, the good cheer of the kitchen, the oceans of excellent ale in the buttery; and when I remember the faith of Edward III., and Henry VI., of Margaret of Anjou, and Margaret of Richmond, of William of Wychcham, of Archbishop Chicheley, and Cardinal Wolsey; when I remember what we have taken from the Roman Catholic religion—King's College, New College, my own Trinity College, and Christ's Church—and when I look at the miserable Do-the-boys-Hall we have given them in return—I ask myself if we, and if the Protestant religion, are not disgraced by the comparison."

To unreflecting Catholics, or to non-Catholics with anti-Papal prejudices, it may appear strange that the British Government should contribute towards the sustention of a College for the education of Catholic Priests in a country where the Church and the people had been persecuted without restraint by the very government that now stepped forward to help Maynooth College. But this is easily explained when it is remembered that the British Government had in its possession a vast quantity of valuable real estate and buildings in the shape of churches, convents, monasteries, abbeys and religious institutions which it had stolen from the Catholic Church in past centuries of persecution for no other reason than because it was "Popish" property. The funds derived from this sequestered property were used to maintain the Protestant Episcopal church in Ireland, which at one time had a revenue of £850,000 per annum, and, very naturally, the Catholics, when they adopted the idea of establishing a College for Catholic young men, reminded the British Government of its ill-gotten wealth, and asked that at least a portion of it should be appropriated for the use of the descendants of the original owners of St. Patrick's Cathedral and Christ Church in Dublin, and a hundred similar institutions throughout Ireland, which were originally Catholic edifices but which formed part of the spoils of the extensive robbery perpetrated during the era of the attempt made to introduce the Protestant Reformation into Ireland, which (thank God!) never succeeded!

The funds appropriated by Parliament were used to maintain *free scholarships* in Maynooth, as by a regulation of the Faculty it was decided to admit two hundred students into the College as *free* scholars, for whose board £20 each should be allowed. These two hundred free places were distributed among the four Ecclesiastical Provinces of Ireland, in the following proportions: To the Provinces of Armagh and Cashel were alloted 60 each; and to those of Dublin and Tuam 40 each.

After the College was established, the trustees made known the fact to the Cardinal-Prefect of the Propaganda at Rome, stating that the institution was designed for the education of young men in Ireland who had a vocation for the Priesthood, and on the 9th of July, 1796, a reply was received from the Cardinal-Prefect commending the undertaking.

From the above brief but authentic account of the origin of Maynooth College, every reader may discern at once that there was not a single iota of "collusion" between the Vatican and the British Government at the inception of that institution. The whole plan originated in Ireland, was managed in Ireland, and the grant came from the Irish Parliament. The Pope (Pius VI.) was entirely absorbed in endeavoring to repel the rising spirit of Gallicanism in France, and in finding means by which to save Italy from becoming involved in the whirlpool of revolution which was then rife in Europe and which was subsequently followed by the triumphal march of Napoleon Bonaparte through the vineyards of Italy.

It is very clear, therefore, that what is said in the book under review concerning the Pope, the British Government, and their secret alliance for the purpose of educating Irish Priests so as to transform them into English subjects, has—like a great many other statements in the same volume—no foundation whatever save the quicksands of malicious falsehood.

WAS THE REPEAL MOVEMENT KILLED BY A PAPAL RESCRIPT?

In the book under review it is stated that Daniel O'Connell organized the great Repeal movement in the year 1829, and had every prospect of achieving success until, in an evil hour, "Pope Gregory XVI. issued a Rescript in the year 1843, commanding the Priests of Ireland to refrain from attending the Repeal meetings." And then the writer continues:

"O'Connell saw in this *Rescript* the doom of his race and country; the blasting of all his cherished hopes. He rose in the grandeur of his almost superhuman power to meet and turn the power of the Holy See. He published a letter to prove that the Rescript was an illegal interference with the civil liberties of the clergy. In the agony of his soul he uttered his famous cry: 'As much religion as you please from Rome, but no politics.'"

This precious piece of bombastic absurdity is a regular jumble of disjointed events to'd after the unusual fashion of placing the cart before the horse!

The Repeal movement was started in April, 1840, under the title of the "Loyal National Repeal Association,"* and as the immense organization preserved its concrete unity up to January 22nd, 1847, when O'Connell left Ireland as a political field for the "Young Ireland" party, it must have puzzled the readers of the book we are reviewing to understand how a Papal Rescript issued in 1843 could have killed it!

The truth is that what this erratic and unreliable adversary of the Pope calls a Papal Rescript was not issued until 1845, and the document was a simple Letter to the Irish Bishops asking them to see that their Priests used less inflammatory language in their political speeches, and cautioning them not to permit religion to suffer through too great absorption in politics. And what was the effect of this Rescript? Here is the answer in a nutshell: "*The only effect produced by the Papal Rescript was, that the tone of the Catholic clergy, in their political speeches at subsequent meetings, was more guarded*"†

It is not true, therefore, that a Papal Rescript killed the Repeal movement, any more than it proved to be "the doom" of O'Connell's "race and country," or that it "blasted all O'Connell's cherished hopes." The Repeal movement met its mortuary end from far different influences than those which radiate from the Vatican. Its death was caused by O'Connell's rash promises never performed, and by the organization of the more active members of the Repeal association into what was aptly called "The Young Ireland Party," in whose ranks were numbered such patriots of unyielding energy as Davis, Mitchel, Duffy, O'Brien, Meagher, and a phalanx of similar Irishmen of unblemished character and undying enthusiasm in the cause of their native land.

The causes which led to the downfall of the Repeal movement, were the natural outcome of the changes in the political sentiments of the Irish people who had grown up in the country during the decade of years in which O'Connell had preached his peace policy from the hill tops of Ireland. But when the Irish people found that the Lord Lieutenant had issued a proclamation suppressing the meeting O'Connell proposed holding on the plains of Clontarf, then they saw that the cry of "peace" towards the English Government could no longer rally the people under O'Connell's standard, and they were ready to adopt any system of physical force agitation which presented itself for their relief from the thraldom of England.

The Clontarf meeting was announced to take place on Sunday, October 8th, 1843, but had to be abandoned in order to save from general massacre the hundreds of thousands of Irish men and women who would have gathered there. One year later, (October 14th, 1844,) O'Connell, his son John, Thomas Steele, T. M. Ray, Charles

---

*Thebaud's *Irish Race*, p. 49.

†O'Keefe's *Life and Times of O'Connell*, Vol. II. page 734.

Gavan Duffy, John Gray, Richard Barrett, and Rev. Thomas Tyrell were arrested and subsequently tried, convicted of course, and imprisoned in Richmond prison. This event was the first nail in the coffin of the Repeal movement.

When O'Connell and the other traversers of English law in Ireland were released from prison on September 7th, 1845, the Liberator was accorded what proved to be the final ovation of the Irish people to the idol of their hearts. Half a million people joined in or witnessed with willing sympathy the procession which escorted the Irish Tribune and his compatriots along the streets and quays of the city of Dublin, and all Ireland was ablaze with joy at the liberation of the Catholic champion of downtrodden Erin.

This day proved to be the full meredian of O'Connell's glory. It was the closing tableau in the Irish political drama wherein he had represented the hero of the hour, and his place on the public stage of Irish politics was replaced by such revolutionary associations as the "'82 Club," the "Phœnix Clubs," the "Young Ireland Party," and instead of preaching the peace policy which Richard Barret of the *Dublin Pilot* and John Gray of the *Dublin Freeman's Journal* had advocated during the time of O'Connell's agitation for Repeal by constitutional means, the *Nation* under Duffy, and the *Felon* under Mitchell, vied with each other in their earnestness to erect barricades in the streets of the Metropolis, to invoke the strong arm of the Irish peasantry, and to wage war to the hilt against the English oppressors of the Irish people. This was the second nail in the coffin of the constitutional movement for Repeal of the Union between Great Britian and Ireland.

Let us now turn to a reliable source* and learn therefrom the causes which led to the final collapse of the Repeal agitation:

The British aristocracy made O'Connell a prisoner in a jail, but the Irish democracy enthroned him as a king in the Rotundo. The ignominy which the government sought to attach to him was removed and melted away in the brilliant splendors of the "levee," and the humiliation of the one was amply compensated by the more than kingly honors of the other. Nevertheless, it is quite certain that at this period—indeed ever since the advent of Lord Heytesbury to Ireland—the tide of O'Connell's popularity was insensibly lapsing and ebbing from him. To accelerate its motion, a very ingenious device was adopted by the deadly enemies of Irish liberty. Highly respectable men, of great influence and large property—men allied to the aristocracy of the country—joined the Repeal movement The thoughtless people rejoiced at their adhesion, and their appearance in Conciliation Hall was hailed with shouts of transport. But the rising of these men amongst the Repealers, like that of certain constellations at sea, was but the signal of storm and wreck. This was inevitable—they belonged to that class who have strong material interest in maintaining the present state of things. One of these was the son of a Protestant bishop, the owner of large landed property in the North of Ireland—Grey Porter. He published a pamphlet, immediately after joining the Association, which delighted Davis and all the young men of Ireland, for he propounded that Ireland ought to have a national militia of one hundred thousand men. To a people like the Irish, "delighting in wars"—the most military, and therefore the most unfortunate people in Europe—such a proposal was in the highest degree seductive and gratifying "Honor to Mr. Porter," exclaimed Davis, "for having had the manliness to propose what thousands thought but spoke not." Porter seized upon the weak point in the Irish character, and became for a time eminently popular. He conjured up visions of military glory which enchanted the poetic minds of young and cultivated men. * * * * *

Porter's pamphlet attracted general attention, and as a consequence his accession made great noise ; and a world of discussion ensued which was not serviceable to the cause of Repeal. Many were at a loss to account for Porter's conduct. It was rather surprising, they said, that this son of a Protestant bishop who had accumulated vast wealth by the excoriation of Catholic poverty, should be so scrupulously careful of the money of the "Popish Repealers." It was certainly a tendency which did not run in his blood. In the meantime, however, the minds of many were filled with suspicion and doubt, *and great damage was done to the Repeal.* The enemy was enabled to fling bitter taunts at the Association and tarnish patriotism with the imputation of sordid motives. The whole affair contributed powerfully *to break up* what Sir Robert Peel termed a "formidable confederacy against British government and British connexion."

When the leader of a political organiza-

*Life and Times of Daniel O'Connell, by C. M. O'Keefe. Vol. II, pp. 728-9.

tion has failed in achieving the political rights which for years he has struggled to gain for his country, and when the men who stood by him begin to doubt his ability to make their rulers redeem the promises he has made to his own people—then it may truly be said that the dry-rot of political decay is destroying that party. Such was the case in 1844-5, the time when "great damage was done to Repeal," and when both the enemies of O'Connell and the friends of physical force were contributing—by different courses of procedure—"to break up" the last remnants that remained of the Repeal Association.

About this time, as if to add additional fury to the waters which lashed around the base of the rock of Irish politics, a Letter or Rescript was received from the Sacred College, declaring that whereas it had been reported to his Holiness that some of the more ardent patriots among the Irish Priesthood had become absorbed in politics and had spoken too rashly in public concerning affairs of State, they were requested thereafter to attend more exclusively to their religious duties and to leave the angry agitation of politics to persons in civil life.

This is the Rescript regarding which the author under review says that O'Connell, "in the agony of his soul uttered his famous cry : 'As much religion as you please from Rome, but no politics.'" The "agony of soul" in this instance at least, is entirely a myth ! Daniel O'Connell never experienced any such "agony" over the Papal document, *nor did he ever give utterance to the "famous cry"* attributed to him ! The sentiment "as much religion as you please from Rome, but no politics," was given expression to by O'Neill Daunt, a member of the Repeal association, at a meeting of that body held in Dublin in the year 1845,* and thus we remove from the hallowed memory of Ireland's Liberator the foul blemish which bigotry and ignorance have cast upon it by attributing to him words he never used.

When once the tide of popularity begins to ebb away from a popular patriot whose star is on the wane, it does not take long until he finds himself standing almost solitary and alone upon a barren strand. Such was O'Connell's fate. In addition to the elements of discord which already existed in the Repeal ranks, Sir Robert Peel's godless College Bill proved a regular apple of discord among the divided Irish patriots. Thomas Davis and his friends were enthusiastic advocates for these colleges which were purposely contemplated for the sole object of secularizing education. O'Connell, the Catholic Bishops and Clergy, as well as the bulk of the laity were opposed to what O'Connell called "the young blood of Ireland," and the result was to widen still wider the fatal gap which separated in hate the people that should have been united in love. This was the last nail in the coffin of the Repeal movement.

Thomas Davis died in 1845, and the death of this great and gifted Irish patriot nearly broke O'Connell's heart. He saw in him a successor to himself, as the great leader of the Irish people, and the high esteem in which the Liberator held the patriot-poet may be judged from the following extract from a letter which O'Connell sent to the Repeal Association when he heard of the death of Davis :

Writing to the Repeal Association, he alludes to this fatal event in the following touching words : "I do not know what to write. My mind is bewildered and my heart afflicted. The loss of my beloved friend—my noble-minded friend—is a source of the deepest sorrow to my mind. What a blow—what a cruel blow—to the cause of Irish nationality ! He was a creature of transcendent qualities of mind and heart. His learning was universal—his knowledge was as minute as it was general. And then he was a being of such incessant energy and continuous exertion. I, of course, in the few years—if years they be—still left to me, cannot expect to look upon his like again or to see the place he has left vacant adequately filled up. And I solemnly declare that I never knew any man who could be so useful to Ireland in the present state of her struggles. His loss is indeed irreparable. What an example he was to the Protestant youths of Ireland ! What a noble emulation of his virtues ought to be excited in the Catholic young men of Ireland. And his heart, too !—it was as gentle, as kind, as loving as a woman's. Yes ! it was as tenderly kind as his judgment was comprehen-

---

*See *Life and Times of O'Connell*, by C. M. O'Keefe, Vol. II., page 734.

sive and his genius magnificent. We shall long deplore his loss. As I stand alone in the solitude of my mountains, many a tear shall I shed in the memory of that noble youth. Oh! how vain are words or tears when such a national calamity afflicts the country. Put me down among the foremost contributors to whatever monument or tribute to his memory shall be voted by the National Association Never did they perform a more imperative or—alas! - so sad a duty. I can write no more—my tears blind me; and after all,

'Fungor inani munere.'"

Early in October, 1845, the first dark shadows of impending Famine began to hover over Ireland All thoughts of repeal of present unjust laws, or of retribution for past political wrongs, vanished from the minds of the masses of the people. Self-preservation became the ruling passion, and the spirit of patriotism languished under the repulsive presence of starvation. The result may easily be conjectured. The Repeal association went into the last throes of dissolution. Conciliation Hall reverberated with rancorous expressions which sowed the dragon's teeth of disunion in many an honest Irishman's breast, and thus Ireland became again a corpse upon the dissecting table of England.

On January 26th, 1846, O'Connell took his departure from Dublin, accompanied by his sons Maurice and John. He went to London, entered the House of Commons in order to try and wring even an atom of justice from the English Government in order to save his people from falling victims to famine. But the only answer he received was the proposition to pass a Coercion Bill! This drastic measure, however, was defeated, the Tories resigned and the Whigs came into power—and then the political cauldron in Ireland was set to bubbling and boiling over to such an extent that Repeal and O'Connell were both almost entirely forgotten.

About this time (1846) a rupture occurred between O'Connell and Smith O'Brien, which brought the latter gentleman into prominence and relegated O Connell to the tomb of the Capulets. To make matters more rapidly approach a crisis difficulties sprung up in the Repeal meetings, held in Conciliation Hall, between Thomas Francis Meagher and Smith O'Brien on one side, and O'Connell and his son John on the other, which ultimately led to an open rupture by the withdrawal from the association of a large number of Repealers who held "Young Ireland" views, and whose departure from the Hall caused tears to flow from many an Irish eye that witnessed the sad scene.

These turbulent scenes were so many swords of sorrow which pierced O'Connell's heart and ultimately hastened his death. He was prostrated by a general breaking up of his system. His physicians recommended rest and medical treatment, but all was unavailing, for what remedy can

"Pluck from the memory a hidden sorrow,
Raze out the written troubles of the brain."

O'Connell determined to make a pilgrimage to Rome, to kneel at the feet of the Sovereign Pontiff, and to ask the blessing of the saintly successor of St. Peter—Pope Pius IX. He was accompanied on his voyage by his son Daniel and Rev. John Miley, as his chaplain, and had proceeded as far as Genoa, when, on the 15th of May, just as the glorious sun had set, the great heart of Irel nd's Liberator ceased to beat, and Ireland lost one of her truest and best sons. According to his last wish his heart was placed in an urn and sent to Rome, where it still rests in the Church of St. Agatha, his body was conveyed back to Ireland, and his soul winged its flight to the bosom of that God Who gave it life on earth, and —every Catholic will pray that it has long since secured life everlasting.

It is to the causes we have succinctly alluded to that we must look for the death of the Repeal movement. Its dissolution could neither be marred nor made by any Rescript from Rome to the few Priests who, unwittingly, were too radical in their public speeches. The Pope had neither hand, act nor part in precipitating the Repeal movement down the precipice which changes in popular opinion prepared for it, and in'o which it would have inevitably fallen even had O'Connell lived for a dozen years longer. There are peculiar fashions in politics just as there are in personal dress, and Ireland in 1845 was becoming tired of waiting for moral force to produce a beneficial change in the prospects of the country. Disappointed and driven to despair, the young blood of the Island deserted O'Connell, and when the Young Ireland Party was born the Repeal Association drew its last breath—as the natural result of the loss of its political vitality.

WAS THE "YOUNG IRELAND" MOVEMENT KILLED BY BISHOPS AND PRIESTS?

The malicious intent of Judge Maguire's book may easily be surmised when it is known that he attributes the failure of every plan adopted, both in ancient and modern days, for the amelioration of Ireland, to the secret or open opposition of either the Pope or the Bishops and Priests of Ireland. Such a sweeping condemnation of Popes, Prelates and Priests exposes every apostate who adopts it to the suspicion that he merely desires to revenge himself upon the Church he has abandoned, hence he cares not how reckless soever his charges may be so long as he can make 'Rome howl," and sow the seeds of antipathy to spiritual authority in the hearts of Irish Catholics.

The "Young Ireland" movement of 1848, following so closely upon the failure of Daniel O'Connell, and the hundreds of thousands who believed in moral suasion as the best argument wherewith to win back Ireland's freedom from the grasp of England, was doomed to failure from its very inception.

In the first place the Irish people were demoralized, disunited, disappointed and cast down into despair by the death of O Connell and the calamitous failure of his constitutional movement.

In the next place the people had just passed through the excruciating agonies of famine and pestilence, and the majority of the agricultural population of Ireland were so reduced to poverty, and so emaciated by starvation, that they had neither the courage nor the confidence to take any active part in the new physical force programme advocated by John Mitchel and those who sided with him in his insurrectionary movement.

It must be also borne in mind that the foundation upon which Mitchel and his compatriots based their plans for Ireland's freedom was designed after that adopted in Paris when King Louis Philippe was torn from the throne of France. The Dublin *Nation* up to this time had been the organ of all the Irish writers of both prose and poetry phrased in patriotic sentiments, but John Mitchel's language and suggestions to the people began at last to be too inflammatory and too dangerous to permit their publication in the columns of the *Nation*, and so he and several other members of the *Nation's* staff seceded and issued a more radical journal under the captivating title of the *United Irishman*.

The columns of the new weekly were filled with full directions for street warfare wherein molten lead was to be poured down upon the devoted heads of the enemy, and every column contained matter calculated to arouse the Irish people to insurrection. This style of literature led to a split in the "Young Ireland" party, one wing being led by Mitchel, and the more moderate wing being under the leadership of William Smith O'Brien, whilst the O'Connellites looked askance upon both wings of the new organization as men who were not in their right senses.

The Catholic Prelates and Priests of Ireland looked upon the "Young Ireland" movement from its very inception, with grave doubts as to its propriety according to the standard of patriotism always held sacred by the Irish Catholic people. In the language of A. M Sullivan,* " they fancied they saw in this movement too much that was akin to the work of the Continental revolutionists, and, greatly as they disliked the domination of England, they would prefer it a thousand times *to such "Liberty" as Carbonari would proclaim."*

"At that time," continues the distinguished Irish patriot from whom we quote, " in 1848, *the power of the Catholic Priests was unbroken, was stronger than ever."* It would seem from this evidence, therefore, that no " Papal influences," thus far had materially affected Ireland's Priesthood, so

---
New Ireland, page 123.

far at least as their love for their native land was concerned.

The result of the deluge of inflammatory literature which the active intellect of the extreme revolutionary element in the "Young Ireland" party poured over the country, was the arrest of Mitchel, Meagher and O'Brien. Mitchel was tried, convicted and transported for fourteen years, and the others subsequently shared his fate. Thus ended the Irish insurrectionary movement of '48, under the ægis of the "Young Ireland" party.

From the foregoing facts it will be apparent to all impartial readers that the "Young Ireland" party was not killed by the Bishops and Priests of Ireland. It was a clear case of self-destruction. Its promoters adopted the anti-Catholic tactics of the clubs of Paris and the Carbonari of Italy. Secrecy ruled every society within the organization, and the cause of its defeat and demise arose from the fact that Ireland was not prepared for any gunpowder warfare in the streets of her cities, nor did the masses of the people have any sympathy with the Continental system upon which it was based.

The wisdom of the Bishops and Priests in Ireland in keeping aloof from this movement was dictated entirely by prudence and not prompted by any lack of patriotism. They saw failure stamped upon it from its inception, and their action saved many a life from being uselessly sacrificed through the evidence of Government spies. Because, as A. M. Sullivan testifies,[†] "*the Government were well informed through spies of everything* that was passing," and all the plots and conspiracies of the "Young Ireland" party were revealed to the authorities of Dublin Castle almost as soon as they were told with great secrecy in the clubrooms of the insurrectionary organization.

Few people can appreciate the terrible misery inflicted on Ireland by the wild rush for revenge which animated the men of '48, and which ended in depriving the Irish cause of many of its most ardent patriots. The closing scene in this direful drama is thus depicted by A. M. Sullivan.[‡]

"Throughout the remaining months of the year (1848) Ireland was given over to the gloomy scenes of special commissions, State trials, and death sentences. Of the leaders or prominent actors in this abortive insurrection, O'Brien, Meagher, MacManus, Martin and O'Doherty were convicted; Dillon, O'Gorman and Doheny succeeded in accomplishing their escape to America. O'Brien, Meagher and MacManus, with one of their devoted companions in danger, Patrick O'Donoghue by name, having been convicted of high treason, were sentenced to death, but by authority of a specially-passed Act of Parliament, the barbarous penalty of hanging, disemboweling and quartering, to which they were formally adjudged, was commuted into transportation beyond the seas for life. Duffy was thrice brought to trial; but although the Crown made desperate efforts to effect his conviction, the prosecution each time broke down, baffled by the splendid abilities of the defence conducted by Mr. Isaac Butt, Q. C. Eventually the proceedings against him were abandoned. Of less important participators numbers were evicted, and hundreds fled the country never to return. 'Forty-eight' cost Ireland dearly—not alone in the sacrifice of some of her best and noblest sons, led to immolate themselves in such desperate enterprise as revolution, but in the terrible reaction, the prostration, the terrorism, the disorganization that ensued. Through many a long and dreary year the country suffered for the delirium of that time."

[†] *New Ireland*, page 125.

[‡] *New Ireland* pp. 129-30.

CHAPTER XXXIV.

Secret Polital Societies.—Their Baneful Influence upon Ireland's Struggles for Freedom.—Reasons why the Church Opposes them.—The Wisdom of Her Opposition Proved by Numerous Examples.

The stern and continuous opposition of the Catholic Church to oath-bound Secret Societies is a fact well-known all over the world. It matters not to her whether such organizations are based upon bigotry or benevolence, or that the objects set forth for attainment are founded on patriotism or politics—the Church alike places the ban of her disapproval upon all congregations of individuals who are sworn to secrecy in order to conspire against the Christian citadel of Salvation, against the State, or any section of human society.

The Catholic Church is inspired by Almighty God in the wisdom which she displays for the moral and spiritual guidance of her children, and even her enemies have been compelled to admit that in her rigid opposition to all oath-bound secret societies she has won the admiration of men who otherwise never could be brought to acknowledge her as truly God's spiritual guide for all mankind.

Every wise mother is careful not to permit her children to fall a prey to wicked companions. The hen hides beneath her wings her chickens from the vulture and the hawk. And for far more cogent Christian reasons—a desire to save the temporal happiness as well as the spiritual lives of the flock of Christ—the Church warns her children not to enter any secret societies where their lives, their liberty, their sacred honor and their Catholic conscience might be jeopardized.

Looking at the baneful influences which oath-bound secret political associations have exercised upon both the politics and the people of Ireland during the past century, the Catholic Prelates of that country have wisely placed the seal of the condemnation of the Church upon all such organizations. From the rebellion of 1798 down to the present day, there never has been any amelioration of Ireland's condition gained through the operation of oath-bound secret society agencies. On the contrary, it is safe to say that more harm has accrued to individuals, to families, and to the fortunes of Ireland herself, from such combinations than from any other cause in connection with Ireland's numerous struggles for political supremacy.

THE SOCIETY OF UNITED IRISHMEN.

In order to demonstrate the evils which befell the Society of United Irishmen a century ago, during Ireland's memorable struggle, we extract from the best and most authentic work on that important era, some passages which will furnish indisputable evidence on that point.

Speaking of the Irish Rebellion of 1798, Dr. Richard R. Madden* says:

"The history of the Rebellion of 1798, like that of every other civil war, whatever traits of heroism may be discovered in the conduct of individuals, is a record of crimes and sufferings, which it is not for the interest of the people and their rulers should be buried in oblivion, however appaling its details. The evils that are inseparable from civil war, require only to be regarded by both orders as calamities which extend far beyond the event of success or failure, and involve considerations of higher importance than those which are ordinarily taken into account, either by those parties who rush into revolt, or the powers who resist the just, or even the unreasonable, demands of the people. It is indeed impossible to exaggerate the evils of civil war; but it is possible to overrate the prospective advantages which are calculated on from its success, and to overlook the sufferings which are the inevitable consequences of its failure.

"It is not alone in the deadly conflict, in the outrages on humanity committed in the frenzy of popular commotion, or party violence, or lawless power, that these evils are to be met with. The direst of them,

---
* *The United Irishmen*, First Series, pp. 406-7.

the most revolting and humiliating to the feelings of all right-minded men, are to be found in the perfidious wickedness of those wretches who rise in troubled times to the surface of society from the obscurity in which their mischievous propensities had previously lain innoxious. These are the men whom the people in revolt must expect to find earliest in their ranks, the most prominent in their societies, violent in their councils, conspicuous where there is security, and backward where there is danger, and who, while urging on their associates, skulk behind them, and bide their own time to betray them to their enemies.

"These are the men whom the leaders of the people must expect to meet in their secret assemblies, to mingle with in private, to suffer the obtrusive familiarity of, unrebuked—whose intemperate activity it is over a task of difficulty to restrain, whose vicious courses they cannot or dare not interfere with, whom they vainly imagine to find steadfast in their cause in the times and troubles which try men's souls, and eventually encounter in the courts of justice, or trace to the portals of the people of authority, shrinking from observation, and lurking about the offices of the underlings of state.

"These are the men whom the agents of government find fit and proper persons, when "the times are out of joint," to defeat the objects of those who are inimical to their principles or their power—wretches whom it is easy to corrupt, being generally not only infamous and dissolute in their lives, but singularly open and scandalous in their infamy. The employment of such men makes it necessary to treat them with consideration, to take the tutelage of their testimony into charge, to condescend to hold confidential communications with them, to wink at their iniquities, to seem unconscious of their venality, to work upon their vanity, to exaggerate their preposterous opinions of their own importance, and to conceal the viler features of their treachery under the veil of a solicitude for the interests of justice or the welfare of their country. If an alliance with such men involve their confederates in danger, the tutelage of their testimony cannot be otherwise than revolting to the feelings of their employers. It is impossible to come in contact with them without loathing the individuals whose services are called into requisition.

"In either case the consequences of the confidence that is betrayed, or the corruption that is practiced, and the use that is made of the infamous agency of spies and informers, are such that it is hard to say whether the danger attendant on the former, or the degradation on the latter, is the evil most to be apprehended or deplored.

"By the reports of the Secret Committees of the Lords, in 1793, and of both Houses of Parliament in 1797, it appears that the Government at a very early period, had a knowledge of the conspiracy carried on by the United Irish Societies in the provinces of Leinster and Ulster, though not of the persons who formed the directory of the former province. A regular system of espionage was adopted so early as 1795, and in 1796 there were few secrets of the United Irishmen which were not in the hands of the Government. It seems to be one of the necessary results of efforts to establish secret societies, that the more the secrecy of their proceedings is sought to be secured by tests and oaths, the more danger is incurred of treachery, and the more difficult it is to guard against traitors; the very anxiety for concealment becomes the immediate occasion of detection. * * *

"Mr. Frederick Dutton, who at an early period was employed in the North as an informer, and had been sent especially to Maidstone to insure the conviction of O'Connor, was a regular informer of this class, a most reckless one in the case of the unfortunate Priest Quigley, in whose greatcoat pocket, by mistake for Arthur O'Connor's, was placed the treasonable papers on which he was convicted. Mr. M'Gucken, the solicitor of the United Irishmen, was another of the private informers, who was intrusted with the defence of the prisoners charged with treason in Belfast, and at the same period was in the pay of the Government—was largely paid, and ultimately pensioned; and during these frightful times M'Gucken continued to possess the confidence of the United Irishmen.

"For upwards of twelve months before the breaking out of the rebellion several members of the Ulster United Irish Society were likewise in the pay of the Government. John Edward Newell entered on his duties at the Castle the 13th of April, 1797, and retired from them rather abruptly, the 6th of February, 1798. Nicholas Maguan, of Saintfield, in the County of Down, a member of the Provincial and County Committees, and also described in the report of 1798 as a colonel of their military system, during the whole of 1797, and down to June, 1798, regularly attended the meetings of the County Down United Irish Societies, and communicated to the Earl of Londonderry's chaplain, the Rev. John Cleland, a magistrate of that county, the treasonable proceedings of those societies after each meeting. * * * * *

"Such were the well-timed measures adopted by the Irish Government to cause the insurrection, in Lord Castlereagh's words, 'to explode,' when the mischievous designs of the United Irishmen had been long known to that Government, and so fully, that one of its leading members declared in Parliament, 'that the State prisoners had confessed nothing which had not been known to them before.'"

THE SOCIETY OF RIBBONMEN.

This plain and straightforward statement is sufficient to demonstrate the danger which lurks in all societies of a similar character, but in order still further to show the dangerous character of such organizations we will quote the sentiments of the great Irish Prelate, Bishop Doyle, of Kildare and Leighlin, on the Ribbonmen*

"The Society of Ribbonmen had, a few years previously (1819) first sprung into vitality. Originally formed in the West of Ireland, it gradually worked its secret way and influence until the confines of Dr. Doyle's diocese were struck by it. Some acts of violence on person and property having been committed, the Bishop devoted several pages of his first Pastoral to an eloquent denunciation of the objects of the society. He concluded with a most argumentative dissuasive, which, though erudite and logical, was clothed in a simplicity of language that rendered it thoroughly intelligible to the masses. The appeal thus terminated : 'Beloved brethren, we tell you in truth and sincerity that these associations are opposed to all your interests, both temporal and eternal; that the oath which unites them is illegal, sacrilegious and unjust; that if observed, it would be a bond of iniquity ; and that though it would be a crime to take it, it would be a still greater crime to observe it by word or deed ; and hence we conjure you by all that is dear to you, your family, your character, your country and your religion, to avoid all connection with these deluded men, and if any of you have been ensnared by them, to abandon their society to repent for the sins you committed in joining them, and, like Paul, 'you will obtain mercy, because it was through ignorance you did evil.' But if there should be found amongst you any persons who, disregarding these salutary instructions and advice, and who would still continue to set at defiance the laws of God and the country, who would still continue to expose our good name to disgrace, our religion to obloquy, and these dioceses, with their peaceable inhabitants, to terror and taxation, let such persons take notice, and we hereby solemnly warn and admonish them that we shall, in case they continue obstinate, resort to the severest chastisements, which the power vested in us from above enables us to inflict." * * * * *

The great Prelate who uttered these words of condemnation was one of the purest, the best, and the most persistent among Irish patriots of his time. But he well knew the dangerous tendencies of such societies and his experience led him to publicly denounce them not only in the year 1819, but also at a subsequent period when that grand Irish Bishop thus addressed the misguided members of his flock for joining the " Defenders"—which was only another change of name for the " Ribbonmen."

"But your object is to make your country free and happy. We will not reason with you on the end which you propose to yourselves, which, even if it were laudable, could not justify the employment of unlawful means, ' as evil,' says an apostle, ' is not to be done that good may happen;' but we will consider for a moment your design itself, and the persons employed to carry it into execution, that if possible the absurdity as well as the wickedness of it may become palpable to you. And first, who are those who would undertake to subvert the laws and constitution of this country? Persons without money, without education, without arms, without counsel, without discipline, without a leader; kept together by a bond of iniquity which it is a duty to violate and a crime to observe ; men destitute of religion and abandoned to the most frightful passions, having blasphemy in their mouths and their hands filled with rapine, and oftentimes with blood. Can such as these regenerate a country and make her free and happy ? No, dearest brethren ; left even to themselves they would destroy each other, but opposed to a regular force, they would scatter like a flock of sheep upon a mountain when a thunderstorm affrights them."†

It is not necessary to moralize upon these sterling sentiments of the great " J. K. L.," so we will proceed at once to inform our readers why the Catholic Church opposed

THE FENIAN ORGANIZATION.

Already we have shown how the ranks of the " Young Ireland" party were filled with spies, and as the Fenian organization was the natural offshoot of the " Young Ireland" and the " Phœnix Club" movements,

---

*Life of Dr. Doyle by W. Fitzpatrick, Vol. I., p. 123.

†Life and Times of Dr. Doyle, pp. 212-13.

it naturally occurred to the Bishops and Priests of Ireland that a large number of innocent people would be placed at the mercy of paid spies and perjured informers in the employ of the English Government if the Fenian organization were permitted to propagate itself throughout the country. Nor were the Bishops and Priests of Ireland alone in their opposition to the new secret society. Such unblemished patriots as Smith O'Brien, John Mitchel, A. M. Sullivan, John B. Dillon, Charles Gavan Duffy, Kevin Izod O Doherty and a very large proportion of the best and purest patriots then in Ireland, were utterly opposed to any plan entailing secrecy upon its participants, for the good and sensible reason that traitors would in time hand innocent men over to the British authorities—and thus work injury to the cause of Ireland as well as bring life-long sorrow upon numerous innocent individuals.

Skibbereen in the county of Cork was the cradle of Fenianism, and the "Phœnix National and Literary Society" was the nucleus of the organization, James Stephens being its sponsor. The secret object of this new organization was to drill Irishmen in military tactics and the manual of arms, then to supply them with the munitions of war from this country, and ultimately to send over from America five or ten thousand men to invade Ireland and to be assisted by "the men in the gap," who were to fight to the death for Ireland's freedom. This was a very heroic programme, but it is far easier to theorize on such important affairs of military prowess than it is to carry them in all their perfection into practical operation.

The great Irish National organ, the Dublin *Nation* came out boldly in opposition to this oath-bound secret organization, and inasmuch as the author of *Ireland and the Pope* has tried to cast odium on the character of the deceased Bishop Moriarty, of Kerry, we will let Mr. A. M. O'Sullivan give us the full version of that Prelate's interference against the Fenian movement, so as to counteract the garbled account in the book under review. Speaking of the notoriety which the Phœnix Society was beginning to attract through floating rumors of the connection of some eminent Irish patriots with its principles, Mr. Sullivan says:

"Meanwhile a new urgency appeared. The Catholic Bishop of Kerry, the Most Rev. Dr. Moriarty, called upon me one day to say that within the past hour he had heard *from a Government official* a minute account of the ' Phœnix Society' conspiracy in his diocese. 'It is no use pooh-poohing such work,' said he: 'the Government are preparing to treat it seriously, and *are in possession of full information* A friendly warning through the *Nation* may disperse the whole danger, and bring these young men back to reason. At all events you will save others from being involved in the catastrophe.'"*

Bishop Moriarty's conduct on this occasion was that of a worthy Christian Bishop who had the best interests of his flock at heart. This Prelate well knew from experience the sad fate which had overtaken and ruined hundreds of families in Ireland by means of secret political organizations which looked very patriotic to the unsuspecting victims, but which proved to be so many traps set by designing informers in order to lodge in prison the best sons of the suffering Irish tenantry and thus entail destitution, exile and death upon many a disrupted family which hitherto had enjoyed lives of rural peace and domestic happiness.

Mr. Sullivan's interview with Bishop Moriarty resulted in placing the *Nation* in direct antagonism to the Fenian organization, and the manner of its opposition can best be told by that distinguished patriot himself in the following extracts :†

"I hesitated no longer ; I not only published Mr. O'Brien's letter, as he desired, but in strong terms appealed to patriotic Irishmen *to avoid the hopeless perils and the demoralizing effects of secret societies.* I was, in the same sense as the national leaders had ever been, as "seditious" as any of them in my hostility to the imperial scheme of destroying our national autonomy, but I had not studied in vain the history of secret oath-bound associations. *I regarded them with horror.* I knew all that could be said as to their advantages in revolutionizing a country ; but even in the firmest and best of hands they had a direct tendency to de-

---
*New Ireland, p. 275. †275-6. ‡323-4.

moralization, and were often, on the whole, more perilous to society than open tyranny. In joining issue on this occasion with the hidden chiefs of the movement, I knew I was setting a great deal on the cast; yet I did not know all. No action of my life bore consequences more full of suffering and sacrifice for me than did this throughout subsequent years. Conducting such a journal as the *Nation*, I had no choice as to silence. An equivocal attitude would have been despicably mean and cowardly. I was called upon to speak and act, under not only the public but the conscientious constraint of duty, and I did so. The result proved that the influence of the *Nation* had been underrated; or, perhaps, I should say, its influence in co operation with the appeals of the Catholic clergy. The enrolment was stopped, and it seemed for a while as if the movement had been relinquished."

Mr. Sullivan devotes a chapter to the Fenian movement, and in order that our readers may fully understand the opposition which that organization met with from many of Ireland's truest, stanchest, and wisest friends, we cull from the chapter before us the following extracts bearing immediately on the causes which entailed the condemnation of the Church upon this oath-bound body :‡

"There were in 1858, on the starting of this enterprise, several Irish-American newspapers ardently devoted to the cause of Irish nationality. In New York city alone there were at least two; one was the the *Irish News*, established by Thomas Francis Meagher; the other the *Irish-American*, then, as now, the leading organ of Irish Nationalism in the United States. Even with these journals the Fenian leaders quarrelled as strongly as with the *Nation*; so they decided to establish a special organ of the movement, which accordingly appeared as the *Phœnix* newspaper, in New York. In this journal they struck out vigorously, right, left, and centre, at everything and everybody supposed to be inimical to their undertaking. They had no need to waste words in rousing the ire of their readers against England. The Irish in America —the maddened fugitives of the dreadful famine and eviction times—hated the British power with quenchless hate. The obstacles that most concerned the secret leaders arose from opposition given to their scheme by the Catholic clergy and the open-policy or anti-Fenian Nationalists. The Catholic Church condemns oath-bound secret societies, —especially if directed to the subversion of the civil power or the overthrow of religion, —for several reasons. First, regarding the sanctity of an oath, it denies that any one who chooses can, for any purpose he pleases, formally administer or impose that solemn obligation Secondly, having regard to the safety of society, of public order, of morals and religion, it prohibits the erection of any such barrier between the objects and operations of a society, and authoritative examination and judgment. Over this critical and important issue the Fenian movement, on its very threshold, was plunged into a bitter war with the ecclesiastical authorities of the Catholic Church "The Priest has no right to interfere in or dictate our politics," said the Fenian leaders; "ours is a political movement; they must not question us or impede us." "You cannot be admitted to the sacraments until you give up and repent of illicit oaths," responded the Catholic Priests; "and if you contumaciously continue in membership of an oath-bound secret society, you are liable to excommunication." "Do you hear this ?—we are cursed by the Church for loving our country !" exclaimed the Fenians; and so for the first five years, from 1860 to 1865, the struggle between the Catholic clergy and the Fenian organizers was fierce, violent, and unsparing. A really active "B," or Fenian centre, had need to be a man who cared little for the Priest's denunciations, and who could persuade the people it was "the Maynooth oath and the gold of England" that made Father Tom so ready to "curse" the cause. The Priests, accordingly, complained that the propagators of Fenianism were men who paid little regard to clerical authority and shunned the practices of faith. One can see how out of antagonistic views thus pressed the quarrel eventuated in the Fenians denouncing the Priests as deadly foes of Irish nationality, and the Priests denouncing the Fenians as enemies of the Church,—men who would overthrow the altar and destroy society.

"Very similar was the conflict between the secret organization and the non-Fenian or anti-Fenian Nationalists; the great object of the Fenian leaders being that the people should have no alternative patriotic effort between embracing their enterprise and siding with imperial subjugation. Indeed, a reference to the pages of the Fenian newspapers, and to the public chronicles of the period, will show that the movement during the four years following 1860 was directed less against the English Government than against those Irish Nationalists, Priests and laymen, whose influence was supposed to impede the organization." * * * *

From the foregoing extract it will be discerned at once that the onslaught made on the Catholic Church by certain unwise leaders among the Fenians could only result in the destruction of the party who proposed to free Erin by means which were not in accord with the Christian sentiments of those most interested in the struggle—the Catholic Prelates, Priests and people of Ireland resident in that land. The folly of such opposition to the Church was subsequently clearly understood by reflecting members of the organization, and the very attitude of antagonism to the Church which was assumed served to weaken the force of Fenianism from the first moment of its existence.

The author of *New Ireland* very clearly points out the fact that at every stage of the conspiracy through which the Fenian organization passed in Ireland, the British Government had for its spies and informers the most trusted members of the organization itself. He describes the cause of the suppression of the *Irish People*, the treason of Pierce Nagle, and the arrest of the principal leaders, and then he adds :*

" It was not the power and arms of the British Government alone that operated to disorganize and destroy the Fenian movement. Dissension and revolt among its leaders broke its power. Before two years Stephens was the object of fierce denunciation from his own followers, and John O'Mahony was deposed and degraded by the Senate of the American Branch, over which he had so long presided. In each case the dethroned or impeached leaders had numerous partisans, so that the unity of the organization on each side of the Atlantic was at an end."

Mr. Sullivan next passes under review the "insurrection" of March 5th, 1867, when the Fenian circles undertook to rise in their might and make an end of Ireland's political misery forever. But here, as in all other attempts made to free Ireland by means of oath-bound compatriots, the spy and the informer spoiled the plans of the patriots at the very moment they sought to bring them to a happy consummation. John Joseph Corydon was one of James Stephens' most trusted agents ; he was not only very high in the Fenian Councils, but he was also very deep in the pay of the British Government—to whom he furnished every secret that the organization most carefully guarded under the impressive form of a forbidden oath.

**New Ireland, p. 369.

Fenianism, therefore, furnishes us with another evidence of the wisdom of the Catholic Church in putting the ban of her condemnation upon oath-bound secret associations of a political character, not one of which gained anything for Ireland—save the disgrace and distress caused by the bloodhounds who "sold the pass" to the British Government.

WAS THE HOME RULE MOVEMENT OPPOSED BY THE CHURCH?

One of the prime objects for issuing the book under review seems to have been the deliberate misrepresentation of the Pope and the Bishops and Priests of Ireland upon every question connected with efforts to restore the nationality of that long-suffering land. No proofs are offered in justification of any criticisms upon the Church, but she is set down as the deadly enemy of Ireland's aspirations for freedom, even though such efforts were grounded upon the laws of the gospel of Christ. The falsity of such a charge has already been made manifest in these pages, and now we will proceed to illustrate still further the vicious venality which prompted such a groundless accusation.

The author under review says that "the finger of Rome" kept back the Catholic clergy in Ireland during the early stages of the Home Rule movement. But the real *cause* which operated in keeping the Irish Bishops and clergy in abeyance for a few months, may be found in the fact that they first desired to ascertain whether the new plan of political action was based upon Christian and constitutional laws, or was it merely a continuation of the secret schemes which so recently had brought exile, destitution, ignominy and death to so many brave patriots who were literally *sold* into penal servitude by the paid spies, iniquitous informers and treacherous traitors of their own race.

As soon, however, as it was made manifest to the over-faithful Prelates and Priests of Ireland that the Home Rule movement was based on legitimate lines of political agitation, that moment they gave it their heartiest co-operation, and the vast majority of them have stood by the standard of Home Rule ever since. This fact is well-known to every intelligent individual and is a sufficient negative answer to the question propounded above.

WAS THE LAND LEAGUE OPPOSED BY THE POPE?

In the work under review we are told that it was, and the author cites, in proof thereof, the following:

I.—Archbishop McCabe published some Pastoral Letters condemning the Land League agitation.

II.—Archbishop McCabe was subsequently elevated to the ecclesiastical dignity of a Cardinal.

III.— On the 20th of January, 1883, Pope Leo XIII., sent a Rescript to the Irish Clergy commanding them to suppress a certain class of societies, the description being broad enough to include the Irish political leagues.

IV.—On May 11th, of the same year, the Pope issued a more powerful and mandatory Rescript condemning and forbidding disaffection to the Government, and forbidding subscriptions to the Parnell Testimonial Fund.

I. The assertion that Archbishop McCabe published Pastorals against the Land League agitation—even admitting that he did so—is no proof that Pope Leo XIII. opposed the Land League. Nor does the fact that Archbishop McCabe was afterwards made a Cardinal indicate in the least that such elevation was caused by his alleged Pastorals antagonistic to the Land League. So much on these points.

II. We now come down to January, 1883, when Pope Leo XIII., *it is said*, issued a *Rescript* to the Irish Clergy, commanding them to suppress a certain class of societies, the description being broad enough to include the Irish Land League.

Here is "the truth, the whole truth, and nothing but the truth," concerning the Pope's actions and utterances regarding the Land League, as we find them recorded in a most impartial work by a disinterested author:*

"The condition of the Irish Catholics, who comprise over four-fifths of the whole population of Ireland, naturally attracted the attention of the Pope at this time. It is not necessary to enter here into any description of the state of Ireland in the years following the coronation of Leo XIII. Everybody is familiar with the story of that home-rule agitation which began to assume definite form after the famine of 1879-80, and the general election of the latter year; and which, though it has not yet obtained the goal of its desires, is, nevertheless, morally certain of winning for the Irish people the inestimable boon of legislative autonomy. When the Land League first began its crusade against alien landlordism, England resorted to all sorts of dishonest methods to create the impression at Rome that the Irish Catholics were being tainted with heresy and false ideas. It was said that they were becoming perverts to the erroneous doctrines of socialism; that they refused to pay their just debts; that they were no longer disposed to obey their Priests and Bishops; and that, in fact, unless some effective barrier were soon interposed, they would lose their faith altogether, and become lost to the Church.

"Naturally such reports as those, which English landlords took good care to get forwarded to Rome, troubled Pope Leo not a little; and hence he summoned the Bishops of Cashel, Emly, Limerick, Cloyne, Ross, and Kerry, to Rome, to consult with them concerning the situation in Ireland. The patriotic Dr. Croke, the Archbishop of Cashel, took upon himself the defence of the Irish agitators; and he assured the Holy Father that there was little or no truth in the alarming rumors that English agents had so sedulously spread in Rome. He pointed out that all the great reforms that had in the past been won in Ireland were carried by just such means as the Irish people were now employing to destroy alien landlordism and English misrule; and he assured his Holiness that there was not the slightest danger of the Irish people either losing their faith, or relaxing that attachment which had hitherto knit them so to closely the Holy See. 'Two things,' said the Holy Father, 'weigh much upon my mind, and are all-important in this question. The first is the preservation of the Catholic faith among the Irish people. Upon this point,' continued his Holiness, 'I confess I have less anxiety; for the past history of Ireland is a pledge for the future, and I have no fear that the Irish, who have preserved their faith through centuries of misfortune, will ever abandon it. The second is the union of the Bishops and clergy with their people, and the imperative necessity that no revolutionary principles should be introduced or allowed to take root among them.' Dr. Croke and the other Irish Prelates assured the Pope anew that there was not the slightest danger of a revo-

---
*Pope Leo XIII. His Life and Letters. Compiled by Rev. James F. Talbot. Boston: 1886. Pp. 230-36.

lution occurring in Ireland. They pointed out to him, that the Irish people were now engaged in a peaceful and constitutional agitation for the acquisition of their rights; and, as they believed that by such an agitation they would eventually win, there was nothing to dread on the score of an armed uprising against the authorities, even if everybody was persuaded that the laws such authorities enforced were unjust and tyrannical ones. The Holy Father had several audiences with the Irish Prelates during their stay in Rome; and he assured them that his sympathies and good wishes went out to Ireland, to the fidelity of whose people to the faith and the Apostolic See he bore willing and eloquent testimony. Later on, the Pope again called the Irish Bishops to Rome, for consultation with them on the Irish situation; but of that more in its proper place. Early in 1881, Cardinal McCabe, Archbishop of Dublin, since deceased, communicated to his clergy the text of a most important Letter addressed to him on the 3rd of January by the Holy Father. The Archbishop asks: 'In what terms does the Holy Father address himself to us? An attempt may be made to *distort his words*, and to make it appear that the Holy See is hostile to the demand of the country for the repeal of harsh laws, which have brought misery and crime amongst us for long generations. Is this the object of the Letter of the Holy Father / *Most certainly not.* He knows the injuries inflicted on our people by the present land code, and he prays that these injuries may be speedily redressed by a change in the laws from which they flow; but whilst he blesses our determination to obtain justice for an oppressed tenantry, there are in the agitation, as carried on, things which he can not approve. No better exponent of the Holy Father's views can be had than the Holy Father himself, who draws a wide distinction between the end aimed at, and some of the means employed to achieve that end.' And then the Archbishop tells how, in his audience with the Pope, 'his Holiness *did not in any way disapprove of the people seeking by legitimate and constitutional means the redress of their grievances;*' but he said that 'in the present agitation, as it is carried on, there are certain things done which I cannot approve of. The people,' he said, 'should be encouraged in doing what is right, but they should be duly impressed with the duty of keeping always *within the bounds of law and religion.*' The words of the last paragraph in the Archbishop's letter are perhaps the most vitally important of all. Regretfully writes his Grace: "Rumors to which we would be unwilling to give credence are already in circulation, that the scheme about to be proposed by Government for the settlement of the land question will be but a half hearted attempt to grapple with the evil they wish to cure. This would be a deplorable misfortune. Unless the cancer which has been eating away the life of the nation be cut out to the last fibre, health and security never can be restored, and sooner or later the disastrous scenes of to-day will return, but with increased violence.' Dr. McCabe calls the evil of the present land system 'a cancer eating into the life of the nation, which must be cut out to the last fibre, or health and security can never be restored.' 'A half-hearted attempt' to grapple with it, Archbishop McCabe designates as 'a deplorable misfortune.'"

THE POPE'S LETTER.

TO OUR VENERABLE BROTHER, EDWARD M CABE, ARCHBISHOP OF DUBLIN, PRIMATE OF IRELAND—

Venerable Brother:—Health and Apostolic Benediction. We read with pleasure your Letter recently addressed to the clergy and people of the Diocese of Dublin, and presented to Us by you when you were in Rome; for in it We recognized your prudence and moderation, since, while Ireland is now deeply moved, partly by a desire of better things, partly by a fear of an uncertain future, you offer counsel admirably suited to the occasion.

The unhappy condition of Catholics in Ireland disquiets and afflicts Us; and We highly esteem their virtue, sorely tried by adversity not for a brief period only, but for many centuries. For, with the greatest fortitude and constancy, they preferred to endure every misfortune rather than forsake the religion of their fathers, or deviate in the slightest degree from their ancient fidelity to the Apostolic See. Moreover, it is their singular glory, extending down to the present time, that most noble proofs of all the other virtues were never wanting amongst them. There reasons force Us to love them with paternal benevolence, and fervently to wish that the evils by which they are afflicted may quickly be brought to an end.

At the same time, We unhesitatingly declare that it is their duty to be carefully on their guard not to allow the fame of their sterling and hereditary probity to be lessened, and not to commit any rash act whereby they may seem to have cast aside the obedience due their lawful rulers; and for this reason, whenever Ireland was greatly excited in guarding and defending her own interests, the Roman Pontiffs constantly endeavored by admonition and exhortation to allay the excited feelings, lest, by a disregard of moderation, justice might be violated, or the cause, however right in itself, might be forced by the influence of passion into the flame of sedition. These counsels were also directed to the end that the Catholics of Ireland should in all things follow the Church as a guide and teacher; and, thoroughly conforming themselves to her precepts, they should reject the allurements of pernicious doctrines. Thus the Supreme Pontiff Gregory XVI., on the 12th of March, 1839, and on the 15th of October, 1844, through the Sacred Congregation of the Propaganda, admonished the Archbishop of Armagh to do nothing except with justice and moderation. And We, following the example of Our predecessors, took care on the 1st of June last year, as you are aware, to give to all the Bishops of Ireland the salutary admonitions which the occasion demanded; namely, that the Irish people should obey the Bishops, and in no particular deviate from the sacredness of duty. And a little later, in the month of November, We testified to some Irish Bishops who had come to visit the tombs of the Apostles, that We ardently desired every good gift for the people of Ireland; but We also added, that order should not be disturbed.

This manner of thinking and acting is entirely conformable to the ordinances and laws of the Catholic Church, and We have no doubt that it will conduce to the interests of Ireland. For We have confidence in the justice of the men who are placed at the head of the State, and who certainly, for the most part, have great experience, combined with prudence in civil affairs. Ireland may obtain what she wants, much more safely and readily, if only she adopts a course which the laws allow, and avoids giving causes of offence.

Therefore, venerable brother, let you and your colleagues in the Episcopate direct your efforts to the end that the people of Ireland, in this anxious condition of affairs, do not transgress the bounds of equity and justice. We have assuredly received from the Bishops, the Clergy, and the people of Ireland, many proofs of reverence and affection; and if now, in a willing spirit, they obey these counsels and Our authority, as We are certain they will, they may feel assured that they have fulfilled their own duty, and have completely satisfied Us.

Finally, from our heart We implore God to look down propitiously on Ireland; and in the meantime, as a pledge of heavenly gifts, We affectionately impart in the Lord the Apostolic Benediction to you, venerable brother, to the other Bishops of Ireland, and to the entire Clergy and people.

Given at St. Peter's, Rome, on the third day of January, 1881, in the third year of Our Pontificate.

LEO PP. XIII.

It would be a work of supererogation on our part to add any remarks to the above loving Letter of the Holy Father to the Irish people, as its plain language, its parental tone, its friendly expression and its general sympathy for the success of every just effort for Ireland's amelioration, proves it to have emanated from the feeling heart of a Pontiff who has never for a moment wavered in his love for Ireland and her valiant, virtuous Catholic people.

It is a plain and palpable fact, therefore, that the Land League movement was *not* opposed by the Church, and we joyfully pride ourselves upon the fact that the foregoing extracts are triumphant vindications of Pope Leo's friendly attitude towards the Irish Land League when carried on in a legitimate manner, and in compliance with the laws of Christian morality —outside of which no Catholic can venture if he desires the blessing of God and His Church to rest upon his struggles for Ireland's freedom.

IV. Let us now pass under review the miscalled "more powerful and mandatory Rescript" which our author mistakingly asserts to have "condemned and forbid disaffection to the British Government." This document introduced with such rhetorical spleen and rabid virulence was not a Rescript in any sense. It was merely a simple Letter issued by the Sacred Congregation of the Propaganda to the Bishops of Ireland, and signed by the Prefect—Cardinal Simeoni.

The text of this Letter stated that *it was sinful to further a just cause by unlawful methods.* Thereby admitting that the *cause* in which the Irish Land League was engaged was *just in itself,* but that some of *the means* employed to attain its end were *not grounded on Christian justice.* Cardinal Simeoni expressed the fear that cupidity had exercised its influence over a portion of the Irish people, that they were adopting false views, and that they were seeking for national prosperity through the instrumentality of remedies which would lead to crime. The Circular stated that class-hatred was engendered in Ireland, horrible crimes were not reprobated, and men were terrorized by the threats of holding them up as the enemies of Ireland unless they subscribed their money to the fund in question. This, in brief, is the contents of the forty-line Circular which has caused so much calumny to be hurled at the Holy Father, who has borne this contumely with model Christian meekness.

Now let us see what this Circular *did not condemn*. There is not a syllable in it condemning the Land League. On the contrary, it explicitly states that it is the perfect right of the Irish people to endeavor to obtain an alleviation of their present troubles, and to agitate for their political rights. Not a word in the Circular in condemnation of Mr. Parnell personally, nor a syllable of censure against his political policy, and the document disclaims any intention of doing so.*

There is not a single reference in the Simeoni Circular condemnatory of the Fair Rent agitation, of the movement for buying out the Irish Landlords, of Home Rule, the Land League, or even entire Repeal of the Union between Great Britian and Ireland. In fine, there is not a single sentence in this document which justifies the extravagant language used in connection with it in the pages of the publication whose malicious errors we have so successfully contradicted. It is clear, therefore, from the irrefutable evidence we have adduced, that Pope Leo XIII. did *not* oppose the Irish Land League.

THE PAPAL "RESCRIPT" OF 1888.

The author whose book we are reviewing seems to have a weakness for calling every document issued by Cardinals or Congregations in Rome by the handy title of *Rescript*, so as to designedly give them an authoritative prominence which, he vainly imagines, they might not otherwise possess. This mistake we have heretofore pointed out and it is only necessary for us to do so again, because the so-called Papal "Rescript" of the 20th of April, 1888, which our author alludes to, was simply a Circular issued by the Congregation of the Holy Office in Rome and signed by Cardinal Simeoni. This document was the Circular which alluded to the "Plan of Campaign" and "Boycotting" as not being considered justifiable by the Cardinals—according to the matters laid down for their guidance in forming their judgment.

In the consideration of this Circular, and in order that our readers may have a clear and authoritative exposition of its real intent, force and meaning, we opine that the better way to reach such a conclusion is to publish the opinions of Most Rev. Dr. William Walsh, Archbishop of Dublin, as that distinguished patriotic Prelate expressed them in an interview with a representative of the Dublin *Freeman's Journal* shortly after the document in question was issued:

Representative: I am fortunate, your Grace, in being the first on your return from Rome to hear what you may have to say about the recent Rescript, and its bearings upon the public affairs of Ireland.

The Archbishop: Well, perhaps so; but I do not think that I have anything of substantial importance to add to what I have already written from Rome upon the subject. Very soon after the Rescript, as you call it, had been published—

R.—Your Grace will pardon me if I ask, then, whether "Rescript" is not the proper term to use?

A.—No; but this is a matter merely of technical accuracy. The word "Rescript" has a restricted technical sense, and, strictly speaking, it is not applicable in the present case. The document in question should rather be spoken of as a "Decree." It is a Decree or decision of the Holy Office, approved by the Sovereign Pontiff. * * *

R.—The news, as your Grace no doubt is aware, first appeared in a London Protestant newspaper, a paper most hostile to the Irish National movements. There is in Ireland, and also indeed, as a matter of course, among the Irish population in England, in Scotland, and in America, a strong and even angry feeling on this point. People are saying that whatever the Decree may be in itself, the fact that it was communicated for publication in the first instance through such a channel, in a newspaper notoriously hostile both to the Land League movement, and to the Home Rule movement, gives it a decidedly political aspect.

A.—To be candid with you, I do not at all wonder that such a feeling exists. If I did not know the facts of the case I should feel very strongly on the subject myself. But the hasty judgments that have been formed on this point do a grievous wrong to the Holy Father. Take the case even on broad, general grounds. The notion that the Pope

---

*"*Quidquid sit de persona Parnelli ejusque conciliis.*"

was in any way influenced by political considerations such as you refer to, rests altogether upon the assumption that his Holiness is in some way opposed to the Irish Nationalist movements—to the movement for Home Rule, or to the movement for obtaining a full measure of justice or of protection against oppression for the tenant-farmers of Ireland. *Now no assumption could be more absolutely contrary to fact.*

R.—It is, I may say, universally believed, your Grace, that many strong influences of various kinds have been brought to bear upon his Holiness within the last year or so, to lead him to take an adverse view of the Irish cause.

A.—People may believe what they like, but I know what I am talking about. It is essential that this point should be fully understood by the Irish people at home and abroad. No matter what influences have been brought to bear upon the Holy Father, no matter through what channels they may have worked, no matter how powerful they may have been, their work has resulted in absolute failure. His Holiness understands the Irish question fully. He knows what is meant by the demand for Home Rule. And he knows what is meant by the demand for a full and effective measure of protection against oppression and of justice for the Irish tenants. That is to say, he knows in the fullest detail what is meant by these demands as I understand them—

R.—Your Grace, it was hoped, would have an opportunity of putting these matters before his Holiness

A.—I had it, and I had it in a fullness which I certainly could not have hoped for. I need hardly add that I availed myself to the fullest possible extent of the opportunity that was so graciously afforded me That, in fact, was what kept me so long in Rome The Holy Father is now in full possession of the Irish national programme. Having said so much I need only add that nothing could be further from his thoughts than any desire to put the slightest obstacle in the way of its success Quite the contrary. It is the firm conviction of his Holiness that the publication of the Decree of the Holy Office, condemning as it does, those points in the practical working of the movement on which so much hostile criticism was concentrated, will be the most decided help in the advancement of the Irish cause.

The following day the Archbishop of Dublin was interviewed by a representative of the *Star*. In the course of the interview his Grace said :

The Archbishop : If you wish to know my views on the land question I shall be happy to give them to you.

R.—The agitation to which the Rescript has given rise turns mainly upon the statement made about the land question in that document The Irish people have been assured by your Grace in the first instance, and afterwards by the recent meeting of the Irish Bishops, that the Roman Decree is a decision in morals and not a political act. But it lays down a number of statements that certainly amount to the condemnation of the present land movement from beginning to end.

A.—No ; excuse me, nothing of the kind.

R.—Does it not practically define that the Irish tenants have no longer any cause for complaint ? It says, equivalently at least, that the rent question is now settled ; that the tenants are under an obligation of justice to pay their rents ; or that at all events there are tribunals in existence to do them full justice if they think their rents too high. It is hard to know what it is, if it is not a sweeping condemnation of the Irish Land movement in every shape and form.

A —But you may take it on my authority that there is no such condemnation. I cannot deny that statements such as you have quoted are to be found in the Letter that accompanies the Decree. But the Decree itself approved as it is by the Pope, is one thing ; that Letter is another.

R.—That is the Letter of Cardinal Monaco ?

A.—Yes. There has been a great deal of foolish writing on this subject in some of the newspapers. It is all very irritating to our people, and I have no doubt that a great deal of it was meant to be so. The Decree itself, as a decision in morals, is binding on the consciences of Catholics. As to Cardinal Monaco's Letter, it is to be treated of course, with respect; but it has no binding force whatever. It is not intended, and indeed, it could not have been intended to have any.

The lucid explanation which the eminent Archbishop of Dublin gives concerning the Propaganda Circular makes it entirely unnecessary for us to say any more on the subject, save to p'ace on record the fact that Pope Leo XIII., is entirely exculpated from all the calumnies cast upon his character by demagogues and doubtful Catholics whose malice has led them into taking sides with the enemies of both Ireland and the Pope.

CHAPTER XXXV.

Some Vicious Falsehoods Regarding "Vatican Politics" fully Refuted—The "Italian Ring" Accounted for.—The Characters of Pope Alexander VI., and other Pontiffs Triumphantly Vindicated.—Conclusion.

There is no body of representatives that have ever existed in the world who have been more caustically calumniated, or more constantly maligned, than the Popes of Rome—the Vicars of Christ, the Vicegerents of God. Catholics may wonder why this is so, since so large a majority of them were pious, pure and prudent, wise beyond their generation, and directed in their office by Divine Wisdom Itself.

The Popes are in the world but not of it, and, representing as they do in their capacity as Chief Bishops of the one holy Roman Catholic and Apostolic Church of Christ, that they should be hated and slandered by the world is precisely what the Son of God predicted concerning all who take up their cross and follow Him. The servant cannot be greater than the Master, and as our Blessed Redeemer was ha ed and reviled whilst on earth for man's Redemption, so also were his chief servants, the Popes of Rome, reviled from the first to the nineteenth century. In a word, to that glorious body of saintly men may well be applied the words of our Lord to His disciples:

"Blessed shall you be when men shall hate you, and when they shall separate you, and cast out your name as evil for the Son of Man's sake. Be glad in that day and rejoice; for behold, *your reward is great in Heaven.* For according to these things did their fathers to the Prophets."

The author of the work under review expresses great anxiety in his last chapter that his readers should have "a general knowledge of the character (religious and political) of the Papal office and of the personnel of its incumbents at various periods, and also a knowledge of the origin, characteristics and personnel of the College of Cardinals," and then follows several pages of some of the most vicious and vituperative falsehoods that ever were framed by apostates, animated by the spirit of diabolical hatred against Almighty God, His Church and His Vicars. Such slanderous and malignant misrepresentations are calculated to exert a most baneful influence in the world if they are permitted to exist without refutation, hence we add a chapter to our work in order to show the slanderous nature of this author's vile repetition of his anti-Christian precursors in the evil work of slandering the Bride of Christ and her chief Bishops.

The apostate antagonist whose work we are reviewing seems to be greatly disturbed in his mind through fear that the Pope and the Cardinals, who constitute the executive organization of the Catholic Church, will commit some overt act which will lead to disasterous consequences, but inasmuch as the writer in question has publicly placed himself outside the pale of the Church by his open apostacy, we fail to see why he is so perturbed on this subject, save that he desires to arouse suspicion in the minds of Catholics so as to change their reverence for their Church into a hatred as intense as that so manifestly and malignantly evinced in his bad book.

The next complaint made is based upon this statement:

"The College of Cardinals for over eight hundred years (ever since it was created) has been composed almost exclusively of Italians, and these have been nearly all members of a little Italian nobility consisting of a very few families."

For the information of our readers it may be well to meet this objection by giving the reasons why a large majority of the members of the College of Cardinals are Italians, which is simply a condition that is enforced by reason of the fact that all the business transacted by the Church is carried on in Rome. It will be easily understood, therefore, that in carrying on the vast amount of ecclesiastical business transacted for the Bishops, Priests and laity all over the world it is most necessary that the Cardinals should reside in the immediate vicinity of the Holy Father so as to receive his instructions speedily and easily.

Rome is the centre and capital of the Catholic Church. Here are received all ecclesiastical and diplomatic documents from every portion of the civilized globe, and if the Pope had to wait until Cardinals could be sent for from different portions of the Christian world in order to transact the business detailed in such documents, the wheels of the Church would be clogged and nothing but delay, disorder and disappointment would ensue.

Under the system of having Italian Cardinals who reside in Rome, the multifarious duties of the different Congregations are attended to promptly, and the vast concerns of the Church run along smoothly and successfully. It must also be borne in mind that men are not born Cardinals. The training necessary to understand fully the particular and peculiar methods employed by the Holy See in its administration of the different duties entailed upon the Vicar of Christ, as well as upon the members of the different Congregations, can only be acquired by a long residence as well as by close and constant study and training in the Eternal City.

It now remains for us only to show why so many Cardinals are members of "a little Italian nobility," and that is very easily accomplished. Cardinals residing in Rome receive only a small stipend which is not nearly sufficient to meet their expenses. Roman Cardinals are compelled to keep up a certain amount of dignity which those in other countries are exempt from. A Roman Cardinal must have a certain number of servants, his own horses and carriage, and all the other appurtenances of his high office, and it is only the members of that "little Italian nobility," so sneeringly and scurriously alluded to, that are able to furnish the means to keep up the expenses entailed on Cardinals resident in Rome. In order, therefore, to sustain the dignity of their high ecclesiastical position, and to be able to contribute the alms which they are constantly interceded for, Italian candidates for the purple have to be either wealthy in their own right, or else members of families whose position in life is such that they are able to assist their relatives with a share of their riches.

Such is the reason why Italian Cardinals happen in many cases to be members of "a little Italian nobility," and it is the same "little Italian nobility," by the way which has given to the Church some of the greatest Saints, Popes, Cardinals and Bishops that ever lived beneath the shadow of St. Peter's. Thus it would seem as if Almighty God had raised up this "little Italian nobility" around the Pontifical Chair for His own wise ends, for His own greater honor and glory, as well as for the benefit of the whole Church.

Malignant-minded writers who thus wantonly sneer at "the little Italian nobility" in Rome, and who allude to the fact that some of the Popes were blood relations as something that is dishonorable to the Papacy and injurious to the Church, evidently forget that in selecting St. John the Baptist as His precursor, and also in gathering around Himself the twelve Apostles who were to propagate His truths, our Blessed Redeemer had among all of these first Christians many men who were related by consanguinity not only to Himself but also to each other. Thus St. John the Baptist was a relative of our Divine Lord; St. James the Greater was a brother of St. John the Evangelist and also related to our Blessed Redeemer; St. James the Less was called the brother of our Lord, and St. Andrew was the brother of St. Peter. Here, therefore, we have the first "colony" of Christians formed by the Son of God Himself, and therein we find a most excellent precedent for "the little Italian nobility consisting of a very few families." The Church of God was founded by "*a very few families*," yet it was the Allwise, Omnipotent and Omnipresent Creator of all things Who thus founded it. And all praise, glory and adoration to Him for having done so!

A VINDICATION OF THE CHARACTER OF POPE ALEXANDER VI. AND OTHER PONTIFFS.

As an example of the "consuming ambition and burning jealousies" which marred the lives of the members of "the little Italian nobility," our author cites the case of Pope Alexander VI., whom he styles "an exceptionally unworthy Pope," merely because he found some enemy of that Pontiff who had calumniated his character.

It is the misfortune of the Catholic Church that Protestant calumniators of the Popes have been allowed to fill the ears of mankind in general with their slanders against the characters of many Pontiffs, whilst Catholic writers remained listlessly looking on and seemingly helpless to stay the assaults of the common enemy. For this reason even Catholics themselves have come to look upon Popes like Alexander VI., with feelings of horror, and to wonder how such "monsters of iniquity" could be permitted by Almighty God to reign over His Church. In this way the demon of detraction has dinned into the ears of the world all the fallacious fables, malicious inventions, and diabolical falsehoods which ancient and modern enemies of the Church have thrown upon the surface of the stream of anti-Catholic literature since printing was invented. By this means cowardice has been engendered in the minds of many Catholics who, in their timidity, imagine that no defence whatever can be made against such assaults upon the characters of Pontiffs like Alexander VI., who is ranked, seemingly by general consent, as "the worst among bad Popes."

It is no discredit to us to admit that thirty years ago we were among those who believed in the commonly-reported iniquities attributed to the Pontiff whose defence we have undertaken. But when we had devoted much time to reading, we began to discover that there were positive reasons which impelled certain individuals who lived contemporaneous with Pope Alexander VI., to blacken his character. These slanders were carried down the stream of time, being increased in iniquity and augmented in number by Protestant and infidel writers who desired to "make bad worse" for the reason that every pang they inflicted upon the Catholic Church was calculated to lessen her influence in the world by undermining the earthly corner-stone of the entire fabric.

One cause why the character of Pope Alexander VI., has been assailed with such virulence may be traced to the fact that in the period of his existence a great degree of rivalry and animosity existed between some of the leading Italian families, each of which had literary hangers-on who were prepared to blacken the character of Pope, Prince or Bishop in order to satisfy the jealousy and spleen of those who hired them, as well as to replenish their fortunes by means of such malignant attacks upon innocent people—who thus became the victims of hatred inspired by misrepresentation.

An idea of the state of Italy at the time when Pope Alexander was called upon to rule the Church may be gleaned from the fact that between the last illness of Pope Innocent VIII., and the coronation of his successor, Alexander VI.—a period of less than two months—there were more than *two hundred unpunished assassinations* committed in the Ecclesiastical States alone. Among the first acts of the new Pontiff was the appointment of four Commissioners to inquire into these horrible crimes, whilst Alexander himself had to devote one day each week to hearing the complaints of the families of the victims. And this arduous and disagreeable duty he did with such equal and exact justice to all that he gave great public satisfaction.*

The State of contention between the prominent families which made up the Italian nobility of the fifteenth century, may well be compared, in its scandalous intensity, to the attitudes assumed by the different political factions in this country about the time when a presidential election is approaching. A person who could con over the contents of the American political press a hundred years from now would form the opinion that both President Harrison and ex-President Cleveland were men who did not possess a single virtue to entitle them to hold for a day the exalted position of

*De Montor's Lives and Times of the Roman Pontiffs, Vol. I. p. 634.

President of this great Republic. The partisan press of each political organization so blackens the characters of opposing candidates that the reader of the future will wonder how the Union continued to exist when certain men were called upon to take the first positions in its government. And, in like manner, the writers of the fifteenth century blackened the character of Pope Alexander VI. through a spirit of spleen and jealousy which caused them to love falsehood better than truth.

During the present century, however, a great flood of light has been thrown upon the character of Alexander VI., redeeming it from the huge mass of filth cast upon it by Guicciardini, Burchardt, Jove, Tomasi, Machiavelli, Voltaire and the school of slanderers who have studiously followed that arch enemy of Christianity with a fidelity worthy of a better cause. Nearly all the calumnies heaped upon this Pontiff's memory have been proved unjust as well as undeserved, and although Roderico Borgia, when a young man, may have been addicted to some licentious habits, yet, *as Pontiff*, his character is free from all carnal corruption. In a word Pope Alexander has been made the scape-goat of the scandalmongers of the fifteenth century.

Now let us glance at the character of the men through whose malignant animosity the character of Pope Alexander VI. has been designedly defamed. Let us ascertain by contemporaneous fact and subsequent evidence whether they are entitled to credit for the slanderous charges which emanated from their malignant imaginations, and when once we have revealed the vileness of the traducers of this Pontiff, the pleasing discovery will be made that they are entirely unworthy of any recognition whatever as the accusers of a Pope whose good name they have buried for nearly four hundred years beneath the debris of diabolical detraction. Here are the principal pensioned or prejudiced witnesses against Pope Alexander VI. :

The first writer whose wicked inventions and innuendos have helped to sully the character of the Pontiff whose case we are considering, is the Florentine, Machiavelli, who was a prototype of the notoriously vile Giraldus Cambrensis—a man whose evidence no person acquainted with his character for falsehood would accept. A pensioned writer who purposely poisoned his pages with putrid charges against the Pope in question, for no higher motive than that which impels a hired assassin to remorselessly stab his innocent victim to death. Like Cambrensis, the hireling of King Henry II. of England, Machiavelli was a noted traducer, whose libelous pen was ever ready to puncture and poison the characters of those whom he was paid to revile and to bring into disgrace.

Guicciardini was only twenty years old when Pope Alexander died, hence his accusations were merely copies of the calumnies of his purchased predecessors. Speaking of the bad faith of this foe of the Pontiff the infidel Bayle in his *Dictionnaire Philosophique*, says : "Guicciardini deserves to be reprobated ; he is guilty of the fault of all scandal mongers," and even Voltaire accuses this hireling of imposture. So vile was his *History of Italy* that when Guicciardini was on his death bed he requested that it *be burned*—a fate that might justly have been applied to many other fifteenth century documents which descanted unjustly upon the character of Pope Alexander VI.

Paul Jove, another traducer of this Pontiff, is described as "a venal and untruthful writer," one who *boasted* that he wielded *two pens*—one of gold, the other of iron— to write of princes according to the favors or frowns he received from them ! He was also noted as one who "mercilessly defamed those who would not pay him for his falsehoods." In this age such a character would be called a professional blackmailer !

Tomasi was paid his price for his perfidious slanders by the enemies of the traduced Pontiff. He thereby became unworthy of credence or respect. Such at least is the opinion adduced by Antoine Varrilas in his work on Louis XII.

We now come to the *Diarium* of John Burchardt. This book is the chief storehouse from which modern enemies of the Church draw their supply of slanders against Pope Alexander VI. which, they inject into the current literature of the century. During his whole life Burchardt was altogether unknown to literary fame. Not a single evidence of his mental labors existed in the world when he died. But *nearly two hundred years after his death*, a French Calvinist claimed to have discovered what is now known as the *Diarium* or document of detraction against the character of Pope Alexander VI. The documents which this bitter enemy of the Church said he discovered, consisted of a motley group of detached leaves, some of them written in Latin, others in French, and others again in Italian. These unauthenticated documents, so suspiciously found nearly two hundred years after the death of Burchardt, were presented to Leibnitz, who gave them to the world as genuine *copies* of some original documents which he regretted he had not been able to become possessed of. Such is the slender and very suspicious thread upon which the traductions of the *Diarium* are strung.

Here we have a vile work attributed to a man who was not known to have ever put a single thought on paper during his whole life. Two centuries elapse after his death when a bitter Protestant produces some odd leaves of manuscript, he passes them to another Protes ant, and he—glad to gather in any literary garbage that would defile the Catholic Church—prints them as the diary of a man dead two hundred years and entirely unknown in the literary world! These circumstances are well calculated to excite suspicion. But to make matters worse—to make "confusion worse confounded"—other Protestant individuals began to discover other detracting documents which they, too, considered as versions of Burchardt's *Diarium*, and out of this medley of manuscript has been hatched many of the vilest calumnies which hitherto have blackened the character of Pope Alexander VI. in the eyes of both Catholics and Protestants alike.

Let us ask, therefore, every impartial reader, if the character of one of the ablest successors of St. Peter is to be weighed and found wanting by the unjust weights of such wicked inventions? The calumnies are contained in a book supposed to be written by a man who was never known as an author. The manuscripts are fathered by French Calvinists—the most bitter and unscrupulous enemies the Church encountered in modern ages. The suspicious documents are suddenly brought to light when two centuries had rolled over the tomb of their reputed author. Do not our readers see the evidences of fraud, fanaticism and forgery in these documents just as plainly as we have pointed them out in the Adrian and Alexander Bulls of a few centuries previous?

Now let us turn away from these suspicious documents and glean from the pages of respectable writers the opinions they held concerning the vile fragments which are supposed to make up the volumes attributed to John Burchardt. Paris de Grassis, a Canon of Bologna and subsequently Bishop of Pesaro, speaking of the vile rubbish said to have been composed by Burchardt says: "Not only was he no man but he was in reality the most detestable of beasts; besides, he was very wicked and spiteful. He has written books which nobody can understand unless it be a sibyl or the devil, who must have been his accomplice."*

Such is the character of the man who is made to appear on the witness-stand of the world to swear against the character of Pope Alexander VI. What think you of him? A fiend with the Father of Lies to help him, could invent any calumny short of convicting the Son of God of error, and it is upon such Satan-inspired testimony that the world has uttered its condemnation of Pope Alexander VI.

The base interpolater who added the forty-second chapter to the *Metalogicus* of John of Salisbury made that Prelate eat, drink and all but sleep with Pope Adrian IV., during his sojourn in Rome. In like manner the conspirators against truth who concocted the loose leaves attributed to Burchardt after he had slumbered for two hundred years in the silent tomb, make his familiarity with the Pontiff of his day, fully on a par—both in fraud and fiction—with that of the vile inventor of the forty-second chapter of the *Metalogicus*. Here is what

---

*Diario ad annum 1506.

Paris de Grassis says on this point:

In reading him one would think he never quitted the Pope for a single instant. He follows him to the chapel, to the consistory, to table, to bed; night has no darkness, the obscurity of which he cannot penetrate. He is a person who does not believe in the existence of virtue, and who by the omnipotence of a ducat would ordinarily explain many a good thought or a good action. Never did a romancer with a *naiveté* so comical sport with the credulity of his readers. Of Alexander VI., who according to him was dissimulation itself personified, he makes the chief personage of a melodrama who publishes his own dissoluteness to the whole Roman people. Only let a Cardinal die and forthwith he examines the drink of the deceased, and almost always finds in it some traces of poisoning. What was the object of this poisoning? It was because Alexander wished to possess himself of the riches of the Cardinal. Voltaire, as a tragic poet, has bitingly jeered at this gross violation of the first rules of the dramatic art. "It has been pretended," says he, "that in a pressing need for money Alexander desired to succeed to the estates of some Cardinals, but it is certain that Cæsar Borgia took away a hundred ducats of gold of the treasure of his father. The need for money, then, was not so real. Besides, how was it possible to be mistaken about that bottle of poisoned wine which it is said caused the death of the Pope? If, when the Pope died, granting that he was poisoned, the cause of his death had been known, it certainly would have been known by the very persons whom it was intended to poison; they would not have left such a crime unpunished, nor would they have suffered Cæsar Borgia to obtain peaceable possession of his father's treasure. . . . It is not difficult to invent falsehoods when persons are determined to calumniate."

Leaving the traducers of Pope Alexander VI. to rest in their own infamy, let us now turn our attention to the life led by that Pontiff, and discover, if we can, a clue to the "infamous deeds" which have made this great Pontiff the cynosure of all Christian eyes—as the vilest character that ever inhabited the Eternal City.

Roderico Borgia, who subsequently became Pope Alexander VI., was born at Valencia in 1431. The family of the Borgia has been so maliciously represented by Protestant and infidel writers that visions of the bloody dagger, the poisoned cup, and the midnight carousal will doubtless arise in the minds of many of our readers. And yet, from this same family whose name is covered with a coating of iniquity by the enemies of the Church, sprang two notable Pontiffs—Calixtus III. and Alexander II., as well as a great saint—the lovable Francis Borgia, one of the Generals of the Society of Jesus.

After acquiring a most thorough education, Roderico Borgia adopted the profession of law, but he soon gave that up for the military camp, in search of glory by feats of arms. Here he remained until his uncle, Alphonsus Borgia, was elected Pope under the title of Calixtus III., when he was called to Rome and placed in a position of trust near that Pontiff. He fulfilled his duties so well that he was subsequently elevated to the purple, although he was then but twenty-five years old.

As yet Roderico Borgia had not received Holy Orders, nor was his case an exceptional one, as there are several instances in former centuries where laymen became Cardinals, although the modern custom is that a secular on becoming a Cardinal shall receive Sub-Deaconship at least.

The enemies of Pope Calixtus III claim that his nephew led a most disreputable life and that he was the father of several illegitimate children. Well, even admitting for argument sake that these occurrences were true, the fact nevertheless remains that *all these children were born fully twenty years before he took Holy Orders, which he did not enter until 1478, when Pope Sixtus IV., nominated him Bishop of Alba.* Fourteen years later—August 11th 1492—Cardinal Roderico Borgia (Lenzuoli) was called to the Chair of Peter—and from the first hour of his Pontificate to the last day of his reign—August 18th, 1503—not a single stone can be cast at him as a transgressor against the virtue of continence.

The Son of God came into the world to save sinners. Thus he changed the persecutor Saul into the personification of a most courageous Christian martyr. In like manner Augustine—the sorrow and the joy of St. Monica—became one of the bright particular stars of the Church of that God Whom he spurned and scorned in his youth. When we reflect on these examples of God's mercy towards men whom even the world called wicked, we will cease to wonder that one who was afterwards Pope had children by Julia Farnese, who was, beyond doubt, legally married to the Cavalier Roderico Borgia.

Julia Farnese came from a family as notable as even the exalted Borgias, and those writers who propagate the idea that such a high-born lady would loosely consort with one of the other sex, know very little indeed of the rigorous Christian chivalry which was one of the main characteristics of the Italian nobility of past centuries, and which is proudly maintained up to our own times.

The intimate relations which existed between the Borgia and the Farnese families is the best proof that the children of Julia Farnese were born in honorable wedlock. Cardinal Farnese (who afterwards became Pope Paul III.) was a great favorite with, and a trusted representative of, Pope Alexander VI. Angelus Ferdinand Farnese fell whilst fighting under the banner of Cæsar Borgia. Is it at all likely, therefore, that if any criminal contumely had been cast upon the character of Julia Farnese, that her kindred would have served the interests of the family who had brought disgrace upon the unsullied escutcheon of her honorable family? It is certain, therefore, that Roderico Borgia's children were legitimate, and were all born fully twenty years before he made his first vows in the vocation of the Priesthood.

But it is not by any means certain that Roderico Borgia had any male or female offspring. M. Chantrel* and the author of a learned disquisition on this important question in the *Dublin Review*, both contend that the children in question were those of the Pontiff's brother, Peter Louis, and this fact was sworn to in Rome on one occasion.

Another learned writer on this subject† makes this important point, showing how the stories concerning Roderico Borgia's children might have originated:

It is well known that in those troublous times it was the custom of the Popes to choose as a General some one of their relations, most commonly a nephew, possessing energy and military talents, to defend the Pontifical domains against the ambitions and grasping princes that surrounded them, and who continually sought to invade them. It was also the custom to give these relations the name of *sons*, and such we can scarcely doubt was the only basis upon which the spirit of enmity supported its original suspicions and calumnies. And need it be remarked that the terms *son* and *daughter*, and their correlative one, *father*, are the ordinary terms of address between all ecclesiastics of the Catholic Church and their flocks, and that these terms are understood in their spiritual sense?

Let us now examine into the behavior of Pope Alexander VI., after he ascended the Pontifical Throne. He was sixty years of age when he first wore the Tiara, and even the enemies of this much-maligned martyr to malignant slanders are forced to admit that he was a man of more than ordinary prudence and whose appearance in public betokened modesty itself. He went about daily doing good, visiting churches, hospitals and similar institutions; and when not thus engaged he was absorbed in affairs of the Church which he managed with magnificent skill and superexcellent success.

In all his actions throughout the eleven years of his Pontificate, Alexander VI., was a virtuous and a just Pontiff. "Under him, says the reputable Audin‡ "the poor as well as the rich could obtain justice in Rome. The people, soldiers and citizens alike, testified great attachment to him, even after his death, because he possessed qualities truly royal. At night he slept scarcely two hours, and from the table he passed almost like a shadow without having made any stay there. Never did he refuse listening to the poor; he liquidated the debts of unfortunate debtors, and he showed himself without pity for remorseless prevaricators."

And yet this is the man whom the foul tongue of calumny has consigned to the attention of nineteenth-century Christians as "a monster of iniquity!" We would ask any candid-minded and unbiased reader, therefore, in view of the character of the traducers of Pope Alexander VI., and the

---
*History of the Popes. Paris. 1862.
†J. J. Barry, M. D., in an article in *American Catholic Quarterly Review* for April, 1878.

‡Life of Pope Leo X.

other facts already asserted in his defence, if there is a civil tribunal in all Christendom that would convict him of the enormous crimes charged against him on the evidence of such witnesses? Every culprit is considered by Common Law to be entitled to the benefit of every doubt in his case, and, we ask, shall the same privilege be denied to a Pontiff whose career whilst an occupant of the Chair of Peter was such that not a single disturbance on the part of the populace occurred in the city of Rome during the eleven years of his Pontificate, and who was so universally esteemed, even when first elected to that highest ecclesiastical dignity, that embassies were dispatched from all the States of Italy in order to express their unanimous congratulations.

Now let us introduce a few witnesses on behalf of the defendant's side of this case, so as to offset in some measure at least the popular prejudice which has long since unjustly prejudged the case before us. Speaking of Pope Alexander VI., a French writer, M. C. F. Chevè§ says:

The more attentively and thoroughly the original documents of the history of that period are studied, the more clear will it become that the memory of Alexander VI. has been fearfully calumniated. To pass an unbiased judgment upon his life, it will be especially necessary to take into account his social surroundings. True criticism has long since cleared the name of Alexander VI. of the charges of poisoning and other horrible crimes that had been groundlessly imputed to him by the revengeful journalists of the ante-room and the scandal-mongers of that age and country. The implacable hostility of the Reformers and the resentment of France because of the political attitude of Alexander VI. have also contributed not a little to blacken his memory. It is not our purpose to excuse the irregularities of his life, but we would invite the reader desirous of learning to what extent he has been defamed to peruse the chapter devoted to him by *M. Audin* (Hist. de Léon X., T. L., c. 2). He was charitable, energetic, fair-minded and moderate. If he incurred so much ill-will, it is because he overcame and kept in check the feudal aristocracy of Rome.

The Abbè Darras, in his *History of the Church*,‖ thus sums up the valueless character of the numerous calumnies circulated by many hireling writers against the moral character of Pope Alexander VI.

The odious charges brought against Alexander VI. himself, in connection with Lucretia, are the inventions of bitter malice: they have not been received by historians of any weight. Their only resource was the license of romance. There are pens which gather up every item of scandal from contemporary libels, and dispense them under the pretence of contributing to the moral education of the public, while flooding the world with immorality. We hold that there were two phases in the life of Alexander VI.: the life of the individual, which was, indeed, but too much like that of most princes of his day; and that of the Pope, which carried out, on the Chair of St. Peter, the policy inaugurated by his predecessors, and preserved in its integrity, the deposit of faith and of ecclesiastical discipline.   *   *   *   *   *

Many serious charges weigh upon the reputation of Alexander VI.; but no one can accuse him of weakness or defection in his Pontifical career. His courage seemed to increase with reverses; the errors of his private life never affected his conduct as Pope; and this is the highest lesson taught by the history of his Pontificate.   *   *   *   *   *

Amid the warring of men and the din of arms, the Pontificate of Alexander VI. drew to a close. "He died," says one of his biographers, "of a tertian fever, after having received the Sacraments with edifying piety; and breathed his last surrounded by the Cardinals." This account differs materially from that of the romances of the day, which state that Alexander died from the effects of a poisoned draught prepared for some Cardinals, and which was, by mistake, given to the Pope at a banquet. His death has been as much belied by calumny as his life (A. D. 1503). Alexander's last days were devoted to a great and noble enterprise. He had used his most earnest endeavors to unite the Christian princes against the Turks; his persevering efforts only succeeded in obtaining help for the Venetians, who were bearing the whole weight of the war. Whatever may be thought of Alexander VI., as as man, it must be allowed that throughout the whole course of his administration he proved himself a skillful diplomatist, and did much for the good of Italy and of the Church.

In view of even the meagre amount of evidence we have adduced, we claim, however, that we have demonstrated the fact that in his character Pope Alexander VI. was made the victim of the virulent assaults

§*Dict des Papes.*
‖Vol. III. pp. 635-639-644.

of hireling writers who had valuable reasons for calumniating him in the blackest manner suggested by their malignant minds. We have also shown that—even with all his faults—Alexander VI., as Pontiff, left such a record behind him as no man addicted to the sensuality charged against him could ever have achieved. Never for a single moment during the eleven years of his Pontificate, did this able successor of St. Peter forget the high and holy ecclesiastical dignity of his sacred office; never did he lose sight of the duties which devolved upon him as the Head of Christ's Church; never did he permit even the smallest and most insignificant compromise of either faith or morals in all the many documents which he has left behind him—and the *Bullarium* of this great Pontiff possesses remarkable value.

It is safe, therefore, for Catholics to rest assured that the calumnies against Pope Alexander's character rest—as M. Chantrel has well remarked—upon these events in his life:

All the accusations brought against him may be summed in the simple one, that he employed Cæsar Borgia to defend the political dominions by force of arms against Italian princes and their foreign allies. What proves that such was the case is, undoubtedly, the significant fact that those who attack him most do so chiefly on account of Cæsar, and show that they do not admit, or at least they pretend to doubt the legitimacy of defending by force of arms the Pontifical patrimony. The accusations of immorality recall those laid to the charge of Boniface VIII. and Sixtus IV., and it is easy to see that they come from the envenomed spirit of party, and that they are fully refuted by their own improbability, their atrociousness, and the absence of all impartial and disinterested testimony. The only things they mention that can be admitted without reserve, are those which have relation to the defence of that patrimony by force of arms. None of those who acknowledge or admit the legitimacy and propriety of this defence attack Alexander. If his case, then, differs from that of some of his predecessors and successors, it is simply in the degree of calumny with which he has been assailed. And yet it may be doubted whether in this respect there is any difference, when one pays attention to the circumstances of the times, and the great resentment which the opposition of contemporary princes excited against that Pontiff, the history of which has consequently been *corrupted in its very source by bribed so-called historians*. When once we give due heed to these circumstances, we find the case of Alexander VI. to be no other than that of the Sixtuses, the Juliuses, the Bonifaces, the Innocents, and the Gregories of the glorious Pontifical line.

The enemies of the Church are imbued with the idea that Pope Alexander VI., died by poison, yet, as De Montor says on the authority of Novaes, "*no diary of the time mentions any such circumstance.*" Alexander, a very old man, died in his bed of malignant fever, and the contrary reports were unheard of until the malicious machinations of Luther.*

Desportes thus speaks of the falsely-alleged poisoning of Alexander :

"The pretended circumstances of the death of Alexander have excited no less doubt. Voltaire himself, whom no one will suspect of partiality in favor of a Pope, exclaims, with the utmost vehemence, against that assertion in his dissertation on the death of Henri IV. 'I dare to say to Guiccardini,' he exclaims, 'you have deceived Europe, and you have deceived yourself in your own prejudice and passion. You were the enemy of the Pope, and you have too easily credited your own hatred, and the actions of his life. No doubt, he took at times cruel and perfidious revenge upon enemies no less cruel and perfidious,' etc. Those few words from an historical discussion, which it is needless to quote more largely, contain an impartial judgment upon that part of the life of Alexander."

Feller thus speaks on the same subject:

"Protestants have often taunted Catholics with the vices of Alexander VI., as if the depravity of a Pontiff could render a holy religion less holy; as if Christianity to be the work of God, must annihilate in its ministers the germs o human passions. It was not the tiara that rendered Alexander vicious; it was his disposition. He would have been the same in whatever sphere he moved. Providence grants that his crimes should not disturb the Church, and that, in these critical circumstances, there were neither schisms nor heresies to battle against."†

A VINDICATION OF SOME OTHER TRADUCED PONTIFFS.

The author whose bad book has called forth this volume, asserts that "no candid historian will claim that Alexander VI.,

---

*De Montor's Lives of the Popes, p. 642.
†See Feller's Hist. Dict. I, p. 112.

was any worse than his predecessors Sergius III., John X., John XI., John XII., John XVI., or John XIX.," but as we have clearly demonstrated the fact that Pope Alexander VI., was not by any means as culpable a criminal as his enemies have painted him, it stands to reason that his predecessors—whom prejudiced writers have charged with horrible crimes they never committed—were not as bad as bigots and bought-up writers of the past have delineated them.

The limits of our book will not permit of any lengthy defence of the Pontiffs who stand charged with being as guilty of criminal acts as Pope Alexander, so we will have to content ourselves with very briefly alluding to each of them, solely for the purpose of showing that these Pontiffs were far from being the bad men fanatics and falsifiers have described them.

POPE SERGIUS III.

It is always prudent for both Catholic and non-Catholic readers of the biographies of the Roman Pontiffs to keep well in mind the fact that some authors who wrote lives of the Popes were prompted to execute that work purely from malicious motives, so as to misrepresent their characters, other writers merely copied what previous traducers of the successors of St. Peter had written to gratify the spleen of the public or the private enemies of the Vicar of Christ. Thus the world has been filled with fraudulent charges against many of the Pontiffs which had no foundation whatever in fact, and many of which have, by recent research, been proved to be purely and purposely fabulous. Even such Protestants as Hurter and Roscoe have assisted in clearing up many such calumnies, and thereby aided Catholic historians like Rohrbacher, Muratori, Fleury, De Montor, Alzog, Darras and Artand in purging by-gone century libels from the pages of so-called "history" filled with putridity.

Pope Sergius III. ruled the Church of God from the year 905 to 911, and here is the character given him by three impartial witnesses:

The name of Sergius III., who was recalled from exile to fill the Chair of St. Peter, is one of those upon which the enemies of the Holy See have most delighted in heaping opprobrium. On the strength of Luitprand's testimony, his morals have been deeply calumniated. The name of Marozia, wife of Adalbert of Tuscany, a notorious character intimately connected with all the scandals of the day, is mentioned in connection with these foul reports, perpetrated by shameless pens. We may quote contemporary writers on the character of Sergius III. "This Pope," says Flodoard, "already proposed for the Sovereign Pontificate at the time of the election of John IX., was recalled amid the unanimous acclamations of the people, and received the consecration long since destined for him. The seven years of this Pontiff's reign were a season of grateful joy to his subjects throughout the world." Another contemporary author, John the Deacon, thus speaks of the same Pontiff: "After his consecration, Pope Sergius III., was much grieved at the dilapidated condition of the Basilica of St. John Lateran, which had fallen into ruins at the time of Stephen VI., and he had recourse to the Divine Goodness in which he ever placed his trust. He undertook to restore the noble pile; he happily succeeded in his holy work, and adorned the new basilica with the most costly ornaments." The epitaph inscribed on the Pontiff's tomb by a grateful people fully bears out the testimony of Flodoard and John the Deacon: "Returning from his exile at the earnest prayer of the people," says this precious monument, "the good pastor showed equal love to all classes of his flock, and met all usurpers with apostolic energy." These three witnesses, who speak of Sergius as a Pontiff not only of unexceptional moral virtues, but full of faith, piety and zeal, are contradicted by Luitprand's partial voice alone. And so ill-informed is that hostile author on this period of history, that he places the Pontificate of Sergius immediately after that of Formosus, and ascribes to him the shocking scene so disgraceful to the annals of Stephen VI. We believe that the dawn of truth is now breaking upon the life of Sergius, and that history has too long been the unsuspecting accomplice of a partial and ill-informed annalist.[*]

It may be well to state here that nearly all the calumnies circulated by the enemies of the Church against the Popes of the tenth century, are copied from Luitprandus, an author concerning whose worth an eminent writer says:

Up to the time that Baronius composed his Annals, the writings of Luitprandus were the only source from which information was to be

[*] Darras, History of the Church, Vol. II., p. 561.

gathered as to the Popes who lived during those dark and evil days; and certainly, as Luitprand told the story, nothing could be too severe for the Cardinal to say of Sergius III., or of the others, as of John X, for instance, whom he similarly condemns. But as was natural enough, the researches of Baronius, astonishing though they were, still left a vast deal in the archives of Europe for the industry of later investigators, such as the Benedictines of St. Maur, and as Pagi, Baluzius, Muratori himself, and a host of others, to bring to light. The result has been that every fragment shedding additional light on the history of the Popes of the 10th century has revealed the injustice that had been done them, by those who had too implicitly relied on Luitprandus as an authority. And certainly, if what this genius of the most profligate of the Dark Ages tells us of himself be deserving of credit, his testimony is not worth a jot against any one else—much less against the Roman Pontiffs. Upon evidence such as his—even if not contradicted, as it is emphatically by witnesses above all suspicion—a packed jury would blush to bring in a verdict of guilty.†

POPE JOHN X.

This Pontiff reigned from the year 914 to 928, and concerning his character a historian of the Church says:

Lamentable in the extreme was the condition of Rome and Italy at this period. In the South, the Saracens, intrenched on the banks of the Garigliano, wasted the estates of the Church. In the North, the princes and municipal powers, far from leaguing against the common enemy, did but help his ravages by domestic feuds. The state of Italy called for a Pope who could lead the imbittered spirits into the ways of conciliation and peace. John X. was elected to the Sovereign Pontificate (April 30, A. D. 914). He had been nine years Archbishop of Revenna, and yet Luitprand does not hesitate to state that he was transferred to the Sovereign See of Rome within a year after his appointment to that of Ravenna by Pope Lando. It is important to correct this error, for upon it depends an entire system of accusations brought against John X. Luitprand himself confesses that he gathered the facts alleged against the Pontiff from a *Popular Life of Theodora*, mother of Marozia. The infamous character of these intriguing and abandoned females plainly shows that his authority could have been but a mere pamphlet. Such is the basis upon which hostile historians have built up all their charges against John X. Flodoard, on the other hand, thus

†Miley's History of Papal States, Vol. II., pp. 270-1.

speaks of the same Pontiff: "His prudent and virtuous life have won for him a throne in Heaven." The reader is free to chose between these two contemporaneous but contradictory statements. Whatever may be imputed to the private individual whose name has been made a mark for the lying calumnies of writers unfriendly to the Papacy, the Pontiff was unimpeachable, and the Church blesses the reign of John X.*

POPE JOHN XI.

This Pontiff reigned from the year 931 to 936, and a distinguished author says of his Pontificate:

John XI., was completely under the control of his brother Alberic, the "Tyrant of Rome," and by Cardinal Baronius, he is styled a *pseudopontifex*. This judgment, however, was not a little influenced by what we have proved to have been the libellous story told by Luitprand. This Pontiff was the son of Alberic and Marozia. There is no proof that his election was procured by violence, though there is in Flodoard a hint to that effect. By one contemporary he is called a Pontiff, *gloriosæ indolis*; this however may have been said in a spirit of adulation. Questioned it cannot be, that in his person, the Apostolic See was completely enslaved. "He was stripped of all influence," says Flodoard, "pushed back into obscurity, and restricted to the mere ceremonies of the Church." His death took place, A. D. 936. He died in captivity, a victim of the ambition of his own kindred.†

POPE JOHN XII.

This Pontiff reigned from the year 956 to 964. Of his character a modern historian says:

I repeat what was said of John XII. in the *Notizie* of Rome for the year 1814:

"John XII., Conti, a Roman, was created Pope in the year 956, and governed the Church about eight years. During that time, and in the year 963, Leo was intruded into the Pontificate. Being subsequently deposed, he again usurped the supreme dignity on the 26th June, 964, and he continued to retain his illegal possession of it until April, 965. Nevertheless, Leo is reckoned in the list of Popes under the name of Leo VIII."

After this preliminary official information, we proceed to details. His name was Octavian, and he was the first Pontiff who changed his

*Darras, History of the Church, Vol. II., p. 567.
†Dr. Miley's Papal States, Vol. II., p. 286.

name. John of the Conti family, grand nephew of Sergius III., and of John XI., was elected, or rather, at the instigation of some Romans, intruded into the Papacy about the 20th of August, 956. He was then only some sixteen or eighteen years old. Such were the calamities of the times, says Baronius, that it was deemed better to tolerate that invasion than to wound the Church by a schism which would be a worse evil still. Therefore the Church accepted and endured him as Pontiff, considering that there would be less evil in tolerating one head, though a monstrous one, than in afflicting the one body with two heads. * * *

At length the end of John's life came. Luitprand, who is hostile to John, bitterly accuses him; but grave authors rightly refuse to admit these latter accusations. Rancor and prejudice sometimes overstep all bounds; having spoken truly on some points, men sometimes fancy themselves privileged to speak untruly on others. Luitprand was the friend of schismatics, and the flatterer of Otho.

We shall close by a reflection of Feller's: "The great number," says he, "of virtuous and holy Pontiffs who have occupied the See of Rome, should make us forget the small number whose morals have ill suited their station. Jesus Christ expressly warns us that the chiefs of religion are not impeccable, and that their faults are no argument against the worship of which they are the ministers, or the doctrines of which they are the depositories. 'The Scribes and Pharisees sit in the chair of Moses: all things whatsoever they shall say unto you, observe and do, but according to their works do ye not.'"—(Matt. xxiii., 23).‡

POPE JOHN XVI.

This Pontiff reigned from the year 986 to 996, and against his character we find no charges of any gravity. Concerning his Pontificate a biographer of the Popes says:

John XVI. was elected at the end of December, 985. He was a Roman Priest, and the son of Leo. Harrassed by the tyrant Crescentius, who, with the title of Consul, occupied the castle of Saint Angelo, John fled into Tuscany, and appealed to Otho III. As soon as the Romans learned the step that the Pope had taken, they recalled him, so much did they dread Otho. The clergy reproached John with yielding to that kind of favoritism which has since been known as nepotism; in fact he enriched his relatives beyond bounds.

This Pope governed more than ten years. He was illustrious as a cultivator of letters, notwithstanding the rudeness of the time, and he is the reputed author of some books on military art. He died on the 30th of April, 996, and was interred at the Vatican, in the oratory of Saint Mary.§

POPE JOHN XIX.

This Pontiff reigned from the year 1003 to 1009. Regarding his character De Montor, in his Lives of the Popes, says:

John XIX., surnamed Fasanus, was elected in November, 1003. He confirmed the institution of the Bishopric of Bamberg, in Franconia, erected at the desire of the Emperor Henry.

Under his Pontificate concord was restored between the Churches of Rome and Constantinople, which had been disunited in consequences of the arrogant pretensions of the patriarch Michael Cerularius, who presumptuously assumed the title of œcumenical and universal Bishop, which exclusively belongs to the Roman Pontiff. John XIX., having forbidden the patriarch to usurp that title, the right of Rome was recognized, and the patriarch Sergius, in its place, took in the Dyptics—i. e., the tables of the Church of Constantinople—the title of the Pope.

Some authors think that John XIX., towards the close of his life, abdicated the Pontificate to retire to the Benedictine Abbey of Saint Paul, at Rome, but modern critics do not admit that fact. This Pope governed five years and five months according to Novaes, and three years and five months, according to the Roman list. It seems certain that he died about the year 1009, and that he was interred at Saint John Lateran.‖

Such were the Popes of the tenth century whose characters have been assailed as "the very worst" in the long line of the successors of St. Peter! Is there anything in their lives which entitles them to the maledictions of mankind throughout the past nine hundred years? Compare their lives with those seculars who surrounded them in the age in which they lived, and the Pontiffs will appear as so many suns shining down upon a sinful world!

These Popes, therefore, have been calumniated. When the Church herself has been misrepresented, when her dogmas have been distorted, when her theological truths have been traduced, when her very Sacraments

---

‡ De Montor's Lives of the Popes, Vol. I., pp. 252-4.

§ De Montor's Lives of the Popes, Vol. I., pp. 261-2-3.

‖ De Montor, Vol. I., pp. 270-271.

have been held up as public scandals to be avoided by all decent intelligent people—it would be folly to expect that those who are at the head of the Church should escape the poison-laden stylus of the hireling, the heretic and the hypocrite.

And now that we have defended to the best of our ability the reputations of the assailed Pontiffs from the tenth to the nineteenth century, the task that we set out to accomplish is finished.

The characters of Popes Adrian and Alexander have been thoroughly purged from the calumnies which have been heaped on them by the falsifying fictions of English forgers. The documents which led to the traduction of these Vicars of Christ have been thoroughly and critically analyzed and dissected. After causing multitudinous controversies throughout more than seven centuries, it may now be said with some degree of truth that both these deceitful documents have been thoroughly exposed and found to be fraudulent in their conception, false in their expression, and fallacious in their character.

But before closing this page we cannot fail to express our joy that we were able to vindicate not only the Vicars of Christ from the aspersions cast upon their character by the author whose fabrications we have fully refuted, but it was also a labor of love on our part to place the fidelity of the Irish people to Rome and their Catholic faith in the true light in which it has always existed and not in the false light in which the enemies of both the Church and Ireland delight to depict it.

As the renowned Dr. James Doyle, the patriotic Bishop of Kildare and Leighlin, has well and truly said: "In Ireland religion has *always* flourished since it was first deposited in her bosom. It is the only country wherein the Christian faith was planted which did not involve the necessity of sowing the Gospel-seed amid blood—a proof that Irishmen were naturally fitted for the exercise of all the virtues of Christianity, and of every moral and social obligation which binds man in community. We have another great and glorious consolation: When infidelity reached our shores, Ireland shook the viper from her bosom and cast it into the depth of the sea. Yes! it were as easy to strip the fields of their verdure as to deprive Irishmen of the fair religion of Christ. * * * * It was an observation of Montesquieu, that the natural disposition of a people, as well as their social institutions, fit them for the reception of Christianity, or dispose them to its rejection. We may account our country particularly blessed, when the Almighty Maker made us particularly disposed for the practice of religion and piety. But as much has been given to us—so, much is expected from us; it is necessary, therefore, that we do good works in a double ratio."

TABLE OF CONTENTS.

CHAPTER I.
Preliminary Considerations regarding the book which called forth this Review and Refutation 9

CHAPTER II.
The Fictitious Bull of Pope Adrian IV.—Education in Ireland.—The character of Giraldus Cambrensis Analysed by Historical Writers.—Abbé MacGeoghegan's Criticism 16

CHAPTER III.
Comments on the Character of Giraldus Cambrensis by Martin A. O'Brennan, James J. Clancy, Thomas Moore and Thomas Mooney 23

CHAPTER IV.
Cardinal Moran's able Historical Essay on the Fictitious character of the Bull attributed to Pope Adrian IV 27

CHAPTER V.
A Historical contrast between the characters of Pope Adrian IV., and King Henry II. of England.—The murder of St. Thomas a'Becket, Archbishop of Canterbury 35

CHAPTER VI.
The Bull attributed to Pope Adrian IV., tested.—Analysis of the Pontificate of Pope Alexander III.—More Historical errors refuted.—The spurious Adrian Bull viewed from a critical standpoint 41

CHAPTER VII.
The Peter Pence Proviso in the Adrian and Alexander Bulls.—The false character of the stipulation.—King John's Surrender of England to the Pope.—Important Documents relating thereto.—Additional Evidence of the Spurious character of the Adrian and Alexander Bulls.—Caustic criticism of Cambrensis by the English editors of his works 47

CHAPTER VIII.
Proof that Giraldus Cambrensis knew that the Adrian Bull was a forged document.—His spiteful and slanderous Sermon in Dublin.—The supposed "Synod of Cashel" critically analysed.—More historical Mistakes made manifest 52

CHAPTER IX.
A description of the inhabitants of Waterford in the Twelfth century.—The favorite abode of Danes, English and other enemies of Ireland.—The period when the See of Waterford was established.—Why no Synod ever met there.—Pope Alexander and the Irish Bishops.—More Historical mistakes corrected 58

CHAPTER X.
The Synod of Windsor criticised.—King Henry's Treaty with the King of Connaught.—The Adrian and Alexander Bulls not known in England in the year 1175.—Cardinal Vivian's visit to Ireland.—The right of Sanctuary in Ireland.—More malicious misstatements melted in the crucible of historic truth 62

CHAPTER XI.
Strong evidence of English Chroniclers, Irish Historians and other writers, from the Twelfth to the Nineteenth Centuries, against the authenticity of the Adrian Bull.—Opinions of Baronius, Bzovius, St. Antoninus, Grafton, Plowden, Bower, and others 68

CHAPTER XII.
Continuation of the evidence of Historical Writers concerning the False character of the Adrian and Alexander Bulls.—Absurd statements of English and Irish Historians.—Extracts from the writings of Abbé MacGeoghegan, Father Thomas N. Burke, Thomas Mooney, Rev. J. J. Brennan, James J. Clancy, Thomas Moore, Monsignor O'Rielly, Geoffrey Keating, Charles O'Kelly, and Thomas Leland 73

CHAPTER XIII.

Additional Witnesses in proof of the Spurious character of the Adrian and Alexander Bulls.—The Misleading statements in O'Halloran's History dissected.—Extracts from the historical works of Hume, Lingard, Rev. J. Thebaud, S. J., and Rev. W. B. Morris...... 78

CHAPTER XIV.

Intrinsic Evidence of the Fraudulent character of the Adrian and Alexander Bulls.—A brief analysis of the text of each.—Criticisms which prove their fictitious origin.—New light on the great Forgery of the Twelfth Century... 84

CHAPTER XV.

Continuation of the same subject.—More historical proof.—Was Ireland ever "Christian only in Name?"—Testimony of St. Bernard, Thierry, St. Columbanus, Cardinal Newman, Archdeacon Lynch, Gorres, and Rev. J. Cogan... 90

CHAPTER XVI.

John of Salisbury dissected.—How King Henry II. concocted the bogus "Adrian" Bull.—Salisbury's "Metalogicus.—Who wrote the Forty-second Chapter?—Strong proof that it was not the work of John of Salisbury... 97

CHAPTER XVII.

Further criticisms on the fictitious chapter in Salisbury's "Metalogicus."—Professor Jungmann's Judgment.—King Henry's oath at Avranches.—An insight into the characters of the two Popes to whom the Bulls are attributed.—Pope Alexander not in Rome in 1172.—Finding the matrix from which Papal seals were forged... 102

CHAPTER XVIII.

Father Gasquet's learned contribution to the "Dublin Review."—Severe strictures on the chapter attributed to John of Salisbury.—The Genuine Letter of Pope Adrian on which the spurious Bull was compiled... 107

CHAPTER XIX.

English translation of Pope Adrian's Letter to King Louis VII., of France.—The Pope's refusal to allow Ireland to be invaded.—A comparison between the wording of the Letter and the Text of the Spurious Bull.—Reasons why the fraud was not exposed in past centuries. 114

CHAPTER XX.

The Papal Court of the Fourteenth Century had no knowledge of the so-called Adrian Bull.—The Letter sent by King Edward of England to Pope John XXII.—Reply of that Pontiff.—Letter from O'Neill, King of Ulster, to Pope John XXII.—Comments thereon.—Proofs that the Adrian Bull never originated in Rome, nor was its genuine character ever admitted by the Irish people... 120

CHAPTER XXI.

The erection of Ireland into a Kingdom by Pope Paul IV.—How English fraud accomplished that object.—Comments on certain expressions in the Letter of Pope John XXII.—Rome's equal and exact justice exemplified.—England's vicious methods illustrated....... 124

CHAPTER XXII.

A new and important witness to the fradulent character of the Adrian and Alexander Bulls.—Selections from the celebrated Historical work "Cambrensis Eversus" by Dr. John Lynch.—Seventeenth century evidence against both the spurious documents...................... 127

CHAPTER XXIII.

Further proof of the spurious character of the Adrian and Alexander Bulls.—Dr. Lynch's criticisms on the Alexander Forgery.. 132

CHAPTER XXIV.

Additional Extracts from "Cambrensis Eversus."—Ireland always loyal to Rome.—More proof of the fraudulent Forgery of the Adrian and Alexander Bulls............................. 135

CHAPTER XXV.

Profound reverence of the People of Ireland for the Vicar of Christ.—Nearly every nation in Europe placed under the ban of the Church except Ireland............................. 140

CHAPTER XXVI.

Ireland's aid to Rome in the Propagation of the Faith.—Irish Saints and Apostolic Missionaries who helped to propagate Christianity throughout every country in Europe...... 143

CHAPTER XXVII.

The Irish Church under the Popes.—How the Holy Union was kept intact.—List of Legates sent from Rome.—Historical Errors corrected by Dr. Lynch.—That author's concluding remarks in which he shows up Cambrensis in the garb of a notorious calumniator of both the Catholic Church and the Irish people.. 147

CHAPTER XXVIII.

Further historical proofs concerning the Letter which Pope Adrian IV. sent to King Louis VII.—Evidence showing that Letter to have alluded to Ireland and not to Spain, as claimed by anti-Catholic writers.. 152

CHAPTER XXIX.

Criticism on the true Letter of Pope Adrian IV., and the False Bull.—Reasons why the Letter "H" applies to *Hibernia* and not to *Hispania* 155

CHAPTER XXX.

What the Popes have done for Ireland.—Help extended to the Irish people.—Important Historical facts.—Correspondence between Pope Pius IX., and the Irish in Rome.—Cardinal Manning's tribute to Ireland's Faith.. 158

CHAPTER XXXI.

The paternal love of Pope Leo XIII. for the Irish people.—How public opinion was prejudiced against the Holy Father—Calumnies cabled around the world—The Pope presented in his true character as the Consistent Friend of the People of Ireland in their struggle for National Independence by rightful means.. 161

CHAPTER XXXII.

Further manifestations of the Love of Pope Leo XIII. for the Irish people.—Address of His Holiness to the Irish Pilgrims in Rome.—The Papal Rescript of 1888 explained.—Archbishop Walsh's Views.—Addresses of his Grace on the Sympathy of the Holy Father for Ireland.—Opinions of Cardinal Pecci, Cardinal Moran, Bishop Keane and Monsignor O'Reilly 170

CHAPTER XXXIII.

Miscellaneous Historical Errors Corrected.—Did Pope John XXII. Excommunicate Edward Bruce and his adherents?—Was Maynooth College founded in order to educate Irish Priests in the interests of England?—Was the Repeal Movement killed by a Papal Rescript?—Was the Young Ireland Movement killed by Irish Bishops and Priests? 178

CHAPTER XXXIV.

Secret Political Societies.—Their baneful influence upon Ireland's Struggles for Freedom. Reasons why the Church opposes them.—The wisdom of her opposition proved by numerous examples.—Was the Home Rule movement opposed by the Church?—Was the Land League opposed by the Pope?.—These questions answered.. 188

CHAPTER XXXV.

Some Vicious Falsehoods Regarding "Vatican Politics" Fully Refuted.—The "Italian Ring" Accounted for.—The characters of Pope Alexander VI., and other Pontiffs Triumphantly Vindicated.—Conclusion 199

www.ingramcontent.com/pod-product-compliance
Lightning Source LLC
Chambersburg PA
CBHW032224230426
43666CB00033B/1120